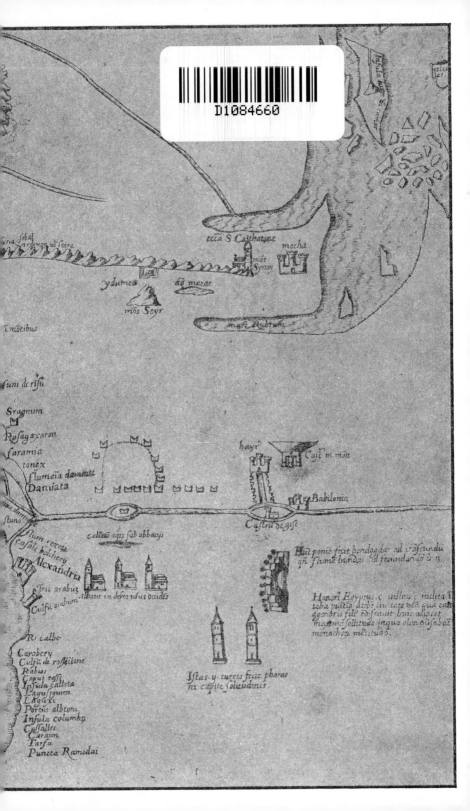

ína sobal aegypten ulstere

tcia S Castharine

mecha

mōt Synay

ydumeā   āq macat

mōs Seyr

mare Rubrum

i mōtibus

ium de risu

Sragnum

Rasagaxaron

Saramia

tonex

flumeia damete

Damiata

hayr

Casꞇ m mīte

Ager Babilonia

Castru de gise

colleta aꞃ sub abbacijs

Huic ponte fecit bendogdar ad trascendu
qn flume hundat ad frecundandū terrā

flum rectū

casale bolchery

Alexandria

Abbate in desto risus occides

Tris arabuꞁ

Culfu arabico

Honorī Egyptus. c uillou c indita ꞇ
teba puilla. dicho ciuitate dcā quia cō
agensbris fuit ēoꝰseauit huic adiacet
maximū sollitudo inqua olim ōꝰsabat
monachoꞃ multitudo.

Ri calber

Carobery
Culfu de rosseilone
Rabies
Caput rossi
Insula calleta
Lagusegura
Laguxi
Portus albtoni
Insula columby
Cassallei
Caraum
Tarsu
Puncta Ramedai

Istas .y. turres fecit pharao
ni capite solicudinis.

Arab background series

Editor: N. A. Ziadeh, Emeritus Professor of History
American University of Beirut

By the same author

Islam and the West, the Making of an Image
Islam, Europe and Empire

The Arabs and Mediaeval Europe

Norman Daniel

Longman
Librairie du Liban

LONGMAN GROUP LIMITED
London
Associated companies, branches and representatives throughout the world

LIBRAIRIE DU LIBAN
Immeuble Esseily, Place Riad Solh, Beirut

© *Longman Group Limited and Librairie du Liban 1975*

First published 1975

ISBN 0 582 78045 4
Library of Congress Catalog Card Number 73-93276

*Printed in Great Britain by Butler and Tanner Ltd,
Frome and London*

In Memoriam

Gerald
our son and friend
who often asked after the progress of this book

remembering also many more
whose lives were completed in so short a time
some of whom are mentioned in the course of this book
such as al-Adid the last Fatimid and Baldwin IV of Jerusalem
countless victims of war or of peace

Contents

Notes on the illustrations   ix

Editor's preface   xi

Acknowledgements   xii

Author's preface   xiii

Chapter 1. Introduction

1. The Middle Ages   1
2. The Mediterranean   5
3. Islam and Christendom in the eighth century   10
4. Arabic and Latin (eighth and ninth centuries)   17

Chapter 2. The Martyrs of Cordova

1. The story   23
2. The background   30
3. The polemic   39
4. Interpretation   45

*Chapter 3. The Central and Western Mediterranean to the end
of the tenth century*

1. Charlemagne and his successors   49
2. Impact of war   54
3. Two personal encounters   62
4. Fragmentary interchange   70
5. Papal policy   75

Chapter 4. Spain in the eleventh and twelfth centuries

1. Principles and practice of reconquest   80
2. Spanish interest in Arab history   88
3. Unacknowledged literary interchange   95
4. Direct literary connections   105

*Chapter 5. European solidarity and the inception of the crusading
idea*

1. General considerations   111
2. Latin aggression and cultural intolerance   113
3. European reaction to the crusading idea   118
4. The morale of the First Crusade   125
5. Aggression in its actual impact   133

Chapter 6. The Central Mediterranean: eleventh–thirteenth centuries

  1. Introductory   140
  2. The Normans in Sicily   144
  3. Frederick II and the Arabs in Europe   153
  4. Frederick II and the Arab World   157
  5. Conclusion   165

Chapter 7. Courtly ideals in the East

  1. Some shared notions   167
  2. The kings of Jerusalem   172
  3. East and West   179
  4. Arab rulers through European eyes   184

Chapter 8. Adaptation and development in the Latin East

  1. The link with the Arab World   192
  2. Self-criticism and self-analysis   202
  3. The Arab World through Latin eyes   210
  4. Merchants, mercenaries and others   218

Chapter 9. The Arabs, Islam and European theology

  1. The conflict   230
  2. Legendary treatment of Islam   232
  3. Serious polemic   237
  4. The holy war   248
  5. Toleration of Muslim communities   254

Chapter 10. Arabic scientific literature in Europe

  1. The rediscovery of the ancient world   263
  2. The thirteenth-century use of Arab sources   274
  3. Common ground: astrology and medicine   282

Chapter 11. The end of the Middle Ages

  1. Themes and topics   300
  2. Geographical areas   308
  3. An attempt at a final perspective   319

Notes   328

Bibliographical note   356

Bibliographical References   358

Index   362

Notes on the illustrations

1. **The war at sea:** Roger II of Sicily earns the title of 'King of Africa' (p. 142): a later mediaeval picture of eleventh-century naval fighting, in the extracts *de passagiis* from the Venetian *Chronologia Magna* (cod. lat. CCCXCIX Bibliothecae ad D. Marci Venetiarum, fo. 76v, see notes to pp. 224–8). This manuscript tabulates contemporary events in parallel columns, one for each separate government in the known world, so that it gives an overall impression of one undivided civilization. The sultans of Damascus and Egypt are given the same crown symbol as European sovereigns; only the insignia of the Eastern and Western Emperors and the Doge of Venice are distinguished.

2. **The Emperor's Arab girl entertainers** (p. 163): on his return to England in 1241, Richard of Cornwall described to the monks of St Albans a performance produced for his amusement by Frederick II; it was drawn from this description by Matthew Paris, with the caption, 'entertainers or dancers: a marvel' (Corpus Christi College, Cambridge, MS 16, fo. 149; see also RS 57 vol. 4 p. 147). The girls were 'bodily beautiful' (*elegantes*) and played musical instruments while balancing on four balls in motion; in the picture, only one each is shown, coloured green. The artist conceived the figures in strictly North European terms; direct drawings of Arab musicians in Sicily can be seen in the roof of the *Capella Palatina* in the Royal Palace in Palermo, and acrobats appear on the capitals of the Benedictine cloisters at Monreale.

3. **Cairo trophy of war from the fall of Acre** (p. 209 and note): this church doorway, shown as it now stands, its Gothic style in contrast with its Mameluke frame, was brought to Cairo during the uneasy period of the immediate successors to Sultan Qalaun, and the mosque in which it was set was only completed by Sultan an-Nasir early in the fourteenth century AD (note to pp. 224–8).

4. **Arab astrology in Europe** (p. 288): the first page of the Latin version of the work of Ibn abi Rijal, an Arab Spaniard in Tunis; it was translated from Arabic into Spanish and from Spanish into Latin, so that it became accessible to all Europe; this manuscript is in Cambridge University Library, Mm. 4. 43. The gowned figure drawn above the initial is holding up an astrolabe. The hunting scene and heraldic

devices also represent aspects of a common culture (see pp. 190, 195, 162). The opening words announce that this is the important and unabridged work by *Aly Abenragel filius*, greatest of philosophers, on judicial astrology; and goes on to relate the history of its translation.

End-papers. This war map of the Eastern Mediterranean is taken from the edition by Bongars, in his *Gesta Dei per Francos* (see note to pp. 204–206), of Marino Sanudo's *Liber Secretorum Fidelium Crucis* (note to p. 222), and derives from a manuscript original. The somewhat detailed illustration of Cairo is visually absurd, but clearly derives from an authentic description. Sanudo's work is a comprehensive compilation of crusading material that dates from the early fourteenth century, when the papal policy of boycotting the Mamelukes conflicted more than ever with the trading interests of the maritime Italian states (p. 222, compare p. 256 and note to pp. 219–20). Sanudo, a well-travelled Venetian, sought to establish an agreed European policy, but he harked back to the Fourth Crusade, and conceived Venice at the head of an imperialist expedition, much as Dubois imagined France (note to pp. 321–2). Sanudo's information is extensive by any standard; we can never speak of plagiarism in the mediaeval context, and such books were written in much the same same way as today we garden, incorporating our predecessors' work. The map exemplifies the common product of mediaeval interests in the Near East.

Editor's preface

The Arab World has, for some time, been attracting the attention of a growing public throughout the world. The strategic position of the Arab countries, the oil they produce, their sudden emancipation and emergence as independent states, their revolutions and *coups d'état*, have been the special concern of statesmen, politicians, businessmen, scholars and journalists, and of equal interest to the general public.

An appreciation of the present-day problems of Arab countries and of their immediate neighbours demands a certain knowledge of their geographical and social background; and a knowledge of the main trends of their history—political, cultural and religious—is essential for an understanding of current issues. Arabs had existed long before the advent of Islam in the seventh century AD, but it was with Islam that they became a world power. Arab civilization, which resulted from the contacts the Arabs had with other peoples and cultures, especially after the creation of this world power, and which reached its height in the ninth, tenth and eleventh centuries, was, for a few centuries that followed, the guiding light of a large part of the world. Its rôle cannot, thus, be ignored.

The Arab Background Series will provide the English-speaking, educated reader with a series of books which will clarify the historical past of the Arabs, and analyse their present-day problems. The contributors to the series, who come from many parts of the world, are all specialists in their respective fields. This variety of approach and attitude creates for the English-speaking reader a unique picture of the Arab World.

N. A. ZIADEH

Acknowledgements

This book was called into existence by the General Editor of the series, Professor Nicola Ziadeh, to whose continuing interest I am immensely indebted; he cannot be blamed for its deficiencies, because things so fell out that we were prevented from discussing it in detail. For constructive criticism, I am also most grateful to my wife, Ruth, who read all the book, and to Fr Gervase Mathew, who read some chapters; in addition, his writings on chivalry suggested to me the theme of my Chapter 7. I alone am responsible for not having made more of my subject. I should like also to record my gratitude to Fr G. C. Anawati, and not least for extending to me the hospitality of the library of the Institut Dominicain d'Études Orientales, at Abbasia, Cairo. My debt to the sources and studies cited in the notes should be clear; I feel under particular obligation for parts of this book to scholars of older generations, Michaud, Dozy, Haskins and others, whose approach to the study of intercultural relations still stimulates their successors. I am grateful, too, to Professor Abdalla el-Tayeb, of Khartoum, for his kind and stimulating exposition of certain Arabic literary themes.

Finally, I owe much to the patience, skill, and experience of the publisher's editorial staff.

For permission to use photographs, the publishers gratefully acknowledge:

The British Library, for the endpaper map and Plate 1;
The Master and Fellows of Corpus Christi College, Cambridge, for Plate 2;
The Egyptian Antiquities Organization, Department of Islamic Monuments, for Plate 3;
Cambridge University Library, for Plate 4.

Author's preface

The purpose of this book is to explore the links between the Arabs and mediaeval Europe. Its technique is to present the impression made by the Arabs, the reactions of the Europeans and some of the ideas that they shared with the Arabs, so far as possible in contemporary words. Because a long book would otherwise be longer, I have also used summaries, I hope always fair summaries, of contemporary opinion. The first chapter, and to some extent the last, are exceptions, because in them I attempt a survey and a comparison of my own. The rest of the book is written so far as possible in contemporary terms, though naturally these have to be carefully chosen and rigidly controlled, and the overall view is inevitably always my own. Sometimes I found that I had to resort to stating an ordinary sequence of events. Some of the material quoted is familiar to any reader of histories of the period, though such passages are more commonly referred to than actually quoted, but many of my quotations are relatively unfamiliar to all but the professional historian. Even he is accustomed to use the material for a purpose different from mine. I am not asking what happened, but what was in the minds of Europeans, and asking it, not as a means to an historical judgement of events, but as an end in itself. I am asking what the world that they shared with the Arabs looked like to them. My book can be called a book entirely about foreign affairs, but the foreign affairs of a whole culture, and foreign affairs as they seemed to people at the time.

My technique is dictated by my purpose, and it would be useful for no other purpose; I must ask to be judged according to what I attempt, and not according to what others have quite differently attempted. I can be judged for choosing the wrong thing to do, or for doing it badly, but not for doing badly something I have not set out to do. Nevertheless, the book is tentative and incomplete, even in terms of what I mean to do. This is inevitable in any attempt to allow other people to speak for themselves; to do themselves justice, they would expect to be quoted in full, and that is obviously impossible; it is not even possible to quote at length. Yet this book does try to catch the events of a long period as they passed through men's minds at the time, and not as we may interpret them according to the changing fashions of historical judgement. We can always probe more deeply into the complexities of a human relationship. It is in this, as I am well aware, that I have only partially succeeded at best. I must hope that I have not proceeded so summarily as to deprive the reader of the opportunity to judge for himself the material I offer him.

Notes

Note references are not used in the text. The reader who wants to check an authority or source has only to refer to the notes at the end of the book, under the page number of the main text.

Transliteration of Arabic

Arabic names in the text are relatively few and mostly familiar, so that all diacritical marks (on consonants as well as on vowels) have been omitted. Arabic-speaking readers ought not to be inconvenienced, and others may be relieved. After some hesitation it was decided that the consonant *ain* and the *hamza* should also be omitted.

Chapter 1

Introduction

1. The Middle Ages

What we may mean by 'the Middle Ages' must in our day be a subject for deep disagreement. At any rate for English readers, Gibbon defines the traditional opinion: the age between a fixed classical civilization and the modern world which inherits its culture. That urbanity which once made Gibbon admired now strikes some readers as unctuous, but his concepts still dominate us, even when we think ourselves free of them. Again and again a historian who rejects many or all of Gibbon's ideas, and especially his prejudices, reflects his historical perspective. One reason may be that he was himself the disproof of his conscious argument. He showed his readers, not a dark abyss between lighted peaks, but a story whose unbroken continuity has never been more clearly demonstrated. His interpretations can be retained, and often are retained, while his superficial cleverness and arrogance are discounted. His historical perspective is spoiled for us rather by the future he could not possibly foresee. Renaissance and Reformation seemed important for him, as leading on to his modern age, the Enlightenment in which he lived. As C. S. Lewis so well argued in his inaugural lecture, *De Descriptione Temporum*, the real close of the Middle Ages comes somewhere in the industrial age, with the new "assumption that everything is provisional and soon to be superseded". It is legitimate to set the modern age at least no earlier than the French Revolution, and, rightly or wrongly, many nations do look back to the series of European revolutions as the beginning of our own times.

The Middle Ages have been indefinitely stretched in both directions. Classical studies are now themselves a special discipline, certainly no longer the whole, or even a rough framework, of our education. The survival of the classical past has become relatively unimportant for a world suspicious of anything that can have been good enough in a less technological age. Even our nineteenth-century historians, conscious of the progress their society had made, were still fairly sure that they had reached the main peak; but our current outlook is based on obsolescence—that is, technological obsolescence of ideas. The continuity of European history remains unbroken. Some distant past is so remote that we are sure that it barely affects us now. Between such a past and the present moment is the Middle Age. If we have to choose a date to end the western European Middle Ages, we might do worse than take 1939. Our successors will have to choose a still later date. The only modern age is the constantly disappearing present. Its roots are in the past, but it is hardly more useful to ask how long is a root than to ask how long is a piece of string.

For the Arabs the customary perspective is a different one. They see no Middle Age, only an age of glory followed by a slow deterioration, first under foreigners who were still Arabic speakers, then through the foreign but still Muslim rule, Arabic influenced, of the Ottomans, into the wholly foreign and degrading colonialism of the Western powers, whose civilization was alien, and unwelcome on any count. For them the only light in the recent perspective which the West dominates is the light of the French Revolution. In the person of Bonaparte it threatened Egypt, but at the same time claimed to liberate it, and introduced that nationalism which the Arabs soon made their own. As they look back upon their relations with the West, they have sometimes seen in the aggression of modern times the substance of which the Crusades were a shadow cast before. We shall see that the Crusades were both more and less than that; but it is true that for most of their history Arabs and Europeans were physically in conflict. The history of much of the world may be said to have begun a new and recognizably distinct era when the Europeans began to expand, from the beginning of the sixteenth century onwards, and this applies particularly, of course, to the West and East Indies. The Arabs were not affected on a significant scale until the nineteenth century, although Portuguese attacks in the Gulf date back to the period of eastward expansion into India. Islam and Christianity have experienced nearly fourteen centuries of living side by side, and so the history of Arab relations with Europe is much longer and more complicated than that of relations with any other non-European people, except the Jews. Indeed, Europe's notion of any foreign culture has been profoundly affected by its longer experience, up to the colonial age, of no other culture but the Arabic; but, for all non-European peoples, this much is common: that the concept of a Middle Age has no relevance, at least for their internal history. Any relevance it may have must be in relation to Europe.

European historians have still not adjusted to this non-European perspective, but they have tried to adjust their minds to a wider world-view than they inherited from their predecessors. They have not altered their viewpoint so radically that the concept of a Middle Age has disappeared; the definition of the classical age has changed much more. The first age, that which preceded the 'Middle' Age in Europe, is now seen on a wider scale, and is often presented as the European culmination of those many ancient civilizations which have been more extensively or successfully studied, after excavation, in the last quarter-century than they had been earlier. Few now expect to learn wisdom from it, or will even still sit uncomfortably at the feet of Plato and Aristotle. In spite of this, the concept of a 'Middle' Age survives in a traditional form, as the age which prepared the development of our present civilization. There has been an honourable attempt to modify this by introducing the history of the other 'ecumenes' than our own; but no one really thinks that any history matters save the history of Europe; this at least must be the opinion of those—including most Europeans—who believe that a civilization determined by Europeans and others of European stock not only dominates but (in whatever form it may develop) will continue indefinitely to dominate the rest of the world. The Middle Ages in this perspective, essentially still the same as Gibbon's, are simply the periods in which our modern world originated; they are 'preceding' ages, and the use of a plural form clearly admits that they are certainly not one single age.

Mediaeval studies found their motivation in the desire of the post-French Revolutionary world to identify national origins; the urge already existed, as Muratori's *Rerum Italicarum Scriptores* exemplifies, but, of course, the Revolution itself was only one more obviously good example of a tendency which grew with accelerating momentum. Collections like the *Monumenta Germaniae Historica* and the English *Rolls Series* show how the search for national origins intensified. It is now an ordinary point of derision that Macaulay and Stubbs could see the Middle Ages of England as a predestined triumph of parliamentary democracy, but the notion of an inevitable progress in one direction or another is common to them, to Marx and Engels, to most evolutionary theory and to any belief in progress as that is commonly understood.

I cannot pretend to be free of the cultural framework of my own day, or claim that I can break out of the tradition of the last few centuries. Nevertheless, it is legitimate to follow a number of specialized historians who, in the course of the present century, have in different ways questioned the accuracy of our traditional perspective. In the present study we cannot suppose that we are dealing with a single period, or with different periods necessarily resembling each other. I am concerned with certain connections between the Arabs and the Europeans during a long series of different ages. My theme is one, because it has to do with a particular relationship; and because it is limited in time, at the beginning by the rise of Islam, and at the end by the old conventional definition of the modern age. That conventional date is nothing more than a convenience; if there is no real Middle Age in Europe, there is certainly none in the relations of the Arabs with Europe. Even that date, however, leaves me a long period and a large subject to compress into a small space; much abbreviation, oversimplification and omission are inevitable.

I intend only to use the techniques of history, but do not mean by that to imply that the new techniques have nothing to offer to the historian; sociology most obviously has, though it is difficult to find anyone who can combine the two disciplines. Nor should I pretend that I am, any more than any other writer, uninfluenced today by the characteristic studies of the age, which, especially psychology, have affected our language as well as our use of the critical method. It remains a fact that, without any arrogance, or jealousy towards others, the historian retains a method, and a valid method, and has his own contribution to make. He has one advantage in making himself understood, though it may add to his difficulty in getting people to listen: he can use ordinary language without recourse to the technical terms which belong to the newer disciplines, all founded on method rather than subject. With the historian, the language, like the subject, preceded the method. Only those who cannot distinguish substance from jargon will complain.

The book is not a definitive study of the relations between Arabs and Europeans; still less is it a study, even tentative, of Arab influence on Europe. I do not believe the time has come to write a definitive history of the reciprocal influences of these two great cultures over nearly fourteen centuries of their existence together, nor for any considerable part of that time; there is too much yet to be published, let alone examined and discussed. The European debt to the Arabs is interesting, and a salutary reminder that European and American power, prosperity and self-confidence are made up of many borrowed elements. Yet it can be inherently more interesting, and also more useful for its practical illustration of current issues of today, to note conscious reactions and to try to trace parallel developments. Two great cultures have developed side by side, but not usually step by step, in the area of, very roughly, the Roman and the Hellenistic empires combined. The more men disown even the immediate past in order to claim a new future, the more clearly we can see that the history of a thousand years ago, of a hundred years ago, and of ten years ago, all go to make up the present; and, if some regard all these as equally irrelevant, we may infer the corollary, that all are equally relevant. No historian could endorse quite that claim, but all the past can pretend to some relevance, and the lessons of the nearer past are often more obscure and ambiguous than those more distant. However patchily and unevenly, a few peaks stand out clearly from the mists.

2. The Mediterranean

In any consideration of Arab relations with mediaeval Europe the key fact is that only the Mediterranean area was common ground. Here if anywhere we will find a justification for carrying this study only as late as the Turkish conquest of the Levant. It is less the European 'Middle Ages' that are significant than the start of Ottoman rule over the Arabs. Both for Europeans and for Arabs the continuing conflict between Europe and the Muslims, or between western Christendom and Islam, was different when the Grand Signor became the protagonist of the play. After that, northern Europeans and non-Arab Muslims played a much larger part than previously in the conflict. Many, indeed, had long been involved, at least during the crusading age; Godfrey of Bouillon and Louis IX of France are Christian examples, and Salah ad-Din or Baybars among the Muslims. Nevertheless, the Mediterranean was the whole of the arena. Islam made no direct impact in any mediaeval period on northern Europe, where the Arabs were a distant bogey, not a present danger. There was no considerable European penetration beyond the coastal regions of Africa and Asia until after the Ottoman conquests, and the virtual disappearance of Arab governments. Within the Mediterranean area, the frontiers shifted to and fro; only Greece and the Balkan peninsula were undisputed by the two religions, until the Ottoman invasions. Mediterranean trade has always reached out to the Atlantic, to the Red Sea and the Indian Ocean, to North-West Europe, to East Africa and South-West Asia; and there have been land and river routes, through Russia to Scandinavia, into Nubia and across the Sudanic belt of Africa, or across the Syrian desert and the Iranian plateau, even into China. These routes were peripheral as long as the centre was the Mediterranean.

It was obviously the centre for the Romans, as *mare nostrum*; though in Roman days it was disputed with the Carthaginians, and even with Greeks and with pirates. It may seem as though it was united in Roman hands for a relatively short time only, but still the Mediterranean had been a channel of communication for long centuries before the Arab conquest; and certainly it was the centre of the areas inhabited by Europeans and by Arabs. Pirenne believed that the northward shift in power which was marked by the imperial coronation of Charlemagne was caused by the Arab disruption—for European use—of the Mediterranean channel of commerce. Others have seen different reasons for the northward shift of power; and it was paralleled by an eastward shift in the Arab World, to Baghdad, and then, in consequence, to Khorasan. No final consensus has yet determined the extent to which European sea trade suffered under the Merovingians, the extent to which the differences between Carolingian and Merovingian economy have been exaggerated, and to which, exaggerated or not, they may be imputed to Arab control of the Mediterranean, or to the weakening of Byzantine control.

The steady expansion of the Arab empire under the first few generations of Muslims made it the heir of most of the Hellenistic and Sassanian world, controlling much of western and central Asia (particularly Iran, Iraq and Syria) and North Africa, with, in particular, Egypt. Arabs controlled the machinery of government, although the machinery itself was largely and for long unchanged. They used Christian clerks. At first they felt no need of foreign literary skills or knowledge; they immediately and extensively employed the arts of those they had conquered. Their expansion to the north-west was checked by the Byzantine defence. Nowhere did Arab power in the seventh century of the Christian era extend to what is now European soil. A rapid survey of the eighth century shows a great change, and a clear foreshadowing of many subsequent developments. Politically and militarily this was a century of developments and crises in and around Europe. The Berbers had been converted to Islam at the end of the preceding century, and in 711 the Arabs and Berbers entered Spain, and quickly overcame and subjected the Visigoths. In 717 the Arabs raised the siege of Constantinople; the Emperor Leo the Isaurian would soon set about enforcing the iconoclasm which was especially the religion of the army. The greatest opponent of iconoclasm, St John of Damascus, was free to attack it because he was a subject of the caliph; but, although Islam had then existed and ruled for a century, he did not take it seriously, know about its teaching or, apparently, suppose it anything but a variant of classical paganism. He neither recognized it as an Abrahamic religion, nor foresaw that it would survive to dispute the world with Christianity. 732 is the date of the famous defeat of the Arabs by Charles Martel, which Gibbon over-stressed as decisive, in order to tease the theologians of Oxford about their escape from interpreting the Quran; but it did so happen that after that date there was no serious northward prosecution of *jihad*, or holy war. There were many raids, and some temporary Arab colonization, but the northern climate never attracted the Arabs seriously. The year that the Emperor Leo III died, 741, was the year of a great Berber revolt. It was in 750 that the Umayyad dynasty was overthrown in the East; the Abbasids established their power at Baghdad, a new city which developed during the decade following, and Arab power came increasingly under Persian and later Turkish influence. The Umayyad amirate of Cordova (caliphate only from the tenth century) was founded in 756; it was later in the century that independent governments in North Africa developed. In the meantime Pepin the Short, son of Charles Martel and father of Charles the Great, deposed Childeric III, the last Merovingian to reign. Within a year or two he had intervened in Italy to establish the temporal power of the papacy, and to defeat the Lombard kingdom; and that, in turn, had only just taken Ravenna from the rule of the Eastern Emperor.

This period of unsettlement, in Europe, in North Africa and western Asia, is the time of the first great impact of the Arabs upon the Latin Mediterranean. It is a period of retreat from the central Mediterranean by Byzantium. There was never again a unified government in the Arab World; the future lay with separate, but often powerful, Arab states in Spain, North Africa, Egypt, and ultimately Syria too. The Italian peninsula was at war, was divided, was, and had long been, subject to invasion; and now, to the attacks of Lombards, Arabs and Byzantines, was added the persistent intervention of the Frankish monarchs. Europe would yet suffer other attacks than those of the Arabs; Magyar invasions and Viking raids still lay in the unknown future. The frontiers of Greek, Arabic and Latin cultures in the Mediterranean areas would shift backwards and forwards, but the main areas were determined in the eighth century; the formation of Latin Europe and that of Arabic-speaking North Africa coincided. Can the Arabs be said to have reoriented European development at this date? We can leave the economic arguments to the specialists; at any rate it seems clear that the monetary system depended on the sources of precious metals which lay on the periphery of the caliphate, in Sudan, and in central Asia, and so were passed into Europe through Arab trade. Nothing here suggests that confrontation with areas under Arab control affected Europe decisively. The shift of political power to what is now northern France had already come about, not as a result of Arab domination, but when the Salian Franks defeated the Visigoths, the Burgundians and other Germanic tribes in Gaul, a process completed long before the birth of the Prophet. Technological historians tell us that the eighth century was a decisive time for northern and western Europe, but developments were independent of the Arab conquest. The widespread adoption of the stirrup in Europe has been dated to the period immediately following the defeat of the Arabs by Charles Martel. It has been suggested that this happened after, not because of, the battle; the increasing use of cavalry, deriving from the power of impact which the new device conferred, and which turned mounted infantry into cavalry, was at least roughly coeval among the Arabs and among the Franks. Probably it originated in eastern Asia, but there is in any case no evidence that it was transmitted to the West through the Mediterranean.

It is plausibly argued that the stirrup stimulated all the technology of heavily armed knights, and thus the social structure of feudalism which supported these expensive fighting units. If so, it did not have precisely the same result among the Arabs. The use of the heavy ploughshare has also been dated to about this period, although its full effectiveness depended on the subsequent development of the horse-collar, the harness and the horse-shoe, and the adoption in many places of three-field crop rotation. This new agriculture would ultimately divide Christian Europe of the north and west from the whole Mediterranean area, whether Christian or Muslim. The horse-collar made it feasible to exploit equine energy, but the Mediterranean rural economy, dictated by the quality of the land, could not bear the expense of the horse, a machine more efficient but more costly than the ox; those who cannot afford a costly technology will do better with what they can afford, but in the north the horse made the double sowing of spring and winter possible, and the double crop made the horse practicable. It has been said that the new diet of lentils gave the undernourished peoples of Europe the energy which they later expended on crusades. Be that as it may, we can see, if we bring our thoughts back to the eighth century, that Europe was on the verge of economic development which had little immediate effect on Mediterranean trade, though it was part of a process that ultimately led to European expansion. The greater productivity of the North made itself felt slowly. In the eighth century trade with the Arabs meant exports of furs, slaves, timber and metals, all of which had long been the staple of trade from the land mass to the inland sea; slaves, as always and everywhere, were the product of war. Much of the material exported originated in Scandinavia; it passed by two routes, through France and Spain, or through Russia and Byzantium. Although later centuries would of course see increased trade, it was at this time that the foundations of Venice were laid, and its trade established. The Arab civilization was dominant, but there was already the promise of the rapid development of the great wealth of northern Europe.

As we saw, the centres of political power had in any case receded inland, north and east, to the Franks, the Danes and the Normans, to the Germans, always apt to interfere in Italy, and to their enemies the Slavs, who would drain strength away from Byzantium; and finally to Baghdad: all the future rulers over the Arab World, excepting Spain and North Africa, would come from Iraq, or through Iraq from central Asia. In this general perspective the Mediterranean loses its unique importance, but not all its importance, and not quickly. We must think in terms of gradually developing and changing cultures, not of abrupt transitions, and not of any absolute demarcation between Arabs and Europeans. We shall take it that the decisive factors in cultural development at this time were the acceptance of either Christianity or Islam by the peoples who came to inhabit the former Roman and Hellenistic worlds; nothing has been said to shake this traditional opinion. We shall not assume that the Christian and Islamic cultures were necessarily different from each other. The cultural element in a religion is that which differences of outlook, manners, customs and interests make in the practice of the basic doctrine; Islam knows cultural differences, but there have doubtless been greater differences within Christendom, both from place to place, and from time to time. At any one time or place, the cultural element may be very large. The differences between the two religions are fewer and smaller than the points they hold in common; in the course of time much greater differences have accrued from the way the cultures understood and practised the two religions. We shall be mistaken if we assume that there were as many cultural differences between eighth-century Christians and the early Muslims as we are accustomed to suppose. I shall try to take none for granted. We must concern ourselves with the two areas, where the language of religion and literature was Arabic or Latin; we must bear in mind that a third area, the Greek, affected the other two; and we must look with an open mind for cultural differences and similarities, and for the way in which new examples of either develop.

3. Islam and Christendom in the eighth century

In Gaul, by the eighth century, the process of conversion to Christianity was well advanced among the Germanic peoples who had conquered the old Roman province, though it was not completed till after the conversion of the Arabs to Islam. The conversion of the Arabs to Islam and that of the English to Christianity happened at the same time. The Prophet was a young man when Augustine was sent to England; his last years coincided with the first conversions of the Northumbrians and the East Angles. The two processes are in no way comparable in their importance to the history of the world, but the parallel between macrocosm and microcosm can be instructive. Birinus began to convert the West Saxons in the year that Umar ibn al-Khattab took Damascus; the first siege of Constantinople and the early expansion of the

Arabs in North Africa took place at about the same time as Theodore of Tarsus was consecrated in Rome, travelled to England and reached his see of Canterbury. It was hardly fanciful to say that while the Arabian peninsula reached out to seize the Mediterranean, the Mediterranean was reaching to link itself to the offshore islands of the North. The conversion of the English was a slower process than the rise of Islam, but the spread of Christianity in England was roughly contemporary with the Arab and the Islamic conquests; leaving out the scale of these events and their importance, can we compare the history and effects of these contemporary conversions?

The differences are naturally what strike us first. After the scale, which need not necessarily imply a difference of quality, the most obvious difference is that Islam was carried by the Arabs to ancient, articulate, literary, and even religious civilizations or cultures; Christianity was taken to an illiterate, though not unsophisticated, society, as its prompt use of literacy would show, and one certainly not without ideas of its own; still, it was a society that must inevitably be the recipient, not the donor, of intellectual development. There can be no greater technological loan than literacy. By our standards, the Latin Mediterranean literary culture of the day was limited in worth, a decayed remnant of the classical inheritance, whereas the Greek-speaking, Syriac and Pahlevi worlds which Islam absorbed contained all that was most 'advanced' or 'cultured', or even 'progressive', within an area of direct influence that excludes China and India. In both religions the Revelation was above all *written*, but the Quran was the writing of all writings, because the writing of God; the Arabs brought a new language to the classical world, whereas the Latin church was carrying the ancient language of the West, and the essential skill of writing it, to a new nation.

The Islamic theologians always set their faces against popular beliefs in saints, relics and miracles, but the Germanic peoples, including the Franks, the Visigoths and the Anglo-Saxons, were exceptionally attached to the cult of relics, even secondary relics, as when the ground into which drained the water which had washed the bones of St Oswald had the power to expel devils from the bodies of the possessed. The Umayyad caliphs, excepting Umar ibn Abd al-Aziz, are often thought of as a secular and almost irreligious tribal aristocracy, patrons not only of a literature which continued the love poetry and satire of pre-Islamic Arabia, but of paintings and carvings at Mushatta and Qusayr Amra, and of the mosaics at the great mosque at Damascus and at the Dome of the Rock, which represent the ancient secular cultures of Syria, Byzantium and Persia. No one could form such an image of the Anglo-Saxon aristocracy from the existing records; Queen Etheldreda, for example, who, twice married to a king, preserved her virginity throughout, as the incorruption of her body after death would demonstrate, and who only used hot water to wash in on the greater feasts of the church, presents a contrast from the dancing girls and hunting scenes of the court of Damascus. Probably she presented the same contrast to her unregenerate compatriots, but they found no historian to celebrate their resistance to the new fashions, and we must infer their existence from other evidence. It was chastity and austerity which were 'in' in her day, as much as the contrary is true of the Anglo-Saxons of our day, though the sum of actual behaviour may always be much the same. Anglo-Saxon Christianity then was essentially monastic. When Drycthelm had a vision of hell, he did not simply mend his ways; he divided his property between his wife, his sons and the poor, and became a monk at Melrose, where he used to stand in the Tweed, sometimes up to his neck, breaking the ice in winter, and letting his clothes dry on him. It is not only in climate that this seems to contrast with contemporary Islam. It is well known that, though the early caliphs had been strict and simple in their lives, the mortification of the flesh was no part of Quranic revelation. Too much could easily be made of this. Al-Hasan al-Basri had already taught asceticism, and given impetus to a long and honourable Muslim tradition. In spite of this, it is undoubted that the image of an ideal which Bede's *Ecclesiastical History* reflects—and Bede was no fanatic to exaggerate or distort—is remote from anything in contemporary Islam.

On the other hand, the Christian and Muslim concepts of sanctity and martyrdom were probably closer at this period than they would be again. Even up to the present day, Christians and Muslims have shared each others' shrines; for long in Egypt at the Nile flood Muslims used to take part in a Christian commemoration of martyrs. 'Canonization', the close Roman inquisition into a petition for the declaration of a dead person's sanctity, had not then come into being. A saint was declared a saint by a popular cult on a national or local scale. Kings who protected Christians were apt to receive national canonization of this sort, whatever their character, an Olaf, even a Canute. Kings who died fighting pagan enemies were at once recognized saints and martyrs, whether an Oswald or an Edmund; neither of these was required to deny Christ, but both died because in a general sense they were Christian. Islam has never enjoyed a systematical process of canonization, and there have been many local cults. For the early Muslims there was little need (as in northern Europe there was for Christians) of protection against other religions: they were riding the crest of success; but the unhappy descendants of the Prophet were recognized as martyrs (some presumed poisoned) by their Shia followers. Islam certainly assumed that he who died in battle against infidels was by virtue of doing so a martyr; and for them the assumption had a better warrant in theology than the comparable assumption for Christians. The Arabic words for 'martyr' and 'witness' are variants, although this came to be lost sight of. In Christian practice the two meanings were equally inextricable, but gradually each acquired its distinct definition. From the reverse tendency in the Muslim world— "in the end almost anyone who had died any violent death and aroused pity was considered by the general public to be a martyr"—the Christian church moved steadily away. Islam, perhaps wisely, left the recognition of sanctity to the people; the Roman church judged it better to turn it into a process of law.

It was resemblance, and not difference, that dominated the dogmatic, liturgical and moral bases of the two religions. Islam taught then, as now, one God and the duty to exterminate polytheist belief; worship by prayers to be said at fixed hours during the day; by an annual pilgrimage, to be observed by all who were able; by an annual fast of a month; and by a fixed gift or tax paid to the poor. Christianity likewise opposed polytheism and was satisfied with nothing short of its destruction; we have already seen that a Christian king killed by pagans in battle was a martyr, like the *shuhuda* of the *jihad*. Some centuries later Peter the Venerable looked back at the conversion of England, and contrasted its peaceable character with the forcible conversions that he attributed to Islam. He meant the peaceable conversion of some ruling families. The new religion was introduced from above as much in the one case as in the other, and of course there was no forcible conversion of Jews and Christians under Islam. We shall see how among the occidental Christians in Spain this very preservation in a subordinate position was actively resented, but oriental

Christians flourished for many centuries after the Arab conquest and, of course, survive today. Europeans, too, made some effort to accommodate themselves to non-Christians who lived among them, but they employed means which modern liberalism would describe as a 'persecution'. We shall see more of this in a later chapter, but already in the sixth century Merovingian church councils were dividing Jews from Christians in daily life. Jews were not permitted to own Christian slaves or employ Christian servants, nor to hold public office over Christians, or teach Christians, or share a meal with them, or appear publicly in Holy Week. For Latins, however, Muslims 'persecuted' by virtue of ruling at all, and their rule was for ever forcible, by virtue of having come into being by conquest. To a visitor from Mars the most obvious difference might well have been the tolerance by Muslims, not only of the true 'Peoples of the Book', but also of the Zoroastrians and even the pagan 'Sabaeans' of the Harran. Yet this distinction between the two religious areas was not greater than the different circumstances of western Europe and western Asia might be expected to dictate. There was not a total contrast.

The characteristic institution of Christendom was the monastery, and at this date there was nothing in Islam even comparable. Yet the life of the Western monk bore a close resemblance to that of the Islamic community. The prayer at fixed hours of the day shaped the pattern of daily life for the Muslims and alike for the monks. To the imaginary outsider again, surely the basic institutions must have seemed the same; the difference would have been that in the one case fewer people said more prayers, and, in the other, more said fewer. Later Christians used to attack the ritual washings that precede prayer in Islam, as if Muslims maintained that such washing cleanses the soul. In fact, the Latin church still shared an inherited Semitic respect for ritual, almost sacramental, washing. St Gregory the Great was the Prophet's contemporary—he was thirty years the elder, but both of them lived into their sixties. He advised St Augustine of Canterbury that, although the intention must be the decisive factor, "the man who has cleansed himself with water after intercourse with his wife is allowed to approach the mystery of Holy Communion." The distinction between good and bad acts and those that are 'lawful yet not good', while it was borrowed from St Paul, is another point in common with the Islamic distinction into good, bad and permitted. Gregory also speaks of ritual impurity; and just as the woman in menstruation is ritually impure in Islam, so Gregory says that it is not blameworthy if women in this condition receive Communion, but commendable if they refrain. There are other points in common between Muslim religious practice and the religious practice, not only of the monks but of the whole Christian community of the time. Gifts to the church were combined with gifts to the poor. There was no ecclesiastical organization in Islam quite like the Christian church, and Christian alms were not as closely regulated as Muslim *zakat*, but the gift to God was institutionalized in both cases, and the emergence of the tithe system in the West in the eighth century made the resemblance closer. *Zakat* and *dime* are variations on a single theme. Finally the pilgrimage, so cardinal to Muslim devotion, had much closer Christian parallels in those days than it would have later. Then it was possible to speak of pilgrims going to Jerusalem "because they desire to fulfil their religion" (*legem eorum adimplere*), a phrase which more exactly describes the sentiment of the Hajji. However, this is told as an explanation made to a Muslim, and may represent a simple kind of spontaneous syncretism. One of the pilgrims smuggles balsam in a gourd sealed with petroleum; if caught, he would be 'martyred'. Pilgrimage to Rome was frequent, and kings would make it. Missionary labour was thought of as a kind of pilgrimage, and the eighth century was a great age of missions. Christians in later ages have criticized Islam as excessively juridical; it would hardly have been possible for the Christian of the eighth century, or for long after, to do so.

The Christian and Muslim worlds were close also in their pagan inheritance. Neither the populations of Europe nor those of what is now the Arab World were suddenly freed of their inherited ideas. Levison printed a missionary sermon about European superstition, dating from the eighth century. The preacher attacks the country people who believe that there are such people as witches who can ill-wish children or cattle. This belief "remained from the custom of the pagans", and, he goes on, we believe that it was taught by the worshippers of idols. Diana ('Deana') was just a woman, possessed by a devil, who practised divination. Another woman was 'Iunae-Minerva' the whore, for whom it was not enough to fornicate with others, but to do so also with her father, Jupiter, and her brothers, 'Mars' and 'Venus'. There is also, he says, an idea that a soul, when it leaves one man, can enter another. We, he concludes, believe that nothing exists except what we can see, and except the demons who have a thousand arts to harm. This passage, which marks the extreme of ignorance of the classics—possibly only in the twentieth century could an educated person again be found to know so little of Venus as to mistake her sex—also records the struggle against the old beliefs which the Christian missionaries carried on, and which good Muslims of the day, had they known of it, could only have applauded. It is clear that this sermon represents at one and the same time the loss of formal Mediterranean culture, and the great effort to destroy paganism which was conducted from all the centres of religion, whether Muslim or Christian, which surround the Mediterranean.

I have contrasted the cult of saints so characteristic of the West —from its root in asceticism to its perfection in the cult of relics— with the Muslim emphasis on the direct worship of God. Even the Christian pilgrimages (except that to the Holy Land) were tied to the cult of saints. Yet this was—and to a large extent deliberately—an attempt to convert to good ends the worship of holy wells, springs and groves which everywhere retained their importance. In Islam also the veneration of saints, their relics and holy places has survived, and it is sure that many practices have been tolerated quite naturally throughout history by both religions; such things were absorbed without conflict, in spite of an obvious continuity with the days of darkness. Certainly not all the Anglo-Saxons were standing in the winter waters of the Tweed. Bede tells how a heavenly messenger visited "every room and every bed" in one monastery, and found with one exception that men and women were alike unprofitably sunk in sleep, or else awake to no good purpose. St Boniface told Archbishop Cuthbert of Canterbury, "there are very few cities of Lombardy, Gaul or France where there is not an English adulteress or prostitute," to the disgrace of the English church; this must have been concomitant to the pilgrimage. The mass of ordinary people doubtless behaved in much the same way everywhere. On the other hand, we have seen already that even from the first century (Hijra), asceticism began to get a hold on zealous Muslims such as Hasan al-Basri, and the doctrine of *zuhd* developed the idea of abstention from sin into that of abstention from all created pleasures. This was a doctrine of the élite; but so in effect was Latin monasticism the practice of an élite.

Probably we should not think of the area from Europe across

western and central Asia as neatly divided into two at this date. It is more apt to suppose a series of active nuclei of civilization in the early eighth century, extended from Byzantium to Persia; the Arab centres in Damascus, Kufa and Fustat were closely linked together among a number of disparate cultures grouped in a rough similarity over the old empire of Alexander, and extended westwards. The European and Arab, Semitic and Iranian groupings exhibited a great diversity within a common pattern, and many interwoven strands met together in the Mediterranean. North and West Europe, the Franks and the Anglo-Saxons, constituted a remote provincial example of this loosely associated group of cultures.

4. Arabic and Latin (eighth and ninth centuries)

The contrast is greater when we consider, not the life of the community in general, but the articulate literate culture of the Arabic and Latin worlds. The point of departure was different. The *Etymologies* of Isidore of Seville, the greatest doctor of the Visigothic church, define the Western literary inheritance of the seventh and eighth centuries at its best. They were compiled at about the time of the Hijra. Of course, we cannot compare this book with the Quran; but, at a lower level, neither can we compare it with the relatively small corpus of pre-Islamic Arabic poetry. Much of the Latin culture which the *Etymologies* epitomize, the Arabs would never come to share. In time there would be shared ground in Greek philosophy and science, which Arabic would acquire in something the same way as Latin had done in the Hellenistic age, and which Latin would later recover from Arabic. There would always remain a vast area, especially in the humanities, where the Arab and the Latin worlds would never meet.

It was natural that the first reactions of the Christian cultures to the Arabic should have been uncertain. Just as John Damascene thought of the Arabs as a passing phenomenon, so perhaps the Spanish Christians at this date supposed them also. One minor figure, a continuator of the history of Isidore of Seville, known as Isidore Pacensis (Beja), was a Mozarab whose *Epitome imperatorum* ends just before the arrival of the first Umayyad, Abd ar-Rahman, in Spain; his book, subtitled *Arabum ephemerides*, is a curious example of hostility and indifference. It is in the form of annals, dated by the Spanish era, by the regnal year (Roman or Arab) and the Hijra year as *anno Arabum*. In spite of this, when speaking of the people, the author generally uses the word *Saraceni*, and this can have come from no Arab source; the simple phrase 'Amirulmuminin' (*sic*) he mistranslates as "governing all things fortunately". On the other hand, many details are quite uncontroversial, and they show a knowledge of Arab history lacking in Europe during most of the Middle Ages; to take just one example, the paragraph on Yazid I and Muawiya II; and the account of the Prophet, while quite plainly hostile, lacks the venomous scurrility of later Christian tradition. There must have been both Christian and Muslim sources. The Latin is obscure, and the work suggests a hybrid culture and an uncertain background.

If we compare the religious controversies of the Muslims in the eighth and ninth centuries AD with those of contemporary Christians, it is certainly once again the differences that strike us first. The great arguments of early Islam related to the caliphate—to political and social questions; Shii and Khariji ideologies were the expression of national and social discontents. In the Umayyad period, Islamic cultures were still dominated by Arabs close to their roots in Arabia, and non-Arabs began to look for self-expansion in the unorthodox sects, just as non-Greek Christians had adopted heresies unacceptable to the Emperor in Constantinople. In Syria and Iraq the Christian cultures long continued unaffected. John of Damascus, as we have noted, thought of the Arabs as temporary intruders. Within the Islamic world, different cultures existed side by side in isolation; it was only gradually that Arabic culture began to take account of the cultures that had existed before Islam and remained in its midst. In spite of the remoteness of the ruling minority of Arabs at this date from the preconceptions of the cultures that had preceded them, their concerns are easily intelligible to the modern European mind; though their religious belief may be alien, their preoccupation with government and its relation to ideology is within our own immediate experience.

The great controversy in Anglo-Saxon England was about the date of Easter, and the seriousness with which Bede and other Christian English writers harp on this theme separates them from us, who cannot share it. We realize that it involved a conflict between Celtic and English cultures; but we lack sympathy here too. We know, but Bede apparently did not, that King Cadwalla of Gwynedd, who was "set upon exterminating the entire English race in Britain, and spared neither women nor innocent children," represented a people who had suffered greatly at English hands. Gregory of Tours earlier adopted much the same attitude to the Bretons. A later generation of Englishmen understood this better, and stories of King Arthur won English sympathy for British resistance. At the time, Roman usages in liturgy and church discipline meant closer links with the Mediterranean world to which men like Theodore of Tarsus and Hadrian the African belonged. The Anglo-Saxons shared their religion of saints, miracles and relics with the Franks; this is the picture we receive from Gregory of Tours.

The effect of the conversion of the English was to bring them immediately into the literary tradition of the Latin world. The Anglo-Saxons quickly produced their own strange contribution to the literature of the ancient world. Caedmon and Aldhelm wrote in English, but Aldhelm wrote also in Latin—verse, of a curious stylistic quality, for example in praise of virginity, and his famous *enigmata*; he cared for language, and wrote on prosody. His works were known to the Mozarabs of Cordova, who prized them, and had existed in the library of the church at Pamplona in the ninth century. Far more outstanding was Bede, declared a doctor of the Christian Church by the Pope in 1899. His most remarkable quality is the width of his interests, within the limits of the Europe of his day; equally, the narrowness of that European culture is measured by the limits of Bede's interests. Grammar and prosody interested him, as the vehicle of Christian knowledge; also chronology, in order to defend the Roman doctrine on the date of Easter, though incidentally he did much to establish the present Christian reckoning of the calendar. His book *On the Nature of Things* is an encyclopaedia of the scientific knowledge available to him, and was intended to be educational, rather than polemic; in his many scriptural commentaries he used Greek and different Latin versions, and collected the opinions of the Fathers with additions of his own. His historical writings were his most original work, especially the *Ecclesiastical History of the English People*; this is the most esteemed of his writings today, although it was the least esteemed by his contemporaries. Although his knowledge was less than that of the great Arab writers on science, whom he antedates, he simply had access to less valuable material. His scriptural commentaries and his histories represent the same kind of interest as Arab historians and Quranic commentators of the early period. He was provincial, but he was the same sort of person as Arab writers of his day and a little later.

Alcuin, who at seventy years just survived into the ninth century, held a key position in the transmission of the higher Latin culture of England to Europe, when it experienced its great Latin revival in the reign of Charlemagne. Alcuin carried to Europe the characteristic interest in grammar, history and theology. His liturgical interests, which he passed on to his many famous students, have no obvious Muslim parallel. He was active in the controversy which condemned the Spanish bishops, Elipandus of Toledo and Felix of Urgel, for their Adoptionist heresy. In spite of living under Muslim rule, the Spanish hierarchy supported the heresy at synods which were held in Europe, and attended by Spanish representatives, including Felix. Communication between the Spaniards, the Emperor and the Pope was uninhibited by the religious barrier. It has been conjectured that Adoptionism was thought by the Spanish bishops as likely to be more acceptable than orthodox Catholic doctrine to their Muslim rulers, and Alcuin himself seems to hint at this; in fact it is very unlikely that the Arab authorities would distinguish between different forms of Trinitarian belief.

All the Carolingian writers of the ninth century cared deeply for the Latin languages. Amalarius of Metz, Rabanus Maurus, Paschasius Radbertus, Servatus Lupus of Ferrières, Ratramnus, Hincmar of Rheims, Gottschalk, Walafrid Strabo and John Scotus Erigena, all were clerical in their interests, both monastic and courtly. The theological controversies of the day were about predestination, and about the sacrament of the altar; liturgy and ritual were a preoccupation, but canon law, the Scriptures, and the lives of the saints were the chief interests. Erigena was the only original thinker in Latin of the age; he and his other contemporaries concerned with the predestination controversy were dealing essentially with the same problem as Muslim theologians with the *qadar*, or power, of God, but Arabs and Latins approached the problem quite differently, and there is no sign or possibility of mutual influence. Three writers, each in his own language outstanding, follow each other: St John Damascene, who died in the middle of the eighth century, Erigena, born sixty years later, and al-Ashari, whose lifetime just overlapped Erigena's. There are notional links between them, but any actual connection is tenuous. Yet all belong recognizably to a common culture. Still another parallel is in the area of religious law. The eighth and ninth centuries were a creative period in the development of the Roman canons, including the famous forgery of the Donation of Constantine. The eighth and ninth centuries were also the creative period of the great Muslim jurisprudents, the founders of the major schools of religious law. These four fields, grammar, prosody, religious law and predestination, were common interests to Arabs and Europeans, but the linguistic and religious barriers make them all nothing more than parallelisms. There was and could be no actual link.

The first century of Abbasid rule is the classical period of the absorption of the conquered cultures into Arabic. This coincided roughly with the Carolingian Renaissance. While the surviving Latin culture purified itself, but made little advance into new territory, Arabic widened its range to the Hellenized culture of Syria, to the Iranian culture which had Hellenic influences of its own, and to some extent to Indian sources. It is curious that when, much later, Europe came to translate large numbers of Arabic texts, it did so largely from the range of subjects now chosen for translation into Arabic. Mostly this was scientific, with exceptions such as the fables of *Kalila wa Dimna*—exactly the exception later to be made by the Latins. The Arabs did not translate the poetry or drama of ancient Greece, as later the Latins would not translate the classical poetry of the Arabs. At this time translations included the *sirr al-asrar, secreta* (for *secretum*) *secretorum*, which would ultimately be equally popular in the West, and some Indian works; the principal heritage of the ancient world, usually in Hellenistic form, was translated into Arabic in the fields of mathematics, astronomy, natural science, geography, and, above all, medicine. Of original writers, the astronomer, al-Farghani, the encyclopaedist, al-Kindi, and the great medical writer, ar-Razi, belong to the eighth century, but other great names of the original thinkers of the classic age of Islam, for example al-Biruni, al-Farabi, Ibn al-Haytham, al-Ghazali and Ibn Sina, were yet to come. The names, both of the translators into Arabic, and of the great Arab writers themselves, unknown to contemporary Europe, became well known in the twelfth century.

The two areas were alike at this time in submitting to a similar process. In both cases several different nations had to learn a new religion, and, still more difficult, a new language. In the one case those nations were 'barbarian', Germans, Franks, Anglo-Saxons;

in the other, already long civilized, Iranians, Semites, Egyptians. In either case there were exceptions, the remnants of the former Romans in the Latin Christian world, the Berbers and other new nations in the Arabic. The differences gave all the immediate advantages to the Arabic-speaking area, which took in both Iranian and Hellenistic cultures. The rest of the Greek-speaking area remained under Byzantium. Europe inherited only the Latin part of the ancient world, and in conditions of maximum difficulty. Intellectually both sides were dominated by a small minority, a minority that consisted of the best men and was moved by the best intentions, so far as such a thing can ever be true. On neither side was the majority more self-interested or venal than on the other. It is true that ordinary men are not usually conscious of how much they have in common with strangers they do not know, and there seems to have been little sensitivity on either side towards the other. Yet with similar interests, and starting from conditions and with characteristics not very dissimilar, the two societies have gradually diverged. How far did this process go, during the course of the conventional mediaeval period? We have to gauge the rate at which a difference, less of attitude at the moment of separation than of language and social and religious organization taking effect with the passage of time, can lead societies, almost accidentally, in different directions.

Chapter 2

The Martyrs of Cordova

1. The story

There has often been ill-feeling between Christendom and Islam, but there has never perhaps been greater hatred than that which those Christians who supported the martyrs' movement felt in Cordova in the ninth century. In the form of *odium theologicum* many kinds of discontent were concentrated, the hatred of the unprivileged for the privileged, of the once-privileged for their successors, of a minority for their surroundings, of one cultural tradition for another, of the users of one language for the users of another. It was further complicated by the strange psychology in which it was expressed. The extreme ascetic Christian ideal which we have already considered found in this movement its logical fulfilment.

The bare facts are astonishing enough. They are illustrated by the stories of the earliest of the martyrs, which I will tell in a little detail. The movement was stimulated by two victims whose attitudes led them accidentally into conflicts with the Muslims. In that, they were untypical of their successors who more deliberately sought their own destruction. Perfectus, the protomartyr, was a monk who used to do the shopping for his House in a market in Cordova. A group of Muslims in the market were curious or mischievous enough to ask him what Catholics thought of Christ and of Muhammad. No doubt this was in Arabic; some of the martyrs bear names that are certainly of Latin origin, others, like 'Servus-Dei', which can only, and very thinly, mask 'Abdalla', seem to have had Arabic names. Perfectus is likely to be one of these—al-Kamil. Perfectus (our Latin sources tell us) immediately confessed the divinity of Christ, but excused himself from speaking of the Prophet. (Our source says *vates*, a soothsayer, not *propheta*.) The group talking to him may have been just amusing themselves at his expense, but in any case they continued to press him, and he finally responded by a scurrilous attack upon the Prophet, following the citation of the Gospel, "many false prophets shall come in my name." He cannot have expected that this would not bring him into trouble, but the sources accuse his interlocutors of bad faith. In fact it is more surprising that apparently they recognized their own faults in this, and let him go. The next time he came to market, the same people called out that he was the rash fool who cursed the Prophet (may God bless him and save him)—the source breaks off to explain this invocation. Then the whole mob in the market rose against him, like bees disturbed in the hive, and hurried him off to the judge. The monk was frightened, and tried to deny the facts. He was sent to prison, where he "began to attack their whole religion." It seems that he alternated between a very natural and even commendable prudence, and a rash itch for destruction. In the end he was executed, publicly among the holiday crowds at the *Id al-Fitr*, at the end of Ramadan, in the Christian year 850; he used the opportunity to abuse the Prophet again and to threaten his hearers with hell. A pleasure boat capsized in the river, drowning two of its occupants; a judgement on the Muslims, some of the Christians considered. They were allowed to take away the body, and this began a considerable trade in the relics of the martyrs. Though often frustrated by official precautions, this gruesome salvage was successful to the point that later two monks came from as far as France, to look for relics which it was said were now easily obtainable in Cordova.

The second episode concerned a merchant called John (Yahya? Yuhanna?), who used to swear by the name of the Prophet, when he was selling his goods, no doubt to attract the good-will of the Muslim customers. In any case he attracted the ill-will of Muslim rivals, who said that he so often swore by the Prophet that he represented himself as Muslim. This is so reasonable that the sources concentrated on the disproportionate punishment, rather than on the offence itself. John was now understood to curse anyone who pronounced the name of the Prophet; the crowd got angry, and he too was hurried off to the Cadi. Again, the simile of angry bees is used. The heart of the accusation against the merchant seems to have been that he was a "particularly subtle scoffer" who took the name of the Prophet lightly, and pronounced it in derision. The alternative must be that he had a serious intention of becoming Muslim; a much worse accusation, if untrue, because he would then become a formal apostate from Islam if he insisted he were still Christian; and that would be a capital offence. He denied that he derided the Prophet, and pleaded that he was accused by rivals in trade. The Cadi compromised by ordering him four hundred lashes, and having him paraded round the town on a donkey with a town crier calling out that "this is what anyone must suffer who derogates the Prophet of God." It seems that he was given the chance of escaping punishment by declaring himself Muslim; in the circumstances of the crime, logical enough. The punishment was hard, but normal by standards then universally accepted. It seems to have helped to arouse the consciences of lapsed Christians in the town.

It was at this point that the true martyrs' movement erupted, in the person of a man called Ishaq—Isaac—a remarkable personality in his own right. He was "born of wealthy parents" and of noble stock; as he grew, "he lived softly amid wealth and good things;" and "as he was accomplished and learned in the Arabic language, he held the office of *exceptor reipublicae*," a *katib*, or secretary, in government. From his comfort and the good prospects of a worldly career the young man suddenly revolted; he was seized by spiritual ardour and became a monk. The monastery in the mountains to which he retired was a family concern; it was maintained by his wealthy uncle and aunt, and her brother was the abbot. It is possible that we should infer a different attitude on the part of his parents, who had apprenticed him to service in a Muslim government, and had indeed given him one of those names which are equally suitable for a Christian or a Muslim (or, of course, a Jew). After three years of ascetic discipline Ishaq was again suddenly inspired, this time to return to Cordova, and to go to the court, where he told the Cadi that he wanted to "become an active member" of his religion, if he would just kindly expound its "order and reason". Our Christian source describes the Cadi's exposition, with an attempt at fair representation. Ishaq replied, "You have lied," and, after first abusing Islam himself, invited the Cadi to become Christian. The Cadi was "confused by so great a shock" and slapped Ishaq on the face. There was some commotion, and Ishaq, evidently in a state of elation, said, "How dare you strike a countenance like to the image of God?" The jurisprudents present disapproved of the Cadi's irregular behaviour; the latter justified himself, supposing that Ishaq must be drunk. This the "intrepid monk" denied; he was just burning with zeal, and only waiting to extend

25

his neck to the executioner. The Cadi did not in fact order execution; Ishaq was committed to prison, but the amir insisted on the death sentence, and had the body cremated, in order to prevent its use as a relic. Ishaq's story suggests emotional and perhaps mental unbalance, the sudden rejection of a good career for the monastery, and of the monastery for deliberate martyrdom. We must imagine Ishaq brooding in his government office upon worldliness, brooding again in his fasts and vigils upon the fate of Perfectus/Kamil and John. His example proved infectious. The abbot-uncle and five other monks followed Ishaq's example; we must again suppose an atmosphere of religious enthusiasm in the monastery. These people were all great seers of visions; one such announced that the sacrifice of Ishaq had been accepted as Abraham's of the first Isaac, and immediately a messenger arrived from town to announce the fresh martyrdoms of the uncle and his companions.

Our intimate knowledge of this and the other individual cases derives from the exceptionally interesting Christian sources, all apologetic, written rather as a party manifesto, for the benefit of moderate Christians who disapproved the self-immolation, than for outside consumption. The two writers concerned were friends; one a layman, Alvaro, a writer with some classical pretensions, who contributed an apologetic work, the *Indiculus Luminosus* and a hagiographical account of his fellow-apologist, Eulogio. Eulogio was a priest, and ultimately, when elected archbishop of Toledo and primate of Spain, himself one of the martyrs. He wrote a number of accounts of the martyrs and exhortations to two of them; but he was in no hurry to become a martyr himself, and Alvaro, so far as we know, was never martyred at all. Both recognized that Ishaq was the prototype of the movement: the first of "those who came really of their own accord," said Eulogio; the first of "our spontaneous martyrs," said Alvaro. Executions deliberately forced upon a reluctant government constituted a kind of violence that was hard to defeat, because it was turned upon itself. This was the course of action that these two writers defended, and in the course of so doing they epitomized the polemic of western Europe against Islam.

We gain a clearer picture of Eulogio by looking closely at one more of the martyrs, the best, however, because of the attachment Eulogio felt for her, the virgin Flora (also a name with an obvious Arabic counterpart); we learn more of him than of her. Initially she was a courageous victim who did not create unnecessary trouble, but in the end she was seized with the real martyr fury. She was the product of a mixed marriage. There seem to have been three children of this marriage, two girls and a boy. The Arab father came from the south and died young, and Flora was brought up in this Muslim household under the sole influence of her Christian mother. Her brother was a practising Muslim, as keenly religious as his sister, but, as she followed their mother, so did he their father. As Eulogio tells it, he was just a persecutor, and we do not know his motives; he may have interfered with her less from religious zeal than from a sense of family duty or of public duty, or under pressure from the neighbours. Alone in the family Flora and her brother shared this feeling for religion; of her mother we hear nothing more than that she imparted her Christian preference; Flora's sister was evidently attached to her, and willing to accompany her and live with her as a Christian, but not to the point of martyrdom. Before the division in the household became open, Flora used to meditate on the text, "He that shall deny me before men, I will also deny him before my Father," and so she decided, without consulting her mother, to leave the house and live among open Christians. She must have already made her brother suspicious, because he went looking for her when she disappeared, disturbing convents and getting clerics arrested; and so, to spare the Christian community further embarrassment, she returned home, but publicly as a Christian, defying her brother. He tried to change her mind, by kind words, by threats and beatings, and then took her in front of the Cadi. Giving witness, he said that she was the youngest of the family; "together with me she always showed a proper compliance with the worship of our religion." Flora denied this, claiming to have always been a Christian, but other evidence from Eulogio shows that this was a prevarication at best. The punishment for apostasy from Islam was death, and prevarication was natural; at this stage Flora was not seeking martyrdom. Flora's apostasy being unproven, she was held by the officers of the court and whipped till the bone of her neck was laid bare, says Eulogio, and so taken home half-dead; left in the charge of the women of the house, she felt well enough after a few days to escape over the roof and into the darkness. She blundered into a Christian house, and so found shelter.

There Eulogio first met her: "I, that sinner rich in iniquity, with both my hands I touched the scars of her most worshipful and

27

delicate neck;" so he wrote after her death; and while she was in prison he wrote to her to recall this time:

> "I gazed upon the skin of your holy neck, torn by the blows of the whip, and the wound from which your beautiful hair had been bared, and which you condescended to show me . . . I touched the wounds with gentle hand, because I did not believe that I ought to caress them with kisses."

He went away, and "for a long time sighed and meditated deeply within myself." Later, Flora's sister joined her and they lived for a while quietly in the country. At the next stage of the story all Flora's family, even the sister who went away with her, disappear. Instead, by accident she encounters in a church a like-minded girl called Mary, sister of one of the six monks who immolated themselves in imitation of Ishaq. This girl was deeply attached to her brother and wished above all to share his death. To Eulogio she is "blessed" where the incomparable Flora is "sanctissima".

These two went back to the Cadi to denounce themselves. Flora asserted that it was she who had been so terribly beaten to make her deny Christ, adding that she "was born of Arab stock"; perhaps this means that she now admitted to having been brought up as a Muslim. Mary proclaimed herself her brother's sister and united herself with him in denouncing Islamic worship as the "figments of demons". Eulogio, himself then in prison, where he wrote his *Documentum Martyriale* to confirm their resolution, says that the Cadi was enraged and consigned them to "the squalor of prison and to the brothel." That they were seriously threatened with prostitution does not seem likely and would certainly have been extra-legal; a threat of enslavement, carrying with it a danger of concubinage, is more likely; or the phrase may just belong in that ambience of virginal sexuality and a taste for pain with which Eulogio invested their story. The Song of Solomon provides the text: "Enter into the bridal bed of your spouse, whom you have so loved that you feared not to die for him. 'For winter is now passed, the rain is over and gone.' " There was a further court examination and further threats. Flora told Eulogio afterwards that, when the Cadi challenged her to explain how she could be a Christian if her brother were Muslim, she finally admitted that she had once been "possessed by the darkness of ignorance", practising her father's religion, and "a slave to the errors of the Arabs". Pressed to say if she were firm in apostasy, she attacked the Prophet "with abstruse arguments" in the court; the two women were ordered to execution and decapitated. The bodies were partly destroyed by dogs and birds, then thrown in the river; parts of Mary's body were found, and served the cult of relics then still so popular. Eulogio did not rush into the bridal bed of the spouse as insistently as he recommended to his followers; he and other Christians then in prison were released.

It would be excessive to recount many of the martyrdoms; but the last of which we have a full account is Eulogio's own, and of this I must say something. In 859 Eulogio was elected archbishop by the Christians of Toledo, but, before he could be consecrated to the see of the Primate of Spain, circumstances brought him to martyrdom. A girl who was the daughter of Muslim parents, but who had Christian connections, was converted by a nun, a relative. The girl was baptized Leocritia. She ran away from home, found lodgings and sought instruction from Eulogio, and became friendly with one of his sisters. Staying late one night, she thought it safer to stay on till the following evening, but a spy reported her presence, and in the morning all the household were arrested. Interrogated, Eulogio said that it was his duty to instruct a neophyte, "as I would gladly do for you also," he added to the Cadi, who sent for rods. Eulogio asked him what he intended these for, and the Cadi said that he meant to educate Eulogio with them. "Sharpen your sword," said Eulogio, "so that you can return my soul, freed from the chains of the body, to Him who gave it. Do not think that you can tear my limbs with the lash." The account is given by Eulogio's friend, Alvaro, who says that "when he reproached the untruth of their Prophet and their religion with clear invective and sufficient eloquence" he was hurried to the palace of the amir and dragged in front of the Council. One of its members was intimate with Eulogio, and tried to talk him out of the course of action on which he was embarked.

> "If fools and idiots are carried away into this deplorable and fatal self-destruction, whereas you are endowed with suitable wisdom and are renowned for your way of life, what madness has compelled you to risk a fatal misfortune and to forget the natural love of life? I beg you to listen to me and I ask you not to destroy yourself as a result of something you have not properly considered. Just say one word in your hour of need, and afterwards you can enjoy your faith wherever you can. We promise never to examine any further."

These terms are obscure; if we understand that Eulogio was offered his life on condition of withdrawing his attack upon Islam, he reacted with the fervour he had preached to others; if he was being asked to apostasize publicly, but not privately, he took the only course open to a Christian. He died courageously on the fifth before the Ides of March, on Saturday at the ninth hour; Leocritia followed him four days later. The Christians tried to keep the birds away from his exposed body; at night a heavenly choir was seen to hang above it; both head and body were recovered, as was the body of Leocritia, after it was thrown in the river. Eulogio had celebrated the stories of forty-eight martyrs; he and Leocritia bring the total to fifty.

Eulogio's death is not typical of the movement; he died in doing his duty, not as the result of going out of his way to attack Islam. He did this only when he was going to be humiliated by public beating. It is clear that none of the leading men of the amirate was aware that he had been for long the champion of the martyrs' movement; on the contrary, the notables knew him as an influence for moderation. Even using only the evidence of men who believed in this fanatical attitude, and who hated such fellow-Christians as wanted to live in peace and quiet, again and again we note the reluctance of the Cadi to condemn the accused, until they leave him no choice; in one case they provoke the whole assembly of Muslims at prayer in the mosque, and the Cadi's authority alone saves them from being torn to pieces. The authorities do not know how to check the movement; they can even hardly control the trade in the relics they are forced to create. They assume that Eulogio, who, with his friend Alvaro, has done most to stimulate fanaticism, is an influence for moderation; and our witness is this same Alvaro, who celebrates his friend's triumphant entry into the glorious army of martyrs. The inconsistency is inexplicable, but it throws into clear relief the hatred for Islam which a quiet, unobtrusive exterior habitually masked. This was an attitude inevitable in a religious minority which constituted a social grouping without privilege.

2. The background

An approach to Islam which contributed to the common European tradition grew out of a seed-bed of resentment. The Christians were too many to forget that they had once been the masters. For some individuals the strain of living on the margins between different communities was intolerable. The difference could only draw attention to those aspects of Christian life which were flourishing in other parts of Europe, but which were not shared by the dominant Muslim community—especially monastic asceticism and the cult of relics. These three factors gave Christians their vivid sense of being persecuted, even when nothing could be further from the facts. The Christian who did not attack Islam was sure of being left undisturbed, but he must always know that he was not free to attack: the limit to aggression was the limit to freedom.

From Eulogio's own account we know that this was no sudden growth of resentment. His grandfather, of the same name, had hated the sound of the call to prayer, to which our Eulogio also refers only offensively; the elder Eulogio would make the sign of the cross and pray, "Neither be thou still, O God;" but the younger prayed, "Let them be confounded that adore graven things." In two generations, so far as this evidence goes, feelings had grown more bitter. Eulogio certainly knew that Muslims do not worship a graven image, but it is also likely that he knew—and if he knew he certainly resented—that Muslims think Christian worship impure. The stages of this argument were probably from 'false worship of God' to 'worship of false God' to 'worship of idol'; if so, he would have seen a theological equivalence which would come to be widely believed in Europe to be the literal truth. We shall have to return to this point later in this book. Here the point is that one God implied one people of God. In days when religion could only be seen as the function of the whole community, the call to prayer was a special provocation of Christian intolerance; it was the public avowal of an insupportable, and even inconceivable, division. Alvaro showed the same hatred of it—beyond all reason— as his friend Eulogio.

The Christians seem to have been generally aware of the throng of Muslims pressing on them; for example of the mob which picks on Perfectus/Kamil in the market, and again on the merchant John, and the description of the execution of Perfectus on the days of *Id al-Fitr*, the feast which ends the month's fast of Ramadan, the holiday crowds and the overturned boat-load of merry-makers who were drowned. Eulogio bears witness to popular hostility at least towards the Christian clergy. "None of our people," he said, "can go among them safely or cross their quarter without being shamed;" those who are recognized as priests are followed by cries of derision, as imbeciles are, and the small boys shout obscenities at them, and throw stones after them. Eulogio is angry and humiliated; he knows that he disobeys the Gospel, but he cannot help himself; it is not wrong, he argues, to curse those who hate the servants of God. "We are calumniated by them often, incessantly in fact . . . many of them think us unworthy to touch their clothes . . . they think it pollution if we mix in their affairs in any way." He quotes Arnobius: "Act and fight with those who fight." We may see the whole martyrs' movement as a violent reaction. In one aspect it may be seen as a sustained effort to break the few links that existed between the two religions. Alvaro wanted to see communication interrupted. He complained that those Christians who worked in government offices ('palatine office'—the *serai*, or palace) were openly implicated in Muslim errors by not making a public profession of their religion, by not praying in public, by not making the sign of the cross on their foreheads (as presumably was a Christian custom) when they yawned. We may see in this a lack of sense of proportion, but in any case this movement lacked proportion; it was a total rejection of the Arab World. Moderate Christians, born in the Catholic faith and brought up in the bosom of the Church, if they wanted peace, had turned to the bed of a prostitute. One of the best-known passages in his works is that where he deplores the young Christians who are learned in Arabic, who "avidly discuss the writings of the Chaldeans" (a circumlocution for Arabs); they despise as worthless the rivers of ecclesiastical beauty which flow from Paradise. He complains of Christians who study the schools of philosophers, or, rather, he corrects himself with heavy sarcasm, philocompers, not lovers of wisdom, but of big words, "not in order to prove their errors, but for the sake of their elegant wit and the fluency of their speech;" they even read Arabic poetry. Yet we shall see that it is characteristic of Alvaro and Eulogio, as of Christians throughout the ages, that they too did not even read Arab authors in order to refute them, but preferred to refute errors that no one in fact put forward.

Perhaps naturally, they equated the fanaticism of their own attitude with loyalty to the Christian religion. Eulogio resented even "the liberality of the king", and the patience of Muslims, to which Christians owed their liberty of worship; he preferred to attribute this liberty to divine providence, as if that were an alternative incompatible with Muslim patience. His strong sense of the calling of the martyrs was allied to a feeling of Visigothic superiority and of personal and family pride; the Christians who publicly disagreed with this spiritual élite were vulgar, "chatterers in the market", a mass without discipline. The Arabizers only half-defend Christianity, Alvaro argued; "and shall we not curse, shall we not detest, Christians who compete for the royal favour, and for commercial rewards and in defence of the Arabs; or shall we instead anathematize and ill-wish religious men who are struggling on behalf of the true God?" He made it very clear that his object was to make a *modus vivendi* for Christians impossible. There should be no assimilation. A Council of bishops held under Reccafred, Archbishop of Seville, condemned voluntary martyrization, and seems to have created a crisis of confidence among the extreme party. It is understandable that it was hard to maintain morale in defiance of common sense, at least for long. Eulogio was specially angered by Christians who collected the taxes on Christians, and so "daily crucify Christ in his members," but he saw that some Christians became Muslims "of their own free will." Occasionally Arabizers might experience revulsion, like the martyr Ishaq who had once been one of the royal secretaries; but the secretary who seemed the very type of the Arabizers was another man who became Muslim at the accession of the amir Muhammad I in 852. Even before that, "he was called a Christian only by name," said Eulogio, "wicked, inflated, haughty, proud and corrupt;" and after he had "conformed to the sect of perversity," Eulogio says that he "frequently entered the temple of impiety" (this means the mosque) "as if he was one of the ministers of the devil, expelled from the Temple of the Lord, which, when he was faithful, he used to visit late and reluctantly." That is, he seemed more religious as a Muslim than he had as a Christian. It is interesting that Eulogio does not seem to imply anything other than that he was genuinely converted, and of course there is no reason why this should not have been the case. The attraction of the dominant culture would be quite sincere; and this was just the reason for the strength of the reaction against it.

Two aspects of the cultural reaction are curious. One was a determined Latinism which does not seem to be patristic in sentiment. Both Eulogio and Alvaro use a strangely inappropriate terminology derived from classical antiquity. The example of St Paul may justify the figure of speech which describes the martyrs as 'athletes' and 'soldiers' of the Lord, or even as actors (*agonistae*), and the Christian effort in general as a 'gymnastic competition' (*palaestricum luctamen*); it was reasonable to speak even of an Arab state as a commonwealth (*respublica*); but when we read that churchmen attacked members of the martyrs' party "in the presence of the Cynics, of the Epicureans even" (that is, before the Cadi) should we understand a reference to the faith and morals of Islam? When Eulogio gives a date as "in the twenty-ninth year of the consulate of Abd ar-Rahman" or speaks of Muhammad's accession as "the very day that he was adorned with the fasces" we recognize a conventional imagery, perhaps a kind of make-believe: "They appear before the consuls," "the fasces are exhibited," "he spoke to the lictors," even, more intelligibly, "the satraps." There are hints of attitudes borrowed from Eusebius and the lives of the martyrs. Latin authors of whom our writers must have disapproved were admired because theirs was the language of the Western church. Eulogio brought back from a visit to Pamplona copies, not only of the *City of God* and of works of Aldhelm, but also of the Aeneid, Juvenal, Horace and Arrian. He disparaged the style of "milky Livy", the sweet tongue of Cato, the eager spirit of Demosthenes, the divine eloquence of Cicero and the flowery Quintilian, only in comparison with the writings of his friend Alvaro. Both use the language of Arnobius, 'nations' and 'Gentiles', not 'Arabs' (*ethnici* and *gentiles*, with *gentilicia*, rather than *arabes* or *arabica*). A compromise was *gens Ismaelitica*, at once Roman and scriptural. The rejected Arabic culture becomes 'Chaldean'. There is a nostalgia for antique forms, and for Roman rulers as types of the persecutor. Alvaro refers obscurely to Donatism. Voluntary martyrdom, of course, was actually condemned at the early fourth-century Council of Elvira (Granada); perhaps there was an unbroken Spanish survival, a minority sentiment authentically classical.

With this classical sentiment went also a frustrated feeling for military imagery. I have already mentioned Eulogio's quotation of Arnobius: "Fight with those that fight;" he thinks naturally of the martyrs as "soldiers of God". Alvaro speaks of them as "gallant men and warriors" (*viri strenui et bellatores*). 'Virile' is a favourite word of praise with Eulogio also; and the Prophet is not 'virile'. Images of war as well as of the gymnasium persist in both writers, *certamen* and *praelium* and *pugna spiritualis*. "Bitterly they resist the enemy." It is crucial that these people were many of them frustrated soldiers, and to remember that their martyrdom was their best or only means of aggression. Psychologists who see asceticism as a death-wish and suicide as an aggression must see in this movement the epitome of their theories.

In terms of social origin the membership of the movement is unsurprising and corresponds naturally with the ideas that characterize it. Some of the martyrs, like Aurea, daughter of Artemia and sister of Adolf and John, are certainly of Roman or Visigothic ancestry, probably both, and explicitly are 'noble'; Aurea "held Arab stock in contempt." A Visigothic name was not a guarantee of pure descent. Mary, Flora's fellow-martyr, was primarily motivated by her deep attachment to her brother Walabonso, one of the six monks who became martyrs in the wake of Ishaq's example; her mother, and presumably though not necessarily his, was a Muslim who was converted by her Christian husband. This marriage was contrary to Islamic law, but it seems to have been made possible because the family lived beyond the reach of government, in the mountains around Cordova. Two martyrs called Nunilo and Alodia were the children of a Christian mother and a Muslim father; this was the normal form of mixed marriage. Flora herself, as we saw, belonged to the same pattern of a mixed marriage. Leocritia, Eulogio's fatal protégée, was an Arab, "noble by birth, more noble by mind, sprung from the dregs of the Arabs," a curious turn of phrase where "dregs" must be used to mean its opposite, for rhetorical reasons. Yet even she had Christian family connections. Saloman (Sulayman) had adhered to Islam for a time, but we do not know his background. His fellow-martyr Roderick had a Catholic and a Muslim brother (apparently a convert) in whose quarrels he became involved. We have seen that many Latin names are ambiguous, giving reason to suspect Arabic originals, an irresistible conclusion in the case of the two martyrs called Servus-Dei (Abdalla); but names irreproachably Latin may belong to mixed marriages, or represent the baptismal names of converts to Christianity. Aurelius was the son of a Christian mother and a Muslim father, brought up to Christian belief in secret, and, according to our text, by his father's, not by his mother's, sister; at the same time he was also brought up to be learned in Arabic literature. He married a girl whose parents were both Muslim, but whose mother, as a widow, had remarried, choosing a man who "retained the faith of Christ in secret." He persuaded his step-daughter to be baptized in the name of Sabigotho, while still publicly practising Islam. Aurelius had a

35

relation called Felix (another ambiguous name) who had wavered in the matter of religion, had become a Muslim, and then wished too late to return to Christian practice. He married a girl called Liliosa (again the name is culturally ambiguous), who was the child of "secret Christians"; they were an affectionate couple, intimate in mind, "holy, lovable, worthy of respect; as they loved one another in life, so in death they were not divided." These four were first stimulated to a public confession of faith by the sight of the punishment meted out to the merchant John. For them the martyrs' urge may have been a need to give public expression to certainty, after years of shifts and deceit.

Their state of mind is more easily understood than that of the more wantonly aggressive martyrs. The background of many of these is not clear, but for some of them, too, the seed-ground of their actions may have lain in the indeterminate margin between the two peoples of God, between the Muslim and the Christian communities. The final witness of death resolved uncertainties. This may be a clue to those, like Ishaq, whose family situation was not mixed, but whose cultural allegiance was obscured by a public career. Intermingled with this thread is also that of pride in the purity of family and race and culture of those whose stock was clear and free of Arab intermarriage or of conversions to Islam. There was one case of presumed Frankish stock, a palace guard converted to Islam, a slave whose home town was Albi, who must have been a prisoner of war or, more probably, the victim of slave-traders. Among those of Spanish origin there were few who were themselves converted to Islam, but several who reacted violently from Arabic culture. Another like Ishaq was Argemirus, a senior official in the royal service who retired into monastic life in his later years. He was 'noble' by birth as were Emila and Jeremias, young men who were learned both in Latin and in Arabic, the one destined for the church and the other for lay life; their attacks on the Prophet were so much more effective than any others that those which had been uttered before theirs were forgotten. Other young men were the pupils of Eulogio himself and presumably formed intellectually by him. This group forms a certain contrast with the peripheral Christians of the mixed marriages, but they must have felt the same need of assurance. Among them the element of humiliated pride which is so strong in Eulogio himself may have been the characteristic motive.

The monastic element, ascetic and (we can hardly escape the word) fanatical, was a strong influence, though probably it was the expression rather than the source of the martyrs' motivation. Ishaq, whose story is told so graphically, appears periodically manic, as when the Cadi believes he can be so elated only because he is drunk, and perhaps depressive too. He not only threw up his career as a government secretary to become a monk, but also his life as a monk to become a martyr. The monastery was a family affair under the control of his paternal cousin and his wife. The atmosphere was certainly overheated; the example of Ishaq was immediately followed by six others, and there was a history of wonders and visions. A beautiful boy from the East appeared to one monk in the night to announce that Ishaq's sacrifice was accepted like Abraham's; Ishaq had spoken from the womb, and when he was seven a virgin saw a ball of light descend on him from heaven. These may admit the influence of Arab legends and even Quranic elements, but it is certain that they represent the effects of constant brooding in fasting conditions. There seem to have been a number of these monasteries, of no great size perhaps, in the hills out of reach of the Capital. They reached back to urban life to find a spectacular death. It was the logic of a monasticism in which stability and obscurity were not admired. "What amazing renunciation of the world," said Eulogio, *O stupenda mundi renuntiatio.*

The history of Cordovan martyrs would never be exactly repeated, though it has its echoes. Ramon Lull sought the same kind of martyrdom, which the Muslim authorities in North Africa steadily refused him, and which he finally provoked in his old age at the hands of an irritated mob. We shall see in the next few pages how the intellectual base of the movement prefigured, though probably it did not engender, the attitude of Europeans, and especially of the more educated, towards Islam, throughout the Middle Ages, and survived even into the present century. The Cordovan martyrs acted in a situation where they needed to establish for their own assurance a clear communal identity. Some must identify themselves with the Christian community unequivocally because their own position was equivocal. The rest, belonging without doubt to the Christian group, needed nevertheless to assert the group's identity against that of the dominant Muslim community. Resentment is one of the sentiments at the basis of this attitude. This assertion was not only expressed as death, and by death, and in death. It was expressed also by the total cultural rejection of Islam and of Arabic history and literature. It was expressed also in terms of asceticism and of the virginal sexuality which may accompany some kinds of asceticism. All these elements recur throughout the formative period of European opinion about the Arab World; even martyrdom is the theme of the Crusades, however illogical it may appear that a military aggression should be in the image of martyrdom, in the mind of the aggressor. Yet martyrdom would be more a theme in the thinking of ordinary simple Christians when they were attacking Arabs, than it was in an earlier time when Arabs were chiefly attacking them. The Cordovan martyrs rightly saw themselves as aggressive soldiers of God when they attacked the Prophet so fiercely, so unreasonably and so savagely; but they were most aggressive in compelling their own executions.

Where so much importance was attached to acts of renunciation, to a life of abstention and even a total abstention from life itself, it is obvious that there could be no appreciation of the positive virtue of a catholic, a tolerant or a moderate approach. The most sustained invective, the most contrived rhetoric and the most spontaneous contempt are all, in the writings of Eulogio and Alvaro, reserved for those Christians who do not share the martyrs' frenzy and who look for the means to live ordinarily and quietly; who, above all, in justifying themselves, criticize the martyrs. There were personal qualities or defects in the writers which harmonize with their ideas, and which we suppose must have given rise to them. Was Eulogio just an ambitious cleric who made himself a leader of a party and rose on the bodies of his victims to ecclesiastical preferment? The suggestion seems grotesque when we recall his own death; and yet that contrast between his extravagant partisanship of self-destruction, and his own reluctance until the very end to endanger himself, must find some explanation. There can be few accounts of personal emotions so frank or revealing, at such an early date; Augustine's work is disingenuous beside Eulogio's candid descriptions of his times of panic, of his humiliated pride, of his strange yearnings for Flora and his obsession with her physical scars and her hair and his fantasies of the heavenly bridegroom and the earthly brothel. It is also evident that Eulogio was brave and humble and charitable and chaste. There seem fewer contradictions in the character of Alvaro, the more professional writer, the more accomplished, much the more reserved of the two; also, as he realized himself, the less attractive. Yet in him too is the painful contrast of a careful man who exhorts others so eloquently to martyrdom. He had a contempt for marriage, and for his own marriage, which is exactly described by the sense which English writers of the last century gave to the word 'monkish'. "I am made up of the mud of lust and desire; earthly, I am suddenly carried to this point." Not having been gifted with continence, he could see no virtue in the alternative of marriage. In both writers there is a tension. Alvaro must have accepted that he would never be a martyr himself, in much the same terms as he accepted that he would never be a monk. Both the martyrs' movement and its literary expression were born in psychological and social tension. Out of this tension came a characteristic approach to Islam.

3. The polemic

We must complete our little survey of this extraordinary episode in the history of the relations of Arabs and Europeans by a short look at the conscious ideas about the Arabs and their religion which Eulogio and Alvaro express. There are ideas which we shall see recur through the centuries. We can recognize two ways in which their writings cast their shadow before. There are certain assertions and arguments which will be unchanged or little changed in form. There are others which do not appear again in the same form, but which methodologically resemble later polemic, and reveal logical faults which would be often repeated.

Eulogio, as might be expected, was polemically the most straightforward. In his longest sustained passage about Islam he applies the words of Saints Paul and Peter to the Prophet and to those who accept him reverently—"although they knew God, they did not honour him as God"—"men who by their wickedness suppress the truth"—"no prophecy ever came by the impulse of man"—"and because of them the way of truth will be reviled." It is interesting that in applying these texts to Islam he finds it necessary or useful to adduce the support of "many of the most expert" opinions, as well as that of the Gospel: "Many false prophets will arise and lead many astray." We should probably be right to infer that the application of these texts to Islam was questioned in Christian circles. Eulogio bases himself on the authority of the Apostles, to question the Muslim claim to follow reason, or worship in truth. His method is to attack the authority of the Prophet to teach, as it would be the method of most later Christian attacks on Islam. He tells us that when he travelled to Pamplona he looked through the "unknown books" in the monastery, and found a short anonymous history of the Prophet. This life is directly ancestral to most of the subsequent attacks on the Prophet, and even begins with the same words as many of them do, a precise (though slightly inaccurate) dating, *tempore Heraclii imperatoris*, putting the rise of Muhammad in 618 (AD— Eulogio actually uses the *aera* date in Spanish style) and citing his Spanish contemporaries, notably Isidore.

The book includes supposed events of the Prophet's life which we may place in three categories. The first covers the misrepresentation of actual facts, for example, of his relations with Khadija, his first wife, or with Zayd, or with Christians (the latter based presumably on the Islamic apocrypha about Bahira). The second category includes total misstatements, as about the Prophet's capture of Damascus. Even if we allow for the inference that Muhammad's history has simply been run on into that of his successors, there is the most confused account of how the Muslims killed "the brother of the emperor of that land." In the third category we find misrepresentations—equally fictitious—of the teaching of the Prophet. The idea, for example, that the Prophet expected to be resurrected must be compounded of a supposition that Muslims conceived him to be a kind of Christ, and a dim knowledge of the dismay which the death of the Prophet did indeed cause, until Abu Bakr reminded the faithful that Muhammad had always taught that he was a man like other men. This same 'little history' argued that the Prophet taught an incorporeal God as a kind of trick to deceive men into accepting other dogmas which were not true. There is ridicule of the Quran which could be applied with equal unfairness to the Bible. "He made up a story of spiders and mousetraps to catch flies" seems to represent *sura* 29: "The likeness of those who take other patrons besides God is as the likeness of the spider, which maketh to herself a house: but the weakest of all houses surely is the house of the spider." The real interest in these passages is that in type, and often letter for letter, they foreshadow the arguments of the twelfth- and thirteenth-century polemists.

The martyrs, as Eulogio describes their acts of defiance, either attack the life and person of the Prophet, or stress Christology and the unity or Trinity of God. Eulogio himself gives an account of Muslim belief about Jesus which is sympathetic.

> "He taught that Christ is the Word of God, and his Spirit, and indeed a great prophet, but with no power of Deity, like Adam, not equal to the Father; who was filled with the Holy Spirit on account of his merits, by the power of God was renowned for miracles and distinguished by signs and portents, prevailing nothing by his own majesty or Godhead, but adhering to God like a just man, he deserved to accomplish many things from the Almighty by humble prayers."

There is no misrepresentation here, and little bitterness. Again, however, it foreshadows a future when Christians would puzzle over the high regard of Muslims for the Messiah, and the Quranic praise of Jesus. The Quranic praises, of course, extend to the mother of Jesus, and it is the more curious that Eulogio writes that he will say nothing about the horrible sacrilege about Mary, queen of the world and mother of the Saviour. Here Eulogio perhaps confused Muslim beliefs with stories from the Talmud; later mediaeval writers did not follow him here, but knew that the Quranic revelation was wholly reverent towards Mary. Eulogio also inveighs bitterly against the building of mosques and particularly against the call to prayer. It seems illogical that he should object more to the public worship of Islam than to Islamic rule itself, and yet this hatred showed itself again and again in later ages.

Ideas that would have a long history appear also in Alvaro; for example, that Islam is a conglomeration of heresies—that is the idea that parallels, while it reverses, the Muslim concept of Christianity as a falling away from the truth of Islam. Another example is the argument that the truthful element in Islam introduces the untruthful, the 'sugared poison', a concept, as we have seen, also in Eulogio. The Quran is a deliberate "weaving of stories together" and "in a false style". The approach most characteristic of Alvaro is that which argues on the basis of what the writer believes Islam must really be; and, of course, he puts into their mouths intentions that they never had. He decides, for example, that he knows better than the Arabs what the *muezzin* (*muadhdhin*, the man who calls to prayer, or utters the *adhan*) really is. He expounds the Old Testament prophet Daniel: in the Vulgate, "He shall worship the god Maozim in his place" (AV— "shall he honour the god of forces") . . . "and he shall do this to fortify Maozim with a strange god." This refers actually to Antiochus Epiphanes, and the god of fortresses, perhaps, to Jupiter Capitolinus, for whom Antiochus, while a hostage in Rome, acquired a devotion. To Alvaro it prophesied Islam. Since 'maozim' means strong, Alvaro can say, "Maozim whom they call Cobar"—*cobar* is *kabir*, or, since he refers to the call to prayer, *akbar*, 'God is great.' "With the ritual of wild animals, their lips apart and their throats wide open, they cry out as if they had the stomach-ache, and make their announcement bawling like madmen." As a description of the *muezzin*, this is grotesque, and the argument that Arabic has changed the form 'Maozim' to 'almozem' (i.e. *muezzin*), which he seems to take for a name of God, hardly less so. All this absurd speculation could easily have been corrected by reference to any Arab, or even perhaps an Arabic-speaking Christian with no axe to grind. It was one of the characteristic polemic positions that Christians believed they knew the real facts which Muslims sought to obscure. Both Alvaro and Eulogio, however, translate correctly a phrase which in later centuries would be exploited polemically against Islam. It can be translated by the literal-minded as "May God pray over Muhammad;" our authors say, "Lord, have mercy on our prophet" or "May God celebrate and save him" (*psallat Deus super eum et salvet eum*). Thus happily they let slip the opportunity for a very superficial polemic advantage; meantime it became clear that both had access to, or had early acquired, accurate information about religious phrases in Arabic. They had not cut themselves off from their surroundings as completely as they pretended.

For Alvaro and Eulogio the Islamic revelation had been contrived to an end, and that end was self-indulgence of all kinds, but mostly of the sexual kind. In our own world, both Christianity and Islam are condemned for setting limits to the use of sexuality and other pleasures; it must seem the more unaccountable that Christians once set so high a store on sexual abstention as to attack Islam violently for its laxity. Yet such is the case. Alvaro followed the same general lines as his friend, but in his own way. He took as his text Ezekiel: "And she was mad with lust . . ." and Jeremiah, "They are become as amorous stallions." For both our writers the confirmation of their arguments by Old Testament prophecy was important, though the texts in which they find what they seek are often more obscure than those in the Quran that they attack. Alvaro's attack is directed against plural marriage and the legality of concubinage in the status of slavery. (Christianity forbade concubinage, at least in theory, but not, of course, slavery.) Probably he also refers to divorce in the phrase "all are made adulterers" but his meaning is often obscure. He even attacks Islam for "uncleanest delight . . . and an incestuous bed", and there is no slightest colouring for such criticism. He also speaks of encouraging things to be done with women "usurping the natural law and seeking new ways of desire;" perhaps this refers only to sexual postures. Alvaro's invective is consistently violent. It is always clear that his objection is to sexual pleasure as such and in any circumstances. He is outraged by a tradition of the Prophet's sexual prowess, because he cannot associate sanctity and sexuality even in a legitimate context. Sex is "from Venus the ridiculous, the spouse of Vulcan, that is, the wife of fire, who, because of the foamy liquid, is also called Afrodin: *qui et opus venereum assignatur*, alkaufeit *idem impudicus nominavit*." The text is corrupt, but the sense is clear, and also the play of words. If there is something of a game in the classical references, biblical citation is wholly serious. Identification of Old Testament meanings as prophetic gives a confidence that can withstand the visible success of Islam in the world around. "Behold Behemoth" —Islam lacks true religion; "he eateth grass"—not wheat; hay stands for the empty people Behemoth devours. The images become tortuous: "Finding them empty he devoured them and tied them to him by everlasting chains." Job's "His strength is in his loins, and his force in the navel of his belly" Alvaro refers to the boast of the Prophet's sexual power. All the strands of his thought run together; on "The sinews of his testicles are wrapped together" he comments, "running with desires and satiated with germination." On "His bones are like pipes of brass" he says, "All his uncouth people make the admirable style of Arabic into something senseless . . . Like metal, they have the style of speaking well, without the sense . . . "

The same thoughts pass through every subject he considers. The Arabs fight against other nations "as if it were the command of God," but the psalmist says, "Scatter thou the nations that delight in war". Christians observed the day of the Lord, but Islam dedicates Friday to "the stomach and to lust", when it ought to be given to sadness and fasting. Christ taught frugality and fasting, Islam "jollity and the allurements of feasting . . . it applies no legal brake for the repression of shamelessness." Christ restrained the natural motions by his laws, Islam encourages licence; Christ ordained abstention even from the connubial bed in the time of fast, but Muslims at such times especially consecrate themselves to "venereal reward". This is a fair indication of the purely rhetorical quality of what is being said: Islam in fact is strict in requiring total abstention during the hours of fast. Eulogio describes the *Id* following the fast as given over to "the debauchery of gluttony and the flow of wantonness," a severe and depressing, but not necessarily a false, description of much human celebration. His comment illustrates another characteristic polemic trick: to contrast Muslim practice with Christian ideal. Practice for practice there would be no such contrast. Alvaro sums up the whole of Christian criticism in his interpretation of Job, when he applies the verse, "or speak soft words to thee". The words of the Quran are "soft", easy, pleasant: *verba sunt mollia*. Eulogio has a genuine gift for description, and in one of his martyrdom accounts he tries to present the Muslim case as the cadi stated it. It begins fairly enough, and slips finally into the usual Christian image of Islam, soft and sexual. "The cadi preached Mahom the author of this sect, who, illuminated by the teaching of the angel Gabriel, received the word of prophecy from the Most High to announce to the nations, established a law, treated of paradise and taught the kingdom of heaven, full of feasts and streams of women."

Eulogio and Alvaro were not direct sources of later mediaeval polemic. This whole extraordinary episode of the Cordovan martyrs seems to have been generally forgotten; yet all that they say falls within the main pattern of the later polemic, and much that they say would reappear later, unchanged in detail. We can even claim that the substance of later Christian polemic against Islam is contained in the Cordovan corpus; but we have no ground to suppose it the original invention of the two friends. We know that their teacher was the abbot Hope-in-God, and that he had written a little book against Islam, from which Eulogio quotes a passage (*"non erit paradisus sed lupanar"*). The monks, clerics and laymen of Cordova had the same schools and education, and the monks seem to have been unstable by Benedictine standards of *stabilitas*. We infer a variety of cenobitical ways of life, both in the town and outside it; in the mountains, a prompt awareness of what was happening in the town, but, in the town, a solid ignorance of what was happening among Muslim fellow-townsmen. Perhaps the real division was not between the clergy and the laity, but between those Christians who renounced and those who accepted Arabization. In the nature of things, the renouncers were destined to disappear from the Spanish scene, but they had received and passed on a tradition. We may recall the "old book" of Pamplona which Eulogio quoted at length. If this was not his own invention (and it is not probable that it was), this manuscript, with its genuine if imperfect knowledge of Islam, savagely twisted by malice, is not likely to have come from a French or other European source. In any case, the sources of Eulogio's knowledge were Spanish. Everything points to the existence of a continuous Spanish Christian tradition which existed before our authors, on which they drew, and which survived long after them. Almost certainly, there was a common stock of half-knowledge about Islam, repetitions at third hand, misinterpretation of things seen and misrepresentation of things heard. Above all, there was a well of resentment, constantly replenished.

4. Interpretation

The evidence for the existence of this long tradition is important to the historian of opinion, but the writers themselves took it largely for granted; for them, the important thing was to justify 'spontaneous' martyrdom. This to us seems too untypical to be equally important; Spanish perhaps, in the sense of quixotic, but almost unparalleled in the main stream of European history. Alvaro refers obscurely to the uncomfortable precedent of the Donatists. Yet even these arguments are worth some analysis. In the face of all the facts, our authors tried to believe that the martyrdoms were not unprovoked. Somehow they had to show that the martyrs responded to a pre-existing persecution of Christians. Alvaro said that if a Christian denies that there is persecution in Cordova, "either he bears the yoke of slavery asleep and dreaming" or he shares the position of the persecutors. His opponents "say that the martyrs proceeded without any hostile stimulus; I, by declaring what they claimed, will confirm that they were oppressed by the zeal of the Arabs." He makes his point by describing in detail the cases of Perfectus/Kamil and of the merchant John. By our standards and his enemies' evidence, the Cadi did everything possible to avoid treating Perfectus severely. John was cruelly beaten, but he was not executed, and his punishment would not have seemed out of the way to a sailor in

45

Nelson's navy. On the other hand, the same evidence convinces us that the Muslim crowds were often hostile and easily roused to attack Christians. Muslim domination was a 'persecution' because it was a domination, not because it was intolerant; we have seen that Christians resented its very tolerance. There was a total opposition of almost Manichaean proportion: *nihil quippe veritati nisi falsitas contravenit.* "We have used the Gospel against the Gospel, for whoever forbids cursing also orders blessing." With heavy sarcasm Alvaro portrays the attitude of tolerant Christians: "They (the martyrs) are the persecutors of the Arabs (*ethnicorum*); we are the persecutors of the worshippers of Christ." The sense of the word 'persecute' becomes clearer. It does not mean more than 'be in opposition to'; the martyrs were provoked, and the martyrs persecuted, by the existence of Islam and the presence of Muslims. The Arabs are 'cruel' but cruelty is wrong only when and because it is used against the church. The Prophet gave the Arabs a sword to kill the people of God, but Islam was instigated by God to winnow the chaff. The chaff are the Christian compromisers. There exist only the truth and the lie.

Eulogio's arguments are similar but they give us a better picture of what the Christian critics were saying. Their first point is the failure of the relics of the martyrs to work miracles. It is indeed a wonder that this movement of fanatics produced no wonder; perhaps thaumaturgical sanctity presupposes a basis of belief among the masses, whereas this, so far as we can tell, was an élite movement. The same reproach was levelled both by Muslims, who did not believe miracles necessary to true prophecy, but recognized that Christians did, and by Christians who demanded confirmation by miracles before they would accept the holiness of the movement. Eulogio could only say that this was to "distract attention from the intention of our martyrs." Many of the faithful and even (*heu proh dolor!*) of the priests did not want the martyrs to be admitted to the catalogues of the saints. These quoted Scripture: "But I say to you, love your enemies;" "Do violence to no man;" "Who, when he was reviled, did not revile;" "nor railers shall possess the kingdom of God." To these he replied with others such as "a little leaven corrupteth the lump" and they "have turned aside into vain babbling," "they have laboured to commit iniquity." We might think that it is the quotations chosen by the critics that are directly to the point, but Eulogio says that such people "are not content to understand the Scriptures in a sane

sense, but expound them according as they please." He complains
that the critics "carry their opinions through the market-place"
and "desert the line of sane doctrine on election by their own
judgement." Can this mean that they thought salvation possible
for Muslims? More probably that they did not confine salvation
to an élite. Eulogio returns to the real point when he says that the
critics argue that "those who are not dragged violently to
martyrdom should not be, or be taken to be, martyrs;" and "they
rebuke those who come by their own will, in that they have been
in no way molested." He argues the existence of persecution from
the destruction of churches, insults to the clergy, the poll tax on
Christians. The soldiers of Christ must confess Christ before the
Arabs: it is understood here that confessing Christ means insulting
Islam. "For he that shall confess me and my words in this adulterous and sinful generation, the Son of man also will confess him."
This misquotation is itself revealing. It is a conflation of two
parallel passages in the Gospels. Eulogio has naturally preferred
the more strongly worded passage, but this actually has "he that
shall be ashamed of me . . . the Son of man also will be ashamed of
him." Put in this correct form, it could by no stretch of imagination have been made to justify the aggressive "confession of
Christ".

Eulogio seems desperately to be hiding his own doubts. "If hell
holds those who openly profess holy things," how much more
those who preach the truth in hiding? If it is useless to wrestle in
the public gymnasium, it is more so to proclaim the truth in
secret. Justice requires a public outcry against the author of crime.
Christians owe no obligation to the Muslims; admittedly Christians
are "allowed freely to bear the standard of the Christian faith by
the followers of the same prophet, as one of the privileges of their
rule," but this must be attributed, not to Muslims' patience, but to
the providence of God. Yet his own arguments may have seemed
specious to him. The motives of the martyrs worry him. Can they
like dying for its own sake? No, he says, they died to escape the
pains of hell, and in doing so went surely to heaven. He must
always return to the same point; the confession of Christ and the
attack on Islam are necessarily involved together. The martyrs'
intentions were good, so their actions must have been right; and
their actions were right, and so their intentions good.

It is the presence of Islam that is a 'persecution', and Christians
must persecute Islam, even by dying in order to denounce it. The

new custom of dying to attack Islam disappeared; it could only be the fashion or the mood of a moment of history. The other ideas survived, and came to determine in due course the Christian attitude to Crusade and to Muslim minorities. The martyrs implied a political theory which in less disadvantageous terms affected the lives of thousands; not always obeyed, yet it was preached by the Church for centuries. It was practised when Islam was originally extirpated from Sicily. It was practised by the Crusaders. It was practised in the Reconquista, and found its ultimate expression when the Spanish monarchs expelled the Moriscos. Its logical and legal expression was in the Inquisition. The theory was simple: Christianity cannot exist side by side with any other religion; and the martyrs practised the theory with a logic untempered by common sense. They applied within a community living under Muslim rule the logic which Christians would later apply in Europe from a dominant position, and continue to apply until the imperial age. Applied from a position of dominance, the theory was very practical, more practical, though less attractive, than the tolerance which Islam still showed to Christians while Europe expelled over its frontiers the few aliens it had not been able totally to absorb.

The over-insistent pursuit of an acceptable orthodoxy, with its resulting tensions, occupied Europe for many centuries, resulting ultimately in a cultural disintegration. This long history did not originate with Eulogio and Alvaro and the Cordovan martyrs whose great renunciation they celebrated. It happens that a small, limited, but extremely interesting literature illuminates one brief episode of Christian resistance to absorption. We should see this literature not as the source of a great tradition, but as the illustration of a phase in its development.

Chapter 3

The Central and Western Mediterranean to the end of the tenth century

1. Charlemagne and his successors

We have seen that the peoples of the Mediterranean world in the eighth century were linked together less by conscious interests than by underlying resemblances; we have also used the magnifying glass on one small area for one short time, and have recognized the festering hatreds of conflicting communities. I want now to look at the actual relations of Europeans and Arabs during the main period of Arab greatness, when the Arabs in fact had their least close relations with European communities. There was a story of St Willibald's pilgrimage towards the middle of the eighth century which illustrates the remoteness of parts of Europe from the Mediterranean community. Landing at Tortosa in Syria from Cyprus, Willibald and seven other Englishmen were soon, at Homs, arrested by the "pagan Saracens", who "did not know of what people they were, and thought they must be spies." Willibald, himself the ultimate source of this statement, seems almost to sympathize. He and his friends were rescued by the intervention of a Spanish chamberlain of the "Saracen king"; this official visited them in the prison, doubtless to establish whether they were indeed spies. They were brought in front of the Caliph; he asked them where they came from, and was told that "these men come from the Western shore, where the sunset takes place, and we do not know of any land beyond, and nothing but waters." The ruler answered, "Why should we punish them? They have not committed any offence against us. Put them on their road . . ." There are several points here of interest. There is no real animosity, apparently on either side. The remoteness of England in physical terms is stressed in much the way any traveller would do, but the underlying argument is the disinterestedness of foreigners from really distant parts. This was not a lack of interest, and there is

49

no suggestion of a sense of difference, but rather one of the community of all whom chance has brought together.

A tone of remote attention is maintained whenever writers from the north are talking about the Mediterranean or the Arabs in it. The Carolingian House was proud to think of itself as cosmopolitan, even before Charles the Great boasted of his exchange of embassies with Harun ar-Rashid. In 692 Pepin boasted of receiving embassies from all the surrounding nations, "Greeks, Romans, Lombards, Huns, Slavs and Saracens." Arab rulers in Spain are often mentioned in the northern annals, and their names were as well known at least as those of Byzantine emperors and commanders. In 777 the King was recorded as having received Ibn al-Arabi, ruler of Saragossa, and other Spanish Arabs. A pride in cosmopolitan connections shines in such annal entries as that for 797, towards the height of Charles the Great's power, which records that Abdalla, a refugee from his brother's rule in Morocco, was received at Aachen, and also that Theoctistus, the legate of the patrician Nicetas, procurator of Sicily, brought letters there from Constantinople, from the Emperor. In 817 the (Western) Emperor received the envoys of Abd ar-Rahman at Compiègne, and sent them ahead to Aachen, where others had already spent the winter. They were kept waiting for three months, and were sent away just as they began to fear they would never be released. It is idle to speculate whether guests or hosts found time or inclination for intelligent discussions; no evidence for it has survived. Alcuin's vague uncertain reference to Spanish Islam as the possible cradle of Adoptionism must surely register the lack of precision in his mind; the Spanish bishops were safe from Frankish pressures because they lived under a foreign prince, but in other ways Adoptionism was handled as though no barrier between Mozarabs and other Europeans existed.

The most famous of Arab negotiations by Charles the Great were those with Harun ar-Rashid, the historicity of which has been seriously doubted. That no Arab reference to this exchange exists is evidence only that Harun or his historians did not think it worth recounting; this does not mean that they did not think the manipulation of a peripheral barbarian state against the Umayyads worth doing. What interests us is unquestionable: the European belief that the embassy occurred. At Ravenna Charles heard that envoys from Harun ('Aaron'—correctly translated), the Commander of the Faithful ('amir munmilin' and other variants, for *amir al-muminin*; it was probably taken for a personal name), the King of Persia, had landed at Pisa. Charles met them near Vercelli; there was one "Persian from the East", and a second envoy from Abraham, amir ('amirati'), ruler at the limits of Africa in Fossat (i.e. Ibrahim ibn al-Aghlab, recently confirmed ruler of Ifriqiya, i.e. Tunis, not Fustat in Egypt). They announced the return of Charles's own envoy, Isaac the Jew, with a fleet burdened with gifts, including the elephant whose journey across the Alps would cause much trouble. As subsequently written up by Eginhard in his *Vita Karoli Magni Imperatoris* (modelled on Suetonius), the exotic aspect was stressed. Later came further gifts, "textiles and aromatic spices and other riches of the countries of the East." Again, there is name-dropping on a grand scale; there were embassies from the Emperors Nicephorus, Michael and Leo. The court at Aachen needed to seem cosmopolitan to itself.

A realistic assessment of politics and war underlay all this, though for Charles the Holy War would always be the war in the East against the Saxons; there, rather than in Spain, the permanent extension of empire was waiting. For his predecessors, for himself and his successors, there were Arab wars in what was later France, as well as in Barcelona and Saragossa; there was no clear frontier, and the area was still thought of as the *Gothic* borders. It was not abnormal for a Christian noble to make Arab allies, or for an Arab rebel to turn for help to a European ruler. The famous invasion of the Franks which Charles Martel turned back in 732 was supported by Eudo, duke of Aquitaine, who invited Abd ar-Rahman, as the Metz Annals put it, to "defend" him from Charles. No annalist recounts the subsequent fighting around Avignon, Narbonne and Nîmes in terms of holy war. If a Saracen is described as '*perfidus*', this may often be only a technicality, hardly more emotive than 'non-Christian', sometimes its best translation. It is true that in 752 Pepin is said to have "liberated the Christians from the servitude of the Arabs," but in spite of references to the heavy yoke of the Arabs, Charles the Great's wars in Spain were the product of political alliances with dissident Arab rulers; the famous disaster of Roncevaux was the work of Basques. The Arabs were just one kind of alien; the *Annals of the Frankish Kings* note under 820 that the treaty with the Arabs in Spain ceased to be useful, and was broken by Christian attack; eight merchant ships returning from Sardinia to Italy were taken by Arab pirates and sunk; the Northmen were in Flanders and at the mouth of the Seine and were devastating the west coast. Attitudes are realist and rarely pious.

There are endless examples in the eighth to the tenth centuries of alliances that linked Arabs and Europeans. In 891 a group of Arab raiders seized and fortified the villa at Garde-Freinet (Fraxinetum, near Fréjus), and this settlement long flourished, purely as a base for raiding. The historian Liutprand of Cremona explains:

> "Those of the Provençals who were the nearest neighbours of those people began to disagree among themselves from envy . . . and because each faction could find no satisfaction for its jealousy and resentment by itself, they called in the same Arabs—no less cunning than faithless—to help them."

Liutprand distinguishes invaders more carefully than some writers do, and he judged the Aghlabids from Tunisia who settled in southern Italy as worse than either the Garde-Freinet Arabs or the Magyars; but he did not single out Arabs as such, and he describes the settlement of the Aghlabids in Italy as having been in response to the request of the Emperor Romanos to quell revolts in Apulia and Calabria. Throughout his lifetime and after, the wars and alliances of Latins, Greeks and Arabs in Italy would continue, but Arab alliances had been more important in the preceding century. The advantage was not necessarily to the Arabs. Liutprand himself, after discussing Pope John's mistresses, describes without comment how a disgruntled Arab defected, and obtained a commission from the same Pope to lead a band of young Roman soldiers. In the total disarray of Italian affairs, and among considerable disorders in the church, the Arab invaders constituted a normal factor, and only one among several. It may be that the unedifying impression given by some tenth-century Popes helped to avert the concept of holy war, which their predecessors had begun to fashion. It can be argued that in a crude form the notion survived, as in Liutprand's grudging account of John X's part in the Byzantine alliance leading to the defeat of the Arabs at the Garigliano in 915. In advance, the Pope was advised to impute a victory to God, and a defeat to the sins of the Christians. Otherwise, although Liutprand often and with reason invokes the judgement of God, any active concept of holy war is remote. He remarked that at the Garigliano some Christian believers thought they saw St Peter and St Paul in the battle line—like Theseus at Marathon— but for himself he said only that it might be reasonable to suppose that the prayers of these saints had brought about the victory. It is a long way from this careful judgement to the concept of crusade. When in 942 King Hugh was in a position to destroy the Arabs of Garde-Freinet, his fear of invasion from the north made him prefer to make a treaty with them instead. Liutprand could not forbear from speculating how many afterwards travelling to Rome as pilgrims shed their blood in consequence. Perhaps in practice more paid ransom. This is sound rhetorical moralizing; but, again, it is less than crusading talk.

Liutprand sometimes speaks of 'Carthaginians' (*Poeni*) rather than of 'Saracens'. By this certainly he means to designate specifically Aghlabid forces, and other writers were usually less exact. The word used for 'Arab' by most of the chroniclers of the time is 'Agarene', though 'Saracen' is also common. Later, 'Saracen' would become the more common. 'Agarene' means 'Arab', as 'descendant of Hagar'. The Greek word 'Saracen', on the other hand, is of unknown etymology, and was thought to imply a claim to descent from Sarah, so that 'Agarene' was often used as a corrective. In pre-Islamic Greek usage, 'Saracen' is synonymous with 'Arab'. 'Ismaelite' has, obviously, the same sense as 'Agarene' —"Ismaelites, who are called Saracens by a corruption of the word," says the continuation of Fredegar. 'Agarene' and 'Ismaelite' are more specific than 'Saracen', which would ultimately come to be used as a portmanteau word with no clear significance, as when a group is said to contain Arabs, Turks and Saracens. Then it means an unspecified residuum of Arabic-speaking Muslims. When from the twelfth century onwards there were more specific ideas of Islam, 'Saracen' in many contexts—in a discussion of Islam, or an account of the time of the Prophet—meant 'Muslim'. If sometimes we must use the one word, and sometimes the other, to translate it, probably both ideas, 'Muslim' and 'Arab' (i.e. a native-speaker of Arabic), were usually present in it. 'Saracen' is never used to refer to a Christian Arab. 'Arabs' and 'Arabus' are rarely used, but, when used, mean an Arabian, in the classical sense, or a Bedouin. No mediaeval writer seems ever to have realized that 'Saracen' has no Arabic equivalent form. It is safe to say that in the period we are discussing, and up to the twelfth century, 'Agarene' and other such words have very little meaning beyond the designation of a race or society only roughly identified. This usage reflects the political situation with its indeterminate frontiers. We shall see that the first ideas of holy war were clearly formed in the ninth century (though forgotten or diluted in the tenth); but in these three centuries the general attitude was in every way more relaxed than it would be later; at once more feeble from a military point of view, and politically more open and un-committed.

We form two clear impressions. During these centuries there is no real development in the European assessment of the Arabs; perhaps there was none from their first arrival in Europe until the Crusades. The picture of a world of violence and devastation, however, was even older: "the struggles of the kings against the nations, of the martyrs against the pagans, of the churches against the heretics" reflects European experience in the sixth century, when Gregory of Tours wrote these words, and until at least the early part of the eleventh; when a change did come, it took the form of an infused emotion of aggression directed against the Arab World and evoked by the thought of it; but the arrival of the Arabs centuries earlier had not created it, and their presence on what is now French and Italian soil does not seem to have changed the quality of life for the natives; Arab violence was not distinct from any other violence, and it brought no new experience.

The other impression is of a difference between northern and Mediterranean attitudes, even at this early date, which modifies any other generalization. North or south, the Arabs were only one of several enemies, but in the Mediterranean, and especially in central and southern Italy, there was a closer experience of Arab invasion, and a much sharper impact of actual warfare. In northern Europe any sense of the presence of the Arabs became increasingly remote after the time of Charles the Great. The Arabs were generally recognized to be a peculiarly Mediterranean problem.

2. Impact of war

In fact this was a 'killing time', and a killing time that endured for long. If Europeans did not yet distinguish the Arabs as their particular enemy, still in the south their main impression of the Arabs was one of violence. The ninth and tenth centuries were a period of sustained attacks on Europe on all sides. We have spoken of the silent agricultural revolution; the astonishing thing is that it gradually took place, and prosperity increased—for example, in East Anglia—against a background of increasingly serious Viking raids on the British islands and on northern France and Germany.

The date of Alfred's standstill agreement with Guthrum, accepting the Danelaw, is 878; the siege of Paris was in 885–6. Arnulf of the East Franks defeated the Danes at Loewen in 891; the foundation of Normandy came in 911. In the course of a century the Danes had overrun much of England, penetrated deep and often into France, made several unsuccessful attacks on Moorish Spain, and even, in one famous episode, sacked the Italian city of Luni, already the victim of Arab raiders. The Magyar invasions of Europe began in 889, and were to trouble central Europe and the Adriatic for over a century. Meanwhile the Aghlabids, whose independent rule in Tunis dates from 800, the year of the coronation of Charlemagne, had conquered Sicily between 827 and 831. Settlements and raids on the mainland began soon afterwards, and in 846 Arab armies were in the outskirts of Rome. Warfare lasted throughout the century, with fluctuating fortunes; Arab attempts at permanent settlements in Italy ended with the victory of combined Greek and Latin forces at the Garigliano in 915. The small Arab colony in Provence, established originally from Spain in 891, lasted for more than eighty years; and raids on the Italian mainland lasted throughout the tenth century and even into the eleventh.

Aghlabid and, later, Fatimid rule in Sicily was settled, peaceful and beneficial, over a mixed society in which the Greek and Latin elements are disputed; it was as well established, for a time, as Arab rule in Spain; but the Arabs could not appear to the citizens of southern Italy under Byzantine or Langobardic rule in the capacity of civilized rulers, but only as colonists who never succeeded in establishing themselves, and as raiders. The relation of the raided to the raider is very different from that of the ruled to the ruler. In Provence, too, although there was a settled colony, in all its eighty odd years it was only a base for raiding. Although Arabs contributed less than Norsemen to the total harassment of the shores of Europe, in these areas their relationship to those who could only fear and fight them must be unproductive. Their very failure to settle prevented fruitful contact. The inherited memory of these two centuries of warfare is a factor, only one out of several, but a factor all the same, to take into account in explaining the characteristic Christian intolerance of Islam, and the aggressive attitude of Christians, in succeeding centuries.

Quotations will illustrate the impression made upon the European mind. Our chroniclers are often monastic and are always clerical, so that they give us the literate not the folk memory, and their experience is not wholly representative; but its tone is cumulatively convincing of the impression left behind, although no doubt it falls well short of the total contemporary experience. In the permanent records of the age, the word regularly associated with the Arabs is 'devastation'. Erchembert, monk of Monte Cassino, writing in the eleventh century, remembered the Arab invasion of Sicily in these terms:

> "About these times, the people of the Arabs, with all the appearance of a swarm of bees, but with a heavy hand, came fast out of Babylon and Africa into Sicily; they devastated everything and all around, and at length took the famous city called Palermo, which they inhabit up to now, and overthrew many cities and towns in that island, and soon they subjected almost all of it to their rule."

Babylon here means Babylon on the Nile, with Fustat (and, later in the Middle Ages, it would mean Cairo); Africa is Ifriqiya, modern Tunisia; a swarm of bees, therefore, from Egypt and Tunis. In fact the invaders were the Tunisian Aghlabids, Liutprand's 'Carthaginians'.

Most chroniclers reflect an image of perpetually repeated devastation. There is some suggestion that at the first mainland impact in about 840 their military techniques were almost as striking as the consequences. The "most astute nation of Arabs" landed troops which

> "as they are cunning by nature, and more forward-looking in evil than others, examined the fortifications of the place (Bari) more minutely, and made their way into the city by hidden places at night-time when the followers of Christ were resting, and partly they slaughtered the innocent people by the sword, and partly took them captive . . ."

There are entries to balance this; there was always a pride in reprisal: "Out of an innumerable force of the Pagans" (we read a little later) "scarcely any escaped." We are not in any case assessing comparative misfortunes. The impression left behind on the European side seems naturally enough to have been overwhelmingly one of Christian devastation. "They crossed to the city of Ancona, which in like manner they consumed by fire, and thence carried off with them many prisoners." "Numberless farmers having been killed, Naples, Benevento and Capua were in part depopulated." "The vilest and most infamous of the

Arabs cruelly laid waste Benevento by fire and sword and captivity."
"The land was reduced to a desert, and the monasteries were
without the holy liturgy." "They laid everything bare . . . destroyed everything." These refer chiefly to the 840s and 870s, but
the same sort of complaints continue in the tenth century.

> "In the year 924, Oria was captured by the Arabs in the month of
> July, and they killed all the women, and took all the rest of the
> people off to Africa to sell for slaves . . . In the year 986 the Arabs
> seized the holy city of Chiriaco and destroyed all Calabria. In the
> year 988 . . . the Arabs depopulated the neighbourhood of Bari and
> took men and women captive to Sicily."

This continued even into the earlier eleventh century; in 1016
the long-suffering town of Luni in Liguria was again attacked and
the Arabs "in strength and safety stayed in all that area, and
misused the women" (in this case the raiders were destroyed).
These extracts are taken almost at random. They can tell us little
more than what was in the minds of the writers. There is little
suggestion that these wars were worse than other wars, and there
is no reproach against the Arabs as Muslims, but only as the
devastators of the moment. Attacks were frequently repeated,
largely because the Europeans lacked the power to mount an
effective counter-attack. The Arab invasions were seen as a
misfortune, but it was one which was not forgotten, as all these
chronicles testify.

A period of devastation which the popes at least were unlikely
to forget was that of the attack on Rome in 846. A Venetian
chronicle rather understates the memory: "The aforesaid Arabs
even dared to approach Rome, and to loot the church of Saint
Peter; but when they came to that of Saint Paul, the Roman
citizens killed them nearly all." The episode is best studied as a
legend, and Benedict, a monk of St Andrew's at Monte Soracte,
gives us the received image, perhaps all the better for being inaccurate, confused and ungrammatical. He says that some scoun-
drels left Rome and invited the "king of Babylon" (Egypt) to
come and take possession of the kingdom of Italy; the Arabs came
and covered the face of the earth like locusts, or like corn standing
in the field. The Romans were in such fear that they dared not go
outside the walls; Rome was closely invested and the church of
Saint Peter was taken and plundered. The enemy surrounded the
altar and one of them took a little spear and threw it at a picture of

the Lord in the apse; it penetrated the plaster, and the image bled as if it were a living man in the flesh; and stayed so forever. (Later the Arabs boast: "We have seen the blood of the Christians' God.") The Pope

"inspired by the holy flamen [*sic*], and daily comforting the Roman people by the power of the Holy Spirit, contrived a plan, how God Almighty should carry away the nations of the barbarians, and should clear the church of Saint Peter the Apostle, which is the head of all the churches, of the pestilential peoples."

He sends messengers to the Frankish king and to the Marquis Guy; the Franks are frightened, but Guy and the Romans destroy a tenth part of the enemy, who embark at Civitavecchia with their loot. The Romans have ever since (Benedict continues) held the Franks in derision. This whole account, with its strong local partisanship, is often inaccurate; not only are Egypt and North Africa confused, but Popes Gregory IV, Sergius II and Leo IV are not distinguished. The passage is primarily emotive. The Arabs are usually called '*barbari*', a word which has often in its history meant little more than 'enemy'. Benedict is very unlearned, yet we can hardly deride his ignorance of contemporary Arab civilization. This was not the aspect which had been shown to the Romans: war is war.

The later invasion of Rome in 875 he describes as inaugurating a thirty-year occupation of the Roman territories. Hincmar, a genuine historian, writing in Germany some forty years after the attack of 846, says:

"The Arabs and Moors assaulted Rome on the Tiber, and when they had laid waste the basilica of the blessed Peter, the prince of the apostles, and carried off all the ornaments and treasures, with the very altar which was situated above the tomb of the famous prince of apostles, they occupied strongly a fortified hill a hundred miles away from the city" (Garigliano).

So far as the danger of permanent colonization was concerned, threats to the west coast and to Rome were the most serious. East-coast settlements were vulnerable to naval attack, both Byzantine and Venetian. It was the thought of a threat to Rome that lay behind the accounts just quoted, and behind Liutprand's most sustained passage on the Arab invasions.

"At the same time Arabs came from Africa with ships and occupied Calabria, Apulia, Benevento and almost all the cities of the Romans, so that the Romans held half, and the Africans half, of each city. On the mount of the Garigliano they established a fortress in which they could safely enough keep their wives, children, their prisoners and their goods."

This with reason seemed particularly dangerous to Liutprand, and he saw that the theology which tells us that God makes the enemy victorious in order to punish our sins must have a military limit, if morale is to be preserved. "Yet lest the Arabs should behave insolently too long, and say 'Where is their God?', God turned the hearts of the Christians, so that the desire was stronger in them to fight than, before, it was to run away." In this way he leads up to an account of the alliance between Romans, Greeks and locals which stormed the Garigliano stronghold. The dividing line between raiding and colonizing was a narrow one. As in the case of the Danish invasions in northern Europe, permanent colonies might have developed where raids succeeded, but this did not happen. A small invading army could not do much in isolation, and the Arabs made no really serious attempt to send reinforcements. From the bridgehead at Garde-Freinet, land-based expeditions to Acqui were not very successful. One such, in 931, coincided with a profitable naval raid on Genoa, when the churches were looted; the fleets operated safely from distant bases.

Memories of fighting from Rome to Salerno survive in the *chanson*, *Li Coronemenz Loois* (about 1130); by then the Arab leader, *"li gentilz amirez"*, could be imagined to have become Christian. The most curious evidence for the European tradition of the times of killing is the story of St Placidus. In the eleventh century, Peter the Deacon, a monk of Monte Cassino, included in his book, *Of the births and deaths of just men*, associated with his monastery, an account of the martyrdom of Placidus and his companions in Sicily. It may have been written to elicit support from Roger of Sicily for the interests of Monte Cassino on the island. There is a stoic account of the martyrdom by Mamucha, the Arab leader of an army 16,700 strong that was devastating Sicily. They cut out Placidus' tongue and broke his teeth and tore his windpipe, and beheaded his whole party. Placidus is unambiguously described as contemporary with St Benedict, and it is made equally clear that the Arabs were Muslims ('Saracen' and 'Ismaelite'); thus the story is set actually a century before the Hijra. It has been acclaimed as one of the most outrageous of forgeries. Our interest is to find the memory of Arab devastations provided convincing background colour for the forgery.

Christian morale was better early in the Carolingian period than it would be again till the eleventh century. Those Arabs who were not killed in battle in Charles Martel's 737 campaign were pursued into the sea and drowned; there was great booty because they had themselves devastated so wide an area. It was not only that sometimes the invaders suffered from the chances of war. Although there were so many reports of piratical raids on a large scale in the Mediterranean, there were often reports of European successes, the capture of Moorish standards in the Balearics, for example, in 799. There was at this period a real fluctuation of success. The Arab fleet which "as usual" attacked Sardinia in 807 was defeated, "and there three thousand are said to have perished," adds the annalist cautiously; they went on to Corsica, where they lost thirteen ships and many more men were killed; it was an unhappy year for them, because, as they themselves admitted, the year before they had taken sixty monks off Pantellaria and sold them as slaves in Spain. This was ill-viewed apparently on both sides. The monks were redeemed by the Emperor and returned to their island, presumably confident that no one would again be unsporting. Yet in 810 the Arab fleet from Spain found both Sardinia and Corsica without defence. In 828 Lothair moved south with a strong force to meet a rumoured Arab invasion of the Frankish coast, but found that the enemy "was either afraid to come or did not want to," and he retired. In the same year the Count Boniface, in charge of the protection of Corsica, sailed with a small fleet to the North African coast, landed between Utica and Carthage, and caught a large body of the inhabitants unawares. Yet on the whole at this date the advantage was with the Arabs, and, as we have already seen, later and in the century following it was more markedly so.

Naturally annalists make much of death and devastation. In practice, probably the most serious factor was the capture of slaves rather than the killings. These raids were business operations and were managed for profit. The effects of the ninth-century wars in southern Italy resulted in a considerable export of slaves, a movement of labour which the country could ill afford. The economy is illustrated by the account of Bernard the Wise, who made the Jerusalem pilgrimage in 870. He and his friends took a passport from the Sultan of Bari ("the chief man of the city, named Suldanus") and took ship at Tarentum, where they found six vessels in the harbour. There were 9,000 captive Christians—we need not take the figure to be exact—of whom one-third were to go to 'Africa' (Ifriqiya, or Tunis), one-third to Tripoli and the rest to Alexandria. Bernard took passage on one of the Alexandria ships. In Egypt he found a Bari passport of little use, and there were heavy disembarkation charges. Licence to move on cost yet more; gradually as he progressed from town to town he got into the way of buying short-distance passports cheaply. The pilgrim was safe enough; the commercial exploitation of travellers and the mobilization of slave labour from the wars went on side by side but separately. There was a greater element of business and trade both in war and in government than there was of religion or abstract principle.

Liutprand, describing the resistance of Henry I of Saxony to the invading Magyars—he calls them Turks, which at that date cannot have had an Islamic implication—puts into his mouth a verse peroration against the enemies of Christ, whom he characterizes emphatically as after ransom tribute. It is the same economy as in the England of the Danegeld. It seems that often it was not permanent settlement that the Europeans feared. Certainly in the tenth century commercial or economic loss was a dominant factor. The Arab coastal raiders had security enough to organize the ransom business on the spot; there is little evidence of prisoners who return, once caught, from overseas, and none of regular ransom missions, as in later centuries. One chronicler tells a story of his own grandfather and great-uncle in 972. His great-uncle was a soldier. Coming down to Vercelli, he heard rumours of a "barbarian" raid which he discounted as improbable, but he found himself suddenly surrounded by "infinite multitudes" of Arabs, and was captured together with some of his men. His brother, the writer's grandfather, knowing nothing of all this, found one of the slaves for sale at the bishop's court. The slave cunningly said nothing about his master's having been captured, and the grandfather redeemed the slave for the price of the breast-plate he was wearing. Then the slave told the rest of the story, and the one brother had the greatest difficulty in raising enough money to ransom the other. It seems likely that the raiders always preferred ransom to slaves. A man must necessarily tend to fetch more from a bereaved family or even a familiar master than, often inexperienced and untrained, on a glutted labour market. In either case there was a drain on European resources, but it was irregular in incidence and even spasmodic. A productive interchange of influences need not presuppose unbroken peace, but it can only exist between permanent bases of settlement.

3. Two personal encounters

We read a number of personal stories which shed a little light, a very little light, on the relations between Arabs and Europeans coexisting in this state of endemic warfare, and illustrate some of the points I have made. Among the populations of Provence or southern Italy there is little sign of curiosity about the ideas of the Arabs who lived among them and fought them, made alliances with them, and fought them again. Negative evidence is not conclusive, but the absence of histories of the Arabs, however travestied, and even of polemic against Islam, among the surviving documents of the period, justifies our assuming that there was a lack of interest, and a failure by two cultures in conflict seriously to penetrate each other. The willingness of many Christians to make alliances with Arabs should be associated precisely with an indifference to their culture and religion. The later ages of fierce aggression against the Arabs coupled a violent dislike with a vivid interest, often but not always erroneous, and never lacking in vitality. So far as the evidence goes, the earlier period was an age of intellectual indifference, when the chief interest was in personalities, and the clerics who wrote the books had no knowledge even of individual Arabs, and often barely differentiated their leaders. We can infer just something from a few stories.

The most famous kidnap for ransom was that of Abbot Maiolus of Cluny, one of the great series of early abbots of that powerful organization. The story is well told by Rudolf Glaber. In 973 an Arab army had boldly pressed inland and for a time occupied some of the more defensible places in the Alpine passes, raiding the countryside around. Maiolus, coming up from Italy on his way home, was surprised with all his following. They were taken off to a more remote place for security; the holy father, says Glaber, with a nasty wound in his hand, from the blow of a javelin meant for one of his men. The Arab captors made their enquiries; while the Abbot insisted that he possessed nothing in this world, he freely conceded that those who were under his command were rich; the ransom was fixed at a thousand pounds of silver, and one of the train was sent to raise it. "While the holy man was held prisoner by the Arabs his quality could not be hidden." As prisoner, he presented at once the image of a great lord condescending— "excelling in the dignity of perfect politeness"—and of an ascetic. "When it came to lunch time, the Arabs offered the food they usually ate, that is, meats and a rather rough kind of bread, and said, 'Eat.' He answered: 'If I go hungry, it is for the Lord to feed me; but these things I will not eat, for they are not what I am accustomed to have.' " Again, side by side with the piety of the man of God, we recognize his sense of the way of life appropriate to a magnate.

> "So one of them, recognizing the respect due to a man of God, and inspired by a sense of duty, bared his arm and at the same time washed his shield, on which he prepared bread in a clean enough way, in the sight of Maiolus. Quickly baking it, he took it to him most respectfully; and Maiolus, accepting it, and refreshing himself from it after the usual prayer, gave thanks to God."

More interesting still was an encounter over belief.

> "Another of these Arabs, when he was whittling a piece of wood with a knife, placed his foot without hesitation on a manuscript belonging to the man of God, a Bible in fact, which he was accustomed by habit always to carry about with him. The holy man, beholding this, lamented, and some of the less insolent among them, observing this, rebuked their companion, saying that it was not right that great prophets should count for nothing like this, that their sayings should be scattered under foot."

Later the same day, for some unknown reason, the others turned angrily on this same man, and in the struggle his foot was mutilated: "really by the judgement of God," says the text, and "that the holiness of the blessed Maiolus should shine forth." Here too we seem to see the association of status with sanctity which underlies all this account, and is assumed to be common ground to the Arabs and the French monks. Also interesting is the explanation of the Muslims' reverence for the words of Jesus the prophet. The author explains that actually the Muslims read the prophets of the Hebrews rather than those of the Christians, "saying that whatever the holy seers of all things foretold about the Lord Christ was fulfilled in a certain man of theirs called Muhammad." This, he says, they prove by an erroneous version of the genealogy of Christ in St Matthew, which replaces Isaac by Ismail. This

obscure and inaccurate assertion seems to be a correction introduced by Glaber, who perhaps does not easily credit the respect
Muslims paid to Jesus; it should be seen as defining the limits of
the knowledge of a later generation rather than that of Maiolus,
and the contemporary interpretation of the episode is rather that
the Arabs perceived and revered, perhaps intuitively, the holiness
both of the Gospels and of the saint. The agreed sum was paid,
the monks were released, and finally the writer notes (on what
authority is not clear) that all the Arabs concerned were killed at
the reduction of Garde-Freinet by Duke William of Arles, and
none returned home.

This encounter came late in the period of Arab advance. It
belongs to the age of the Ottos, to the age of Liutprand. Liutprand,
too, saw the Arab World from the outside; it did not catch his
imagination, and it had nothing, for him, to compare with the
cultural ascendancy of Byzantium, then in the final period of its
military triumph over Muslim forces. He has no stories to tell of
Arabs, like his stories of Greeks. Tenth-century encounters with
Arabs, even so nearly barren as that of Maiolus, are rare, and
even more obviously unfruitful of an exchange of thought of any
kind. Of quite exceptional interest, therefore, is the mission of
John of Gorze to the Caliph and Commander of the Faithful,
Abd ar-Rahman an-Nasir, at the height of Umayyad power in
Spain. It is no meeting of cultures in the sense of an intellectual
interchange, but it is full of interest for the different ways in
which the two cultures could be seen to conflict or diverge. The
Byzantine ghost is always present; we cannot but compare
Liutprand's almost contemporary mission to Byzantium; and
Abd ar-Rahman was himself, of course, supposed to have modelled
his ceremonial on the Byzantine example. In those days diplomacy
consisted of occasional missions, complimentary in character, and
largely exploratory in intention. An embassy took several years
about a single exchange of views and, like all diplomacy, might or
might not have practical results. At almost exactly the time that
John of Gorze was setting off for Cordova, Liutprand was returning
from his first embassy to Constantinople, this one (on behalf of the
Marquis Berengar) before he joined Otto's court, and before
Otto intervened in Italy and became Emperor. Some years after,
Liutprand was to become friendly with Recamund of Elvira,
Abd ar-Rahman's Mozarab ambassador to Otto. To Recamund,
Liutprand dedicates his *Antapodosis*, and occasionally, when he

speaks of events in which Arabs of Spain or Garde-Freinet are involved, he makes a personal reference to Recamund. It remains true that Arab affairs did not greatly interest him.

To understand the story of John of Gorze we have to consider first the religious aspect, which was relevant to a mission to Spain, but not (at that date) to a mission to Constantinople. The clergy surrounding Otto condemned letters sent by Abd ar-Rahman, who, "as a Muslim and altogether foreign to the true faith, although he sought the friendship of a Christian prince, vomited forth several blasphemies against Christ." It is, of course, out of the question that orthodox Muslim letters can have been intended to attack Christ, but in the very wish to be courteous, perhaps, they may have called down the blessing of God on the Prophet Jesus, or in some other way unintentionally have raised the hackles of orthodox Christian believers. Although Otto's advisers admitted that the Caliph's intention was friendly, they considered that letters should be returned to him which would 'correct' his errors. There is some mystery about the Caliph's embassy; we know that he later made use of a Mozarab bishop, and, if he preferred to use a Christian subject in a mission to a Christian potentate, it is evident that he saw the danger of giving unintentional religious offence, and perhaps realized that offence could be taken at some minimally Muslim formula. Otto in any case had no Muslim subject to send to Abd ar-Rahman in return, and was certainly less sensitive to the danger of being offensive. There was some difficulty about the choice of envoys. John's abbot finally allowed him to go, although he had wished at first to frustrate John's "desire to be martyred". Perhaps this desire was an unsuitable predisposition for an ambassador.

The sense of the letters had been leaked in advance. The central feature of the way the embassy was received was the attempt by the Caliph to prevent John from presenting letters which it was known would be offensive (in their turn) to Islam, and would endanger the lives of the members of the mission. There are echoes in this story of the drama of the martyrs in this same Cordova of exactly a hundred years earlier. The probable assumption is that the reply composed by Otto's advisers did not content itself with asserting the doctrine of the Trinity, but that it also followed the usual line of Christian polemic, attacking the Prophet; or, at any rate, that the authorities in Cordova had reason to believe that this was so. "An irrevocable law binds them, that what was fixed in antiquity

for the whole nation may never be dissolved in any way;" a fair
description, though a little *outré*, of the *sharia*. King and people are
"tied by one knot" and, as the king punishes any transgression by
the people, so the people punish the king. Their "first and dreadful
law is that no one may ever dare to say anything against their
religion;" without a chance of intercession and without mercy, the
offender must be punished by death, and, if the king delays doing
so, he will himself be promptly executed. It is not clear what the
source of this misapprehension is, but it adds a certain bureaucratic
equity to the concept of persecution.

This question is also discussed by John and a Mozarab bishop.
When the latter is reminded that Otto's letters are a riposte to the
"blasphemous" letters sent to him, the Mozarab appeals for a
little realism:

> "Consider under what conditions we labour. We are fallen
> into these things because of sin, that we are in the power of the
> Muslims (*paganorum*). We are forbidden by the Apostle's word
> to resist power. Only one bit of comfort remains, that in the evil of
> such calamity they do not forbid us to follow our own religion; and
> when they see us diligently observing Christianity, they honour
> and understand us, the more so that they are drawn that way by
> their own conviction, since they are completely horrified by the
> Jews. For the time being, therefore, we should keep this counsel,
> that since nothing of our religion needs to be given up, we should
> obey them in all the other things, and observe their commands, so
> far as these do not conflict with faith."

John immediately reacts heatedly; "somewhat roused" he says,
"It would better have become another than you, who seem to be a
bishop, to propose these things." This is the quick response of the
European who has not the habit of living in an inferior position,
and so cannot bear the notion of compromise. His actual arguments
are rather irrational. He says that the whole Catholic church has
found it hateful that the Mozarabs should be circumcised, as he
hears is the case, and he quotes Galatians 5:2 (strictly to the letter
and out of context). Then he objects to their abominating any
foods as unclean, because of keeping in communion with Muslims,
citing Titus 1:15, and 1 Timothy 4:5, and another conflation of
Timothy and Titus combined. These are only partly to the point,
and can be taken to bear in any way in which the speaker cares
to interpret them. Still, the Mozarab seems to have been cowed—
the account derives from John himself, we must remember—and

says weakly that "necessity constrains us." John responds with the expected tirade, "I shall never approve of transgressing the divine laws from fear, or love, or any mortal favour . . . I shall openly resist, and not run away from witnessing the truth out of love of life itself." All this is very sincerely meant, we may be sure; but when it came to the point, John was charmed instead of threatened, and ended up chatting happily with the Caliph himself.

At one point during the long period while the ambassadors are waiting to be received, a letter is sent on parchment, on one of the few days when the party were allowed to go to the church. (They were normally kept in isolation.) Realizing that it was likely to prove critical, John put off reading it till after the service was over. "As he turned things over in his mind, he found certain terrors were able to touch him, but he never admitted that he was smitten by any fears." Among other things the letter threatened death for all the Christians of Spain if John persisted in delivering his own letters. To this a defiant reply was sent, arguing largely from John's duty to Otto ("would keep inviolate his loyalty," etc.). The Caliph was not enraged this time, and discussed the reply with his Council. Someone suggested that an ambassador as steadfast as John might also be prudent; might he not himself suggest a way out? John does usefully suggest that an embassy be sent to Otto to obtain milder letters, and this was in fact done. The emissary was Recamund, and so there was effectively no further religious conflict; John's religious views and his perform- ance of the task that his king had sent him to perform coincided as long as the letters to be delivered were in some sense a Christian manifesto, but the practical solution suggests that John had tired or grown out of the attitude of the would-be martyr. There is something characteristically European in an aggressive reaction which is positively evoked by a situation of inferiority. It found religious expression much as with Eulogio and Alvaro; but there was now this difference, for the foreign priest at least, that he had a diplomatic and world job to do, besides seeking martyrdom.

So much for the religious and polemic expression of hostility in terms of conscious argument. Some points better classed as social behaviour are also interesting. The Caliph (he is never called Caliph, but always *rex*) is seen as both ceremonial and cunning. Apart from the idea that he was subject to popular control, there are implications of formal and time-wasting ceremonial which are no doubt more just. The Caliph will not admit that he knows of the letters attacking Islam (because of the supposed law that would enforce him to execute or be executed) but can in any case only be approached through messengers or by letters handed to the household slaves. When the emissaries arrived, they were told they would have to wait three times as long as the last mission, who waited three years. In the end they too waited three years, but not all of this was ceremonial delay by the caliphal court. Apart from the negotiations about presenting the obnoxious letters, the mission of Recamund to Otto seems to have taken a year alone. When Recamund was appointed, he visited John to ask him about Otto (always called, prematurely at this date, Emperor)—"about the customs and institutions of our country, about the clemency of the Emperor, how moderate to his own people, whether he was quick to be angry, irrevocable in decision and much of that kind," and Recamund also wanted to know "finally whether he might be released and not held there for as long a time as John had been." He does not indeed seem to have been long detained by Otto, but he spent a long time visiting Gorze, both coming and going. At least as John's information went, Otto had quickly decided to send new presents and milder letters. These Recamund tried to present direct to the Caliph, who, however, insisted that John should be rewarded for his persistence by making the presentation now agreed on all sides.

The period before Recamund's departure on the compromise mission has some interesting aspects. The authorities seem to have sent a series of envoys to gain intelligence of John's intentions. The first was a Jew, who had apparently been sent informally to encourage the mission and to brief them about local custom:

> "He impressed on them much concerning the custom of the people, and how they ought to observe it in public. The people themselves restrained the young men from all silly and wild action and talk; there was nothing, however trivial, that could not be brought to the King's notice. If they were allowed out, they should not so much as nod at women, even as a joke; nothing could more threaten disaster for them . . ."

The Jew probed carefully to find out about the letters, and John apparently held nothing back. The Jew advised against sending the letters; John insisted that he must present Otto's gifts (then an essential part of every embassy) and Otto's letters together. It was a few months after the Jew that the Mozarab bishop came. The discussion that resulted I have described already. After the hints came the threats—the parchment sent to the church—and then the request for a compromise solution. John clearly felt that he had given each messenger of the Caliph the appropriate reaction—to the Jew candour, to the bishop theological intransigence, to the direct threats a firm reply, and so to the compromise. He may have been right, though he told his story to the writer in a way that suggests that his attitudes were spontaneous rather than calculated. Yet he was accustomed to the diplomatic fashions of his own day, and he seems to have had at least no more to complain about than Liutprand had in Constantinople. He may even have felt more at home; he gives no hint of surprise at new sights or ways, but rather accepts them as normal. In the final meeting with the Caliph he refuses to wear robes of honour, because he is a monk, but even this may have been well calculated. There was a ceremonial entry into Cordova from the suburb where he had been held for so long; once he had been accepted it was as though his status had changed. There were soldiers, crowds, troop exercises, demonstrations, in the dusty road of midsummer. At the palace entrance, carpets and cloaks were laid down. He was brought into a small room where the King sat alone, "as if he were a god (*numen*) accessible to none, or to few." The walls as well as the floors were covered, the King reclined on a luxurious couch, "for they do not use chairs or stools, in the fashion of other peoples, but they recline on beds or couches, talking or eating with their legs crossed, one over the other." The Caliph gave John the palm of his hand to kiss. John admits very frankly that he had entered feeling bitter about the treatment he had received, but that the Caliph's gracious reception made him feel "that he could not have been more equable in spirit." John was later taken back to see the Caliph again, to chat about the strength of Otto's position. There seems to have been a straight discussion, but doubtless planned to extract information. John was sometimes tactless in insisting on his own Emperor's power, but he tried to be tactful; he "replied little and such as might soothe the King's mind." There is no mention of an interpreter, though there must have been one, perhaps Recamund; John's group had been held in isolation, and could not have learned Arabic, even if they had wished to. John notes differences and peculiarities, and leaves us somewhat impressed to think that he did not find more things strange. There is no more suggestion of strangeness or hostility than in Liutprand's Byzantine embassy, and there is much similarity in the treatment the two received, especially the remoteness and grandeur alternating with an intimacy of personal discussion with the monarch. It was customary to treat an embassy rather as a dog sniffs at a strange creature, slowly and prudently examining it from a distance with careful testing. The absence of any real appearance of alienation reduces the importance of the religious dispute. The similarities between Cordova and Byzantium mark the continuing unity of Mediterranean society.

4. Fragmentary interchange

If we return to the Arab settlements in Italy of the previous century, we find less evidence of a spirit of resistance; there are records of personal encounters, but still only occasional hints of knowledge or of understanding between the cultures. The Chronicle of Salerno suggests some spirit of rivalry, an almost sporting element which prefigures, if it does not actually caricature, a later phase of chivalry. This comes out in one anecdote about the siege of Salerno in 871. The chronicler describes two Christian victories in single combat. The desperation of the Christians contrasts with the bravado of the Arab chivalry. We get the impression that the stories were told because they were about Christian successes, and that that was unusual. One of the outstanding leaders of the Arab army, we are told, came and jeered aloud, "You son of perdition, Peter, come and have a hand-to-hand fight, and you will find out what the powers of the Arabs are." To summarize the text in its own phrases, the Arab exulted for a long time, repeating the same words, while Peter put his faith in the mercy of his Redeemer, and went out with a bold spirit to meet him. The Arab came nearly up to the city walls, in a coat of mail and heavily armed, and charged at him. The Christian managed to dodge the impact, but the Arab with his light horse came in again; the Christian continued to evade the wild attack with agility and in fear, and called hastily on God and the martyrs Cosmas and Damian; he stuck out the spear which was in his hand, and hit the Arab between the shoulders; the Arab's vital warmth immediately departed, he clasped his horse's neck, fled to his own people and died immediately. This vivid picture of the over-confident and lively Arab and the reluctant Christian hero appears so frankly only because of the unexpected result. It strikes us now that the morale of the Christians was terrible, and this is rubbed in immediately by another, similar story. Halim had four sons, one of whom, rasher than the others, called daily to the Salernitans: "One of you come out and take me on in single combat, and then you will find out what a son of Halim is like." A man called Landemar came out, ready for battle; the son of Halim came at him with great strength and hit him hard, "but, the Lord not permitting, he in no way wounded him." The Arab rode round Landemar fast, trying to get at him, but the Christian kept his pike facing his opponent and managed to hit him; he too rode back, and died soon after. "O the incomprehensible judgements of God! He punishes, and he saves." The champion of Salerno in this episode makes a much better showing, but the whole struggle is seen in terms of divine intervention, and the Christians seem as mesmerized as rabbits by a weasel, although, not so long before, the Lombard aristocracy had been the great scourge. All the same, the Arabs are shown as real people; they are not just an indistinguishable enemy.

Another story about the same siege is more personal still.

> "The prince Waifar went to the bath; while he was deciding to return to the palace with his people, an Arab staying in the marketplace of the city of Salerno greeted him and said: 'I beg you to give me the covering that you are wearing on your head.' And Waifar straightaway bared his head and presented the wrapping to the Arab on the spot."

The Arab returned to Africa, and found the fleet preparing to sail for the attack on Italy. In the course of the siege he came across an Amalfi man and asked him if he had seen Waifar or knew him. The man replied that he saw him often. The Arab then sent a message: "By Mary's son, I beseech you, as you worship God, faithfully to report my words to him." He went on to tell him how to strengthen the fortifications. "And if he asks you, who passed such things to you, say to him that the Arab to whom you presented the head-covering disclosed the message: only let him believe promptly." Waifar took the message at its face value and built his defences as advised; the siege of Salerno failed, so that we must assume the message was accurate and in good faith. The motivation is obscure. Why the head-covering, why asked and why given? Was it a recognition signal? Was the Arab traveller employed by Waifar as a spy? Whether this was so or not, the story with all its unexplained elements yet suggests the persistence of effective, and perhaps normal, relations between Italy and North Africa in all these wars. The phrase "by the son of Mary" is quite convincing; certainly it represents accurately Arabic and Muslim speech. There must always be something in common between those who take the son of Mary to witness to the truth of what they say.

The kinds of legends and even atrocity stories that were remembered are also an indication of the impression that this period of Aghlabid attacks made upon the Italians. Thus in retrospect the story of Euphemius, the Byzantine leader who invited the Arab invasion of Sicily, was romanticized. Euphemius was a rich man persecuted, whose beautiful bride was given to another man. "You have defiled my wife," he said; "may I die this year if I do not get the wives of many men defiled." Hence his invitation to the Arabs. I do not think that this is a reference to the usual Christian claim that Muslims were characteristically lascivious, but just a long experience of the usual concomitants of warfare of this sort; we can even say that this period is marked by the absence of any special hatred of Islam. The story would have been the same if the invaders had been Vikings.

The same may even apply to another story of the just punishment of a rape. At the siege of Salerno the Arab commander Abdalla made a church his headquarters,

> "and there he raged with riotous living and sundry impurities, so much that he ordered a bed to be prepared for him on the most sacred altar, and there he used to sport with girls whom he had licentiously taken in plunder. Yet not long did so monstrous a contagion last . . . For when a girl was offered to him, a Christian and very beautiful, he immediately ordered her to be carried off to his bed; but while it was all he could do to rape her, and she resisted him with all her energy, still he said to her in his own language, 'I shall defile this most holy altar before I die, because many sacrifices have been offered upon it;' and suddenly a beam was dislodged from a height, by the hands of angels, and fell on Abdalla the general, and immediately he died; and by the wonderful power of God that girl was hardly touched by the beam, and remained unhurt."

The chronicler argues that the Muslims might suppose that this was an accident, not the hand of God; but why—he asks—did beams dislodged in many old churches never fall on the altar? In a tale which has so many probably legendary elements it is useless to argue about details; yet there are points of verisimilitude. For example: "he said to her in his own language"; and yet, did Christian girls from the country round Salerno follow a phrase in Arabic at a moment of stress? If so, they had been culturally absorbed; if not, perhaps there was some such episode, with some kind of witness, and something said which was translated, but we cannot say more. No doubt in this story the suffering and the righteousness of the Christian girl are contrasted with the wickedness of the enemy, but except for the name 'Agarene' there is nothing said of the enemy that seems meant to be characteristic of Muslims as such. They are here again considered as barbarians indistinguishable from other barbarians. There is the simple relation of enmity dissociated from any communication.

The story of the ultimate reduction of the Arab settlement at Garde-Freinet curiously reverses the legend of Euphemius and the Arab invasion of Sicily. One of the companions of the swarthy garrison (*fusci*) was called Aimo, no doubt some such name as Haymar, assimilated to a familiar Latin form.

> "With the others, he went out to lay that country waste, and they took gold and horses and cattle and sundry treasure, and girls and boys. It happened that they drew lots for what they had taken, and a certain exceptionally beautiful woman fell to the lot of Aimo; but someone more powerful than he came and took her away, and so in a state of rage he stayed apart from the others."

Accordingly he worked his revenge by going secretly to Count Robald of Provence; the Count brought a sufficient force together on some pretext, and the Arab camp was successfully surprised. Aimo's family lived long in the district. Again it was clear how unlike the feelings of the day were to the later spirit of crusade. These stories are simply good stories of fighting men and weeping women, adventure stories, often with a pious moral, but different in kind from the polemic and propagandist literature of later ages.

We read incidental references to negotiations, consultations, even discussions arising out of alliances constantly made and remade, but there is little that sheds light on the quality of the relationship of Arabs to Italians or Provençals. There are passing references to the artefacts of a shared culture, as when the Arabs attack, "resounding and making a great noise with trumpets", "they played the pipes and sambuks and all kinds of music." A genuine scholar of the age who published historical material about Arabia was the Greek-speaking anti-pope, Anastasius Bibliotecarius, whose *Chronographia* brings together in Latin a number of Byzantine sources, but at the time had little impact. To this period belongs the legendary story that the medical school of Salerno, the Hippocratic City, was founded by four masters, a Jew, a Greek ('Pontus'), an Arab ('Abdalla') and the eponymous Latin, Salernus, each teaching in his own language. The legend came later and there is not much evidence of the character of the school before the early eleventh century. Earlier, Salernitans penetrated France, but Richer, who would undertake a rare journey for a chance to read the Hippocratic *Aphorisms*, despised their scientific training. The real sources of Salernitan medical knowledge appear to have been primarily Latin and Greek. There was a clear Arab influence in the eleventh century, but in the tenth there seems to have been just one Jewish medical writer (known as Doumoulos in Greek) who had been an Arab prisoner for some time, and who lived and wrote in Otranto.

All this is very thin. The fact is that whatever interchange there was between Christian—either Latin or Greek—and Arab cultures, it has left almost no record at all. Some such contacts were disgraceful by the standards of any age, and the sale of Christians as slaves to Muslim Spain was one such. Verdun, in the north of France, was a centre of trade in *carzimasia*; these were boys who were castrated by removing both penis and testicles, and the traders, says Liutprand, "take the boys into Spain and make a large profit." These Christian traders left no account of their cultural exchanges, although their wares were prized in Constantinople as well as in Spain. The whole weight of evidence of the Latin sources is negative. There is no clear image (either true or false) of an Arab or even Muslim identity. We shall shortly see how the Popes did something to segregate the Arabs in Italy, but in the letters of Pope John VIII, for example, we shall find nothing to suggest that Muslims were distinct in his mind from peoples of polytheist belief or primitive habits. The circumstances of the Arab presence were such that nothing of contemporary Arab civilization (then at its peak) penetrated the Latin consciousness: no idea of its wealth, or power, or extent; none of its nature or its quality; hardly even an awareness that it existed. In Spain, of course, Arabic literature was known and understood, and either accepted or resisted, but nowhere else. Outside Spain, a little was known of the rulers of Arab Spain, partly as a result of the exchange of embassies; but there was only a vague impression (before 868 quite mistaken) of a 'king' of Babylon (Egypt) and of greater rulers beyond; the Abbasids were just 'the Persians'. We saw that, in the time of Charlemagne, Arabic titles and names were confused. So too later; thus Erchembert speaks of the "king of the pagans" named "Calphus", i.e. Khalifa, Caliph.

Communication rarely went beyond the recognition, implied at least, of a certain common ground in morals. In 876 the men of Salerno swore a league with the Arabs, and then attacked a small group of Arabs treacherously. The Arabs, we are told, appealed against the Christians to the Christians' master: "O Jesus, son of Mary, by this we shall know truly whether you rule heaven and earth and are the lord of all creation, if you overthrow these perjured men effectually." Although the Arabs were few, they destroyed their enemy. Here the Christian writer extracts theological triumph out of a military and moral defeat. Muslims do not think that Jesus rules heaven and earth, but this could have been said ironically. The teller, on his side, at least observes that there exists a common morality, as well as a common recognition of Jesus as holy. In considering all this evidence, and it amounts to very little, we can only feel our way among elements of legend.

5. Papal policy

Alliances between small Christian states and Arab forces were essentially haphazard. The Arabs were not welcomed in Italy, as they had been in Egypt, as liberators, nor was their government accepted as a *fait accompli*, as it had been in Spain; sentiments of loyalty were more localized and less sophisticated than in seventh-century Egypt, and in Italy there was no unitary state like Visigothic Spain. The fragmentation of Italy militated against both the acceptance and the rejection of Arab rule. Military alliances seem to have been a form of co-operation at the lowest possible cultural level, though they would indeed lead on to the long history of Arab military employment in the peninsula as mercenaries. At first, alliances with Arabs were not made against united ecclesiastical disapproval, as in the crusading period, when popes and councils denounced every suggestion of co-operation; in the ninth century this attitude was only coming into existence.

It is precisely in the formation of papal and clerical policy in this period that the crusading concept (though not yet crusading enthusiasm) began to take shape.

We can study this in the ninth century in some papal correspondence. Leo IV succeeded to the pontificate in 847, after the Arab pillage of St Peter's and the Roman suburbs. He wrote that the Franks who die faithfully fighting the Arabs would not be denied the kingdom of heaven; the Almighty knows when men have died "for the truth of faith, for the safety of their country and the defence of Christians," and they will have the reward to which they have justified their claim. This is hardly a declaration of holy war, though it is a statement of a just war, and it does specifically endorse resistance to non-Christian attack. It tends to a European and Christian rejection of the Arabs. Papal policy in Italy, while it sought every possible ally, attempted in the same process to isolate the Arab invaders.

The struggle of Pope John VIII against Athanasius, duke and bishop of Naples, who for many years balanced Arab, Byzantine and local interests against each other, illustrates this point. Where later the Normans for a while would attempt a similar balance in their own way and under their own rigid control, within a framework of nominal respect for papal policies, Athanasius accepted Byzantine suzerainty, and was indifferent or unsympathetic to the Latin *nexus* and the Roman interest. He resisted the papal attempt to cut off communication with the Muslims. "I beg you to remember what you are," remonstrated Pope John in 881; "remember what you will be, unless you come to your senses, and bear in mind the judgements of the Lord, lest you be forced to render an account to God for as many as are destroyed through your failure to act, and, after being led captive, perish by various deaths." Athanasius, complained John, had not only promised to break off relations with the Arabs ('Agarenes') "but also to arrest the Arabs ('Saracens') and send them to us." One wonders whether captured Arabs in Rome would find better employment than captured Italians in Arab Sicily, but persecution and oppression only bear those names when they are suffered, not when they are inflicted. Soon John was circularizing the other bishops to announce his excommunication of Athanasius, who, "making an alliance with the sons of Ismail, has reduced this land to nothing," so that those who used to live in it certainly no longer existed. Southern Italy did indeed suffer from the contentions of those who sought to control it, Arab commanders, the Byzantine and German Emperors, the local rulers and the Pope himself. John reproved the motive: "alas for the advantage of shameful gain," and so determined: "we anathematize him, until such time as he separates himself wholly from these same Arabs, as the enemy of all Christianity."

Some of the neighbours of Athanasius supported the papal policy. The Salernitans expressed disapproval, less of the betrayal of Christendom, than of that of the Christians of Salerno. "By the just judgement of God," the Arab commander invited by Athanasius "rising up against him first of all, began seriously to damage Naples, and to swallow up everything round about, and to levy exactions on the girls and the horses and the arable lands." In this turmoil, the subject of the Pope's anathema, Athanasius, was only too glad to call in the help of Waimar of Salerno, and the Arabs were driven off. However, as soon as he was freed of Arab oppression, Athanasius quarrelled with Waimar, and it was then that the Arabs established their settlement on the Garigliano. (We are all the time paraphrasing the Salerno Chronicle, of course.) Capua, Benevento, Salerno and Naples were all attacked, "but Athanasius, getting up to his usual tricks and entering into a peace with the Arabs, together with them did great damage to the land of the Salernitans."

The excommunication of Athanasius is best understood in the context of John VIII's plans for the total expulsion of the Arabs from Italy, which dates from 877, when they had once again seriously threatened Rome. To Charles the Bald he wrote of "all the suburbs of Rome even having been so plundered that no inhabitant or resident of any age whatever seems to remain in them." In another letter to Charles he says that what with the "pagans" and the iniquitous Christians it is now too dangerous to send northwards either by land or by sea; such are the evils that "our age does not remember the like." He describes the devastation with all the rhetoric he knows; words fail him. Within the fortifications of Rome a ruined peasantry looked glumly out across a desert; no misfortune could further befall, except the fall of the city itself. He sought material reward for any commander of troops who would break with the Arabs; and alliance with Arabs (he told the rulers of the southern cities) was essentially an *impium foedus*, and the Neapolitans, once a people of God, were now by such alliance become a people of the prince of darkness.

The Arabs are "sons of fornication", though it is not clear if this is a reference to their different marriage laws, a theological condemnation in Old Testament terms, or simple abuse. Probably the phrase is associated with "vessel of wrath". "What use is it to us," he asks, "to know the way of justice, when after knowing it we turn backwards, and join ourselves thus freely with the enemies of the Christian name?" He tried to make the Emperor's flesh creep by describing the alternative which must result from any failure to defend him:

> "either we shall be made subject to the pagans, or (what the divine power forbids) we shall perish by a cruel death, to the total ruin of Christianity, and in consequence both the name of Christ will be blasphemed among the nations, and we shall be given over to oblivion . . ."

Peace among Christians and their unity in Christ he associated with the total withdrawal from "the fellowship of pagans". He begs the bishop of Parma not to delay coming in strength to discuss a general plan by which "the impious nation may be driven out of our territories: that is what we demand, that is what by special prayer we earnestly beseech beforehand." To be truly free of them, a fleet action, he was well aware, was also necessary. Above all, he wanted tough fighters (*robusti proeliatores*) and inveighed against neutrality or indifference.

Two years after the great crisis of 877, when the Pope wrote his imperious demands for help to so many allies, the northern bishops asked about those who fall in defence of "the holy church of God and the Christian religion and Commonwealth." He replied that he was confident that those who were killed while struggling hard against pagans and infidels *cum pietate* for the Catholic religion would be received into eternal rest. This was rather carefully worded, and for one who was quick to anathematize any co-operation with Arab forces, perhaps surprisingly so. The popes were prompt in organizing Italy for the Latin rite, and in exploiting both Arabs and Byzantines, but they were rather slow to develop a theology of holy war, or to endorse the notion of martyrdom by crusade. To fight the Muslims was essentially a good work, not really unlike other good works, and it must be done with the right disposition. This is not to deny that the popes put the fullest possible support of religion behind their efforts to impose their rite upon the peninsula. In the tenth century the papal policy was the same, although the popes spoke with less authority, as being personally so much less reputable than their immediate predecessors. This may be one reason why the theology of holy war did not develop further until Urban began to preach the Crusade. It is certain that the conquest both of Spain and of Sicily proceeded in the eleventh century without much emphasis on religion; the rulers set severe limitations to church influence. It was at all times the work of the church to cut off communication with the Muslims. Yet even prescinding from church influence, we can ask whether, during the eighth, ninth and tenth centuries, when the frontiers between western Europe and the Arabs were more uncertain and liable to fluctuate than ever again, a multi-cultural society was ever possible. It is difficult to think so.

Chapter 4

Spain in the eleventh and twelfth centuries

1. Principles and practice of reconquest

No one could question that the biggest impact of the Arabs on mediaeval Europe was in Spain, or that through Spain the rest of Europe received its most accurate impressions of the Arabs. No one could question that it was in Spain more than anywhere that for so long the two cultures developed in parallel. There were indeed four lines in parallel, Europeans under European rule, Arabs under Arab rule, and the two converses, the Mozarabs and the Mudejares. Spain was the chief source of knowledge of Arabic philosophy and science and of Islam. For some centuries, the impact of Arabs on Europeans in Spain was the history of Spain, and yet we cannot say that it accounted for the whole Arab impress on Europe.

Europe was more aware of the East, although less passed between the two cultures there at the educated level. There was always traffic to the East, pilgrim and mercantile as well as military. Crusading hysteria affected the whole European attitude to Arabs, and most perhaps at the less conscious and less articulate level. Crusade was a matter of emotion and imagination which the clergy merely rationalized. From the East came the threat of cataclysmic horrors, in turn the 'Saracens', the Seljuk Turks, the Mongols and the Ottoman Turks. In Spain the emotions were pitched in a lower key, although there were pilgrims and there was a theological campaign. The recovery of European fighting morale in Spain and Sicily in the eleventh century preceded the true crusading impulse, and it always contributed to it more than it owed. Spain was not Jerusalem, and, for an obvious religious reason, had less hold on the imagination, but it also seemed less dangerous to Europe, where only the Berber invasions, Almoravid or Almohad, aroused universal interest. For the most part, the

Spanish Reconquest was too steady for European fears to focus on the south-west corner of the land-mass. This may even have helped Spain to become the passage through which so much cultural development passed. So far is this the case, that I must deal separately with the two great themes of which Spain is the chief home—the transmission of Arabic philosophic and scientific literature, and the formation of the ideological polemic against Islam. Here I am concerned to indicate rather how Spaniards and their other Frankish allies thought about their Arabic-speaking neighbours, enemies, and often allies.

It was Dozy who first contrasted the Cid, *mio Cid el Campeador*, of modern Christian legend and the Cid of the Arab histories. He quotes Ibn Bassam's description of the Champion as "a Galician dog . . . a man who made a trade of chaining prisoners, the flail of the country," but not a Crusader in any sense; the ally of the Banu Hud, their help gave him the chance to become powerful, "and there was no countryside in Spain that he did not pillage." Through the alliance, "this tyrant whom God curse" was able to secure the great *coup* of his life, the capture of Valencia, and to hold it as a champion of local Spain against the Murabiti advance. Yet the legendary hero of the *Cantar del Cid* is himself (like his prototype of real life) frankly professional: "The Moors offered three thousand silver marks, a proposition which satisfied the Cid—

> Asmaron los moros—tres mill marcos de plata
> Plogo a mio Çid—d'aquesta presentaja

—and it was paid in full on the third day." We need not think of the Cid in terms of criticism or rehabilitation, of opposition between the ideas of Menendez Pidal and of Dozy. The fact is that the contemporary Arab and European pictures of the Cid do not really conflict. The Cid of the poem, like the poem as a whole, is delightfully free of humbug. The theme of loot is almost always present, and in the *cantar* fighting is barely considered in any other context. Booty is not something to accept as a gift, but should be honourably acquired by fighting until the blood drips from the elbow. Fighting is a sport also, worth doing for its own sake. In the foreign bishop Jerome it is an amiable eccentricity that he should want to fight only for the honour of Christendom, but he is no Crusader; his motive is the honour, rather than the extension, of Christendom. He wants more chivalrous adventures, more tournaments, more *provezas*. For everyone else the sport is also the profession. The game is fighting the Moors, but the Christians get their living by doing so:

si con moros non lidiaremos,—no nos daran del pan . . .

The Moors are deliberately terrorized; the poem makes no bones about it. They dare not work in the fields. The Cid, sleeping by day and travelling by night, raids indiscriminately for three years, till the people of Valencia have no food supply. Most Moors are the objects of a contrived terror, to be robbed, slaughtered or sold as slaves.

Yet the villains of the story are Europeans, Christians, and nobles of ancient lineage; cowards, not adventurers. Moors are occasionally allies and may always become friends. They may be more truly noble, and 'my Cid' cares what they think of him (though neither the real nor the fictional Cid can have been under much delusion about this). Treachery to an allied Moor is despicable; the Moor 'Avengalvon' is the Cid's only friend among his peers, his other friends are followers. A time when Spain will be no longer divided between Muslims and Christians is not envisaged. Thus, an emphatic way of saying that no one should know is to say: neither Moors nor Christians shall know, *moros nin cristianos*; and when the Cid swears not to cut his beard, he adds, "whatever anyone says," expressed in the form, "whatever Moors or Christians may say." Moors and Christians seem more than anything like rival football teams. The total candour of the poet and his creations wins our sympathy, but the poem is quite amoral; the Cid is essentially "he who was born in a lucky hour", *el que en buen ora nasco*.

Before we compare the Cid of the chroniclers, we must glance at the historical background. Until the arrival of the Murabiti Berbers, the Almoravids, under Yusuf ibn Tashufin, Spain of the eleventh century was a patchwork of minor powers (kings of the 'taifas' and the Christians of the north) of which it was only generally, but not always, true that the Europeans were aligned against the Arabs. Yet Dozy argues that Europeans had to be told to treat Arabs as human, and cites a law of Sancho of Aragon in 1090, that a man who receives a 'Saracen' slave must feed him, because he is a man who cannot be allowed to starve like a beast. Dozy draws our attention to a passage from Ibn Bassam, quoting

Ibn Hayyan on the capture of Barbastro by Spanish and French knights in 1064. According to his account, the sack of Barbastro by the Franks differed from other sacks, whether by Franks or Arabs or others, largely in its orderliness. After the capture of the town, all the Arabs were ordered back into their houses, so that their new masters could share the booty according to a fixed plan. In this sort of account Christians usually describe rapes as taking place in the churches; the parallel horror for the Arab was to describe the rapes of their women by the Franks in front of the master of the household—husband and father. Perhaps we may very roughly equate the Christian church with the Muslim home. The passage cited is most interesting for its account by a Jewish merchant sent in to ransom the daughters of a leading Arab from the Frankish victors. Dressed in his predecessor's clothes and reclining on his predecessor's cushions among girls, their new master will not sell; he has all the riches he wants from his share of the loot. In a well-known passage the Frank indicates one of the girls, and says:

"I swear to you that I will not give her up, for she is the daughter of the former master of this house, who is a man highly regarded among his own people. That is why I have made her my mistress, not to mention that she is specially beautiful, and I hope that she will give me children. His fathers acted in the same way when they were the masters; now the chance has turned, and you see that we take our revenge."

Then he offers to show the Jew, to whom he talks French, the singer of the former master, also beautiful, to whom the Frank talks in pidgin Arabic; the girl takes her lute; she is crying, but the Christian furtively wipes her tears, and then drinks continually while she is singing, all very gaily, although the Jew, who understands classical Arabic very little himself, is sure that the Frank understands none at all. The Jew sees there is no business to be done, and leaves. Next year the Arabs recaptured Barbastro, killing everyone they found, except children and the leaders worth ransoming. The point that Dozy wishes us to understand, and that these extracts make abundantly clear, is the shared way of life of Frank and Arab. The Frank finds nothing strange or abnormal in taking over the Arab household. The language rather than any fundamental custom is unfamiliar; the Frank is at home in what is only variant behaviour within a common area.

This does not at all presuppose fraternization in a sense of mutual understanding. "I kill you, you kill me, I rape your women, you rape mine" is clearly not a high order of understanding, though beating time to the same music, even drunkenly, may imply something more. However tyrannical the Cid, the very name by which we know him is the Arabic *Sidi*, 'my lord'; it is not the Spanish. There is an unending alternation between alliances of a flimsy character between Moors and Spaniards and massacres and murders on both sides. With the Cid the emphasis in the Spanish sources is always on booty rather than on massacre, though *devastavit et destruxit* is often present. I have already given an example, but the theme is recurrent. The natural sequence is victory—thanks to Christ—magnificent profits; this is true both in the *Poema* and in the Latin *Historia Roderici*. In the *Poema*, the Cid dreams of conquering all the lands of the Moors, "where the mosques are," but realizes that the hope of tribute is more realistic than the temptation of the conqueror's infinite loot. The *Historia* tells us of the capture of Valencia in 1094, of silver and gold and strings of pearls and gems set in gold and silken garments; there is both relish at good business achieved, and a genuine taste for elegance and splendour. The Cid and his men were "richer than can be described." Immediately after, at the Battle of Cuarte, again there is a satisfactory profit: gold and silver and precious clothing, war-horses and riding horses, mules and different kinds of arms and masses of food supplies and treasures indescribable. Three years later, the battle of Bairen produced less abundance, but at any rate enough gold and silver and mules, arms and other wealth. The Cid saw his enemy as a field to be harvested and was willing for good tactical reasons not to exhaust the soil: to the garrison of Murviedro, very near the end of his life, he says: "Take your wives and children and households and all your property, and go in peace with all your things, wherever you please." At the capture of Valencia he did not threaten the freedom of Islamic worship. Perhaps not the least attractive side of the Cid is, unexpectedly, his piety, which is never unctuous. When he was threatened by a major advance of the Murabitin under Muhammad, the nephew of Yusuf, he "encouraged and strengthened his men firmly and with his accustomed braveness of heart," and he also earnestly prayed the Lord Jesus Christ for divine help; but he takes care of his men's spirits first, and he prays like any man in a jam, not like a Crusader with a pre-emption on heavenly support. If to the Arab writers he seemed a cruel tyrant, they yet admired the heroic character of his life, and his love of glory, though we might substitute 'booty'. His stature was heroic both in legend and in fact; he was not a charlatan.

Alfonso VI, the Cid's sovereign, had a good reputation with the Arabs, though he was a formidable opponent; his worst enemies were his own nobles, whose unruliness contemporary legends glorified. In the next century the chronicle of Alfonso VII shows a distinct change of tone in what is admired. He, too, protected his Arabic-speaking subjects, but enemy Arabs and Moors suffered. Thus we read that in the area of Jaen the Christian armies

> "pillaged all the land . . . set fire to all the villages they found, and destroyed their mosques; and all the men learned in religion that they found, they cut down with the sword; the vines and the olives and the figs and all the trees, they had cut down, and everywhere that their feet trod, they left devastated behind them."

When the Christians are cut off by a large army of Moors and Arabs ('Moabites', i.e. Almoravids, and 'Agarenes'), they appeal for help, but are cut off by the river. They are advised to confess their sins to each other, pray, communicate with blessed bread, "and may God have mercy on your souls." "Then the Christians, well prepared by faith and by arms, killed whatever Arab prisoners they held, men, children, women and the beasts they had with them. And immediately the Arabs charged on them and all the Christians died . . ." This is a bitter kind of fighting, and the same chronicle gives many examples. When Coria was taken by Alfonso, the mosques were destroyed, and the city cleared of the 'contamination' of Islam. After the victory of Munio Alfonso at Montiel we are told three times of his Roman triumph:

> "the royal standards aloft, and the heads of the kings on the ends of spears, and then noble knights, prisoners in chains; after these, the Arab people, with their hands tied behind their backs; there followed Christian footmen leading the horses of the kings and the mules of the leaders and princes with their best saddles in gold and silver . . . and camels laden with arms and all the spoils."

After a few days the queen Berengaria, "moved by great pity," had the heads taken down, and embalmed by Arab and Jewish doctors with myrrh and aloes, wrapped in the best cloth and set in gold and silver, and sent to their wives in Cordova. If it is anachronistic not to accept that pity was the motive, there was some recognition of common humanity in a war which was becoming more savage than in the previous century. There are obvious reasons for this. On the one hand the Almoravids had presented a more serious danger than the kings of the Tawaif; on the other, the Eastern Crusade was now a familiar notion, and religious duty was boosting the collection of booty. There remains in spite of this something more down to earth, more human and less pretentious, however brutal, about the fighting in Spain. The Moors were always taken for granted as a natural phenomenon, as the Arabs and Turks of the East were not.

Nevertheless, the technicalities of crusading were introduced into Spain. It is instructive to compare a ninth-century royal monastic endowment with one of the tenth. Alfonso the Chaste of the Asturias, a steady but not outstandingly successful fighter against the Arab caliphate, introduces the details of property with a long prayer to the King of Kings, who, in distributing the kingdoms, gave not least of them by a shining victory to the Goths in Spain, but when they displeased Him, withdrew the glory of their kingdom; they deserved to sustain the Arab sword; now the people were rescued and the enemy struck by His power through the Christians and Asturians. In the following century Sancho and Tota, in a parallel document, also conscious of the long religious conflict in Spain between two peoples, are more rhetorical and more confident of achievement. He rehearses at length how all the fortresses, cities, towns and countryside of Spain used to belong to the Christians; how because they and their fathers sinned persistently (*assidue*) God brought in a barbarian people; how "by the infestation of this unbelieving people and their rabid persecution, Spain was almost wholly depopulated of Christians, until God, looking down upon the affliction and oppression of his people, put down their (Arab) impious audacity" and now conferred the victory on the unworthy king whose prayer this is— leading up to the endowment of a monastery at "the place which in the Chaldean language of those unbelievers is called Albelda." In the same century, from Frankish outsiders, less conscious than natives of the special history of Spain, we find the beginnings of a pre-crusading attitude, as the expanding Spanish monarchies begin to employ foreign soldiers. Indulgences are granted to the warriors of Christ in the later part of the century, and Gregory VII claimed suzerainty over recovered territory. That this was a recovery was never forgotten. The Council of Toledo held in 1086 naturally speaks of the Toledan church "liberated from Arab tyranny." In the twelfth century the Spanish Reconquest was totally assimilated theologically to the Crusade in the East; after recalling how the Spanish church "has been constantly eroded by the deaths of the children of God through the oppression of the pagans," Calistus II grants to those taking part in the proposed expedition "the same remission of sins as we have done for the defenders of the Eastern Church." The slaughter of the centuries guided both sides into habitual resentment and so the habit of renewed slaughter. Yet the crusading touch never wholly replaced, even for professional soldiers from outside, the hard slog of a natural and local bitterness. Indulgences were an additional bonus, but they were not the primary inspiration.

The English account of the capture of Lisbon in 1147 contains an interesting exchange between the bishop and a sheikh, which, whether or not it reports an actual conversation, is remarkable for the way it modifies normal attitudes. The bishop, in trying to persuade the defenders to surrender easily, promises them freedom of worship under Christian rule, unless they choose to "increase the church of God;" and he does so on the ground of "long usage". The sheikh replies,

> "Certainly, this city, I think, was once yours; but now it is ours, and perhaps in the future will be yours. But this will be in the gift of God. When God wished, we had it; and when he shall wish us not to have it, we shall not have it. Indeed no wall is impregnable against the judgement of his will."

He is resigned to the "misfortunes and sorrows and injuries" which God, who holds all evils under him, may inflict. For a European to write like this is to contradict the whole spirit of crusade which animated Christian theory, and the spirit of revenge which inspired Iberian warfare. The writer makes the Christian bishop concede a right to religious freedom based on long usage; he makes the Muslim speak with a true piety equally acceptable in Christian or Islamic terms—which it was unusually imaginative to understand in an enemy's situation. The success of an enemy was a difficult theological problem for both sides throughout the long history of their contact. And if the conversation actually took place, then it is still more remarkable, even if it is only a conventional formulation of some actual talk. We can but say that the twin motives of revenge and holy war were sometimes overcome or neglected.

If the quality of attitudes rarely changed, so too did the scale. In the European imagination Spain was a small stage, and the East was a large one. Once at least, however, the Spanish drama was watched with anxiety from a distance. The 'Almohads', al-Muwahhidin, were a mass movement of Berbers inspired by the religious leader, Ibn Tumart, who claimed to be the Mahdi, who was a really learned sheikh and a brilliant teacher. The Almohad advance along the North African coast did not particularly interest, let alone alarm, and certainly not seriously, the people of Italy or the Christians of Sicily. Yet Salimbene builds into his narrative an account of the battle of Las Navas de Tolosa—which did indeed decisively defeat the Almohads—which seems to concentrate dramatically into the one year of 1212 nearly seventy years of Almohad history in Spain. "In the same year the Commander of the Faithful, the King of Morocco, coming into Spain, with an infinite multitude of Arabs threatened to take, not only Spain, but even Rome, and Europe itself." He refers briefly to Innocent III's intervention, gives a brief but vivid account of the battle and ends:

> "And by the grace of the Saviour, and with the most Christian Kings of Aragon and Navarre and Castille butchering them, the enemy turned tail; of whom the swords of the followers of Christ devoured endless thousands . . . sixty thousand of both sexes of the gentiles they killed."

2. Spanish interest in Arab history

How wide and how close a knowledge do the Spanish Christians show of what was happening among their Arab and Berber neighbours? From knowledge we can safely infer interest. There are two subjects of historical writing where we can look for examples. There are descriptions of major movements among the Arabs; and there are accounts of local politics and the decisions made by neighbouring commands or states in the wars in progress all the time. The great historical collections of Alfonso the Learned in the thirteenth century are so eclectic in their sources, compiled rather than edited, that we can assume that no material has been deliberately excluded. The version of the arrival of the Almoravids in Spain, an event of very great temporary importance, in the *Cronica General*, based partly on Roderick of Toledo's great history, and partly on earlier legendary material, is confused, often imaginary and, one would have thought, obviously improbable.

According to the story, taken from a lost *Cantar de la Mora Zaida*, Alfonso VI, the captor of Toledo and the sovereign of the Cid, fell in love, after the death of his fifth wife (the facts about Alfonso's women are obscure), with the beautiful daughter of the king of Seville, Muhammad al-Mutamid ibn Abbad. The chronicle, while crediting this romantic story, realistically points out the strong places held by the prince. Zaida is equally made out to be in love with Alfonso; both these fallings in love occur in the contemporary courtly manner of romance, since in each case the one falls in love with the reputation of the other. There is an element of fact; Zaida existed, though the daughter-in-law, not the daughter, of Muhammad Mutamid of Seville. In the story as derived from the *cantar* she is willing to give up her religion for love, rather than for policy, and Cuenca came with her as dowry, also, therefore, for love. If Alfonso seems to us to have had sound, business-like reasons, it is true that he really did have a good reputation "among both Moors and Christians." But there are many errors of fact. The Seville alliance took place after the Almoravid invasion. Worst of all, in the *Cronica*, it is Alfonso himself, on the advice of his friend Muhammad Mutamid, who calls the Almoravids into Spain as mercenary troops, under Yusuf ibn Tashufin, because they are the best of the Moorish knights. That Alfonso did so is quite untrue, and the reason for saying so difficult to understand; the source is again the *cantar*. The Almoravid army is made to attack both the Moors and Christians of Spain with one Moorish ally, thus defeating and reversing Alfonso's support plan of making use of their services; this was necessary, in order to bring the account into line with the known fact of Alfonso's defeat by Yusuf. According to this legend, Muhammad Mutamid was killed by the Almoravids for giving Zaida as wife to Alfonso, and for being his friend. The title, *miramomelin*, though recognized as a title, and not, as usual, supposed to be a name, is translated, not 'Commander of the Faithful', but 'Lord of all the other Lords', perhaps a realistic interpretation of its imperial implications. Ali the son of Yusuf is represented as an unrelated rival who proclaims himself in his Lord's place. Later chapters are more accurate. The little kings of the Moorish states are represented as deciding that if they are to be ruled by strangers, strangers of their own kind and religion would be better than the Christian Europeans, and so they invite in Yusuf and his Murabitin. This explanation follows a passage extracted from an Arabic Muslim source. The confusion in the story is the result of an exceptionally bad use of the sources, and Roderick of Toledo, usually the stand-by of the *Cronica*, is here himself confused by his source.

The facts are very much jumbled. There were too many conflicting interests at this date; on the Christian side, the king and the aristocracy, and on the Arab, the remaining *tawaif* and the Murabitin; a compilation which reflects the interaction of all these must lack clarity. The personality and reputation of Alfonso VI were just such as were most likely to give rise to legend. His relations with women were evidently more complex than the sources make clear. He was a 'protector' of the conquered Arabs, and his anger when, against his promise and will, the Friday mosque in Toledo was turned into a church and the "uncleanness of Muhammad turned out," and bells rung in the minaret, is in no way minimized by Roderick of Toledo or by the *Cronica*, following him. As such he was remembered also in Arab sources. He was also a Romanizer, who brought in French monks and substituted the Roman rite for the Mozarab. In the *Poema del Cid* he is seen as an oppressor. A king who is an object of suspicion to an ungovernable aristocracy, who conciliates his newly conquered subjects and makes use of foreign clergy is perfectly consistent, but the account of his reign was obscured essentially by the mixture of sources, by the inclusion of legendary material in the *Cronica*, and equally, by contrast, through the inclusion of an important Arab source. The use of this Arab source, first identified by Dozy, a local history of Valencia from Alfonso's capture of Toledo to the Cid's of Valencia, results in an exceptionally well-informed and objective series of chapters, in startling contrast to the legendary elements. The Arabic material stands out like a chain of rocks in the sea. The very detailed picture of the Cid's relations with Valencia, and of Arab politics in the city in the years before its capture, and even the inclusion in the *Cronica* of an Elegy on Valencia in Arabic, with Castilian commentary, produce an unexpected effect. When we read these chapters of the *Cronica*, and, indeed, the parallel passages of Roderick of Toledo which include less material, we cannot fail to be struck by the confusion to which the memory of such an important event as the Almoravid invasions had been reduced in only a century and a half. Some of the muddles are easily understood in themselves; for example, the simplification of Yusuf ibn Tashufin's several incursions into Spain into one. The interpolation of so much private motivation of a romantic kind may be comprehensible in the sense that private motives do affect historical events, because rulers have other motives besides public ambition; the wide line of history may not be diverted, but the details of the process can. Yet the deliberate choice of an obviously fictional course of events—fictional in contemporary terms even—indicates a rapid passage of history into folklore, and the use of the single written source in Arabic brings this out more strongly by contrast. We need not criticize the writing of the history, but we must admit that all this, if we take it as a reflection of Spanish European interest in the Arab World in Spain, shows some genuine interest but very little discrimination. We have only written sources taken from written sources, or from poetic sources fixed in a professional oral transmission. Oral tradition of a casual kind is slight. In the end Yusuf ibn Tashufin, the greatest of the Murabitin, earned an encomium that we only occasionally find paralleled in Christian European historians: "This king, Yusuf, protected his land and his people, and maintained justice for them all; those who resisted him in different strong places he fought until they submitted to his rule." (Ali his son is contrasted as weak and indolent.) Roderick of Toledo carries his *Historia Arabum* only as far as the Almoravids. To this extent therefore he did the Murabitin historical justice.

It would be reasonable to expect a clearer memory of the Almohad, than of Almoravid, intervention in Spain; it was more recent, perhaps more dangerous, more ideological. There is the same confusion about Arab politics at the end of the Almoravid period in Spanish historical writing of the thirteenth century that there is about its beginnings. The disturbances which marked the years immediately preceding the Almohad arrival under the governorship of Yahya ibn Ghaniya are described in a muddled way. In the Chronicle of the Emperor Alfonso, one thing that stands out is Alfonso VII's care for his reputation, like his namesake's, for keeping faith with his Arab allies. The rise of Almohad power in the persons of the Masmuda Berbers is seen in terms of national pride.

"King Tashufin" (the grandson of Yusuf) "went off overseas to the city called Marrakush, in the home of his father King Ali, and he took with him many Christians who are called Mozarabs, and who have lived since ancient times in the lands of the Arabs; and similarly he took with him all the prisoners whom he found in all the land under his rule, and he placed them in towns and fortresses with other captive Christians, in the face of those people who are called Masmuda (*muzmutos*), and who were making war on all the land of the Murabiti (*moabitorum*)."

When their leader died, all the Christians "scattering dust and mud upon themselves, mourned and said, O Reberter our leader, our shield and breastplate . . ." However, Abd al-Mumin, the 'King of the Assyrians' (the Almohads), rejoiced, and now felt free and able to destroy the power of the Murabitin. This he did first in Africa and then in Spain. Here is a natural patriotic pride, but not an objective historical assessment of the Christian troops employed in Africa.

The actual account of the genesis of the Almohad movement and of the teaching of Ibn Tumart is given in Roderick's *de rebus Hispaniae* and in the *Cronica*, which seems to doubt the truth of what it reports, so often does it insist on Roderick's authority for what is said. The story starts well, representing the Arabic legend at first not unfairly. Ibn Tumart is supposed to have recognized in Abd al-Mumin by secret signs that he was the man destined to lead the Muwahhidi reform of Islam. This is stated by the Christian text fairly enough, except that Ibn Tumart is described, not as a man learned in religious law, but as learned in "astronomy and natural sciences", i.e. astrology. The Spanish Christian version goes more and more wide of the mark. Ibn Tumart also knows a man who is learned in Quranic knowledge and who preaches against the doctrine of the Caliph of Baghdad; he is called Almohadi; he too wants to fight the Murabitin. The preaching of Almohadi, the advice of Ibn Tumart, enable Abd al-Mumin to destroy the Almoravid power in Africa. Here, of course, 'Almohadi' is a second *persona* of Ibn Tumart, who was in fact very learned in the religious sciences, had studied long in the East, and who gradually adopted unorthodox views (from a Sunni point of view) and finally announced his Mahdiship. Almohadi is now "honoured in all things as a Prophet of God." Abd al-Mumin crossed to Spain and subdued nearly all the Arabs—this was true enough. Almohadi died, was buried near Marrakesh, and people would come to his tomb when in trouble for miraculous assistance. This was why they were called *Almohades,* after his name; others say that Almohades means 'united' (says Roderick). Almohad is, of course, a form of al-Muwahhidin, 'those who affirm the unity of God,' and the character 'Almohadi' totally imaginary. The second explanation of the meaning of the term comes nearer to the fact than the first, but this too is quite inadequate. We need hardly wonder at the curious legends that Christians believed about the life of the Prophet Muhammad when we see the invention of this eponymous prophet 'Almohadi' in the case of events which took place barely a century earlier; this probably represents the contemporary Christian Spanish tradition of the facts. The rule of the Almohads continued in fact into the time when the *Cronica* and histories of Roderick of Toledo were written; theirs was the age of Ibn Tufayl and Ibn Rushd who, as Averroes, was to have more influence on Christian Europe than on the Arab World. In spite of this, we have this lack of interest which alone can explain such careless myth-making.

Before we leave the subject of what we must call isolationist history-writing we may find a glance at historical method worth while. When we speak of a lack of interest, we cannot altogether blame the individual writer. We can say that anyone so learned as Roderick Archbishop of Toledo (Jimenez de Rada) can be blamed—as we shall suggest William of Tyre may be blamed— for not investigating more closely the supposed facts he was relating. There is no anachronism in saying that he wanted to be accurate; in many fields, as we shall see, Spain was the scene of an increasingly careful search for accuracy which reached its culmination in the lifetime of Roderick. The refusal to distinguish between sources, the acceptance of everything handed down, lay at the root of the matter. The Spanish historical school combines the real risks of an encyclopaedic approach with an apparently deliberate refusal to suspect established and hitherto unquestioned facts. This is far from being true of all, or even many, mediaeval historians. We have to suspect isolationism in this sense, not particularly in the writers of history, but in the whole new Christian community in Spain as a whole. Often we can detect a longing for authentic material, and the single example of the incorporation of Arab material in the text of the *Cronica* is the proof that such a desire existed, but it is overwhelmed by folklore history.

This comes out most clearly in Roderick's history of the

Prophet, based on local European legends, to which the *Cronica* adds more. All these seem to be the creation of Spanish Christians, perhaps picked up from their Mozarab co-religionists by the new conquerors and worked over by them. If so, much of the substance of these legends would derive from deliberate, resentful misrepresentation of half-understood Muslim history in Arabic, sometimes, but not always, orally acquired. The misrepresentation of the Prophet as a 'mage' (soothsayer, magician, someone learned in hidden arts) may be an unconscious recognition of the greater learning of the Arabs, inspired by communal suspicion, and taking shape before large numbers of scientific, medical, astrological and other works were translated in the twelfth century. Here again we have the determination to see in Christian legends about the Prophet, however they evolved, the same authenticity as in Arabic sources, and this must reflect the defiance of the Arab World by the newly forming European community.

There is also a lack of immediacy, often a total lack of conviction, in writing about events in the Arab World. This more than anything marks the refusal to accept Arabic civilization as something shared. In the writers and compilers of histories this contrasts with the realities of Spanish coexistence between the two cultures, and belongs rather to war propaganda. The history of Alfonso VII which we have already quoted is curious in its constant use of biblical phraseology (including the use of Moabite for Almoravid, Murabiti). This is used to give verisimilitude—as well, no doubt, as a suitable theological parallel—to episodes and conversations which in fact are conjectural. Thus there is a passage which purports to describe the appointment of Yahya ibn Ghaniya, the last Almoravid governor of Spain. King Tashufin "was saddened and troubled and all his kingdom with him, and calling to himself all the chiefs of the Christians that he had with him and of the Moabites and of the Arabs, said to them . . ." (cf. Matthew 2:3 and 4). He asks them who should be governor, and they unanimously recommend Ibn Ghaniya. Tashufin gives instructions which the editor identifies as substantially Nebuchadnezzar's to Holofernes in the Vulgate version: "Take gold and silver in abundance from my treasuries" (Judith 2:10); ". . . Let not thy sword spare any of their country, and every fortified city and the towns thou shalt subjugate to me and to thee" (*ibid.*, verse 6). In the next chapter Alfonso is lent the language of Judas Maccabeus,

"Take charge of this people" (Maccabees 5:10). This style continues through the text—the whole tone is often scriptural, like a
parody, even when actual passages are unidentifiable. The biblical
trick is something additional; but much of the great *Cronica* is a
lifeless citation of imaginary conversations. When we get a sentence
that goes back to the original experience, it contrasts vividly with
all the unimaginative fictional conversation. Here are the Arabs
besieged by the Cid in Valencia: "In all this the Murabitis
delayed; and one day people said, 'At last they are coming' and
the next day, 'They are not coming after all;' and they waited for
them." Very rarely was there an immediate authenticity in the
European Spaniard's ideas of his Arab compatriots.

3. Unacknowledged literary interchange

We have been looking at examples of isolation and rejection. We
have been forced to acknowledge a violence which at most seems
almost to imply that Arabs and Europeans did not share a common
humanity; and which at best was based on the usual intolerance
and cruelty of war, and the unscrupulousness of a business in
which the profits derived solely from loot and ransom. We have
seen the unreality which divided historians from the facts to which
their histories ought to have gone back, apparently because the
Spanish Franks and Arabs were too cut off from each other, even
in a society where intermingling and interalliance were commonplaces, to have much knowledge of the other side of the hill. We
must now glance at a different kind of evidence. Literature presents
us with a remarkable contrast—one great unacknowledged debt,
and one conscious and deliberate effort of propaganda. Both these
subjects have been, and will doubtless continue to be, areas of
controversy. It was denied at one time that the poetry of the
troubadours was indebted to the poetry of the petty courts of the
taifas of the eleventh century. Similarly, the origins of the corpus
of the *chansons de geste*—of the 'matter of France'—have been
disputed. It is not my intention to examine these problems in any
detail, but rather to draw from them one or two points relevant to
my main theme.

The best-known fact about European knowledge of Islam in the
Middle Ages is that Muslims were frequently believed to worship
a series of idols, one of whom was *Mahom*, and the origin and
attribution of the others, especially *Apollin* and *Tervagan*, is

disputed. These idols are literally idols: thus an amir offers these three 'gods' splendid images:

> *Li amiralz recleimet Apolin*
> *E Tervagan e Mahumet altresi:*
> *Mi damnedeu, jo vos ai mult servit:*
> *Tutes tes ymagenes ferai d'or fin.*

This absurdity occurs regularly in all the *chansons de geste*, including the *Antioche* and *Jerusalem*, which relate to the First Crusade, whereas the rest are primarily concerned with the Charlemagne cycle, and so with an imaginary version of the Emperor's intervention in Spain. *Roland* itself culminates with the battle of Roncesvalles, magnificently told, retaining much of the old Germanic theme of the outnumbered war-band fighting to the end. The whole has been turned to war propaganda against the 'Saracens', or, as they are most often called in the *chansons*, the 'pagans'; after all, the real Roncesvalles was an attack by barbaric Basques, and not by Charlemagne's allies or enemies among the Arabs. Yet it is not altogether true that in *Roland* "the only good Saracen is a dead Saracen." In the poem, the amir "looks like a real baron . . . he is a learned man in his religion, and in battle proud and tough." The enemy's disasters also are lent some dignity.

> "The heat is great, the dust is rising. The pagans run and the French harass them . . . Bramidonie has climbed to the top of her tower; with her are the clerks and the canons of the false religion, which God has never loved; they are neither ordained nor tonsured. When she sees the Arabs so confounded, she cries aloud, 'Help us, Mahum! O gentle King, our men are defeated and the emir killed in such great shame.' "

When Marsilius hears her, "he turns to the wall, his eyes weep, his head falls forward. He has died of sorrow, with the weight of sin upon him. He gives his soul to the devils." There is a certain respect in all these lines. Throughout *Roland* the enemy are indeed better dead, but they are generally noble. The difference between 'them' and 'us' is that they serve false gods, and that the devils have their souls. Their religion is conceived, not only as serving richly adorned idols, but as managed in parallel with the Christian one. There are 'clerks' and 'canons', but they are not priests and not monks. It is relevant that the list in *Roland* of the nations that make up the enemy army includes real pagans, or former pagans—

Huns, Canaanites, Magyars, Avars, Slavs (as well as unidentified
peoples); none of whom were ever Muslims—they are all just
"a people that God has never loved." In France especially, the
Arabs, as *'pagani'*, seem to have been somehow associated with
antiquity, itself only dimly perceived; in Spain they had been seen
in the rôle of ancient Roman persecutors, and often their philosophers would not be distinguished from Greeks. Sometimes in
the *chansons* there seems to be some faint reflection of fact, but the
entire religious establishment of the Saracens there is a total
fabrication. There is just nothing at all true in it, and we are so
accustomed to this that only occasionally has the question been
asked, why? The obvious answer is that the *chansons* are war
propaganda; a subtler version of this is Bédier's, that they are
pilgrimage propaganda, exploiting attitudes of war. Only the
topography of shrines is not wildly inaccurate.

A question that interests us here is, were these gods deliberately
invented by an individual writer, as H. Grégoire suggested, or do
they only reflect Christian folklore about the enemies of Christians
in Spain? Whatever solution we accept, there is difficulty in understanding the absurdity of the names of the various 'gods', but,
above all, the absurdity of supposing Muslims idolators is almost
beyond conjecture. If the Saracen enemy can be treated with
something like respect, and if the descriptions of battle bear some
resemblance to the scenes described in the histories, why is there
this total divergence from reality about the religion? If the propaganda is to convince those who actually fight Muslims, how can
they be expected to credit what their eyes can disprove? When the
Cronica speaks of the conversion of the great mosque of Toledo
into a cathedral, the episode that angered Alfonso VI, the text
refers to ejecting the "uncleannesses". The parallel exercise in
Roland occurs when the French take Saragossa:

> "With a thousand Frenchmen they have searched the town, the
> synagogues and the mosques. With blows of steel hammers and
> axes they break the images and all the idols; no evil spells or magic
> will remain."

We must here distinguish. Muslim religious men, the Prophet
himself and, as we saw, Ibn Tumart, were associated with magic
and astronomy (astrology). This is an easy accusation, of its nature
incapable of proof or disproof; moreover, Christian attitudes were
ambivalent; there was evil divination, but there was also good

scientific astrology. The idea that the Franks found and broke up actual idols in the mosques is, of course, quite a different idea. Obviously it cannot correspond with the actual experience of those Franks who from time to time had occasion to 'clean' mosques of their former usage in captured Spanish cities, before turning them into churches; nor do the chronicles claim that idols were found. The audiences for the *chansons* were living quietly in monasteries or courts or trading towns in northern Europe, where any fable might amuse, and reality need not intrude. Actually, we are talking about 'escapist' literature: Wild West material. But *Roland* and other *chansons* can also have been recruiting songs; war propaganda, but only for those who have not yet reached the scene of war. It is part of their unreality that they should also apparently have been used for Compostela propaganda. This literature is French, the product of the employment of foreigners in the Reconquest. It is about Spain, but it is not in Spain; the men of the *chansons* are all from northern Europe, and in them the Reconquest is European rather than Spanish.

Associated with *Roland* and the group of related *chansons* is the 'Chronicle of the false Turpinus', that is, an historical novel, written at some time in the first half of the twelfth century, perhaps about the end of the period of Almoravid rule, as if by Turpinus, Archbishop of Rheims to Charlemagne. We are not concerned with its relation to the Compostela church, but we do note immediately that the Turpinus Chronicle belongs to the same world of legend as the *chansons*—it is even more legendary than *Roland*—and, like them, it looks forward to a golden age when there will be no more 'pagans' in Spain. There is a sort of duel for Spain, or, better, a judicial ordeal by battle. Ordeal by battle, where justice is submitted to a providential control of chance, must be preceded by appropriate ritual, and this is in fact well exemplified in *Roland* itself, when Tierry appeals the traitor Guenelun: "When they are ready for battle, they are confessed and absolved and blessed. They hear their masses and receive communion." So the Archbishop (no other than Turpinus himself, who in the *Roland* version of events is killed) blesses the army before battle: "Confess your sins, I shall absolve you to save your souls. If you die you will be holy martyrs . . ." For penance, he orders them to strike. "The French stand up . . . They have been absolved and are free of their sins." Indeed, the whole argument of *Roland* is a judgement of the right, and a shade more subtle than the famous line, "Pagans are in the wrong and Christians have the right," would suggest. The same case is explicitly, almost formally, argued in the Turpinus Chronicle. Charles himself is supposed to have been brought up in Spain at the court of the amir Galaffrus of Toledo, who knighted him, and there seems to be a faint echo of history in his helping this Arab king against his Arab enemies. Therefore he speaks Arabic well, and so he is able to enter into fluent controversy with the Muslim Aigoland; the conflict is reduced to simple but unusual terms. Aigoland asks why Charles has taken away from the Arabs their land, which did not belong to him by hereditary right from his father or his fathers' fathers. Charles replies: because Jesus Christ the Creator has chosen the Christian people above all other peoples, and established them to rule all the nations of the world; and so that the Muslim nation may be converted. Aigoland answers that it would be unworthy that "our people should be subject to your people, when our religion is worth more than yours. We have Muhammad, who was the messenger sent us by God and whose precepts we hold. What is more, we have almighty gods, who by command of Muhammad reveal the future to us . . ." "Aigoland," says Charles, "in this you are mistaken;" it is the Christians who serve God, and the Muslims serve the devil "in his *simulacra*". Thus the Christian religion is worth more. They agree that the way to prove which is worthy is to fight; and Aigoland says that if the Muslims win the Christians will be oppressed for ever, but if the Christians win he and his people will be baptized. They fight again and again, twenty against twenty, forty against forty, a hundred against a hundred, and so on, and always the Christians win; the Muslims are all killed, except Aigoland, who agrees to be baptized. Here we have the legal case clearly stated, and the judgement worked out in terms of ordeal by battle.

Although the date of Turpinus is certainly twelfth century, and perhaps well advanced in the century, the normal crusading argument, that the Christians are taking back their own, that this is a restoration of their own land, is not used at all, although to modern minds the case would be a stronger one in Spain than in Jerusalem. In fact, the very opposite is conceded; it is the Arabs who have the right to the land by inheritance. The Christian right is a right conferred by the truth of their religion, and the Arabs may be converted. It is not clear whether, in that case, they will share in the natural dominion of Christians over others, and

99

this problem is not resolved, or even considered; it is evaded by the death of the Arab contestants. I think that the author always conceived the Christians as European, and did not or would not consider the logical results of a putative Arab conversion. Turpinus imputes idolatry to the Muslims, but more subtly than the *chansons* do; the 'almighty gods' receive their orders from Muhammad and are *simulacra* of the devil. Muhammad, in short, is being presented as a necromancer. The author must know perfectly well the true Muslim confession of faith, because he also uses the formula, "the Messenger of God sent us by God". His, in fact, is an ingenious attempt to correspond with known facts, without denying the ordinary absurd background of the *chansons*. In the last resort this is a clerical fantasy of victory. Europeans in the twelfth century had proved, not indeed invariably victorious, but still steadily successful, throughout the Mediterranean. It was possible to see the conflict as an ordeal by battle, not yet concluded, but progressing reasonably hopefully. The days when men would rack their brains to understand why God should allow victory to the Muslims in the East—however great the sins of the Christians—were yet to come. Even so, the often acute writer of the Turpinus fiction is careful in the bargain he allows Charles to make with Aigoland by which Muslim victory is to result in Christian subjection, but Christian victory in Muslim conversion.

The *chansons* have no monolithic attitude. They are often grotesque. The Arab Gormont is an honoured enemy, the renegade Isembart joins him in his kingdom at Cirencester. Arabs, surely, are here confused with Vikings. The *chansons* did not exclude a female interest, even a love interest, though this was strictly subject to conversion. The 'Queen of Spain', Bramidonie, in *Roland*, is a heroine conceived after the model of such European ladies as Adela of Blois. After the victory of Charles, all the Arabs are brought to the baptistery; they can become Christian, or be hanged or be cut down or burned to death; but Bramidonie is taken prisoner to France, that she may be converted by love, not force. And in the end she did become Christian, under the name of Juliana, a Christian 'by true knowledge'. In *Anseis de Cartage*, the love of the Arab princess Gaudisse for the Christian King of Spain (under Charles), her escape to him, conversion and marriage, are as much as religion the cause of war.

Et Franchois ont ma fille gaagnie.

Such stories may reflect the story of Zaida and Alfonso VI, or at least marriages and other unions between Christians and Muslims, and the unions with slaves on either side. Is there seepage into the *chansons*, orthodox and pious, and mostly clerical or clerically inspired, of a literary exchange which fitted less readily into the war situation?

There has long been controversy about whether Europe is indebted to the Arabs of Spain for troubadour verse (no longer seriously in doubt), and for the notion of courtly love. These questions relate to the eleventh century; the more serious fighting of the twelfth, and the more effective Arab organization under Almoravids and Almohads is justly reflected in the serious atmosphere of the *chansons de geste*. Honour, not controversy, had moved the Cid; on the Muslim side, the petty kings of the *taifas* inherited civilization, but not strength, from the Umayyad caliphate. The absence of fanaticism on both sides made an interchange easier than earlier or later in Spanish history. Arabs were often feudatories of Europeans, who might send their sons to spend some time in Arab households. There is a body of macaronic verse of this period, the Arabic *muwashshah* and *zajal* with their Romance *kharja*, or envoi, a plaintive love lyric which implies performance by a Mozarab girl professional singer.

> *Aman ya habibi*
> *al-wahsa me no feras*
> *Bon beja ma boquella*

Women probably often passed from one side to the other. The results could be exaggerated. The knight at Barbastro who swayed drunkenly to the dancing of a slave-girl whose song he could not understand exemplifies a strictly limited cultural interchange. Female slaves must nevertheless have played a considerable part. It has been suggested that the large number of Christian slaves in Arab cities resulted in a degree of freedom for women to move about that has always been unusual in Muslim countries; the customs of the Spanish Arabs may well have been as much influenced by Christian infiltration, often involuntary, as the other way round. On the other hand, though the numbers of women captured at Barbastro may have been exaggerated, many must have gone to Provençal courts on many such occasions. The formal indebtedness of early troubadour verse to Arabic originals does not seem to be seriously in doubt.

The history of the relations of the sexes, of the development of some sexual equality, of courtly love, of the service of a lady by a knight, and of the whole romantic tradition, is made up of problems not quickly solved. Prejudice, patriotism, the width of linguistic resource necessary for an adequate judgement of materials reaching across centuries, even perhaps millennia, and across many divergent cultures, have left many aspects obscure. What debt is there specifically to Spain by Europe? How much did Europe develop of its own? What kinds of meeting, what methods of communication, does a considerable debt of literary themes imply? We must begin by the assumption that, if verse forms were transmitted, there was a serious communication between Arabic and Romance languages in the eleventh century. Even allowing for the possibility that warfare in the eleventh century was a little less devastating than in the twelfth, how could there be a fruitful transmission of ideas in an atmosphere of rough and tough pillage, murder and destruction? If we can accept that persistent devastation was no seed-bed for cultural exchange when the Arabs were raiding Italy, why should it have been so when the European Spaniards were making their steady, and far from gentle, advance through the Peninsula?

There are more partial answers. Nykl points out that the transmission of a melody not only presents no problem, but may provide additional motivation. He also points out that there would be no difficulty about finding interpreters. On the other hand, the interpretation of a song is one thing, the copying of the fine points of its metre quite another. We have to presuppose men of determination and some originality who might be sufficiently attracted to give close attention to the songs and verses of the Arabs. William IX of Aquitaine, who stands in the key position at the head of the line of Provençal poets, was at least a man of individual and almost eccentric character. It is credible that he might have made such an effort as would have been needed. It is relevant here that he was himself a rich and powerful, if bellicose, magnate, able to command others to help him to any extent he required. If we were to question his possessing the concentration, we must reply that the author of his poems must by hypothesis have possessed a fine ear for metre and a capacity for hard work. There was one fundamental difference for the Europeans between the Spanish Reconquest and the period of struggle for dominion in southern Italy; in Spain the Europeans were winning. They were not struggling for existence, but for richer and richer booty. They were expanding, and taking in more and more Arab country, and though there was much depopulation, the Arab farmers were the greatest sufferers. Rich Arabs (or Europeans) could always expect to survive, in order to be ransomed, and skilled singers and poets and courtiers were themselves rich enough for ransom, or worth saving for their skills. We hear of the killing of Arabs learned in the religious law, not of those who were learned in secular accomplishments. The conquerors, if their position is reasonably assured, can usually afford to learn from the conquered. We should expect that Spanish poetry and singing would be influenced by Moorish sources, as in fact they were.

What is more surprising is that the first appearance of the troubadours should have been in Provence. The closeness of the Catalan and Provençal languages, and the similarities of life at petty courts whether in the Peninsula or in southern France make any transition less surprising. War was an occupation for a gentleman in Aquitaine before it fell into the hands of administrators from the north. William of Aquitaine fought his co-religionists; then he fought and nearly died in Asia Minor; finally he fought in Spain; if he could not plunder the Saracens, he plundered the church at home. He, and the patrons of troubadours, and troubadours of gentlemanly status, all provided a demand which must explain the rapid development of their verse, more rapid, at least in surviving written form, than anything Spanish of the same nature. Yet, if the *Poema del Cid* is totally different in character, it is easy to see that the society it describes is one in which poetry fitted to the *muluk at-tawaif*, the petty Arab kings of the eleventh century, would flourish.

On the whole, it seems undeniable that courtly poetry in Arabic, often trivial, yet ranged much more widely in theme and treatment than troubadour verse. If the latter had not a special position in European literary history, it might well be regarded as no more than a provincial and decadent offshoot of the court poets of Spain. It was a particular contribution of European poetry to stress the joys of war, for those who fought as a sport: "I am well pleased by the gay time of Easter, which gives birth to leaves and flowers . . . I have great joy when I see the armed horsemen and horses ranged upon the plain." This is not complex literature, although there is much skilled craftsmanship. There is much of

politics, largely personal and often vituperative. Political generaliz-
ations may be orthodox to the point of banality: "All goes ill for
the four kings of Spain, because they do not want peace among
themselves;" they ought to turn their arms "against the people
who did not believe in our religion, until Spain is all of one faith."
The troubadour attitude to crusade is often almost indistinguishable from the clerical, since in this matter courts and clergy were
agreed at least on the need to fight. William of Aquitaine himself
went crusading, unsuccessfully, like so much that he did. Marcabru repeats orthodoxy when he is imagining the sadness of the
Crusader's deserted lover, the daughter of the lord of a castle.
"Jesus," she said, "my great sorrow grows through you, *because
of the outrage you suffer*, for all the best people in the world have
gone to serve you ... With you has gone my friend, the fair, the
noble, the brave, the strong." In another poem he pleads for help
in chasing the Arabs out of Spain and out of the Holy Sepulchre.
The meanness of powerful men beyond the mountains *"Als
Amoravis fai conort,"* encourages the Almoravids; let them wait
till the warm weather returns, together with the lord of Castile,
"and we will make the people of Cordova grow thin." All this
literature is agreeable, but as thin as the people of Cordova.

If, however, European concepts of courtly love derive from the
petty courts of the *taifas*, the whole romantic tradition in European
literature owes an almost disproportionate debt to eleventh-century
Spain. It has been argued that there is evidence of Platonic ideas
in Provence at this period, conjectured to derive from Ibn Hazm.
It has also been argued that, on the contrary, ideas which occur
widely in the poetry of the world cannot be certainly attributed
to particular sources. From the anthropological point of view,
Nelli has stressed that chastity or spirituality (in no Christian
sense), or at any rate refraining from sexual acts, was accepted as
the highest form of love from the middle of the twelfth century;
at best it is an ideal of companionship rather than of domination
by the lady. He sees it as deriving from many possible sources,
Celtic, Germanic, even Byzantine, as well as Arab; and possibly,
therefore, from them all. The development of ideas of friendship
and equality in heterosexual love he sees as an extension of the
fraternities of blood which originated among men of many cultures, and the introduction of impediments to sexuality in a literary
ideal would derive from contexts that were already, or were meant
to be, sexless, love for a mother or among male companions. He

argues that though ancient misogyny survived, the old tradition that continence strengthens warriors helped the new ideas. The unreasonable domination of her lover by the lady would have roots in Celtic and other customs of a remote past. All Nelli's possibilities suggest the ambiguity or multiplicity of the origins of European romanticism, in which Arab sources would be some among many. From the sociological point of view, Duby identified the twelfth-century problem of *juventus*, the unmarried errant knights seeking booty and women in the short run, and wives and lands in the long; the over-production of sons in the aristocracy would obviously favour romantic troubadour themes. This much at least we can say: the existing traditions of Europe were favourable to the new ideas; in particular, a dominating Lady is 'feudally' intelligible, and the discursive, scholastic treatment of the theme, as by Andreas Capellanus, although it has Arab parallels in the love debates, is paralleled equally by contemporary philosophical methodology. Secondly, certain of the ideas that became popular in the vernacular literatures of Europe from the twelfth century have close parallels in eleventh-century Spanish Arabic literature; besides the love debates, just mentioned, there is also the domination of the male lover by the woman, and the idea of chaste sexual love as well; another example is the character of the jealous figure. In the person, not only of a husband, but also of the guardian of the women of a household, servant or eunuch, this fits Islamic society even better than the freer society of Germanic Europe. Yet if these ideas did come from Spain, they were speedily acclimatized, because already half-formulated. Thirdly, we must add that later developments of European literature, such as allegorized psychological verse, do not seem to have an Arabic parallel. To sum up a bare conclusion; there were certainly some parallel developments, and these were probably related.

4. Direct literary connections

The influences just discussed are the subject of speculation. We cannot define them accurately in detail; supposition has to replace records that do not exist. Except for Wolfram von Eschenbach's absurd attribution of the Grail legend to the Moors, the debt of the romantic writers of Europe to the Arabs, whatever it was, was unacknowledged. We nowhere find an explicit admission that there was an alien source for the new ideas of western Europe in the twelfth century in the lay world. In the clerical world concerned with the translation of scientific and philosophical material from Arabic, the situation is very different; there the debt is clear and defined, and was always acknowledged. It is so large a subject that I leave it for another chapter. Much the same is true of the mediaeval study of Islam, in yet another chapter. Outside these areas of thought, it is hard to say how far Europe at different periods was aware of Spain.

There are some aspects of Spanish life or literature which passed in isolation into the literature of Europe. The first was the *Disciplina clericalis* of the converted Jewish writer, Pedro de Alfonso. In this translation from the Arabic he was the first to introduce the genre of fable, a kind of subdivision of Wisdom literature. These are pleasant, even amusing, though grave in style; they also mock their own genre. It is surprising that they did not become more popular, or give rise to a large body of imitations; as it was, they found many copyists, and, in due course, printers. Pedro, named after his patron Alfonso VI, may possibly have visited the court of Henry I of England in the capacity of physician; his treatise against Judaism (in the form of dialogue), with a chapter on Islam, is a serious work; but, although the author has good Christian reasons against his old faith, his arguments against Islam are rather in the Jewish than the Christian tradition. For the rest, his story belongs to that of the spread of Arab science. The *Kalila wa Dimna* collection was translated late in the thirteenth century by John of Capua, from a Hebrew version; this translator's main interests were medical, and he did a Latin version of a Hebrew translation of the Arabic of Ibn Zuhr, physician at Almoravid and Almohad courts. This is a long gap and a surprising one, and it is not obvious why the Hebrew element should have been so strong in the purely literary field. There was far more original writing in the vernaculars, Catalan, Castilian, Portuguese, Galician, and especially in verse, than there was translation. The contact between Spaniards of the different races and religions was clear cut only in scientific fields; for the rest, it was often tenuous.

'News from Spain' was another way in which Spanish events reached Europe. According to Salimbene, as we saw, there was widespread fear of the Almohads; this refers to the campaign of 1212, but an earlier chronicler had already spoken with awe of "the King of Morocco, in whose power is all Africa, and even the

Arabs who are in Spain." The kind of killing to which we have constantly had to refer was also known from a distance, and the St Albans Chronicle notes under 1184 that the Archbishop of Compostela managed to kill three hundred thousand Arabs at dawn, on the feast of St John and St Paul, with only twenty thousand men; in the month following, the Arabs killed ten thousand women and children at Alcobaza. We must hope that foreign news reaching England, then as now, was sensationally exaggerated. With the turn of the tide of war, there are not many complaints of Saracens who slaughter Christians, in the old style, though we find Ralph of Coggeshall referring to the Alarcos campaign of 1195 as a time when the Almohads "depopulating several provinces with fires and pillage, spared neither age nor order" (i.e. priests). Usually, by now, the Christians could claim, and much preferred to claim, the opposite; and this marks the remoteness of Coggeshall, despite Cistercian settlements in Spain, from the contemporary spirit of the Reconquest. Even St Albans, rest-house for kings and all but metropolitan, misses the new note of domination. Earlier, Orderic Vitalis had responded to the recruiting need with the right note of triumph, speaking of "great rewards" and "rich booty" to be had in Spain. If we go back to a still earlier date, we find some grotesque stories of Spanish campaigns that reach northern chronicles, as the early eleventh-century story of the Count of Urgel in Catalonia, who lost his life in an attack on the Arabs, and whose victor carried his head about, 'aromatized' in a gold setting, for luck. My examples are taken almost at random. Events in Spain receive frequent mention, especially as victory becomes more frequent than defeat, but naturally foreign histories are vague, obscure and unrelated to context. A reference in a European chronicle is an annalist's reference, and as such shares the quality of a present-day newspaper or television report.

One or two such foreign accounts have a special character of their own. The revival of learning in the twelfth and early thirteenth centuries included a revival of astrology, and the popular love of sensation could find satisfaction, not only in religious prophecies, but also in rumours started by, or blamed on, astrologers. We shall see that an apocalyptic atmosphere was characteristic of Frederick II's Italy; and the anxieties of the day spread far into Europe. Irrational panics had already reached the north. Hoveden tells us how the astrologers foretold a great pestilence, and all, clerics and laymen, rich and poor, were seized with fright as the prophesied date approached; then he copies into his text (under 1184) the *Epistola Pharamellae filii Abdelabi Cordubensis*, written from the court of the Almohad caliph, called Ibn Yaqub in this text (in 1184 Abu Yaqub Yusuf was succeeded by Abu Yusuf Yaqub al-Mansur), in Marrakush, to John, Archbishop of Toledo. Farajallah (?) wants to reassure Christians who have been unnecessarily alarmed by unscientific astrology. Some peculiarly dressed merchants had arrived in Marrakesh, selling tolerably good coloured cloth; they came from a distant country, the kingdom of the Franks; a Toledan prisoner called Ferrando interpreted for them. They explained that the astrologers foretold for 1186, or 572 Hijra (but 572 Hijra was 1176), a wind from the west which would destroy everything erected on the earth, and would be followed by a horrible stench which would kill men. The text continues to give complex and very technical astrological reasons why this is wrong. One manuscript does not print the text, but just mentions the arrival of this letter "of consolation". The chronicler may have been more interested in the astrological niceties than his public, who may be supposed more interested to know just that the astrologers at home have caused a great deal of alarm to no purpose; but he seems to have meant to stress the technical superiority of the Spanish Arab. Perhaps there is a satirical element. Many Englishmen had returned home from studying in Spain during the preceding half-century, and there may have been an intellectual snobbery in citing Spanish Arab sources; or perhaps a local resentment which took pleasure in seeming to cite the real thing against spurious claims to a superior knowledge.

Perhaps the satirical use of the Spanish setting was never more ambitiously attempted than in the story about King John of England which Matthew Paris inserted into the St Albans Chronicle, as having immediately preceded the campaign which ended with the Almohad defeat at Las Navas de Tolosa. John sends three envoys, the third of whom, a cleric called Robert of London, Paris claims as his source in conversations at St Albans. An embassy of three (two laymen) go to seek the Almohad caliph's support for John, against a promise to give up the Christian religion and pay tribute to Marrakesh. The Almohad caliph at this date was Muhammad an-Nasir; he is called '*admiralium Murmelium* (or *Murmelin*)', and '*Miramumelinum*' (one of the infinite varieties of *amir al-muminin*) is said to be his name "among the ordinary run of people" (Hoveden had said it was his family name, *cognomen*). It seems that Spain was pretty well as remote to the Englishman as Jerusalem. The *admiralius*, or king, receives them after their entry through three guarded gates, all very circumstantially described. So is the king himself, "a man of middle age and stature, quick in gesture and fertile in speech, and discreet." He says that he has read and been pleased by the letters of St Paul; but one thing about him displeases the king, that he did not remain in the religion in which he was born. The same applies to King John, who proposes to leave the "most pious and most pure religion" in which he was born. If the *admiralius* were going to be an *exlex*, a renegade, it is Christianity he would embrace. The story continues through a general discussion, and is followed by a more intimate talk between the *admiralius* and Robert of London. It is chiefly concerned with abuse, often crude abuse, of King John, and doubtless that is the whole purpose of describing the episode. For us the chief point of interest is the choice for this purpose of an Almohad ruler whose attack on Spain is about to be related, as well as the attempt to give it verisimilitude by descriptions which are, of course, generalized, and not such as could apply only to Marrakesh or an-Nasir.

Certainly the great victory at Las Navas de Tolosa made a considerable, wide impression, and Paris next relates it. If news from Spain had its place in chronicles with other chief interests, Giraldus Cambrensis tells us that the fame of Henry II of England reached Spain (as well as Byzantium and Syria).

> "Indeed all the princes of the lands, Christians as well as non-Christians, and, like the German Frederick and the Greek Manuel, so Nur ad-Din in his time, and afterwards Salah ad-Din; and, like those of Asia, so those of Europe, of Spain that is, as much those of the native faith as the unbelievers, used to honour and visit the same with frequent messengers."

Spain was one of the four corners of the earth, but it was not perhaps the most important of them. We must not let ourselves be mesmerized by the fact that it was the principal channel for the scientific and philosophical development of Europe for two centuries, into according it the same hyperbole as Giraldus gave Henry. We can say quite truly that Spain was by far the most important area for the contact of Arabs with Europeans. We can say with equal truth that Europeans were less impressed by the Arabs and Berbers of Spain than by the peoples of the East: Arab, Seljuk,

Turkish or Tartar. Through Spain came very many specific influences which we can trace, not only in learning and literature, but equally in the plastic arts, in administrative techniques, and in other ways known or suspected. In spite of that, events in Spain occasionally impressed, rather than constantly dominated, the European imagination. Above all, Spain was a European success, and once this was clear, much of the interest had gone out of it. It largely ceased to be news; and in a business sense also, it ceased to be a speculation. Spain was firmly in the hands of its new owners.

Chapter 5

European solidarity and the inception of the crusading idea

1. General considerations

The ideas characteristic of the First Crusade survived long after it, but appeared at its first preaching. Memories of Urban's words were confused, but some arguments are clearly distinguishable and constant. Most mediaeval historians of crusade begin with Urban's sermon at Clermont, as though it were itself the text of the greater sermon of the whole Crusade. To the devout clerical thinker the history of crusade was homiletic because it told the story of how God acted through his people, through the Franks; later they would have to say that it was also homiletic because it showed how God must punish his people for their sins. At the beginning, the leaders and the people themselves felt a sense of salvation, a kind of revelation, the binding force of a supernatural purpose and power. The excitement of clerics, lords and people was the same: *Deus lo volt*. So long as sincere conviction supported it, it was a great propaganda success for the clerical interest; the people might now be bound to a holy purpose, a people of God who, like ancient Israel, would now use their talents for the advancement of the kingdom of God, of the church of the reformed papacy.

The idea was not that the people of God would be rewarded because they virtuously fought the Holy War; God would act in them and so recover for himself his own land. They would be only its guardians. The material advantage derived from the Crusade by lucky members of the ruling class (and not all were lucky) has evoked a chain of criticism from those first days until our own. Among the poor and on the lunatic fringe there were chiliastic hopes and revolutionary urges which were the expression of a more pathetic self-interest. After the first excitement had spent itself, however, it was not difficult for contemporaries to penetrate the pious justifications of unscrupulous interests. It was natural to think theologically and to attribute failures, small failures at first, greater ones later, the permanent loss of the territory that had been gained, the fall of Jerusalem, the fall of Acre, and finally the advance of the Ottomans, to the sins of unrighteous Christians.

Yet the crusading concept could have come to no other result. This is clear enough from the most cursory examination of the beginnings of the movement. The Lords of the army, not only Raymond of Toulouse or Duke Godfrey, but Bohemund and Tancred too, were as much 'pilgrims' as any in the army. There must be lords if the land was to be captured, and still more if it was to remain in Christian hands. The function of a pilgrim lord was to command the band of pilgrims: in a feudal world, this must mean to establish feudal holdings and the usual network of marriages and allegiances. It must mean the adaptation of the economy and the law of Mediterranean Europe to the Levant. There is no need to think crusading lords hypocritical, or merchant houses cynical; if the pilgrims were the *populus Dei*, they were the same people, working and living through the same institutions, at home and *outremer*. Any criticism of the Crusade as an exploitation of religious sentiment is anachronistic; we owe it to the theoretical temper of the Enlightenment when, like Gibbon and Talleyrand, we see an association of land-hungry war-bands and mercantile interests who cloak their motives with religious pretence. Although this is an absurd simplification, it is true that theology was the natural expression of the times, and that the doctrine of the holy war was perfectly suited to the establishment of the Latin states. The anachronism is to suppose the religious sentiment a mask, even, or especially, when Crusaders failed to maintain the attitudes preached and expected by an Urban or a Bernard.

It is interesting to see how the idea of the people of God worked out, in theory and in practice. That the King was substituted for the Advocate of the Holy Sepulchre, Baldwin I for his brother Godfrey, amounted to a formal admission that the people of God were a colony, not a theocracy. Nevertheless, we may say that the lay sentiment and the clerical were in alliance. When we read of angels in the battle-line, we think of popular myth, of Marathon or of Mons. Belief in a God who actually takes part in the war his people wage must represent a wave of solidarity and communal feeling, and the ultimate survival of the Franks justified their notion of God by success. The First Crusade was one of the principal events in the history of the European consciousness. This is obvious enough from the number of second-hand accounts of it that were written; and there has never been a time when Europe has not, in one way or another, remembered the First Crusade. Accounts of later crusades are ordinary histories and travels; the first was the response to a clerical idea which satisfied a wider—and powerful—emotional need. The precise distinction is less clear between the ecclesiastical contribution and the lay, between the parts played by the different classes and interests, by the higher clergy, the theologians, the lords, the merchant republics, and the proletariat of poor pilgrims. Many different origins went to make up the attitude of Christians to the Arabs they invaded. What began as a common enthusiasm broke up immediately into its constituent parts, and yet a certain common attitude, which was pan-European, remained.

2. Latin aggression and cultural intolerance

Fulcher of Chartres attributed to Urban the deliberate intention to revive Christianity by means of crusade. If Urban was principally motivated by the thought of how the Christian faith was diminished among clergy and people, of how the princes of the land were warring against each other, then his object was primarily European, not missionary; not to extend religion abroad, or even to defend it from invasion, but to make its rule effective at home. There is no more authentic account of Urban's preaching than the selective, or imaginary, accounts of his hearers and his hearers' hearers; these certainly represent at least accepted ideas of the crusading impetus. A generation after the event, William of Malmesbury's version stresses the historical danger to Christendom, the loss of Asia and Africa; Europe only remained, and even there the threat was instanced by three centuries' occupation of Spain and the Balearics. The supposed need to repel an attack upon the Christian religion is common to all the accounts, but it is quite compatible with a wish to turn the taste for arms to any other end than internecine warfare. Earlier wars against the Arabs, as well as the situation in Spain, had prepared men's minds. A fund of xenophobia was latent in the homogeneous culture of Europe.

One feature of this is the contrast between the theory that the crusading purpose was the liberation of Oriental Christians and the actual hostility most Latins felt in their encounters with their co-religionists of Greek, Syriac or Coptic allegiances. It is not clear how far—if at all—the Latins in Europe realized that the eastern rites were different from their own. Their encounter with the Byzantines would arouse both political and cultural hostility on each side; and when the Latin states were established, the Christian Arabs were treated without respect by the Latin Church. In Europe, xenophobia was easily aroused, and its contamination infectious; expressed at first in the belief in an Islamic aggression, it quickly became indiscriminate, as the pilgrims realized that the world was made up of many nations, and all of them alien. Only when they reached the Arab World were they reoriented to their first hate, and even then only partially. From the first arrival of the undisciplined troops and camp-followers of Walter Sans-Avoir and Peter the Hermit in eastern Europe, there was acute conflict. This was still true in the case of relatively disciplined armies. The author of the *Gesta Francorum*, who followed Bohemund, describes at first hand how the people of Thrace "were really afraid of us, not thinking that we were pilgrims, but that we wanted to plunder the land and to kill them." The local people refused to trade, and so the Franks did plunder them. At Monastir the pilgrims attacked a castle of heretics, and burned it and its inhabitants together; the Emperor's troops attacked the pilgrims, and Bohemund lectured his prisoners, "Why do you kill Christ's people and mine?" Here all the symptoms of cultural misunderstanding are suggested, each side increasingly indignant with the other. If Bohemund had not been conciliatory under political restraint, mutual offence would have continued to mount. The failure of the Franks to mingle with their often involuntary hosts can be measured at different levels; there were the real horrors in the Balkans, pillage, rape, murder and actual battle; at another level there was the failure of the Latin leaders to respect, or to earn the respect of, the Byzantine Emperor. It is possible to exaggerate the barbarism of Frankish behaviour. The Frankish leaders were sophisticated, and their followers were probably no more ignorant than Byzantine mercenaries and peasants; but it is impossible to exaggerate the cultural intolerance of the Franks. Perhaps the clearest evidence is their insistence on Latinizing the churches whenever they obtained power, and ultimately, of course, in the thirteenth century, in Greece itself. They never earned the loyalty of their Christian Arab subjects in Palestine and Syria.

All the cultures involved in the Crusades, Arab, Greek, Syrian, Latin, thought of each other as in some sense 'barbarian'. This is traditional usage; the word describes an alien culture and alien institutions, as the ancient Greeks used it of the Persians. This is how the Latins used it of the Arabs and Turks; Guibert of Nogent in fact set the Crusades consciously in the context of the wars of the ancients. The conviction of a superior culture comes out clearly in Urban's urging that the Franks are the natural leaders of the Christians, and in the idea of the *Turci et Arabes* as *barbari* at the frontiers of 'Romania' (i.e. of East Rome). The same idea is inherent in the words *pagani* and *gentiles* used of the Arabs. The Latins saw themselves in the Crusade as the heirs at once of ancient Athens, of Alexander, of imperial Rome, of Judas Maccabeus, and of the early Christian martyrs; all their disparate cultural inheritance was blended into one by the notion of holy war. Very rarely was their complacency disturbed, and the exception marks the rule. Some seventy years after Urban preached, William of Tyre, himself the product of the new states, imagined how the first Crusaders must have looked to the Fatimid rulers of the day in Egypt:

"The Egyptian prince, most powerful of Eastern rulers . . . gathered vast armies together, saying that it was disgraceful that a barbarian people, sprung from the furthest ends of the earth, should enter his kingdom and violently occupy a province subject to his rule."

William may have found a hint for this speech in a passage of the *Gesta*, but there the drift is very different. Emphatically the first Crusaders did not think of themselves as barbarians.

The norm was cultural arrogance, firmly based on a conviction of right which was elaborated in a complex and fully articulate theory of defensive war. The liberation of the Holy Places was the basic idea and theoretic justification of the Crusade; the Holy Land was Christian land and must be recovered from the barbarians. If the Franks were the natural leaders of the Christians, the recovery of Jerusalem was a Frankish duty. The Holy Land was always seen as God's own, *terra sua*. The Roman curia always referred to any land which had once been Christian (Spain, Sicily) as 'restored' to Christianity, and this applied above all to the Holy

E

Land. "Almighty everlasting God, who by thy marvellous power hast plucked out Jerusalem, thy city, from the hands of the pagans, and hast given it back to the Christians . . .": so began the collect of the feast of the Recovery which was celebrated in the Church of Jerusalem in the twelfth century. The attitude was not so rarefied as to occur only in liturgy and papal bulls and recruiting homiletic. Caffaro in his Genoese Chronicle gives a good example of the official and clerical justification of the war, almost on the field of battle, and in any case in discussion with Muslims. Two Muslims come out of besieged Caesarea and approach the Patriarch and the Legate. "Lords, you who are masters and doctors of the Christian law, why do you command your people to kill us, to invade our country, when it is written in your religion that no one must kill anyone who is in the image of your God, or carry off his goods?" And the Patriarch replies,

> "It is true that it is written in our law that you shall not carry off another's goods and shall not kill him, and we neither do nor commend the one or the other. But this town does not belong to you, it is and must be St Peter's, whom your fathers chased out of Caesarea. That is why we who are St Peter's vicars want to recover his land, and not to take away your property. As to murder, we reply that he who fights to destroy the law of God must be killed in just vengeance . . . We ask you to give up the land of St Peter, and we will let you go safe and sound, your persons and your goods. If you will not do so, the Lord will kill you with his sword . . ."

The length and the detail of this official Christian reply recognize the importance of the Muslim accusation. It hardly matters whether something that actually happened is truly recounted. It would be an even more remarkable conversation if the speech of the Muslims had been solely the invention of the Christian conscience. What these Arabs say is interesting, too, as a remote ancestor of the arguments of modern anti-imperialists.

If there is nothing in Caffaro's account that might not in fact have happened, a comparable story in the *Gesta* clearly represents talk circulating in the army of Bohemund. This is a version of the embassy of Herluin and Peter the Hermit to Kerbogha, after the fall of the city of Antioch and before the decisive great battle with Kerbogha, and the capture of the citadel. The Frankish leaders in council instructed their envoys to ask "through some interpreter", *quamobrem temere ac superbissime in Christianorum introistis terram,* "why have you so rashly and arrogantly invaded the land of the

Christians?" The ambassadors asked Kerbogha, in the name of their leaders, if he had come to be baptized; if not, to remove his army promptly from "the land of God and of Christians, which the blessed Peter the apostle long since converted to the worship of Christ by his preaching." The Franks offered to permit Kerbogha (and by implication the Muslim Arabs of the country also) to take their flocks and other goods and all kinds of possessions away with them. The issue as these Crusaders saw it comes out even more clearly in the reply this story allots to Kerbogha. "We neither like nor want your God or your Christianity (*christianitas*) and we utterly reject you and them." Kerbogha was surprised—and was so reported—that the Franks should call theirs a land that the Turks had taken away from an effeminate people (presumably the Greeks); if the Franks will renounce the God they worship and become Turks, the Muslims will give them this land and more besides; the foot-soldiers will all become knights, as the Turks all are; all will be welcomed in the highest friendship. Otherwise they will be killed or led into captivity for ever. Thus the crusading army was perfectly clear about both the claim and the counter-claim.

Through all the history of Christian relations with Islam, at least until the imperial period, Christians would insist upon the material gains that conversion to Islam would offer, no doubt because it was polemically the best way to explain why it should occur at all. In the present instance, it is interesting that the offer—as it was understood by the Crusaders themselves—would most benefit the foot-men, and the poorer knights who had lost, and at that stage could not replace, their horses. The writer was himself a soldier, and he held, not a proletarian view, but not that of the most privileged either. He recognized the temptation to enter as a valued professional into a different society with new opportunities; but the fate of those who surrendered with Rainald at Xerigordo, said to have been sold as slaves all over the Arab World, would have deterred him. In any case, he was a sincere Christian who accepted the clerical position.

We do not often find an Islamic point of view put forward at all. Fulcher of Chartres, an army chaplain attached to Baldwin, later the first king of that name, was a mild man who disliked cruelty and had no taste for fighting. He took for granted the accepted view of a Latin right to ownership of the Holy Land, even when most critical of Christian behaviour. "What is there surprising if

Muslims or wicked lords take our lands from us, when we reach out rapacious hands to the lands of our neighbours?" Urban's view of the Crusade as Fulcher recounted it reflects a whole world torn by warfare, both the bitter fighting between Christian men who will not observe the truce of God, and the incessant and remorseless attacks on the outer edge of Christendom by the Turks who reach even to the Mediterranean shore. This is characteristic of Fulcher, who declaimed against the horrors of fighting, a pacifist kind of Crusader. There is no evidence that anything like an accurate chronology of Islam was yet widely known; the translation of Theophanes by Anastasius was soon to influence and correct most writers who chronicled the history of the world, but it is unlikely that Fulcher and most of those concerned with the First Crusade had seen it. Embrico of Mainz had placed Muhammad in the fourth century, more probably by a wild guess than a reasoned error. In the eleventh century there was still a widespread ignorance of Islamic chronology; the rise of Islam was airily dated as unknown, *quo nescio tempore*, by Guibert of Nogent, although he cared for the facts of classical history; and of the Cairo of his own time he knew (in a rough sense, correctly) that Babylon was the ancient Memphis. We have to assume that there was very little understanding of the fact that Palestine had been in the possession of Islam since the days of Umar ibn al-Khattab. The centuries of Muslim and Arab habitation were forgotten, being part neither of classical nor of sacred history. Indeed, until they left Antioch the Crusaders were in territory that had been Christian till a few years earlier; the Turkish armies were visibly invaders (coming rather vaguely from 'Khorasan' somewhere in the east), and the inhabitants, especially of the coastal plain, were largely Christian Arabs of various churches, none of which were clearly known or understood. The earliest account of the Prophet which has any reflection of history, and which was soon widespread, places him in 'Corozan'. Later generations, both in Europe and the Latin states, knew better; but the earlier Crusaders had no reason to suspect a conflict between the theological theory, the historical evidence, and the observed facts.

3. European reaction to the crusading idea

The myth of the Crusade which treated it as one of the greatest of events in the world's history began with its contemporaries.

Since the beginning of the world, said Robert of Rheims, the expedition of the Crusaders is the occurrence which most merits our admiration—excepting the Redemption—because it is the work, not of men, but of God. All Guibert's argument, and still more his famous title, *Gesta Dei per Francos*, made God the author of the Crusade, which took its place naturally in the sequence of sacred history. As in the Old Testament, so "in our time God has instituted holy fighting." The emphasis is more or less the same in all contemporary historians. To the churchman it seemed almost as though he were taking part in a new writing of Holy Scripture. Not this interpretation, but this perspective of importance has survived many centuries of historical assessment, the Renaissance, the Enlightenment, the Romantic Age, the age of scientific historiography; that is not to say that the assessment is not correct, but one of the reasons that makes it correct is precisely the strength of the impact it made upon the European imagination from the start. The impact remains, in spite of so much that has happened since, and that seems important to us; but at the time, too, it established its place in the sequence of history, not only the sequence of classics and Scripture known to the cleric, but also in competition with King Arthur and the matter of Britain, with Charlemagne, William of Orange and the matter of France, with the matter of Troy and Alexander and Rome the Great; so far as they circulated at this date, they appealed more to the mind of the ordinary man. The Crusader could write himself into epic. According to Robert of Rheims, Urban himself quoted the example of Charlemagne and his son Louis, but for the more literate who supported the crusading appeal, its importance derived from a theological assessment.

Our classic explanation of the strength of the European reaction is, once again, Gibbon's. "Against the private wars of the barbarians, their bloody tournaments, licentious loves, and judicial duels, the popes and synods might ineffectually thunder;" now these "reigning passions" of war and sport were transformed in status into penance. In addition, of course, "fancy already grasped the golden sceptres of Asia," but this is an afterthought. Can we justify this eighteenth-century simplification? It strikes us immediately that this was essentially Urban's judgement too. From their diametrically opposed positions, Pope and historian have made a congruous analysis of the facts, or perhaps the historian has simply followed the Pope. This continuity is impressive, and yet there are difficulties. What we may call the 'sublimation of energy' theory makes assumptions that are not tenable. Was the age more licentious and bloody than those before or after? Was only the knightly class affected? Obviously not; and Guibert wrote very much to the point when he spoke of the "knightly class and the common people on the move" (*oberrans*). All classes were affected; they were all disturbed. Even when they went on pilgrimage they were still licentious, and still fought each other as well as the enemy, as had always been the case. Whatever the Pope's good intention, the Crusade was not unique in character. The bare idea of crusade was hardly new; in a primitive form, it already existed in Spain, and had begun to take shape in Italy long before. It can be argued that in what actually happened there was nothing new at all; but what was new was a sudden emotional content. Urban fired so immediate a response that we can hardly say whether the preaching started the emotional outburst, or merely gave expression to a state of mind that had reached the point of explosion.

We can argue that the uncertainty about what Urban actually said is evidence that he expressed an already existing communal need, rather than initiated a new idea, or even seemed to his contemporaries to do so. There is some evidence of a predisposition to excitement. Guibert tells us that existing discord was resolved by the heavenly rain of Urban's preaching. Perhaps this is only another form of the 'sublimation of energy' theory; but it looks more as though Guibert thought that there was an abnormal disturbance which was quieted by the idea of crusade. He implies, not the transfer to a useful purpose of a course of action which was satisfying though harmful, but instead the allaying of a sense of dissatisfaction. There seems to have been a movement, some sense of a revelation or of salvation. The author of the *Gesta* begins his story by saying, "When already that limit was approaching which the Lord Jesus daily points out to his faithful, saying specially in his Gospel, 'If any man will come after me, let him deny himself and take up his cross and follow me,' then there was a powerful movement through all the regions of the Gauls;" every sincere Christian realized that "he should not delay in taking the road to the Holy Sepulchre." According to this text, the Pope went north to preach, as quickly as he could; it is as though he went in response to urgent demand, rather than to conduct a reforming council. Here it is not what happened that matters, but what seemed to happen. There are other indications. Peter the Hermit was evidently revivalist in manner; he was himself a strong and 'charismatic' personality, like all great preachers, as well as eccentric. Myths formed around him, as witness the Antioch and Jerusalem *chansons*. His early history is doubtful; it is hard to define what he did or to be sure what set him going. It is not even clear when he started preaching, or how his initiative related to Urban's. It is only clear that his preaching corresponded to the people's wants, that the opportunity he was given exactly suited his obsession about Jerusalem, that he was the man for his time. We have seen that Europe was narrowly intolerant and xenophobic, but in 1095 this xenophobia was like a summer forest, ready to blaze. The frenzied response was itself an indication of a previous disposition.

Robert of Rheims describes the enthusiasm with which Urban's words were received, and his caution in forbidding women to crusade without their husbands or guardians, or monks without the permission of their superiors. Baudri de Bourgeuil (who, like Robert, based his story of the actual Crusade on the *Gesta*) tells how everyone began to preach crusade, the bishops first and the rest of the world afterwards; he claims that fathers rejoiced to see their sons go, wives at the departure of their husbands, and those who were left were miserable because they could not go; he tells us that things went too far, and that monks seized the chance to abscond. Among the common people, there were those who branded the cross on themselves with hot iron, either from a spirit of ostentation, or to give the impression of a miracle. The fever extended from England across France and Gascony to the Italian cities, which prepared their ships to carry their pilgrims. He speaks also of the celestial prodigies which were seen in 1095, always a fair indication of mass excitement. Guibert gives further indications of frenzy; for example, how people sold their property on a buyers' market, as if they were ransoming their lives, for low prices. It is to him that we owe the story of the children who ran away from their families, and asked at every town they came to, "Is this Jerusalem?" In verse, he tells us that women and children and old men went ahead, in order to die for Christ, before the young men came to fight for him. He stresses the strange men who came from a great distance, including Scots with bare legs and a bag of food over the shoulder, and islanders with no known language who could only signify their crusading intention by making a cross with their fingers. Men spurned their honours and treated their beautiful wives like dirt. He tells us that those who at first mocked at the enthusiasm of others caught the contagion and behaved with the same enthusiasm. The preaching of Peter the Hermit restored unfaithful women to their husbands, and peace to men who squabbled; Guibert tells us that Peter was taken for "sub-divine", and he adds that he tells us so, not because it is true, but in order to satisfy the popular taste for sensation. The people shed all their former responsibilities, and rose like a cloud of locusts who "have no king, yet all of them march in rank." There is a note of irony, whether deliberate or not, which makes this passage credible. Many people were made miserable by being compelled to remain behind, among them, as he himself tells us, the historian Albert of Aix. The leaders, he reminds us, no less than the rest, left their homelands, their families, their towns, castles, fields, and all the pleasures of life, for the sake of this good work. Clergy, nobles, all the people, the chaste, the incestuous, the adulterers, robbers, "all who professed the Christian faith," grasped the opportunity for penance. Every description of the European sentiment of the day is extravagant.

It was natural that a vast movement of xenophobic character should be accompanied by manifestations of xenophobia against resident foreigners, and, since the form of xenophobia was religious, the infidel Jews were obvious victims. Raoul Glaber, who died a monk of Cluny half a century before the time of the First Crusade, chronicles the destruction of the Church of the Holy Sepulchre in 1009, and describes how the Jews of Orleans sent a message to Cairo to warn the Fatimid ruler that the Christians were preparing to attack him. The renegade monk carried the message, written in Hebrew, and hidden in a pilgrim's staff; the Jews were drowned, killed by the sword or burned, and the monk also came back to be burned. Glaber says that soon afterwards Europe was stricken by a terrible famine, and as a result vast hordes of pilgrims set out for the Holy Land. Adhemar of Chabannes, writing early in the eleventh century, also claimed that the Jews sent warnings to the Muslim rulers of the danger of a crusade. When the long-conceived Crusade matured, Jews inevitably suffered. The Treves chronicle describes how the local Jews, when they heard that approaching Crusaders were determined to compel them to believe in Jesus Christ, killed their own children, that they might pass to the bosom of Abraham; the women killed themselves; some took refuge with the bishop, who profited from the occasion to convert them. Albert of Aix tells a similar story of the Jews of Cologne and Mainz, where the bishop's protection was largely unsuccessful. Again a few were converted, "more from fear of death than from love of God." They were not attacked by local people, or for anything they had done. Albert comments on the fate of the pilgrims under Emich of Leisingen in Hungary: they were punished for their sins of the flesh and for their cruelties to the Jews, which they committed, not as instruments of the justice of God, but for motives of greed. He derides some for following the guidance of a goose and a goat, as inspired by God. Albert, more clearly than Guibert, perceived the part played by an unrestrained and undisciplined proletariat who at best were ridiculous, superstitious and licentious, and at worst indiscriminate in their cruelty. The following of Peter the Hermit, Gottschalk, Emich of Leisingen and others, probably included many antinomian chiliasts who finally reached Syria, having survived sundry richly deserved disasters.

At home, these pilgrims first "emerged in bands on all sides," equipped themselves with food and arms that they needed to get to Jerusalem, says Albert of Aix, and were "burning with fire and divine love." He goes on directly to say that

> "these people . . . joined up in one force, but did not abstain at all from illicit unions and the pleasures of the flesh; they gave themselves up to gluttonous excess without interruption and amused themselves without interruption with women and young girls who had also emigrated from their homes to give themselves to the same follies."

The reader is bound to think the fire of divine love here rather conventional, especially as it is immediately after this that Albert goes on to describe the outrages against the Jews. Both Guibert and Albert draw attention to the many excesses and outrages committed in Hungary and elsewhere against Christians. It is clear that we are dealing with a social class which could not usually indulge itself in these pleasures without outside restraint. Doubtless great lords so behaved; but they knew how and when to take their pleasures. Here we are dealing with unsettled "knights and footmen", that is, free men, but adventurers, as well as a mass of unidentified men, women and children. If the great lords were tempted partly by the hope of new lands and partly by the hope of heaven, it seems that the masses had a similar dual temptation, but after their own fashion. Their religion was an enthusiasm with little personal application, and the immediate result of their liberation from ordinary social restraints was a progressive self-destruction.

It is a commonplace that the hopes for the Crusade, while they succeeded materially, were spiritually disappointed. The seeds of this failure were sown from the start, even, perhaps, in that very concept; the seed itself was rotten. In the best of the clerical writers there were lapses of taste, even a degree of prurience. Different versions of the *Letter of the Emperor of Constantinople* are variations on a pornographic theme; the worst atrocities attributed to the Turks are sexual, Greek daughters ravished before their mothers, or, in another version, the other way about, and the victims made to sing lewd songs; even more bizarre is the report of widespread homosexuality, extending even to the seduction of bishops. Guibert does not hesitate to believe all this of Turks, but is indignant at the suggestion that the beauty of Greek women might encourage Franks to join in the fight against the infidel. The women themselves, if they could have foreseen the future, might as soon have been raped by Turks as by Franks. The *Letter* contains other less scabrous but still sensationalist bits about the circumcision of youths and boys forced to urinate on the altars. If there was a note of scandal throughout the Crusades, it had been present from the beginning. There was something of hysteria, not only in the European response to the crusading idea, but also in the message itself. Preachers, who included several figures as dubious as Peter the Hermit, shared a common inspiration with their audiences. They found it a short step from the acts they condemned to the acts they committed. To argue from stories of atrocities is to fail to distinguish between 'it has happened' and 'it constantly happens', and may lead to an acceptance that the acts concerned are possible. Rape and loot are the constituents of the sack of cities which would reward the Crusaders, and Albert of Aix was horrified to recognize the true motives behind the preliminary attacks on the Jews by Crusaders at the start of their 'pilgrimage'. Rationalized by the theologians was the underlying xenophobia, and with it were mixed dreams of sex and avarice. These were the foundations of sand on which the Pope hoped to build for peace and the sanctification of Europe.

4. The morale of the First Crusade

If there had been nothing more than the corrupt frenzy which marked the first phase of the movement, the energies of Europe would have been quickly spent, as happened in the case of the crowds who accompanied Peter the Hermit to the east. Europe owed the success of the Crusade largely, of course, to the weakness of the Arab states, but also to the fighting qualities of the knights under the leadership of the great lords. Their morale was occasionally shaken, but it remained sound enough to survive extremes of danger, anxiety and hardships. Here was the real success of the papal policy. The Crusade brought to Europe neither virtue nor peace, but orthodox faith did sustain the determined core of the army. This is still true, when we have made allowance for the hope of plunder and the cynical manipulation of visionaries. In fact, the crusading theology was a workable system with nothing starry-eyed about it. If fighting the Muslims were part of the ordinary struggle of the Christian life, it would be realistic to expect it to exist side by side with sin. The theory was not that crusading blotted sin out. The issue of events, successful or unsuccessful, could be attributed to the reward of faith and works or to the punishment of sins. This is precisely the theory as it was elaborated, from the time of Urban onwards, from the basic theory already existing.

Fundamental to Urban's idea was the concept of the Crusade as a way to earn the remission of sins, and so an extension of the ordinary way by good works; indeed, the Crusade was itself a good work, a holy exercise, and so a suitable penance; it was a pilgrimage in arms. It soon came to be a recognized penance, especially for rich and powerful sinners, and, with perfect logic, it became possible for a sinner to buy his way out of taking the cross. In paying money for the Crusade he was giving it just such aid as by fighting himself he would give, and with greater economy of effort, if his presence were needed at home. It was easy also to transfer the notion to European affairs, to the Crusade in Spain, then to the Crusade against the heretics, and then to aid the Pope against all his enemies, against a Christian Emperor or a Christian republic. Yet, though the battle was meritorious, to die in the process was something short of true martyrdom. It is evidence of theological moderation that death in crusade never became officially martyrdom; the Crusader was given a plenary indulgence, provided he confessed himself with contrite heart and was absolved. The same indulgence was given for paying for someone else to crusade. True martyrdom, however, wipes out all sins in itself; for the clergy, therefore, crusading to the death does not of itself make the martyr.

This is not to say that the people accepted such theological distinctions. The *Chanson de Roland* shows the Christian host confessing itself before battle, and yet speaks of the dead as martyred. To the theologians this implies a contradiction. After the battle of Dorylaeum, the priests prayed for the dead, but it was an important part of the morale of the First Crusade to think of the dead as martyrs who immediately joined the company of the blessed. Probably the inconsistency was never resolved in the minds of ordinary Crusaders. It would seem that the army looked on themselves in an active capacity as pilgrims, in a passive capacity as martyrs. In the first they were at one with the Pope and the theologians; the second is a natural extension, but one which marks the division between the higher clergy with their canon law, and the people generally. The use of the term 'pilgrim' often seems incongruous enough to the modern ear. The army which crossed Europe and Byzantium with such devastating effect and which carved a kingdom and three principalities out of the Arab lands was normally described as 'pilgrim'. The *Gesta* calls the army in adjoining classes *militia Christi* and *Peregrini*, and even in one single phrase "soldiers and pilgrims of Christ". Other examples will enforce the point. Thus after the capture of Caesarea, "the poorest of the pilgrims became rich." 'Pilgrim' remained the term most naturally used by those who had come specially from Europe, after the Latin states were established. The *Gesta Ludovici VII* speaks of the "pilgrimage" (the Second Crusade) to take Damascus. The point is simply the application of the term to an army. The *Gesta Francorum* makes al-Afdal, Fatimid *wazir*, express the point very clearly.

> "I have been defeated by a people of beggars, poorly armed and poverty-stricken, who have nothing but a bag and a scrip. These are now chasing the Egyptian people, who often distributed alms to them when they begged their way all through our land."

This is a European picture of an Arab's thoughts; it is how a soldier, perhaps all the army, imagined an Arab would think.

The frank ingratitude, the implied resentment of gifts received from Arab hosts is natural enough, but characteristic. Robert of Rheims took the *wazir*'s supposed thoughts a step further: if the pilgrims had come with the traditional stick and wallet they would have been welcomed with honours and good things; armed, they must fear the anger of the King of the Persians. Certainly, the great lords were not poor pilgrims armed; but the poor pilgrim might now feel proud to be armed, and beholden to no one, without having to feel any the less a pilgrim.

When the pilgrims were dead they became martyrs in the eyes of their friends. It was not only those who died in main actions against enemy; it was enough to be killed in the course of the war, for example, a foraging party who were surprised and killed just when they had found some barley and bitter pears. It was not only those who were killed, but also those who died of starvation or disease: "Many of our people received martyrdom there," says the author of the *Gesta*, "and many of the poorest people died of hunger for the name of Christ. When they entered Heaven in triumph they were wearing the robe of martyrdom." The same author seems to say that both those who were killed and those who were taken prisoner, "some to Khorasan, some to Antioch, some to Aleppo," received a blessed martyrdom, *felix acceperunt martyrium*. The sense of solidarity with soldier-martyrs of tradition went even further: led by George, Demetrius and Maurice, they were seen to fight at the side of the Franks. That Franks who died in battle were esteemed martyrs goes without saying: "More than a thousand of our knights and footmen were martyred that day," remarks the *Gesta*; "and we believe they went up to Heaven and received the white robe of martyrdom." There is a clear reflection of the liturgy, and a sense of union with the Christian past: *te martyrum candidatus laudat exercitus*. The author of the *Gesta*, because he was a soldier, is our best guide to the attitude of the army. The *Chanson d'Antioche* also speaks for laymen, and refers to death in battle quite casually as *martire*. This was a popular not a theological approach, but it is beyond doubt that the sense of divine support was constantly with the army, not always orthodox, but an enduring consolation and an essential part of its morale. When there was danger of despair, the army fabricated its own solution to its problems.

The visions of Saint Andrew to Peter Bartholomew and the resulting discovery of the Holy Lance illustrate the difference between the leaders of the army and the mass of lesser ranks. Of the secular leaders, only the Count of St Gilles believed in the miracle; but the discovery was made by his men, the revelation to his follower. In any case the Count was unrepresentative of the courts of Provence, aristocratic, secular and literary: William of Aquitaine would make an even less successful, but probably also a less credulous, Crusader. No one would expect the Norman leaders to believe in a miracle vouchsafed to a rival. From the disbelief in visions which Fulcher makes clear, and from his account of the visionary's death as a result of the crucial ordeal by fire, we may infer that Godfrey and Baldwin agreed with Adhemar, the Legate, in doubting the truth or even the sincerity of the revelation. Raymund of Aguilers's account of the affair, even including his account of the ordeal, shows an invincible determination to believe. The author of the *Gesta*, who accepts the visions, says nothing of the ordeal, and stresses the invigorating effect on the morale of the army when it was at its lowest. He may have been influenced by his contact with the Provençals, between Antioch and Jerusalem. It is likely that Fulcher represents the view of the higher clergy and the leaders, and with hindsight; until Adhemar's attitude became known and until the resort to ordeal, the effect on the army may have been general, as the *Gesta* claims. The visions came to a disreputable servant of a Provençal pilgrim; to a contemporary theologian as to a modern critic, he was an obvious fraud; but the association of a good life, or sanctity, with holiness, or a vision, was a relatively new idea. It seems to indicate a division between the educated clerical leaders and the masses. The priest Stephen's vision of Christ was accepted because the visionary was more respectable. Both visions were a popular response to a desperate situation.

We recognize two levels of morale, the official, rational clerical theory, and the more confused, instinctive and popular confidence in supernatural support. There was a third, composed of simple self-confidence and communal pride. The Crusaders felt something of the ethos of the warbands of their Germanic ancestors; they were a small group of people, and fewer fighting men, in a strange world, among the inexhaustible hordes of their enemies. The weakness of Arab and Turkish rulers at the time of the First Crusade was not obvious to the Crusaders in their ignorance of Islamic politics and history. What they achieved was remarkable enough, and it seemed so to them. They had seen the strength, not the weakness, of the enemy. Even with the intervention of God, they had something to be proud of. This was expressed both in direct reference to the enemy and in imaginary assessments of enemy morale. In First Crusade accounts, the Sultan of Nicea warns the Arabs, not that God and his angels fight at the head of the Christian host, but that "their courage is from God or the devil"—Christians themselves realized that angel participants are visible only to the side they help and that what the enemy sees is their good morale. Arabs are supposed to think of the Franks with respect or even fear; ". . . this innumerable people, who fear neither death nor the enemy," "the bravest and the most daring," "this determined and cruel nation." This at least tells us how the Christians hoped they were regarded; many of these remarks relate to a time when morale was low among the Franks, and may actually have been written before the final victory; it is remarkable that they imagined themselves to be intimidating. This was whistling in the dark; in fact they were often hungry and frightened. The idea that the Franks must seem innumerable to the enemy may be a hopeful reflection of how the enemy seemed to the Franks. The *Gesta* actually speaks of the Franks, as seen by the Arabs, in almost the same detailed terms as, in another passage altogether, of the Arabs as seen by the Franks. It was realistic to suppose the Egyptians to despise the small number of Franks. Fulcher spoke of the Holy Land as "so to say deserted" by the Crusaders after the fall of Jerusalem; "there was nobody to defend it from the Saracens, if they dared to attack it." He went on to ask why they did not dare; there were peoples and kingdoms of such numbers and strength against Jerusalem, and yet it was left in peace when there were only three hundred knights to defend it. Even to the least credulous this might seem miraculous, the more so in their total ignorance of the political situation of the Arab World. This impression of the multitude of the enemy was very natural; it even suggests a growing realization that after all Palestine was an Arab country. If the Franks felt themselves a war-band isolated by a deep penetration into alien country, it was no more than the truth; this was a situation in which Normans throve, and it was an epic situation, familiar in the poems sung in the halls and courts of northern Europe.

Two aspects are worth stressing. There was that pride in fighting prowess which came to be an essential part of the chivalric code. In a famous passage, the author of the *Gesta* praises the military ability and courage of the Turks who expected to terrorize the Franks with the menace of their arrows, as they had the Arabs, Armenians, Syrians and Greeks. "Yet please God they will never be worth as much as our men." There was admiration and a genuine fellow-feeling for another fighting race. "However, they say that they are of the race of the Franks, and that no one is naturally meant to be a knight except the Franks and them." Did the writer believe that the Turks had once been Christian? Perhaps that all the world had been? "I shall say the truth which nobody can deny. If only they had always been firm in the faith of Christ (*certe si in fide Christi . . . semper firmi fuissent*) . . . it would be impossible to find anyone stronger or braver or more gifted for war than they." Both Turks and the Franks of the Crusade were itinerant professional soldiers, and this bond was real; Arabs and Syrians and the quiet settled people were different. Even so early we find the phrase *effici Turci* for "become Muslims"; and a convert to Islam may be turned *Turcatus*. Islam is essentially the religion of the Arabs, but already military Turkish domination gives us these phrases which would of course be universal in European languages in the Ottoman period.

There was some conscious tendency in the army to think of themselves as a new community. "If a Breton (*britannus*) or a German wanted to talk to me, I could not reply to either of them; but, however much we were divided by language, we seemed to be made one single people by our love of God and charity to our neighbour"—"neighbour" means army comrade. It would be easy to make too much of this; Fulcher, who is speaking here, was an idealist, and the notorious quarrels of the leaders of the different national groups were reflected in their followers. Nevertheless, all the first-hand accounts are full of the sense of dangers and hardships shared; and Fulcher is summing up the facts when he says, "Consider . . . how in our time God turned the West into the East; for we who were Westerners are now become Orientals; he who was a Roman or a Frank has become in this land a Galilean or a Palestinian, he who was from Rheims or Chartres has been made into a Tyrian or Antiochene." Men whose ideas had been limited to a town or village became a small group of Europeans isolated in the Arab World, as soon as they left Byzantium.

It is doubtful how far solidarity extended downwards socially. In times of trouble, discipline was tightened, we cannot say how equitably, by severe penalties for giving short measure (a bourgeois crime, but also a poor dealer's), theft (more tempting to the poor), and fornication (no class monopoly). A public example was made of an adulterous couple who were stripped and flogged round the camp, that the sight of their injuries might deter the rest. The mass of 'poor pilgrims' may have had a rather makeshift morale of their own. The status of the women followers is ambiguous. They brought the men water at the battle at Dorylaeum. They fought in a band against Kerbogha. Some were respectable. There was a real proletariat with the army of which we are only partly informed. Guibert tells us, with other miscellaneous information, that the *Tafurs*, tramps, followed their 'king', a Norman adventurer, and went barefoot and penniless, eating grass and roots. They provided heavy unskilled labour when it was needed. When the Legate, Adhemar, died, the *Gesta* recalls how he used to preach to the knights, "None of you can be saved, if he does not honour and support the poor; without them, you cannot be saved; without you, they cannot live." This was a Christian approach. The Tafurs seem to have provoked a mixed response. The *Poème d'Antioche* tells us that they had their own camp, and stresses their separate organization; Peter the Hermit, after the destruction of the mass of his followers, apparently attached himself to them. Their grossest exploit, allegedly at Peter's suggestion, was to cook and eat Arab or Turkish corpses. Other eye-witnesses refer to this, and to the horror it inspired among the enemy, and editors such as William of Tyre (who says that Bohemund pretended to cook enemy spies, to frighten real spies off) exclude or modify it; but *Antioche* makes it a boast. Killing the enemy men, and raping the '*beles Sarrasines*' in victory is also a boast. From their great moment with the corpses, the Tafurs are represented as objects, naturally, of special fear and hatred to the Arabs and Turks, but perhaps for that reason, are also given a kind of esteem by Christians. As heroes, they appealed to the audiences who listened to these songs, as *ribaldi*, crude but comic. In the *Chanson de Jerusalem* they played an even bigger part, quite unhistorical, but reflecting a social reality. They were tough, and rude, and very much the opposite of *courtois*; crude in their every impulse, and certainly as secular as the most cynical of the lords. They were hungry and dressed in rags, and were easily trapped by a bait of precious stones and riches. These poems, *Antioche* and *Jerusalem*, have been thought to represent the rise of a popular movement, or popular consciousness and pride. We occasionally get glimpses of such people in other writers, as in the *Gesta*, when Kerbogha is shown a cheap, rusty sword, a dirty bow and a discarded lance, which had just been captured from "poor pilgrims", as if they were typical of Frankish arms; or when Fulcher tells us that at the sack of cities "many of the poor grew rich."

In the two poems, Peter the Hermit, a deflated but not wholly discredited figure after his lapse into cowardice at Antioch, is constantly allied to the King of the Tafurs. In the unhistorical *Jerusalem* he is captured by the enemy; the *Jerusalem* is full of the paraphernalia of supposed Muslim gods (Tervagant, Apollin, as in the *chansons de geste*); in both poems 'Mahom' is represented as a splendid idol, a deposit of riches clearly viewed as potential loot. When Peter the Hermit is captured, far from following the recommended practice of refusing to apostatize in the face of death, he 'pretended' to be converted to Islam; he bowed before the jewel-encrusted idol, "but he thought quite otherwise." Still, the poet makes no bones about it: he "adored Mahon," and this is shown as a very smart trick. This total reversal of the Crusader's whole duty doubtless reflects, not only the actual behaviour of many captured 'pilgrims', but the unguarded opinion of some of them, especially at the two social extremes. Here is the humour of the professional 'fool'; it coexisted, however inconsistently, with the belief that any who died were 'martyrs'. It is not necessary to suppose a party of cynics and a party of believers; many people were probably both at different times. Although these poems must reflect an unclerical taste, they do not imply that the crowds could not be carried away by waves of unthinking religious enthusiasm—they could be and were. Perhaps the one constant factor is the crude xenophobia. Even the Tafurs were a part of the whole 'Christian' people, of the new European community overseas. Like the great lords, poor pilgrims came and went between the Latin Kingdom, when it was established, and Europe. Doubtless some Tafurs returned home, some had died of hunger or on the fringes of battle, some were able to find comfortable homes on the loot of the sacked cities, others perhaps ended as they had begun, begging on the streets. The crusading community was complex and contained many strands.

5. Aggression in its actual impact

This very complexity of the army, and the strains to which its morale was subjected, combined with unusual opportunities to satisfy sordid desires which the hope of salvation could not suppress, to make the war more than ordinarily brutal. Often duty seemed to coincide very closely with interest, and, provided the men fought well, they were encouraged to take their reward. Before the battle of Ascalon the Patriarch proclaimed that anyone who turned aside to any plunder before the battle was finished should be excommunicated, but "they might turn back after it was over to seize whatever was destined to them by the Lord." In such cases religion might sometimes fail to stem, but never fail to impel, national passion. Looting in the right place was blessed. Often the Frankish search for loot was taken to grotesque lengths. "They cut up the bodies of the dead, because they would find gold bezants hidden in their stomachs; some sliced the flesh into pieces and cooked it to eat." Fulcher tells us the same thing of the corpses of the enemy after the fall of Jerusalem, where the massacre caused an unparalleled stench: "they split open their stomachs when they were dead, in order to get bezants out of their intestines, which, when they were alive, they had gulped down their ill-fated gullets." Similarly, after the fall of Caesarea, the corpses were burned, so that

> "the good luck resulted of finding bezants which they had obstinately swallowed, not wanting the Franks to get any of their property. Some of them hid coins in their mouths behind their gums. Consequently it sometimes happened, when one of our men hit one of the Arabs on his neck with his fist, that he spat ten or sixteen bezants out of his mouth."

The women also hid bezants in their pubic parts, "which was a disgraceful place to hide things and much more shaming to me to relate"—*nefas erat sic recondendum et multo turpius mihi ad recitandum.* But what of the pilgrims who searched in such places? What gave them the idea of doing so? Yet all this was to become a commonplace of crusading warfare.

In spite of an artificial rhetoric, Fulcher expresses a genuine personal horror of fighting. He refers to the capture of Caesarea; he is speaking specifically of the Crusade, *bellum sacrum.*

"O war, which is hateful to the innocent and terrible to the beholder! War which is not beautiful, named by antiphrasis (*bellum quia non bellum*). I saw war, I hesitated in my mind, I was afraid of being hit. Everyone rushed upon the iron, as if he had no fear of death. There is dreadful misfortune where there is no charity. There was a tremendous noise from the blows exchanged by the two sides. This man strikes, that man falls down. This man knows no pity, neither does that man ask it; this one loses a fist, that one an eye. The human mind, where it sees such affliction, shrinks back."

These gentler sentiments, however rarely, coexisted with the horrors of the First Crusade.

Descriptions of carnage continue throughout the Crusade. We saw that this began with Christian victims of Christian aid; in Greece, for example, we find the pilgrims cutting off a woman's breasts because she was defending her property. This happened, but no writer lets it pass uncritically. With the atrocities committed against Muslims there is no similar expression of disapproval. It is possible that telling it at all, and telling it so often, conceals a sense of guilt; if not horror, then a certain doubt, though evidently there was little enough doubt in the doing. The *Gesta* repeats these occasions almost monotonously: at Antioch "they killed all the Turks and Saracens they found," and "no one could go on the foot-path except over the bodies of the dead;" at al-Bara the Count of St Gilles "killed all the Arabs, men and women, great and small," and then "recalled (the town) to the faith of Christ;" at Maarra, "they killed everyone whether male or female wherever they found them;" Bohemund even killed some of his prisoners, and, once more, passers-by had to tread on the Arab corpses; at Jerusalem "our men waded up to the ankles in blood." Raymund of Aguilers says they waded in blood to their knees; and even if both descriptions are exaggerated, Raymund, who came later to the main scene of slaughter at the Haram ash-Sharif, may state a true ratio.

The scene in Jerusalem is so famous and so horrible, and struck contemporaries so forcibly, that it is worth looking at more closely. "At last, when the pagans were defeated, our men took many prisoners, both men and women, in the Temple. They killed those they chose, and those they chose they saved alive." The Temple here is the Temple of Solomon, by which Crusaders meant the al-Aqsa Mosque; the Temple of the Lord was the Qubbat as-Sakhra.

"Our men rushed round the whole city, seizing gold and silver, horses and mules, and houses full of goods of all sorts, and they all came rejoicing and weeping from excess of gladness to worship at the Sepulchre of our Saviour Jesus, and there they fulfilled their vows to him."

The day before when the Franks had entered the city, they had pursued defenders "killing and cutting them down as far as Solomon's Temple" (it was there that men were wading in blood) and "great numbers of pagans of both sexes" had escaped by crowding onto the roof of the mosque, where Tancred had given them protection, by passing his standard up to them. What the Crusaders did then, after their night of loot and prayer, cannot be excused as done in the heat of battle, or even of greed and lust.

"Next morning they climbed cautiously up onto the Temple roof and attacked the Muslims, both men and women, cutting off their heads with drawn swords. Other Muslims, indeed, threw themselves headlong from the Temple. Tancred was extremely angry when he saw this."

It seems clear that the murderers, doing this in cold blood, felt about the undefended men and women they killed exactly as if they had been destroying vermin; this story, more than any other, suggests the denial of a common humanity. The author's own attitude is ambiguous; the eye-witnesses record without comment. Albert of Aix, who did not leave Europe, tells the most lurid, though generalized, story: children cut out of their mothers' wombs and smashed against the walls. Very likely he exaggerates for the sake of sensation; but he is also prepared to justify by military necessity what he believes did happen; and yet he sees that Godfrey's refusal to take part was better, however eccentric. These horrors of the fall of Jerusalem remained embedded in men's minds. When William of Tyre came much later to record this episode, it had still not lost its shocking character. Like Albert, he sought some justification, and he argued that the massacre happened by the just judgement of God, because of the profanation of the sanctuary of the Lord by profane (i.e. Muslim) rites. The bloodshed and death expiated this wrong. We read this in a cultivated and humane churchman who was familiar with Arabs in his daily life. It is curious how bitterly the clergy resented the use of the two mosques on the Temple area by Islam, although they had been built as mosques, and no previous church had existed on the site.

It is possible to make too sweeping a condemnation. There is little that is new, nothing that has not been often repeated, in the behaviour of the Crusaders; it is the religious association that seems especially incongruous to us. Runciman has suggested that the example set at Jerusalem was that which later the Arabs followed. It is true that when the cities of the coast fell in the thirteenth century to the Mamluk conquerors, there was a great deal of killing. However, this was not new, either in Christian or Muslim warfare, or (as we have seen) in war between the two. It would not seem out of place among the massacres of our own age. The great innovation of Islam was to offer a new alternative to the classical tradition of slavery or death; either conversion, which would give full rights to those who accepted it, or submission and toleration. This gradually became the practice of civilized nations, and the latter alternative was the basis of British and French imperial rule in the nineteenth century; but in the Middle Ages Europe offered toleration only temporarily. On both sides slavery was the penalty of resistance. The Franks gradually began to sell their prisoners into slavery, rather than kill them. Bohemund at Maarra saved some of the population from massacre: "some he had killed, and some he ordered to be taken to Antioch to sell." During the campaigns that led to the fall of Jerusalem we get the impression of haphazard decisions by various leaders, not one of whom was consistent. With the establishment of the Kingdom, practices began to settle into a more orderly pattern. At the fall of Caesarea, Fulcher says:

> "Few of the male sex were kept alive. They spared a good many females, in order that they should serve always at turning the hand-mills. Of those whom they captured, some people bought and sold to each other both the pretty females and the ugly ones; similarly the males. The King kept alive the amir of that town and the bishop (whom they call the cadi); he spared them more for the sake of the money than out of friendship."

On both sides, from this time onwards, the great could almost always count on the possibility of ransom to save them; it is clear that slave concubinage occurred, however uncanonically on the Christian side. In the early days, less important people could hardly hope to remain steadfast in their religion and go free;

"they arrested all the peasants of the place," says the *Gesta* of the Maarra region, "and those who would not accept Christianity they killed, but those who preferred to acknowledge Christ they spared." There would soon develop a more tolerant and realistic attitude. It came to be accepted that the legal fate of prisoners was enslavement, not death, and ultimately "even Christians" would disapprove of great massacres.

In the course of the original aggression, the Crusaders were in great danger, and, what is more important, were unable to assess their danger accurately. Fear goes a long way to explain the psychology of the massacres of the First Crusade. Albert of Aix supposed—and this may reflect actual discussions—that the Crusaders would not feel able to supervise a hostile population in lands they must hold against every attack. Fulcher was astonished that so small a kingdom with such few defenders was not attacked. To be surrounded by unnumbered strangers, alien not only in race and language and culture but also in religion, must have been profoundly disturbing. When it became clear that there would be no effective reinforcement for the colony, those who still remained understood that they must find a way to live with the existing population, part oriental Christian, part Muslim; but the danger from the surrounding peoples and from the subsisting population of the country was perhaps always in the minds of the Latins of the East.

Ernoul, writing in the thirteenth century, when the inland territory had already been some time lost, recounts the stories current in the small area which remained, and which were fully adapted to the ways of the land. He tells how a hundred years earlier than when he was writing, and some sixty-five years after the First Crusaders arrived, King Thoros of Armenia gave advice to King Almalric I.

"Sir, I am very sorry for you and for the country; for you are not king, except only as long as the Muslims wish; you will only keep the country for as long as the Muslims wish. And I will tell you how this is. There are Muslims living in all the towns of your country . . . If it so happened that a Muslim army entered your country it would have help and information from the peasants of the land, both victuals and services. If it turned out that the Muslims were defeated, your own people would help them to safety; and if you were defeated, it would be your own peasants who would do you worst harm."

His idea was to bring three thousand Christians to colonize the land, and to expel all the Muslims. This was not done, of course, but it epitomizes the dilemma of the Latin states from the moment the First Crusaders entered territory not predominantly inhabited by Latins. The northern border-land had been habitually fought over, and was used to frequent changes of ruler. Further south sentiment was against the Franks; an Arab aristocracy ruling a population partly Christian Arab was dispossessed. Thoros was making the distinction, important in our own day, between imperial rule and colonization. The Latin states were colonies in that Europeans settled there, but, outside the main towns at least, an alien aristocracy ruled a reluctant population to which Latin liturgy and strict feudal custom were wholly alien and quite unacceptable.

There is so much that is sordid and cruel in the whole history of crusade, but especially in the story of the First Crusade, that it is tempting to dismiss it simply as aggression. Two encounters between the Arabs and Europe, in Spain and in the central Mediterranean, mark the gradual recovery by Christian rulers of lands largely populated by various European stocks. The third encounter, in the Levant, was, in terms of human populations, a naked aggression. We infer from its temporary success that Europe was ready to colonize, though not to colonize thoroughly; we note the readiness of the home populations to respond to a call, the often hysterical nature of their response, the elements of instability in the crusading community, the ambiguous motivation of so much that was done in the name of the Lord, the savage murder of the defenceless, raping, looting. Albert of Aix often attributes humanitarian actions to a base motive—they are done for bribes, *corrupti pecunia*; and he groups together the motives "avarice, indifference and pity." This is hard, but sensible enough, in a way; these three combine to make a policy. The leaders who foresaw a future in Palestine recognized coldly the practical necessity of conciliating a population that it would be fatal to drive to despair. Avarice and sexuality motivated sacks and massacres. Yet when we have accepted all the uncomfortable facts of aggression, we are free to study the invasion of the Arab homeland by Europeans for its inherent interest, and find that, although they failed in so many ways to provide inter-cultural links, the Crusader states have a use and a meaning for the relations of the Arabs with Europe. They constitute an essential step in the development of the future relations of the two peoples, and they exemplify the parallel development of the two heirs of the ancient world. Above all, the imaginative impact that the Crusades made upon the mind of Europe makes it impossible to dismiss them easily. The existing attitude of Europeans to the Arab World was intensified and fixed. European persecutors and aggressors would always see Arabs in the same capacity. It was as if future European aggression was endowed for ever with a conviction of righteousness. In the long run the Crusades confirmed the European belief that it was not possible to share a culture with the Arabs; it was their own behaviour, as much as Arab behaviour, that taught them this. The experience strengthened the sense of difference which later ages would inherit.

Chapter 6

The Central Mediterranean: eleventh–thirteenth centuries

1. Introductory

The conquest of Sicily by the great Norman adventurers was not a pre-view of the Crusades. It was the reflux of the tide that for so long had ebbed and flowed around the central Mediterranean. This time was final for the determination of political and cultural frontiers in the area. Further European advances into North Africa would fail, and there would be no more serious Arab onslaughts on Italy or France; much of Spain remained to be fought over, and for a short time Sicily had the quite delusory appearance of a multi-cultic and multi-cultural state. It was absorbed by Latin Christendom through simple if arduous military effort. The psychological impact was not comparable to that of the Crusades. It had little to do with religion in the first place, and religion was never more than a political and military factor in the Sicilian situation. Islam, as religion and as a culture, and the Arabs and Berbers as distinct peoples, were very gradually extirpated, because in the long run it was convenient to the Norman rulers, up to and including the Emperor Frederick II, that they should be; in the meantime, and for the same reason, their support was exploited. Much less than appears at first sight was there a useful exchange of ideas or practices.

The tone of the Norman invasion was set by the earlier contribution to the campaign of George Maniakes in Sicily in 1138–40 made by Harald Hardradi, with the Varangians, and a troop of Normans.

> Then the young warrior,
> Scourge of the Saracens,
> Waged his grim game of war
> On the level plains of Sicily.

Harald "gained victory and booty whenever he fought;" "the Varangians killed anyone they could lay hands on, priests and laymen alike . . . They took an enormous booty . . ." This was war for profit, in the end for permanent profit, as the Danish settlements in England had been, and like the Reconquest in Spain; it was cross-cultural in that Christian and Muslim inhabitants suffered alike. Ultimately both Greeks and Arabs would disappear under the relentless pressure. This was made possible by Count Roger, of the inexhaustible de Hauteville family, brother of Robert Guiscard, who first projected the conquest of Sicily; Roger was a much more formidable and persistent invader than the erratic Harald. Yet the Christian flood-tide was not confined to Norman prowess; Genoa and Pisa in the eleventh century destroyed the Arab settlements in Sardinia and successfully and profitably raided North Africa. Investment in such adventures by the merchant cities and the more massive undertaking of the Norman Conquest were supported by papal blessings, but Norman rulers of Sicily continued to sack and pillage on the mainland in the twelfth and thirteenth centuries, with Arab armies whose fathers had done the same thing under their own leaders in the ninth and tenth. It was Frederick II who transferred the remaining Arab population as a body onto the Italian mainland, in order to maintain their professional services as soldiers, while depriving them of the opportunity to rebel as peoples.

The treatment of the Arabs as a people and a culture difficult to absorb into the normal ways of European life was always typical of the Norman rulers of Sicily. In Europe as a whole in the age in which Sicily was conquered there was little serious interest in, and a continuing ignorance of, Arab culture. Such ideas about the Prophet as existed were literary fantasies. The events of the reign of the eccentric Fatimid caliph al-Hakim, honoured by the founders of the Druzes, penetrated obscurely into the annals of the West. Naturally, the destruction of Christian churches makes up most of the story, and, in the chronicle of Adhemar of Chabannes, it loses nothing in the telling. The Jews appear, not as fellow-victims of the Caliph's religious prejudices, but as European traitors who send him word from Europe that the Christians will attack him; it is this that precipitates the great persecution of Arab Christians. Al-Hakim is called "Nabuchodonosor of Babylon, whom they call amir." This may imply confusion of the two Babylons, or may just be a clumsily expressed allusion from the one Babylon to the other; the title *amir* is inadequate for a Fatimid caliph. The "Saracens" repent of the destruction of the churches and they suffer a great famine. The streets and the wastes are filled with corpses which feed the wild beasts and the birds. Then the "people of Arabia" rise up, kill all whom they find still alive and capture the "king of Babylon"; because he had set himself up in pride against God, he was disembowelled alive, and when he was dead his abdomen was sewn up with stones, and his body was weighted with lead and thrown into the sea. In all this, the only words used are *Saracenus, paganus* and *gentes Arabiae* to describe the peoples concerned, and it is uncertain what background the writer or his informants conceived for the events they relate so obscurely. It was still true that the encounters of war seemed to bring no knowledge in their wake. About 1020, a Moorish raid on Narbonne was totally defeated, and the enemy prisoners were either sold as slaves or put to work as slaves locally. In the East, changes in doctrine among Sufi sects are commonly attributed to the influence of Christians absorbed into Islam, but there seems to have been no influence exerted by captured Arabs in Europe. We must assume that their numbers were small and that their social standing remained depressed.

Raiders on either side might be intercepted in retreat, but could rarely be prevented from initial success; a raid on the Italian coast is reported as late as 1113, when Christian rule in Sicily was long firmly established. The raiders were caught and killed in the sea. In 1087 the Genoese and Pisan joint expedition which resulted in the ransom of al-Mahdiyya from the Zirid ruler, Tamim, exemplified both the new European sea-power and the profits it brought. It was already characteristic that the cities concerned should establish their future trading rights, as well as demand immediate loot. Norman Sicily maintained effective fleets throughout the twelfth century, but the Norman rule along the coast of North Africa, based on al-Mahdiyya, lasted only from 1148 till 1160, and was maintained in the face of lively local Arab opposition. It enabled Roger II to die 'King of Africa', as well as of Sicily, and very briefly it resulted in a tolerant Christian government and bi-cultural state which, as in Sicily, would certainly have continued tolerant only as long as was necessary, had it been possible to retain power at all. A final agreement between the Sicilian and Almohad rulers in 1180 included a regular payment to the Sicilian, William II, which continued to be claimed by his successors. The payment ensured the protection of Arab merchants in Sicily, and, like all such arrangements, might be considered a subsidy by the donor and tribute by the recipient. The Sicilians continued to use sea-power, and raids on Egypt, on a scale varying between invasion level and hit-and-run, contributed to the crusading position in the East. The seizure of the 'King of Morocco's daughter' by the Sicilian fleet in 1179 caught the romantic eyes of the chronicler, but illustrates the wide-ranging capacity of Sicilian sea-power, which by this time European historians were coming to take for granted. During this century the rivalry of the Italian cities, themselves in competition with Sicily, shows how Europeans could afford to dissipate their energies and still expect a good profit. Raiding would always continue possible, but a firm power base in Africa was beyond the capacity of Europe in the Middle Ages. The proof of this is the failure of Louis IX's last crusade in 1270, admittedly the attempt of a dying man. It was a crusade, as Joinville said, of "small profit"; after the death of Louis it produced a sum in blackmail which Charles of Anjou could claim proved that the Hafsid ruler, al-Mustansir, was his tributary. In fact, it was the final demonstration, not only of the failure of crusading in general, but also of the military possibilities of serious operations across the sea.

Time would thus prove that the pattern established in the eleventh century would endure. It was an age of major initiatives in the central Mediterranean, and not only on the tides of war. This was also the age of Constantine the African, apparently a nearly isolated phenomenon, but not a negligible one, and conceivably a sign of more that has left no record. Our main account of his life we owe to Peter the Deacon, of Monte Cassino, a natural writer of fiction miscast as historian. The story sheds a confused light on the beginning of a cultural loan from the Arabic. Constantine was apparently born as a North African Arab, who travelled from Carthage (Tunis) to Babylon (Cairo), and then further east, to study the grammar, dialectic, geometry, arithmetic, mathematics, astronomy, necromancy, music and physics of the Chaldeans, Arabs, Persians, Saracens, Egyptians and Indians; the story becomes more extravagant as, after India, he completes his education in Ethiopia. This rigmarole of nations represents the writer's twelfth-century consciousness of the world of ancient learning, but it can be taken also to reflect some proportion of eleventh-century legend about Constantine. His name before his conversion we do not know, but, according to different versions, he aroused jealous hatred at home, and was somehow connected by trade with Salerno. He turned naturally to the prince of the city for protection, became first a Christian and finally a monk of Monte Cassino. What is certain is that he made Latin paraphrases (sometimes claiming them as original work) from the Arabic of Ali ibn al-Abbas, Ibn al-Jazzar, Ishaq al-Israili and Hunayn ibn Ishaq, and from Arabic versions of Hippocrates and Galen, that is, from Muslim, Christian, Jewish, ex-Magian and Hellenistic writers.

This was the first swallow of the intellectual summer of Arabic influence on European learning. Constantine was not a great scholar, but his life shows that there was some slow growth across the Mediterranean of a productive communication. To a lesser extent by land routes, Gerbert had already begun his process, though his achievement was less considerable, and his studies in Spain were apparently unrelated to specifically Arabic material. Yet he acquired the same subsequent legend as a magician as Roger Bacon, Albert the Great and Michael the Scot, and this is at least presumptive evidence of the impression made on the public by new techniques acquired. The eleventh century, which saw a considerable revival of interest in new methods of thought, was not a revolutionary age; it began a process of indebtedness to the Arab World, but not yet on a considerable scale; the epoch of Lanfranc and Berengar was primarily one of internal intellectual development. Amid the usual slaughter there was nevertheless some lightening of the dark failure to communicate, over two centuries.

2. The Normans in Sicily

The invasion of Sicily was based on an Arab invitation, following the pattern of the Arab, Greek and Italian wars of the preceding centuries, with their shifting alliances often under papal disapproval. From now onwards, however, events moved steadily to the advantage of the Normans, who knew more than any other people how to exploit their gains and how to insist in spite of their misfortunes. It is characteristic that the Norman historian, Malaterra, describes the invitation to Count Roger by Ibn al-Tumna, not in political terms, but in personal and domestic ones; his young relative by marriage, "a decent young man", was murdered by his lord. This is politics personalized, but it is obvious that the historian has forgotten to think of aliens as different; he has assumed that there is a common human motivation. His analysis of events is crude, but any religious distinction is ignored. Count Roger certainly recognized and exploited ordinary human motives; at the capture of Agrigento, he won over the Arab general Hamud by saving his wife from molestation. Malaterra also implies a common cultural judgement of values; a 'fate worse than death' is a case in point. An Arab who is fleeing from Norman attack and whose sister becomes too weak to go further, kills her to avoid her being captured and raped. The story is told with conscious sympathy. It is obvious that a moral or conventional concept neither Muslim nor Christian in its origin is shared.

In spite of this a period of war is always a period of brutality, and if we can pick out a few points in common, the ones we meet most often are opportunist tactics and indiscriminate cruelty. It is understood that 'Greeks and Arabs' in Sicily have their specific interests which are obviously not Norman; and Sicilian Arabs are distinguished as 'Saracens' from North Africans, called 'Arabs and Africans', i.e. Arabs and Berbers. These last are mercenaries, having come to the aid of the 'Sicilians' only "for the sake of reward". It does look as though Malaterra thought Normans in the service of the same objective were not in the same category. Very soon, any Arabs in Sicily who continued to fight against Count Roger were classified as "still rebels". Even in Malaterra's account it is clear that there was the normal savagery in the fighting, as much on one side as on the other; the divided Arabs and small Norman armies causing the war to drag on to the destruction of the countryside. If the Arabs had not been divided, the Normans would have found no foothold; as it was, in the course of a generation, a small band of adventurers, irresponsible but pertinacious, had created a united and prosperous kingdom.

The evident Norman lack of interest in religion in one sense was largely counteracted by the interest they could extract from it in another. It is claimed that they were welcomed by Christian populations, who on the occasion came hurriedly up with donatives to explain that they paid tribute to Arab lords, not from love, but fear of death. Where the Normans entered a Christian area, the inhabitants were prompt to explain their devotion to their cause. A Christian population had good reason. The theory was enunciated, an interesting precursor of the crusading system, that what is captured from non-Christians (*pagani*) is free of all canonical prohibition based on the text "If one sacrifices from what has been wrongfully obtained, the offering is blemished," and so Christ's poor in spirit—i.e. the Normans and their Count Roger—might legitimately offer some of their booty, "violently seized", for the building of churches. For less holy ends it was doubtless even more suitably appropriated. When Palermo was captured, the ancient church, now a mosque, was purged, of course, of its "impious violation". In spite of all, there was a certain note of holy war; from the very success of the Normans it was clear that God favoured them: "we could easily tell that God was our supporter." They confessed and communicated and accepted penance before battle, as was recommended in the *chansons de geste* and was to be the pattern of crusading warfare. Pope Alexander provided a holy banner to help defeat the Arabs, and insisted that further conquests for Christ were more important than sending him presents in Rome; he wanted permanent gains in Sicily. The Count hears Mass piously before battle and is duly rewarded by God, although, when he exhorts his troops, he is pictured very frankly and quite naturally holding out the prospect of plenty of loot. Malaterra ends his history with Pope Urban's blessing: Roger has greatly extended the church of God into the boundaries of the Muslims, by the power of the Heavenly Majesty. The surge of aggression was always closely associated with the sense of divine support. The Italian towns were often as avaricious as any Norman bandit, and as the Pisans had made the first attack on Palermo, so they attacked Tunis and gained useful ransom. This was old-style raiding, not crusading. Pisa would soon learn to trust rather in peaceful trading in Africa. They employed God less, or less successfully, than the land-bound Normans.

Because of the blend of Arab, Byzantine and Norman administrative techniques, the splendid churches and other buildings, the continued use of the three languages, and the survival of Greek and Arab titles, Norman Sicily has often been seen as the home of the only multi-cultural and tolerant state of the Middle Ages. Al-Idrisi, the Arab geographer, and the greatest of all mediaeval geographers, found a good patron in Roger II. There were a number of useful translations from Arabic, but more especially from Greek, and a number of scholars from northern Europe, including Adelard of Bath, visited Sicily and shared in its

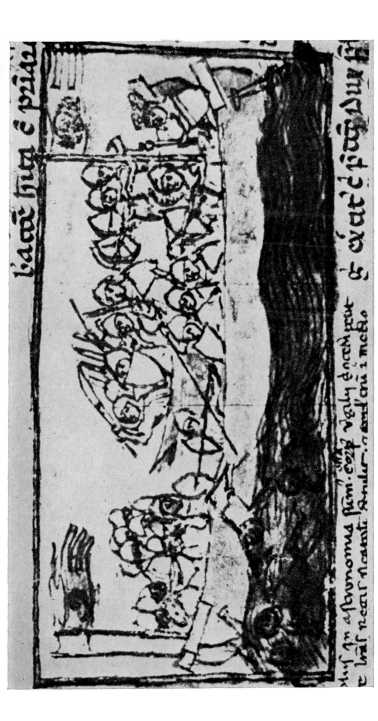

The war at sea (p.142)

ignotoȝ ⁊ iſtimer
ſpatee parabant
obſtupendaſ: unã
Duc eiũ puelle ſa
uimenti planicie
debant. plantiſ ſ
du oſ· ⁊ alia reliqſ
⁊ illuc plaudente
bat uoluentib; ſ
do ⁊ canendo diũ
moduloſ replica
tabellaſ ĩ manil
⁊ prodigialiſ erag
intuentib; tã iſe
Et poſtaliquot

The Arab girls who entertained the Emperor (p.163)

learning. The greatest period of its activity in Latin was under the Emperor Frederick II, but the Greek *Almagest* was translated in the twelfth century, and the translations from the Greek by the Sicilian Aristippus include the *Meno* and *Phaedo*. One original Greek history was written at the court, Nilus Doxopatres on the Five Patriarchates. The Latin writer Hugo Falcandus describes how the Normans attracted administrative or military talent from the north, and St Bernard was personally associated with the foundation of monasteries. There were not only new foundations, but old ones which were gradually taken over from the Greek communities. This is about as much as we can say. The final tally of achievement was rather slight. Historical accident alone brought the three cultures side by side, but they never blended. It is the fact that al-Idrisi was not translated into Latin, or, for that matter, into Greek, at the time of greatest opportunity. Greek and Arabic cultures survived just as long as the kings found it useful to protect them, and to exploit their least independent subjects.

Perhaps the picture of the tolerant Sicilian court is based as much on the account of Ibn Jubayr as on any single source. It is he who tells us how the Muslim eunuch pages at the court of William II ('the Good') enjoyed the King's favour, and openly practised their religion, while nominally acceding to Christianity. They were used in matters of delicacy, including supervision of the cooking; they kept Ramadan, and would pray almost in the presence of the King, who himself wrote Arabic, but they went in fear and would not speak freely in front of the servants. They felt that they were in servitude and they prayed for liberation by an Arab victory. In an earthquake, the King's pages and women were calling on God and His Prophet, when the King came on them. They were afraid he would denounce them, but he advised all to call on the God they worshipped, and so to feel peace of heart. All the palace concubines were Muslim, but they had converted many Frankish palace women secretly to Islam. All these crypto-Muslims were particularly pious and given to good works, including the ransom of prisoners. Ibn Jubayr states specifically that William (who lived in great luxury) acted altogether like a Muslim king, especially in his methods of government, and that he was the gentlest of Christian kings—towards Muslims, is implied. He was much given to seeking advice of astrologers and doctors.

It is natural that Ibn Jubayr should have been impressed by the

F

survival of active Islam among Arabs who could thus preserve their own culture for more than a hundred years of Christian rule, and at the very court of the ruler. It can be argued that he was over-influenced by this remarkable fact, and that he stressed too little the remark that these Muslims went in daily fear for their lives. Indeed, it might be fairer that we should accuse ourselves, rather than him, of the mistake in emphasis. When William of Apulia is describing the capture of Palermo in his *De Rebus Gestis Normannorum in Sicilia* he describes Roger's offer of safety and favour to the inhabitants. At the same time he destroys all the mosques, and turns the principal mosque into a church of the Virgin, so that where the demons had sat should now be the seat of God and a fitting doorway to heaven. This is not a bad summary of the mercy that Europe would always offer to the Arabs: conditional on the destruction of their religion, and, ultimately, of their separate identity. If we read the Latin historians of Norman Sicily we see how little the Muslim culture penetrated their lives, even for the short while that they found it wise to tolerate it. Ibn Jubayr describes the survival of a small esoteric society. Outside the court, the Arabs were driven increasingly from the public places and from the fertile valleys into the hills.

The building of the royal palace in Palermo certainly made a real impression; its splendour was Byzantine, and, though we can justly call it a major achievement of the common culture of the Mediterranean which still flourished, it was not specially Arab. The survival of titles, *emir* (in the usual contemporary form, *ammiratus*) and *gaytus* for *caid*, the use of *duana* for *diwan*, of *defertarii* for books of administrative law (from *defter*), these among others prove the continued use of some Arabic forms. They show nothing more. Instances where Latin monasteries accept an oath on the Quran from feudal dependants exemplify a more practical and a more realistic kind of toleration. Latin authors show the least possible interest in the affairs of the Arabs of North Africa. Thus Abd al-Mumin, the successor of Ibn Tumart and the first Almohad caliph, is described by Hugo Falcandus as "the very powerful Masmuda king", and Romuald of Salerno speaks similarly of the *Mesemuti* (Hugh: *Masmudi*). This is perfectly correct; the Almohads, considered tribally, were the Masmuda Berbers. What impresses us is the total lack of interest in them as a religious movement.

The dangers which Muslim Arabs incurred can be illustrated

from Latin authors, who tell their story with different degrees of approval. In 1146 Roger II's eunuch Philip, first his confidential agent and later successful commander of a sea-raid, was denounced as a hidden Muslim:

"Under the cloak of the Christian name, he preserved a hidden soldier of the devil; while as far as the outward appearance was concerned he showed himself to be a Christian, he was wholly Muslim in mind and deed; he hated Christians and greatly loved pagans (Muslims); he went into the churches of God reluctantly, and visited the synagogues of the malignants (mosques) more often. He supplied them with oil for arranging the lights and other things necessary. Not respecting Christian tradition at all, he did not stop eating meat on Fridays or in Lent; he sent messengers with offerings to the tomb of Muhammad, and commended himself greatly to the prayers of the priests of that place."

This tallies with Ibn Jubayr's account, two reigns later; again we see, in spite of the coexistence of the religions, Christian ignorance of the Hajj: 'the tomb of Muhammad'. Roger gave out that he was very upset to find that Philip, whom he had brought up a Catholic since he was a boy, should so betray him. Philip was handed over to the barons to condemn. He was dragged violently at the heels of a horse to the square before the palace and thrown into the fire to die. His accomplices were also executed. In this way the King was unable to extend his protection and was forced to show that he was "a most Christian prince and a Catholic."

Another pretty story of Norman sentiment relates to the reign of William I ('the Bad'); a revolt in the palace in March 1161 freed a number of important prisoners and raised a riot; the palace was partly sacked and the King imprisoned. The details of the plot, which was foiled, do not concern us. In ransacking the palace, some took gems and rings, others rich clothing or gold or silver, sending it home by friends, or throwing it out of the window to the crowd; "nor were there lacking those who believed that the beauty of the girls was to be preferred to all other gains." Finally none of the eunuchs whom they could find escaped; many were caught in the street on their way to find refuge at the houses of friends, and killed by the knights. A sectarian massacre developed —"a battle arose, and many Arabs were killed and robbed." The knights killed many in their warehouses, or in the fiscal offices (*diwans*), or wandering outside their homes in the streets. After that the Arabs judged it unsafe to live in the centre of the town, and concentrated in a more defensible quarter. In general, the function of the palace eunuchs seems to have been to act as trusted agents of the King, and as secretaries, as well occasionally as commanders; no doubt he trusted them because his knights hated them, and his knights hated them because of his trust. King William now regarded Henry Aristippus with suspicion, apparently because he had given some of the palace girls shelter during the outrages, and kept them for some days. If this is unseemly in an archdeacon of Catania, that does not seem to have been William's reason. It is clear that the court atmosphere engendered suspicion often associated with the surviving Muslim loyalties of the remaining Arab functionaries, courtiers and women.

In the next reign, during the minority, but not really very long before Ibn Jubayr's visit, Robert of Calatabiano was accused of a number of sensational crimes. The courtiers, Muslim and Christian, are naturally seen from a different angle from Ibn Jubayr's. Stephen the Chancellor, as a Frank brought in from outside, held a position which might appear to be intermediate between the unruly mixed European crowds in Palermo and the court, with its Arab servants. Many people were accused of apostasy to Islam, and these he punished; although they had long been protected by "the eunuchs", perhaps meaning all Muslim courtiers. No doubt they were accused because a proved apostate's property would be confiscated. A number of successful accusations encouraged the citizens to accuse Robert. Members of a delegation complained that he had robbed them of land or houses, and one woman accused him of debauching her daughter. It was also pointed out, though in any case generally known, that he had renovated the disused mosque in a sea fortress at his own expense. Perhaps this was in fact an ancient temple; the phrase used is *antiquissimum templum Saracenorum*. He can hardly have been guilty of even allowing Muslims to worship there, because he was not convicted of apostasy, although subsequently tried for all the offences against church law of which he had been accused. It was also claimed that wine-sellers in the town had leased a house from him at a vast price, where, under his patronage, Arabs might even debauch Christian women and abuse boys with impunity, and commit every sort of crime. Large profits accrued, which the inn-keepers shared with the owner of the house. Robert seems at first to have laughed at the accusations, but, as the outcry against him increased, he "turned to the protection of the eunuchs," who begged the Queen to save him, as a loyal servant of the court. The Queen wanted to blame the *caid* Peter, as having ordered the rapes and murders; Peter, an unwilling convert, had already fled from Sicily. Finally Robert was brought to trial for canonical offences only, "perjury, incest, adultery", not for the robberies, rapes and murders; but he was so ill-treated after conviction that he died in prison. This was evidently considered a victory over the court, and in particular over the court Arabs; the European settlers from the mainland were delighted. There were divisions among the Arabs, but those who were attached to the court were hostile to the Chancellor, because he had condemned Robert. The one thing that stands out clearly in this story is the hostility between the citizens and the palace in an atmosphere of suspicion and sensation. What truth lay behind the accusations is impossible to say. It is not obvious that there was any at all. Certainly it was dangerous for a Christian, even or perhaps especially a wealthy one, to have Arab friends, even or especially at court.

It is natural that the will to suppress the minority should have developed first among the general public, to whom Arabs were simply an alien and useless group, rivals, and probably a hostile and sinister influence on the authorities; it developed only later among the princes, who for long could make good use of Arab services. The Christian people, at any rate the knights not attached to the royal interest, and the townsmen, were little disposed to tolerate the survival of Islam or of the Arabs as a separate culture. In 1161, the Lombard settlers were easily roused to sedition "to invade the royal domain and to slaughter the Arabs wherever they found them"—more exactly, "they destroyed both those who lived mixed up with Christians in different towns, and those who, living apart, possessed their own villages, with no distinction of their state by sex or age." A few escaped disguised in Christian dress to the temporary safety of Arab towns in the south. They felt such a horror of the Lombard areas that for generations they would only unwillingly pass through them; it is in this area again that we hear of soldiers massacring Arabs, until prevented by the King's prohibition. In return, it was possible for the King, when he came to punish some rebels, to torture some, and others "he hanged, with Arabs and scoffers to watch." The death of William I seems to have been another occasion of danger for the court Arabs, and one group, including the high chamberlain of the palace, thought it time to escape to Morocco with at least a part of their fortunes. At the death of William II, said Hugh of Falco, "because it is difficult for the Christians in such a disturbance of affairs, with the fear of the King removed, not to oppress the Arabs," it was natural enough that the Arabs, "worn out by many wrongs," took to the mountains for refuge in increasingly large numbers.

It is not easy to sum up the Hauteville dynasty in Sicily. They were certainly great patrons of the arts of peace, and some of them were great masters of the arts of war; they were patrons of original study and of important and unimportant translations, of men of learning and science, especially the applied sciences, medicine, astrology. The kings were not all in the same mould. Roger the Great Count, "his energy never failing," and Roger II, "who did not know how to be idle, in war or in peace," are in contrast to William I; although he was said not to be able to leave any honest woman alone, he not only built churches but cared for them and saw to the liturgy that should be used in them, a much more settled personality. There was a continuity of policy in spite of individual differences. The court was secularized, perhaps not more than the Byzantine court, or the English court or other courts in Europe; certainly it was uncommitted to anything like a crusading ethos, but it was always ready fully to exploit Christian loyalties. It was not ready to give up the support of groups which might balance the intrusive papal interest, or the fissiparous anarchy of the feudatories; it would never fail to exploit whatever opportunity lay to hand. The dynasty needed clerks, whether Latin, Greek or Arab, to maintain the administration which they themselves inspired. They attracted an easy admiration. When William I died, all the citizens dressed in black for three days, and the women, but especially the Arabs, mourned, tearing their hair and ululating and drumming through the city. Romuald says that both Roger II and William I were careful to collect money and—wisely, in their economic position—were not generous in spending it; they knew how to reward the loyal and punish the unfaithful. Romuald perhaps is partisan when he says that both would rather be feared than loved; in Roger's case, feared most by Greeks and Arabs. William II succeeded as a boy not yet fourteen, but his beauty and charm reconciled his father's bitterest enemies. Both Williams were good-looking, as was Roger, son of Roger II, who died young: "a handsome man and an energetic soldier, honest, kindly, merciful and much loved by his people." It is to the peculiar ability of this family to surround themselves by men of their own choosing to serve them in many capacities that we must in part attribute the long survival of Muslims at court, in the face of the hatred of the Europeans. The withdrawal of the royal protection was always fatal to those Arabs who had not emigrated to North Africa. The Hautevilles were opportunists of the finest quality. They used their Arab followers, like their Greeks and Normans and their recruits from all over Europe. They found and took an Arab kingdom, admittedly in great disarray; but they quickly made the Arab element in it almost accidental. The kindness which they showed their Arab subjects for as long as it suited them should not mask a relative failure to make use of their extraordinary opportunity to absorb Arab culture.

3. Frederick II and the Arabs in Europe

Haskins rightly judged Frederick the last of the Norman line. In this book we are concerned with him in relation to the Arabs of Sicily; in relation to his Arab diplomacy; in relation to his crusade; in relation to his interest in Arab learning; and as an example, real or supposed, of alien influences on Europe. It will be convenient to take all these together, especially as his crusading, his relation with the Arab kings and with the popes are all part of his central Mediterranean policy. Frederick can be considered only as a single phenomenon. If he is fragmented he ceases to be credible. His approach to the Arabs seems to spring from the long and usually opportunist Norman attitude in Sicily.

It was Frederick who destroyed the Arabs of Sicily. They had been treated fiercely by Tancred, after the death of William II, and had fought against Frederick in his minority, and been reconciled by Pope Innocent III, who confirmed their existing privileges. Nevertheless, their fighting capacity was now reduced to guerilla warfare based on their mountain refuges in the Val di Mazzara, though some survived in the plains. A desperate nationalist resistance of this kind was anachronistic. For any king they must be indistinguishable from rebels or brigands, and as such Frederick, when he came in 1221 to tackle the problem, treated them, though with a difference. He wanted them extirpated from Sicily, but he still had a use for them which was quite in the tradition of his Norman ancestors. Perhaps no racial group has ever been more callously treated, because these were not only uprooted and re-established in an alien environment, but they were isolated at Lucera on the Italian mainland, where they must be wholly dependent for their safety on the Emperor, who could therefore use them, willing or unwilling, as mercenaries to be expended at his will; the more unpopular they became, the more they were dependent on him.

It was in 1223 that the Emperor could write that he had at last been able to bring down the Sicilian Arabs from "the summits of the mountains and impregnable places" into the plains, the achievement of an arduous campaign. In some areas the Arabs were able to dominate and even to frighten the countryside. Feeling was too high on both sides for any but a radical solution to appeal to the Emperor. Fighting in fact continued for a few years, and Arabs were brought down to camps in the plains, but it appears that by 1226 the Arab population had been largely reduced, and from this date the Arab settlement at Lucera in Capitanata began to provide active troops in the imperial service. The quasi-penal colony was built up steadily, as witness, for example, in 1239, a circular to all justiciars, chamberlains and other officials in Sicily to send "all Arabs generally" in their territories to Lucera. Nevertheless, punitive wars continued for some twenty years against the Arab 'rebels' of the Sicilian heights. The *Annales Siculi* say only in 1245 that "Count Richard of Caserta on the order of the Lord Emperor ejected all the Arabs from Sicily" and sent them to Lucera in Apulia.

The settlement at Lucera created an inevitable conflict with the papal and clerical interest. For Frederick its value lay in its separation, its Arab culture and its Muslim religion, as well as its total dependence on himself; for the clergy it was a scandal that Islam should be freely practised in the heart of Christendom, and, to be fair to them, that so many souls should be lost. Contemporary references to Lucera are sometimes devoid of moral overtone, but only rarely. Already in the 20s Frederick used his Arab troops on the Crusade, their Muslim practice a scandal to Christian Crusaders, and not less, one supposes, to Muslims conscious of *jihad*. In 1233 Pope Gregory wrote to Frederick to admonish him to ensure that the Lucera Arabs, said to understand Italian dialect not badly, "receive in peace and patiently hear" the Dominicans he was sending, angels of peace, to convert them. To this Frederick replied unhurriedly and somewhat disingenuously that he welcomed their ministration, especially as he hoped to be in Lucera himself, where already conversions were taking place; he trusted to the time when not Lucera alone, but the fullness of the nations would have returned to the faith. Frederick, indeed, knew how to be more unctuous than the pope, and with fair words to reduce the impact of the preachers. During the lifetime of Frederick, missionaries were successfully discouraged, and made little or no headway. Frederick himself showed a constant interest. His *diplomata* are often concerned with small details of administration concerning Lucera, where customs and dues accepted under William II were maintained. In one mixed group of craftsmen, Lombard, Greek and Arab, a certain Abdalla alone is *servus noster*. The Lucera livestock included camels, a case of long cultural survival, and its master craftsmen were employed over a wide area.

The annalists often note the use of 'Saracen' troops, including archers, in the imperial armies—"Teutons, Apulians, Arabs . . . and even Greeks". Frederick used them unscrupulously, as, on one occasion, to execute a bishop, which confirmed clerical hatred of them. The papal party accused them, of course, of debauching virgins, wives and widows in churches, and of insulting holy images. To a man who complained of the disgrace when an Arab officer billeted on him raped his wife, the Emperor ambiguously quoted the maxim, "where there is force, there is no disgrace." In a rhetorical way 'Saracens' are referred to in contemporary Italian chronicles as types of cruel savages; as, for example, to speak of cruelties committed by Italians, not, as you would expect, by "barbarians or Indians, by Medes or Saracens, by Sarmatians or Britons, not by Tartars or Chaldeans"—a good mixture of ancient and modern. Sometimes a greater realism reveals the friendless Arab soldiers at the receiving end, "butchered like brute animals," Italian troops "cutting down Arabs in pieces, eagerly wounding them as if they were dogs." As prisoners, they had always been liable to be singled out for exemplary punishment. Of one slaughter (of Christians) it was said that such things "would not be done to Jews, not even to Arabs." Under Manfred, Arab troops from Lucera were heavily involved: "innumerable Arabs", and papal propaganda represented their employment as sending "the host of the Arabs against the patrimony of St Peter." After the death of Manfred, the rumour of the coming of Conradin comforted the Lucera Arabs, who feared French rule and prepared to rebel against it. The unlucky Manfred and Conradin and the Lucera Arabs could only hope to help each other in the face of papal policy and French ambitions. Nevertheless, Charles of Anjou accepted Lucera's final surrender, refusing pardon only to its Christian allies, and it preserved a little longer its quasi-independence, in the service of the new Sicilian house. It was claimed that some of its people were converted.

At the end of the century Charles II put an end to Frederick's experiment, and to the last considerable remnant of Sicilian co-existence. Lucera was depopulated: "uprooting vices and planting virtues, Lucera was wiped out," as "a nest of pestilence," in 1301; "lurid in pollution . . . the stubborn plague and filthy infection of Apulia," so "celestial wisdom" determined, "should vanish away like a clay vessel." Lucera was renamed the city of Saint Mary; and "after some of the Arabs had been killed and the others turned out in that same destroyed Lucera, the mosque was found which was venerated by them according to the cult and the name of Muhammad," but, regarded as a "temple of idolatrous worship", it was (of course) turned into a church. The *diplomata* of the Angevin dynasty are very wordy and repetitive; rhetoric about the destruction of Lucera seems endless in these official documents which compare ill with those of the Hohenstaufen. The city was "subsequently settled with a numerous race of Christians," and it is interesting to find these requesting the same rights as the Arabs whom they had replaced; "it would be unfair" to dispose of rights of cultivation more harshly to Christians than to Arabs. "Let them enjoy the same freedom of grazing, water and woods as the Arabs enjoyed." The new inhabitants were strictly forbidden to shelter any Arabs who might want to return and "no man, whatever his importance" might build dwellings suitable to house them. There is an implication that the Christians were moved less by charity than by the hope of cheap labour. In any case, in 1336 a distinct Arab community, but scattered in different places and exercising different crafts and trades, still survived in Apulia, and by then King Robert was prepared to offer protection against Christians who, without his authority, would persecute and rob them; such Christians were threatened with process of law in cases where they molested those Arabs who "in no way abuse the decency of the Christian faith." All that we can say is that the experiment of toleration, even in the manner by which Islam tolerated the Peoples of the Book, was occasionally conceded, rarely attempted deliberately, and never attempted for long, in Europe in the Middle Ages; the Angevin rulers unwillingly inherited a community which Frederick II had created, not so that it might live in peace, but as a field from which regularly to harvest professional soldiers. Its later history and final destruction were already contained in its foundation.

4. Frederick II and the Arab World

In all Frederick's interactions with the Arab World we find the same unscrupulous mixture of opportunism, secularity and independence of mind. Frederick the Crusader, excommunicated for not crusading, and kept under excommunication for crusading in the wrong way, made his crusading policy part of his general policy of military, commercial and scientific relations in the eastern Mediterranean. To the clerical and papal interests the success of a crusade by negotiation was by itself an offence, but the point of which they made greatest propaganda use, and which seems in fact most genuinely to have made them indignant, was that his agreement with the Sultan left the *Templum Domini* and the *Templum Salominis* for Muslim worship. That there had never been a place for Christian worship on the site of the old Jewish Temple was never understood, although something was known of the work of Umar ibn al-Khattab, who in fact excavated the ruined site and erected the first mosque there. The two *'templa'* were the Qubbat as-Sakhra (the Dome of the Rock) and the al-Aqsa mosque, which still stand. It was generally believed that the Dome of the Rock was the building of the Presentation and that in which the Lord had taught. The Temple was to be in the hands of Muslims, who were to hold the keys, said the Patriarch, in his first hurried attack on the agreement between Frederick and the sultan al-Kamil; "manifest abuse . . . the agreement of Christ and Belial;" Muslims would have free access to the 'Temple' for worship and Franks must enter only with respect. This church, which was the patriarchal seat, was now the seat of Muhammad. Many more Muslims would come to pray at the Temple than Christians at the Sepulchre, so that Christian tenure of Jerusalem would be in danger. In composing this diatribe, the Patriarch omits to consider that without Frederick's agreement there would be no Christian rule in Jerusalem at all. The Master of the Teutonic Knights pointed out that the Temple area would be in the hands of a few old men and under the immediate control of Frederick's armed guards; he had seen with his own eyes that this was so. The Patriarch had other objections: Christians would have to hear Muslim prayers offered and Muslim religion proclaimed without contradiction or objection. In court cases involving only Muslims, the case would be heard by a Muslim judge; that was no sort of jurisdiction for Christians to have in the city. These summarized extracts reflect only palely the venom of the original, which does however succeed in concentrating so many of the emotional themes which prevented rational relationships between good Christians and good Muslims. As we shall see in another chapter, good relations, when they developed at all, did so on a practical, never a theoretical, basis.

Frederick II himself reported his achievement—and, granted the fundamental Christian weakness, a ten-year truce permitting Christian control of the Holy City was an achievement that only petty minds could carp at—in terms of extreme piety worthy of a pope: "O how much is the mercy of the Creator to be praised, and how much the strength of his power always to be feared." He did not omit to point out that the Arabs held the Temple in great reverence and went there to pray according to their rite, as pilgrims, unarmed, without permission to stay there, but, their prayers once said, leaving immediately. The peace had taken a great deal of negotiating, much, it was known, done in advance of the Emperor's arrival in Palestine. It was understood that the Sultan agreed to peace under the Emperor's threat of a war which he had demonstrated his ability to wage destructively; according to one version, the truce would save the shedding "of the blood of many people." The attack on Frederick's crusading policy cannot be dismissed as just an expression of party politics, though it was that; but, in addition, papal policies confirmed the popes—and so orthodox opinion in general—more firmly than ever in an attitude totally rejecting co-operation with Muslims. Frederick's fault in the Holy Land was to have found a successful compromise.

The clerical hatred for Frederick is one measure of the clerical rejection of compromise with Islam and of everything Arab. The attack on him, often apocalyptic in tone, provides a certain orthodox parallel to the literature of pseudo-apocalyptic prophecy of the early thirteenth century. In 1239 Pope Gregory wrote to the Archbishop of Canterbury, slightly paraphrasing the Book of Revelation, or perhaps misquoting from memory, "A beast arose out of the sea filled with the names of blasphemy . . . it opened its mouth to utter blasphemies against God." The Beast was the

Emperor, and his blasphemies were often associated with his Arab connections, relatively slight though these were. Legend collected round the Emperor and round Islam, and the two were associated. In Europe at that time an apocalyptic approach tended in any case to have Arab associations.

The Arab World had a special place in the articulate forms of chiliasm. Among the ages of the world, Abbot Joachim (in Salimbene's summary) put the age in which he lived under the aegis of Salah ad-Din and of the ten kings of the Apocalypse (17:12). There was an astrological chiliasm also. About 1230 it was once again generally understood that John of Toledo had issued a warning, endorsed by all the astrologers and geomancers of Toledo, of Ethiopia and various other parts of the world, "Christian, Muslim and Hebrew, and all the philosophers," that there was going to be a suffocating plague which would destroy the cities of the East, and then of the West, to be followed by the bloodiest of wars; "and there will be doubt and ignorance among the Muslims, so that they will completely give up their synagogues, mosques (*mummerias*) and their secret things." Such rumours were constantly revived with new variations; in an age when astrologers provided a wide service, these scares may have satisfied the same psychological need as the health scares of our own day. Among the inarticulate, we again find this Arab association with momentous changes in the world. The "innumerable multitude of shepherds" who from Flanders and Picardy crossed France in 1251, picking up the miscellaneous proletariat of the towns as they went, demanded to cross the sea in order to kill the Arabs and to avenge the French king, whom they supposed to be still a prisoner, and for whose defeat they blamed the knightly class and the clergy. This movement was in some ways reminiscent of the poor Crusaders, but its dangerously revolutionary violence was directed at the whole established order, and was used particularly in killing the clergy, often with popular approval. Among its enemies it was rumoured that the leaders were in league with the Sultan, who wanted the poor shepherds for slaves. In Italy, Salimbene heard that the common people of France were angry with the friars who had supported Louis' project, and mocked their custom of begging alms, by giving pennies to the poor "in the name of Muhammad, who is stronger than Christ." This pattern with its themes of prophecies of disaster, destruction of the Arabs, illiterate Crusaders, a miraculous passage across the sea, a final destiny in the Arab slave markets, seems to recur in different forms for roughly the first half of the thirteenth century. It is against this background that we must see the impression made by Frederick II on an age which imagined some sinister Arab design in any unusual situation.

It was especially this background that made some of the papal denunciations of Frederick credible to his contemporaries. The characteristic accusation against him, and the most famous, was (in Matthew Paris's version of 1238) that "it is alleged that he said, although this is not suitable to repeat, that three tricksters cunningly and deceitfully seduced the whole people of their own times, in order to dominate the world, namely Moses, Jesus and Muhammad." This classic epigram was given great publicity by the papal party, without Paris's careful *fertur eum dixisse*, and by the Pope himself, who ended his letter to the Archbishop of Canterbury with it, in the better known form that the Emperor had said the world was deceived by three imposters, Jesus Christ, Moses and Muhammad, of whom only the latter two had succeeded when they died. Again—the Pope said the Emperor had said—all who believed that the God who created heaven and earth could be born of a Virgin were idiots, and no one can be born except by the preceding union of a man and a woman. Finally, he had said that men ought to believe nothing but what they can prove "by compulsion and reason of nature." These materialist doctrines were not at all uncommon in the thirteenth century. The third of them has sometimes been identified as an Averroist influence, but there is nothing more than suspicion to support this, particularly at so early a date; nor does it need any explanation. These are all commonplaces of the secularist tradition, which may have been rightly or wrongly fathered on Frederick, but it is safer to assume that the only thing original about them is their being said publicly; and it was the Pope that said them publicly. We know nothing of them from an imperialist source. There can be no implication that Frederick acquired such thoughts from orthodox Muslims; of the three assertions only the first part of the second is not plainly contrary to Islam.

This is not the place to attempt another analysis of the character of Frederick, but one or two points are relevant to his 'pro-Arab' reputation. At the death of the Emperor, Salimbene recounts the various *superstitiones* which have been his defects. These vary from his amputation of a man's thumb, to punish the wrong spelling of his name (he preferred Friderick), to the old experiment of having children brought up without allowing anyone to speak to them, in order to find out whether they would naturally speak Hebrew, Greek, Latin, Arabic, or at least the language of their parents. The children all died, for lack, as Salimbene sensibly points out, of human affection. It is difficult to take many of the stories about Frederick seriously. All the telling phrases and the various experiments attributed to him have a genuinely consistent character, but in the end they only prove that he inspired legends about himself. All stories of a certain character might have begun to be fathered on him. The remark of the French workers, that Muhammad was stronger than Christ, was of the same type, and might as easily have been attributed to him. Another of his telling remarks was that the Jewish God who thought Palestine was flowing in milk and honey had never seen Sicily and southern Italy. Surely here we have an ancient joke from the army, which must have been repeated in one form or another by generations of Crusaders? A sardonic wit, a taste for natural science and an anti-papal policy may have been enough to turn him into the archetype of the scientific sceptic. In the same way his anti-papal policy helped to turn him into the apocalyptic scourge of the clergy that the myth-making followers and successors of Joachim made of him, even centuries after his death. Was 'Frederick the natural philosopher', and was 'Frederick the friend of Arab kings', equally mythical?

Frederick's patronage of learning does not amount to a great deal, apart from his employment of Michael Scot, and Scot, as Haskins pointed out, is a confused writer, not of the first class. Frederick has two greater claims. One is his circulation of philosophical and scientific problems to Arab scholars. The single surviving reply, from Ibn Sabin al-Ishbili, comments quite rightly on the amateur approach which Frederick's terminology reveals. This is an important point, and part of the consistent picture that we have recognized in the stories told about him; they might have been invented to caricature a sincere and intelligent but capricious and undisciplined amateur enquirer, and very possibly they were. The fact of his sending such problems round at all is evidence of something more; not, at that date, of any new recognition of European dependence on Arabic science, but of a willingness to deal direct, and to take the shortest and most practical route. It shows amateurishness also, however, even in patronage; the professional patron sets up a school, but Frederick only asked questions that happened to interest him. Secondly, again as Haskins pointed out, there can be no doubt about Frederick's genuine interest in zoology. This helps to mark his other interests as less serious. His collections of animals are well attested, and depended largely on imports from Africa. This was an interest he shared with his son Manfred. He was alleged to have imported experts from Egypt to find out if ostrich eggs would hatch in Apulia. He had a work on falconry translated from Arabic, and his own on that subject was the product of careful and loving attention both by himself personally and by Manfred. A piece of technical knowledge he brought back from Palestine was the use of the hood in falconry. Scot's translations of Aristotle's *De Animalibus*, probably from Arabic, are not the product of this interest, but may have drawn Frederick's interest to Scot. Frederick carried on the Norman Sicilian tradition, but he was not a great patron. Yet it is worth saying that he thought in terms of the whole Mediterranean world and of all its cultures.

Too much has been made of his friendship with Arab rulers. He was no doubt the most distinguished monarch to have relations of any sort; it is interesting that the contemporaries of Richard I of England admired him for his relationship with al-Adil, whereas papal propaganda was enough to make Frederick's dealings with al-Kamil a matter of reproach. A bare generation separated the two. There can be no question that the negotiations with al-Kamil, resulting in the much hated lease of the Holy Land to Frederick, were a real diplomatic achievement, perhaps one of the most remarkable of purely diplomatic achievements recorded, but they are not unique. For Tunis we have Frederick's treaty with the first of the Hafsid rulers, Abu Zakariya, dated 1231. It shows no essential difference from the Arab diplomacy to which the maritime Italian states, the Catalans and others were already accustomed. All such agreements are based on reciprocal privileges designed to make trade possible. Frederick agrees to an exchange of prisoners; the Muslims of Pantellaria shall not be subject to a Christian, but to a Muslim from Sicily; Latin merchants in Africa shall be free of exactions; the Emperor will make restitution of goods stolen by Christian pirates. He leaves the Italian cities to maintain their own separate agreements. The Almohad caliph is formally honoured. In this there is nothing of exceptional interest. More remarkable, Frederick gave political asylum to Abu Zakariya's nephew Abd al-Aziz, and kept him, in effect a hostage, at Lucera. A number of the *diplomata* witness that he was kept in honourable state. The Pope alleged that he wanted to be baptized, but was prevented by Frederick. There is not the slightest reason to suppose that the Pope was right. All this is evidence that Frederick treated his Arab neighbours with the same realistic absence of scruple with which he ruled, and in that sense he was treating Arabs like Europeans; it is not evidence for the special friendship of which his enemies accused him.

He certainly did not exclude Arabs who were his subjects from his company, any more than his predecessors in the Sicilian kingdom had done; like them he knew how to exploit their services fully. Perhaps the clue to Frederick's reputation is that he simply did and said what many less prominent people had done and said before him, but did it in the light of the publicity to which an emperor is subject. We can trace his changing reputation as he passes through the pages of Matthew Paris. Alleged anti-Christian atrocities by the Lucera troops, following the usual formulae of such outrages, were supposedly committed by his express command. Every treaty or communication with a Muslim ruler became a friendship, though the Cardinal of Viterbo judged that the Sultan (al-Kamil) who sent supplies to the army of the Fifth Crusade at Damietta, in the Nile inundation, defended the church better than Frederick. This extraordinary remark is some measure, not only of the hatred the papal party bore to Frederick, but also of the confusion in the minds of those who condemned his so-called Arab alliances. Matthew Paris says that Frederick's enemies (and Paris was the last man to take the Pope too seriously) claimed that he was more inclined to the Muslim religion than the Christian; that he had a number of loose-living Arab girls as concubines, and that the rumour was spreading that he was more closely allied and friendly with Arabs than with Christians. Paris adds again that his enemies wanted to obscure his fame, and that only He from Whom nothing was hidden knew if they sinned thereby. Five years later Paris noted that the Emperor's fame was being even more darkened by those who said that he would not pay proper attention in church, or pray, or respect the higher clergy, or talk sensibly about the Catholic faith, or stay out of the beds of his little Arab girls (*muliercularum sarracenarum*); worst of all, he was bringing Arabs and others into his empire, and letting them build heavily fortified towns. This last refers to the misfortunes of the Lucera Sicilians, of course. In 1247 Paris records that some discerning men were afraid that Frederick, in his fury and desper-ation, would apostatize, or call to his help the Tartars from Russia, or the Sultan of Egypt, "his close friend, to the confusion of all Christendom," bringing in a multitude of non-Christians. Per-haps this notion relates partly or distantly to the misconception about the Lucera operation. When finally Frederick dies, Paris refers to the wealth he has gained by sending his agents or factors into the East and bringing back merchandise from as far as the Indies, by land and sea. Paris also believes, what it is unlikely the Pope did, that Frederick was forgiven by God, Who wants none who believe in Him to perish. Paris is peculiar only in that his suspicion of the Pope allows him to have charitable thoughts of Frederick; otherwise, he reflects the rumours of European opinion admirably.

It is clear that Frederick was indeed the heir of the Normans of Sicily. Above all, he thought in Mediterranean terms, as did also, indeed, the great maritime cities. The papal policy, which would be later intensified, of boycotting Egypt and the rest of the Arab World, was the antithesis of Frederick's. His crusade was the only thoroughly sensible one, though it was certainly unheroic. His friendships with the Arab rulers were not of course friendships in any effective sense, but he did consistently practise a policy of normal relationships that favoured trade, and in his erratic way he found it natural to promote a scientific exchange. The fluctuation of rumour which would make him now an atheist and next a crypto-Muslim reflected a world where normal relations were hard to conceive and impossible to interpret accurately, and where there was no longer, in spite of a century and a half of translation from the Arabic, one single culture. Frederick was simply detached from any interests but those of his empire and his kingdom of Sicily. He used the Arabs, but there is no way in which he was their friend, except as his interests required. Although the case of the Sicilian Arabs was already desperate when Frederick succeeded to the Sicilian throne, still it was he who ensured, and partly encompassed, their total destruction. He never seems to have thought of an Arab as other than an ordinary human being, and this was a lesson that his contemporaries needed to learn, and most of them never learned. When that is said, we must remember that other human beings were never more to him than instruments of policy or the subjects of experiment.

5. Conclusion

Two centuries saw the total Latinization of Europe in the central Mediterranean. Except for Malta, where the Arabic language, though not the Muslim religion, survived, all the Arab culture, and all Arab interests apart from piracy, were destroyed in the Italian mainland, in the islands and the sea. North Africa was attacked, but it became clear in this period that it would remain an Arab area. In North Africa itself Christianity died out in the same period, except as the tolerated religion of foreigners, merchants and other specially protected persons. In the pontificate of Gregory VII, papal letters dated 1073 and 1076 show that the remnants of a native Latin hierarchy functioned in Carthage (Tunis) and Bone, and the local hierarchy still survived at the time of Norman rule. The period of Almohad rule seems to have seen its end. When Innocent III writes to the Almohad caliph it is to recommend Religious (i.e. members of religious orders) sent to ransom prisoners. Many papal letters of the thirteenth century recommend Franciscans and Dominicans to different rulers; the era of foreign chaplaincies had in effect succeeded that of a native church. The line of demarcation was thus more firmly and definitely drawn than ever before. In future there would be less commingling; Arabs and Europeans in the central Mediterranean would remain on visiting terms to their mutual profit, but would never be compatriots.

We could exaggerate the change. There had been a flux of warfare rather than peaceful living before; and the attempt at coexistence in Sicily was accidental, not deliberate, temporary, while expediency was served, and never accepted by the mass of either population. Probably only the court itself enjoyed a shared culture, and even there it seems to have been compartmented. The actual products of the tripartite culture were relatively sparse, and the Hellenic element was greater than the Arab. Under Frederick II there was productivity in the fields of science, in which we include astrology; but Frederick, with his wide-ranging and diffused interests, made no attempt to create a common culture. We can only say that he was genuinely interested to keep communication with the Arab states of North Africa and Syria open, where the popes wanted them closed. The eleventh century saw in the campaigns of George Maniakes the last Byzantine attempt to recover Graecia Magna, and in the Norman Conquest it saw the first great defeat of Greeks and Arabs alike by a northern race. The Normans, with their infinite energy and versatility, were ready for a kind of cultural compromise so long as it was useful. The succession of the House of France in the person of Charles of Anjou, in alliance with the uncompromising and single-minded policy of the papacy, ensured the destruction of everything that was not Latin. Henceforth the frontiers of the Roman Church were clearly marked, and helped to define the frontiers of Europe; within them there would be no divergence.

Chapter 7

Courtly ideals in the East

1. Some shared notions

There is no question here of attempting to write a comparative history of opinion in Arab and European society in the Mediterranean, not even only of opinion in that small area at the eastern end, where the two cultures came together for less than two hundred years. At the fringe of such a study, I will just examine shortly whether there at any rate existed some overlap of accepted ideals at the top of the social structure. European society was doubtless the less fluid, though far from wholly stable; Arab society less legally feudal, but, despite its fluidity of class structure, still firmly based in chivalry and wealthy landed families. Both societies depended on courts, and in the case of every Arab ruler in Syria, until Salah ad-Din took power, and every Latin ruler, these were little courts limited in influence and wealth. Fatimid Egypt was richer and stronger, but even Fatimid Egypt in its decline was vulnerable, and was the victim of actual invasion by the Latins. If we widen our perspective in time to include the Ayyubids and Mamelukes, and in space to the rulers of western Europe, it remains true that throughout Arab and European society, over a long period we are dealing with a courtly society which can never be conceived as imperial. The scale varies, but it is never the grand scale known earlier by Byzantium and by Baghdad, or the future scale of the Ottomans or the colonizing powers of western Europe. In this chapter I want to consider the standards by which rulers were judged. A fragmented courtly society is particularly vulnerable to an incompetent ruler; and its ideals will tend to be the ideals most readily attained by the individual. To define it negatively, this society is the antithesis of bureaucracy. Chivalry was an individual way of life, which the courts of the day must accommodate, because knightly life was the stuff of which they were made, and the rulers themselves were knights; but there was a limit to this. Personal incompetence must create greater tension even than in a bureaucracy. The character of the rulers was crucial; and this was true equally among Arabs and Franks. It was natural that the ideals of both should overlap.

There is another preliminary point. Without going into the question of interacting influences, should we ask whether the crusading situation in itself affected the code of behaviour? In the Latin states, Europeans lived side by side with both Muslim and Christian Arabs; the latter were a socially depressed class, but the Muslims were knights and lords like themselves. By social position they were entitled to be treated under the code of chivalry. On the other hand, the tendency of orthodox thought among the clergy and at Rome was to believe that the only good Arab was a converted one. How far did living side by side with people who over so long a period must continue to be regarded as enemies affect the standards of behaviour? Prowess, of course, continued to be a virtue, and the qualities of indomitability and audacity would pay an extra dividend in all situations of uncertainty and risk. *Franchise, debonneïrete* were also rather encouraged than otherwise by the conditions of life in the East. Freedom of manner and a deliberately casual approach must be favoured by the uncertainty of life and of tenure and the partial break with European traditional ways of life. *Largesse*, generosity with material things, and detachment from wealth might remain no less an ideal even for those who grasped most avidly at quick and large returns, the rewards of prowess in terms of loot. *Courtoisie*, in the sense of a formal code of manners, may have provided the framework for relations between Arab and European lords. *Pitie*, compassion, seems to have been rarely attempted in any war, least obviously in crusading war. The persistent encouragement of xenophobic attitudes could only militate against compassion, although it is impossible to believe that it was never practised. At least we can say that the chivalric code was always relevant to the situation in the Latin states.

There are some obvious ways in which Arab and Frankish chivalric ideals conformed, a few where they clearly did not. It strikes every reader of Usama ibn Munqidh, conventionally pious except for being devoid of any sense of holy war, that the Latin knights never seemed alien to him, except in their peculiar attitude to religion and in the freedom they allowed their women. This freedom that European women assumed was a Germanic inheritance, and Usama's astonishment at the lack of public decorum of Frankish women was characteristic of traditional Mediterranean society. This freedom is related to the doctrine of *franchise*, which developed (especially at a rather later date) as part of the Western chivalric ideal, though *franchise* in its aspect of generosity of spirit was certainly part of the Arab literary ideal. In other respects the two societies had everything in common, both the sense of *largesse* and the realization that *prowess* is important above all. Its complement was loyalty. To a modern European, these qualities seem essentially feudal, but they are better thought of as courtly, and as belonging to a rural society studded with a few major towns; the ideal king was urban but not yet metropolitan. *Largesse* in particular was an inherited notion in every society, equally the Arab and the Germanic, in both of which it was associated with an aristocratic ideal. A modern anthropologist has put this very well, speaking of the Kababish Arabs of the Northern Sudan: a slave "is one, whose ignoble birth is reflected in his characteristic meanness, and who is mean either because he has nothing of his own to give or because he thinks that nothing is acquired by giving liberally." This associates baseness of birth and baseness of motive, and this also is common to the Arab and Latin societies of the Christian twelfth and thirteenth centuries. For a king the requirements were extended; thus generosity must accompany accessibility, the generous gift of his time and person, as much as of his wealth and honours.

One classic expression of the traditional Arab ideal was quoted by Muhassin ibn Ali at the end of our tenth century, looking back upon the great Muslim age:

> I regret Ubaydallah as more lordly and munificent than Fadl,
>   Yahya or his grandfather;
> They were munificent when fortune favoured; he when fortune was
>   unfavourable.

Largesse is an attitude of mind, for Arabs as for the Latins. The same writer goes on to quote Hasan ibn Ali ibn Zaid, the astrologer: he liked to be praised for his good words: "I assure you I do it for God's glory only; but if it be for show, it is still a good thing, and why should not (my critics) be similarly hypocritical?" The point of this is not that the interior attitude does not matter, but the reverse, that the critics are moved by low envy. In former days, he says, those who envied wealth tried to get rich; those who envied learning studied; who envied munificence adopted a more lavish style; now they want to impoverish the rich, they accuse the learned of errors, belittle liberality as a business oper- ation, and benefactions as hypocrisy. These critics reveal their baseness; the attitude of mind is crucial, nobility is of the soul. In the middle of the tenth century al-Mutanabbi had described the most noble gentleman:

> he who has made time's vicissitudes his prisoners, and the clouds
>   envious of his hands;
> physicking abundance of riches by reducing them to little with acts
>   of munificence, as though wealth were a sickness.

This makes it really important actually to be rid of wealth, although nobility is predominantly an attitude. Perhaps only the heirs who follow a greater age than their own can afford this approach. The Latin West looked back to a series of more distant and often myth- ical past ages, through Charles the Great to the classical age and equally through the Bible to Jewish history. They were also con- scious of their actual capacity for growth. Western nobility was strictly inherited, though it could be conferred, and poor men of gentle birth like William the Marshal rose to the heights of nobility. In any case, in the West, too, nobility must be an attitude of mind to match the noble birth. This was an obvious factor in William of Tyre's estimates of the kings of Jerusalem. It would be difficult to assert that he acquired this from an eastern model, and a parallel attitude of Arabs and Latins probably resulted from their still very similar circumstances. Positive evidence is inconclusive, but William and his like would have been conscious of any difference between their own kingship and that of the Arabs around them. The negative evidence is so strong as to be presumptive that they took it for granted that they shared an ideal which they may well have considered a basic element of all human existence.

The qualities of kingship must evidently extend beyond those of chivalry. A king has to be effective, and we shall see how this criterion naturally modifies Tyre's assessments of the Latin kings. Al-Farabi, writing like the other Arabs we have been quoting, in the tenth century, is realistic in his definitions. He requires wisdom and the power of persuasion and the power to fight the holy war. There is certainly some correspondence between the faculties of persuading and of creating an imaginative impression, which he describes, and the affability which William of Tyre notes in some of the kings. *Affabilitas* is the less precise and the wider notion, containing both the capacity to make an impression and the accessibility to those who want to convey their own needs. The Arab requirement of the capacity to fight the holy war as essential to a ruler is obviously assimilable to the Frankish requirement of crusading prowess. Toughness in itself is required of kings, because they are the essential soldiers, the hub of all men's defence. A summary of William the Marshal's service in Syria is prowess and toughness and largesse. What here applies to a knight must apply still more to a king. This conception lies behind all judgements on the kings.

In talking of the standards of men of business or war it is rash to rely on philosophers. Yet the universal popularity of the *Secreta Secretorum* among both Arabs and Europeans is evidence that cannot be quickly dismissed. The supposed advice of Aristotle to Alexander on the business of government modifies the extreme notion of *largesse,* as liable too easily to lean either to prodigality or to avarice: in a king, it must not extend to his own impoverishment, and so end in his defeat. It is unwise, inappropriate; the considerations are prudential. On the other hand the objection to avarice is to the state of mind. "The name of avarice really disgraces the king and is inconsistent with a king's majesty;" a man's good name also derives from a state of mind, or inherent nobility, "he who truly desires good fame will be famous and glorious, and who falsely desires it will be confounded by ill fame;" again, "envy generates untruth, which is the root of wrong things and the material of the vices." When the text praises learning, Roger Bacon (one of its editors in the West) recalls the saying he attributes to William the Conqueror, "An illiterate king is a crowned ass." There is much advice on the conduct of war; the heart of it is that "there is no victory over people unless they are first defeated by the cowardice of their hearts, and by the intrusion of fear." All these notions, and especially those that relate to the nobility of the heart, are common ground to the two cultures. Some of the recommendations of the *Secreta Secretorum* are less universally acceptable; the advice to a king not to risk his life in battle accords ill with the practice (and still less with the ideals) of either Arabs or Franks at this date. The advice to avoid familiarity with his subjects is hardly in opposition to *affabilitas*, because it is meant chiefly against 'low persons', or against an excess which breeds contempt.

These preliminary observations are very sketchy, and I intend them only to indicate that Arab and Frankish ideas about behaviour belonged at least to the same general field of thought. I cannot give a detailed analysis, but I have offered a few illustrations of a general proposition. I want to give my space to a slightly more detailed examination of the Franks' estimates of their own rulers in the East, and also of the great Arab leaders.

2. The kings of Jerusalem

Not the least remarkable aspect of the crusading states was their lay character. They seem more secular than the kingdoms of Europe, largely no doubt because they were established and maintained by soldiers. The historians have a considerable proportion of laymen, even from the beginning, with the *Gesta* and the poem of *Antioche*; and, for the commercial interest, Caffaro; later there were Ernoul and the continuators of William of Tyre, Philip of Novara and, of course, Joinville. The Latin states did not produce a serious clerical writer who was not himself a courtier; partly this was because of the low condition of the church in Palestine, but that was itself a consequence rather than a cause of the secular character of the state. Jacques de Vitry was the most orthodox of crusading writers of any stature, and he came from the West. Later in the history of the Kingdom of Acre a larger proportion of writers were clerical, often friars. Yet we are not often far from the camp-fires, or even the court itself, at any time in the whole story. The historians are often participants, and even the clergy have been, whether willingly or not, men of action. Fulcher was a priest, but chaplain to Baldwin I; he was consciously a man of peace with a distaste for the fighting, but he belonged to a soldier's court.

Fulcher places *probitas* very high as a military virtue; *militiae probitas* means soldierliness, and is coming near to the cognate *prowess*. Fulcher explains that Godfrey was chosen to command the new nation for his high birth, for his *militiae probitas*, for his patient moderation, and for the grace of his manners. These are military and social virtues. Fulcher stresses in Baldwin I, also, his "accustomed soldierliness"; he is a most accomplished warrior, but Fulcher reproves him for his lack of prudence, for attacking the enemy without adequate support; for relying too much on his prowess, in fact. A king must be moderate, because moderation is among the skills of war, and he must possess them all, not only those which bring personal renown. Fulcher was not a soldier, and his preferences, explicit or implied, may ill represent the opinion of the professionals; but he was familiar with warfare and with soldiers, and his ideal of the leader who is both *probus* and *modestus* is highly professional. His list of the qualities for which Duke Godfrey was chosen is unclerical, realistic and very courtier-like.

William of Tyre, also a priest and ultimately a prelate, was a courtier of great distinction, Chancellor of the kingdom and tutor to Baldwin the Leper, and is one of the greatest of mediaeval historians. The Middle Ages produced many ecclesiastics who were also statesmen, equally at home in the church and at court, but William was the only one who was also a writer. It is to this blend of experience and background that we owe his balanced judgements, appropriate to a churchman of a reforming era, to a high official of a royal court and a distinguished pedagogue whose sentiments we can identify although they were controlled. His history is no exception to the rule that secular interests seem to dominate the history of the Crusaders. His own chief concern is for international relations, almost for international confidence; he feels this more when it is a question of relations with Byzantines or with Arab states than when it is between minor princes. His moderate churchmanship shows in his reluctance to criticize the part played by clergy in his story, and in the way he treats the broad sweep of events—the rise of Islam, the inception of the Crusades—where he employs the accepted Latin conventions. When he is writing about his own times his imagination warms, and his interest in contemporary Arab politics is genuine, though it hardly extends beyond the interests of his own state. Arab history is not his subject; as he several times tells us, we should look for that to his (now lost) history of the princes of the East, which certainly reproduced an eastern Christian view of past Islamic history, but the contemporary part might have been an invaluable source for the history of inter-communal opinion.

In the earlier part of his history, of course, he is only working over old materials, though even this has some interest, particularly selection and omission in the process of editing. The memory of Duke Godfrey does not seem to have attracted him greatly. He was interested that Arab observers were astonished to see Godfrey cut off the head of a camel with one blow of his sword, as much, no doubt, because of the willing expenditure of a valuable beast, as because of the strength and skill of his arm—*largesse* as well as *prowess*. Of the kings who lived before his time, William most admired Baldwin I. He begins his account of Baldwin's early life by explaining that he was educated, had, indeed, started on the career of a clerk, and given it up for no known reason. He describes his features, admits that there was something less than kingly in slight imperfections in his appearance. He praises his gravity of demeanour, "measured in his gait, grave in disposition and in speech", *gravis in incessu, habitu et verbo serius*; his manner and the way he wore his mantle made him seem to one who did not know him more like a bishop than a man of the world, *persona saecularis*. He was said to have suffered from a weakness for the pleasures of the flesh, but managed such business so discreetly he created no scandal and did no great wrong to anyone; only his personal servants knew what he was about. He was "quick to arms and active on horseback; he was indefatigable and attentive to affairs of state whenever they required." It was superfluous to praise in him the qualities of all his family, said William, his high-mindedness, his high courage (*magnificentia, animositas*) and his ability in the discipline of war; he would not allow himself to fall below the example of his brother in these things. There is much in the way of life here described to appeal to the Arab society which surrounded Baldwin; chiefly it lacks the quality of princely generosity, which corresponds to the notion of *largesse*. This was a virtue difficult to practise, for a king whose revenues were inadequate for the *negotia regni*.

William tells at some length a story of Baldwin's courtesy at a very early stage in the settlement of the kingdom, when crusading ardour and intolerance might be expected to be still alive; courtesy and largesse are closely connected. The King had intercepted and captured a caravan in the desert across the Jordan, and he was returning with the captured herds and other loot. There happened to be among his captives the pregnant wife of "a great and powerful prince". Her labour came on her and she gave birth.

> "When the King heard that, he ordered her to be put down from the camel on which she was riding and a comfortable bed to be prepared for the time being out of the spoils, on the ground, and she was given food and two jars of water; and he also gave her, as she wished, a maid and two camels, which she chose, so that she could live on their milk; he wrapped her in the cloak he was wearing and

left her, and set out with his army. The same day or the next, that
great shaikh (*satrapa*) of the Arabs was following in the tracks of
our army, as is the custom of his people, with a great company of his
men, and he was grieving and extremely sad, because he had lost
his wife, a noble matron, and about to give birth; he was reflecting
that all that remained to him was as nothing, when by accident he
fell upon her, lying like that. When he saw and wondered at the
overflowing humanity which the King had shown to her, he began
to extol the name of the Latins to the stars and especially the mercy
of the King."

He conceived an obligation to the King which he in fact discharged
by helping him to escape from the Egyptians at Ramla a year later.
This generous act of Baldwin's is less likely to have been a calculated act of policy than a spontaneous gesture; the King showed
little mercy at Caesarea shortly after, saving only the amir and the
cadi, for the sake of their ransom. The Latin tale is told as an act
of generosity, a gesture such as might be made anywhere; but it is
the kind of act of which Arabs approve, an example of *eryahiya*,
the disposition to be generous. That there is a common standard of
judgement is certainly implied in the telling.

We are frequently reminded of the secular elements in Latin
society, but this does not correlate with the Arabizing factor. In
William's picture of Baldwin II there is little that strikes us as
particularly Arab. William notes his fidelity to treaty obligations,
a point in which he felt a special interest; he praises his clemency
and his humanity; but he is praising him more for his ability to
settle in the mixed world of Latins and Arabs than for ideal
qualities. Joscelin II, of Edessa, is described not only as skilled
in war and liberal, but also as given to excess of drink and women.
This is the same picture of the ideal ruler, but turned to partial
reprobation; William disapproves, but recognizes the secular
virtues. Perhaps the most interesting of William's pictures of the
Latin princes is his long account of Baldwin III. In this, of course,
he was speaking from personal knowledge.

He mentions first Baldwin's natural presence and dignity; he
easily surpassed all the other princes of the realm in the grace of his
person and equally in the liveliness of his mind and his articulate
expression (*eloquentiae flora*). Anyone who did not know who he
was could recognize the dignity of a king in him. That articulate
expression, rhetorical ability, should be one of the signs of majesty
is another quality sympathetic to Arab standards of judgement,

and William goes on to stress this quality further, although his feeling is rather Hellenic than Arab. "The disposition of his well-constituted mind balanced so much corporal grace." He continues:

"For he was quick in his natural bent, to the highest degree, and he had a kind of pre-eminence of his own in fluent speech. He did not seem inferior to any prince whatever in the dignity of laudable behaviour. Indeed, he was extremely tender-hearted and courteous, and, although he showed himself generous beyond his powers almost to everyone, he was not covetous of other people's property. He did not trouble the patrimony of the church; neither did he, in the manner of a spendthrift, lie in wait for the wealth of his subjects."

This seems to be very close to the Arab ideal of the prince, though it falls somewhat short of business efficiency. The original might translate more easily into Arabic than into English.

"What is very rare at this age, and even in adolescence, he was God-fearing, and respectful towards church institutions and the prelates of the church. Endowed with vigour of mind, he achieved the advantage of a faithful memory." This, perhaps, was put in in contrast to his Angevin father, who notoriously could remember neither names nor faces.

"He was appropriately well educated, much better than his brother Amalric, who succeeded him. When in fact he could steal some leisure from his public engagements, he willingly applied himself to reading; he would listen chiefly to histories, and he carefully studied the achievements and the customs of the ancient kings and the best rulers. He took his recreation very much in discussions, chiefly with the learned, but also with knowledgeable laymen. He excelled so much in the gift of courtesy (affability), that he used to address the lowliest people, greeting them casually and by name. To those who wanted to come to him and to those who fell in with him here or there he would freely offer the interchange of mutual conversation and would not refuse what they asked. Thus he earned the favour of the people and of the elders, so that he was considered more acceptable than any of his predecessors. He was also able to bear hard work, and he was especially far-seeing, as is the way of the best prince, in the doubtful occurrences of war. In the greatest necessities, which he very often carried through for the increase of the kingdom, he showed a constancy that was royal and on no occasion did he fall short of the composure of a strong man. He had a deep knowledge of the customary law by which the kingdom of the East is governed, so that even the older lords of the kingdom sought his advice out of his practical knowledge in doubtful matters, and admired the learning and the experience of his mind. His talk was cheerful and witty; he would fit in with any people whatsoever by means of some pleasing accommodation, and he adapted himself happily to every age and condition."

Urbanity was his special virtue, except only that he used to jeer at his friends when they said something to which he objected. He was more given to gambling than a king should be. As an adolescent he was said to have wronged husbands, but he gave this up as he grew older, and, once married, lived continently. He used to say that excess, whether in eating or in drinking, was the fuel of the worst crimes. *Urbanitas, affabilitas, liberalitas*: these seem to be crucial elements in William's picture. A prince who is dignified, generous to a fault, accessible and warm-hearted to all, respectful of learning and himself learned in appropriate fields, history and the law of his land, eloquent and fluent in speech, is close to an ideal equally Arab or European.

The description of Baldwin's brother, King Amalric I, is also instructive. Although it is written with a comparison between the brothers always in mind, the impression that it gives is of a more European prince, both in his faults and in his virtues. He was less well read than Baldwin, but he, too, liked to listen to the reading of history. It was he who pressed William of Tyre to write his history of the rulers of the East. The elders did not come to him for information, but he listened to them willingly if they knew the manners and customs of foreign countries. We form the impression, not of a well-trained mind, but certainly of an interesting personality, unpretentious, pertinacious, a little slow. The dedication to a short divinatory text which Haskins prints refers to Amalric as "unconquered, bounteous", soldier and patron to an astrologer who could guide him towards great successes in Egypt. This hardly differs from William of Tyre's estimate, and an astrologer professionally employed is advertising his own business, not delivering a general opinion. Amalric's was a lettered court, but with little pretension to be a centre of learning. William of Tyre, more disinterested than the astrologer, tells us that Amalric was not liberal with money, but that he showed generosity in another way, refusing to make those to whom he entrusted his business account for their stewardship; for some people, this confidence of his in his servants was a fault, for others it proved his good faith, that is, his loyalty to those whom he employed, certainly a chivalric quality. He would not listen to reports of infidelity to him. William admits that Amalric defended his meanness as necessary to the prosperity of the country, on which he spent what he took from the church and from his subjects. William seems only partly to accept this; it did not altogether square with the facts in some cases of which he knew, and in any case the right to tax the church was one of the European controversies of the day, one in which William was theoretically committed against the royal power. William lays stress on the royal manner.

> "He was more taciturn than is right, and was devoid of any great urbanity. He was almost wholly without the grace of affability which especially unites the hearts of subjects to their princes. He hardly ever spoke to anyone, unless he was forced to, or was spoken to first."

Like his brother, the King detested drunkenness and overeating. His court was not altogether bleak; he used to laugh loudly and with his whole body. Some relaxed social intercourse complemented the history readings and the serious discussions; no doubt it was needed in this little court, decimated by war and disease. With William, the King obviously had an easy relationship; William discreetly relates that the King "was said" to suffer from the lusts of the flesh, and *said* to have assailed the marriages of others, and he interjects, despite his 'saids', "which may God mercifully forgive him," an affectionate prayer. In all this, Amalric is judged largely by the chivalric ideal; manners are closely related to the duty of a prince, which is both to defend the kingdom, and to deal graciously with individuals.

The qualities which William of Tyre seems to be using to measure the monarchs are, certainly, prowess, and to some degree loyalty, largely but not wholly irrelevant in a king, certainly, too, *courtoisie* in the sense of *affabilitas*, and generosity, both of money and of spirit. All these come within the chivalric code. In addition, William tests them against a standard of seriousness which is characteristic of him: by their learning, appropriate to laymen, in literature and in the laws of the realm, and their seriousness of manner—he rates manner high in importance—together with the attention they waste on frivolous occupations. This standard may be thought personal, or perhaps clerical; but it may also reflect his awareness of the Arab gravity of manner which has often in the

Trophy of war from Acre, incorporated into a mosque in Cairo (p.209)

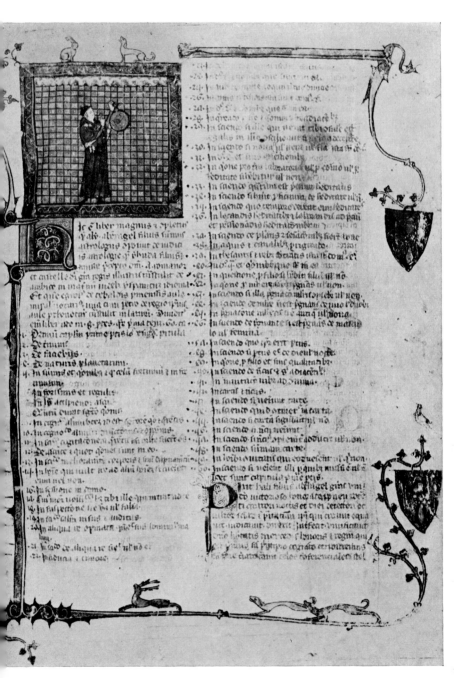

Arab astrology in Europe (p.288)

past been admired by Western observers. In William's sad little character sketch of his pupil, Baldwin the Leper, he uses these same standards, curiously modified by the extent to which they are inappropriate to a boy, and also by his obvious affection for Baldwin. William had taught him from the age of nine, because his father was very anxious about his education. His studies prospered, and he seemed to develop his natural abilities daily. Thirteen at his accession, he closely resembled his father physically. He was frugal, and remembered kindnesses and injuries alike. Quick by disposition, he was slow to find words, but loved discussions, and was an enthusiastic listener to histories, like his father, and blessed with a good memory. He was a better horseman than even his elders usually were. He was really obedient to good advice. Here are the same preoccupations in embryo. All this series of standards is homogeneous; they are secular, courtly, and fit well into the aristocratic ideals of chivalry, a little modified to allow for the duties of kings; and to these gravity must be added. On this evidence, suspicion remains, but we cannot assert positively, that William was influenced by Arab ideals. More confidently, we can say that his standards would be accepted by his Muslim contemporaries. There is nothing in them that is not European, but they are a selection of European ideals that are not peculiar to Europe, and all would suit the Arab World well. They are rarely explicitly Christian, and are never contrary to Christianity. They are at a level of behaviour where Islam and Christianity had never diverged.

3. East and West

The Latin kingdoms were unparalleled in western Europe. The existence of Jerusalem, the most contrived of all kingdoms, was at all times uncertain, however desperately it might be held for a time. Its institutions were theoretical and feudal; it could never hope to be more than a multi-racial conglomeration; nation building had never been possible. When we compare William of Malmesbury's royal character sketches with those of his namesake of Tyre, we realize that they had much in common. Malmesbury betrays a certain conflict between kingliness and state business; thus, of William the Conqueror: "he would say and do . . . almost anything unbecoming such great majesty, where the hope of money allured him;" there is an echo here of Tyre on Amalric.

Malmesbury despised the second William of England for his extravagance, content with a cheap article, if he was told it was expensive. The reputation of his generosity, however, "reached even to the East." The rulers of the Latin kingdom Malmesbury could only judge distantly, but, following Fulcher of Chartres, did so by practical standards: Baldwin I ruled "with less presumptuous haughtiness, but with great and consummate prudence." Malmesbury's ideal ruler was, of course, his own king Henry I of England, Plato's philosopher king, guided by the sweets of learning he had imbibed, his object "to spare the suppliant, but depress the proud." Here Malmesbury seems more the courtier than Tyre ever does. Seemliness and generosity are qualities common both to Tyre and to Malmesbury, as well as to the Arab World. Of the two, Malmesbury even seems sometimes the more conscious of the obligations and problems of a ruler, although he wrote with less knowledge, and seems himself to have avoided the great monastic offices. Tyre was long closely connected with the court, and his personal portraits are naturally more intimate. His standards may insensibly have begun to diverge from those prevailing in the West, but, if so, it is a matter of only a slight emphasis in the qualities which most interest him; and William of Malmesbury shows that at the other end of Europe there was no marked difference of approach, at least in an earlier generation (Malmesbury died when Tyre was a boy). Another comparison that we can make is between William of Tyre and his contemporaries, Gerald of Wales and Walter Map. These two were also courtiers, and could write of Henry II of England with some personal knowledge, though not with the intimacy that William of Tyre enjoyed with his kings. At the English Angevin court we have moved into a new world where the traditional virtues are not at the centre of interest. If the comparison seems to show new tendencies in the West, where Henry tolerated rather than admitted chivalry, the chivalric virtues would continue to be admired in England long after Henry died.

We can compare Latin Europeans of West and East in the person of King Fulk, who came from Anjou relatively late in life into the society of the Latin East. William of Tyre once again draws a king's character carefully.

"Fulk was a red-headed man . . . faithful, gentle and, contrary to the rules for a man of his colour, courteous, kindly and merciful; he was completely free in the works of piety and the bestowing of

alms; . . . he was very experienced in military matters, patient in
the sweats of war, and very far-seeing."

All these are explicitly virtues with which we are told to contrast
the defects which he like other mortals showed—among them,

> "he had such a feeble, weak memory, that he could not remember
> the names of his own servants, nor did he recognize faces, except of
> a few people; so that, if someone whom just a little while before he
> had been paying the highest honour and favouring with familiarity
> presented himself again, he would earnestly ask who he might be."

This is very nearly the portrait of a clown, and Fulk's fault seems
an offence both against dignity and against urbanity. A good
soldier and a good family man, a little like King Mark in *Tristan*,
he was something less than the ideal king. His defects reduced his
professional competence, but were also a falling short from an
inherent ideal of kingliness as the centre as well as the source of
court life. Fulk's personality is his own, not specifically Western
or un-Western, but the standards by which he is being judged
are the same as William judged Fulk's sons by. They are simply
characteristic of William of Tyre.

There are two rulers from western Europe who may be judged
in their dealings with the Arabs. Surely Louis IX's outstanding
characteristic as Joinville sees him is his sense of honour in
dealing with his Egyptian captors; they must not be cheated, and
they must be trusted to keep their own word, as the King insisted
his own must be. With this goes a certain integrity which verged
upon disdain; the King thought it beneath his rank to buy his
freedom with money (as distinct from letting go the city of Damietta); Joinville understood that this refusal to haggle appealed to
the young sultan, Turan Shah, as generosity. After their release,
Joinville advised the King to stay in Acre, because he must not
desert the prisoners left in Egypt. When the King announced his
decision, he gave as his reason the safety of what remained of the
Latin East, but he continued to negotiate for the prisoners,
especially the children. The King's accessibility, which is close to
Arab practice, Joinville tells in a purely French context. There
were things about the king that did not seem common sense to
Joinville: his extravagant love for his mother, his detachment from
his wife and children, his insistence on taking part in chores,
especially indulgenced chores, carrying earth to the fortifications
and the dead to burial. Much of this seemed saintly, but not all of

it kingly. There is a good deal about the king's generosity, in the employment of Joinville himself, for example, or in fortifying Jaffa, but this is always well-spent money with a certain stress on economic use. Louis had all the gravity that William of Tyre could have wished, but Joinville seems to hanker after a less rational chivalry, the extravagant gifts of the gambling Count of Poitiers, or the exploit of the Count of Jaffa, when he captured a rich caravan of cloth and distributed all the spoil to his knights; the count was impetuous in attack, pious, but unimpressed by patriarchal excommunication for holding a tower in the city which belonged to the patriarchate; he prayed for long in his chapel before spending the night with his wife; he died a prisoner, martyred for his religion but also by the malice of the Cairene merchants who had never forgiven his earlier plundering their property. He had set his arms between the five hundred battlements of his castle, *d'or a une croix de gueles patée*, a beautiful sight, says Joinville. There is an absence of magnificence in the life of Louis IX, and it makes even his admiring biographer draw less saintly characters in an attractive contrast. Louis commanded affection that remained critical. Joinville himself made piety serve prudence, and the king covered France with his pious benefactions. Yet in his prudential aspect King Louis was not necessarily unlike the Arab rulers, still less the Mamelukes; but Joinville himself would have made the better Arab.

Sixty years earlier, Richard of England was served by no Joinville, and he himself was no Louis. There are aspects of his legend which are clear and relevant to our enquiry. The *Itinerarium* of King Richard records an acute but ambiguous episode of legend-making by Bishop Hubert of Salisbury, when he went with the third group of pilgrims to Jerusalem, after the peace was made, and was entertained honourably, like other notables, by Salah ad-Din. Saladin asks about the character of King Richard, and about what the Christians think of the Arabs. The Bishop records no reply to the second request; perhaps diplomatically silent, not necessarily so. Of Richard he replied, or wished to be known to have replied, that he had no equal, in the business of war, or in his outstanding courage or his generosity in giving. He suggested that if Richard and Saladin could share a combination of their two characters, there would be no two princes in the world to touch them. Here is a criticism of both. Saladin replies that Richard's courage and daring are well known to the Arabs, his prodigality in risking his life; but for himself he prefers to be endowed with wisdom and moderation, rather than with immoderate daring, and would say so wherever and however he held power: in saying so he took up what the Bishop already implied, that they shared standards of judgement. If Saladin wants to modify prowess by wisdom, he takes largesse for granted (the word is specific, *largitas*). Accessibility with Richard is not quite the same as it would later be with Louis IX; Richard's is a public gesture which may as easily turn into anger, and he is always conscious of the effect he is creating; in Louis we have the steady wisdom which Saladin admired, and a set intention to do justice well. Accessibility in one form or another is common to all, to Richard, Louis, Salah ad-Din, the great Ayyubids, and the lesser Arab rulers, to Fulk and Baldwin and Amalric, to every ruler of the day; and it is certainly normal (as it has remained) in any Arab ruler or official. With Richard the stress on prowess was so great that it lasted into later legend. Arabs would explain the occasional casual shying of a horse by joking that the King of England did it; and they would use Richard as a threat to silence a crying child. So Joinville tells us, long afterwards, and Ernoul recounts the same; it was at least a Frankish legend about an Arab legend. Sometimes English writers rather overdo the extent to which Saladin or his brother, al-Adil, respected Richard. In Richard of Devizes we read a curious account of al-Adil's visit to the King of England. He speaks without dignity; even a remote verisimilitude is inconceivable. He sounds more like an inferior dragoman or even a tout who revenges the humiliation of his position by talking with his tongue in his cheek. Even so, there is criticism once again of Richard's rashness. The king is ill:

"O God of the Christians, if God thou be, thou shalt not suffer such a man to die, as necessary to thy people as he is hasty . . . this Richard whom I love so much, and yet fear . . ."

Through the unction appears clearly the need for moderation which is a new element in the concept of prowess. In the last resort, European opinion, or the opinion of Richard's more chivalric subjects, was that only his unexpected death prevented his achieving a greater crusade and even a kind of world rule:

> *E l'onor e la seingnorie*
> *De Sarrazins, de Crestiens*
> *E de toz homes terriens.*

Even Richard's legend concedes the limitations of the purely chivalric element in kingship, but such a recognition does not distinguish feudal Europe from the Fatimid, Ayyubid or Mameluke Arab World. If the ideals were similar, so was the practical good sense. I do not know how seriously William the Marshal thought that Richard might have ruled the world, but clearly he could envisage one world where one king ruled Arabs and Europeans alike. Any juxtaposition of the two cultures that we identify may reveal similarities of approach, in spite of the years of warfare and separation. European monarchs who come to the East take their natural place there. The chivalrous aspect of European tradition blended particularly well into the situation in the East, especially with William of Tyre's characteristic addition of the quality of gravity. Chivalry and gravity combine to stress that side of Europe which remained closest in its development to the Arab World. A religious aristocrat in Europe might come close in spirit to the good Arab leader; even with his faults, Louis was wholly intelligible in Arab terms; Richard too, though he lacked seriousness. In the twelfth century similarities in the way of life encouraged similar attitudes to develop; in the thirteenth century this was still largely true, but they would disappear again, as gradually the two cultures turned again into different paths.

4. Arab rulers through European eyes

William of Tyre naturally does not, because he cannot, describe the characters of Muslim leaders as he did those of Latin kings. Some of his references are minimal. He quotes as apposite—but not as his own—a couplet on Zangi, at his death, punning on his name, as *sanguineus*; a close enough pun, and perhaps commonly made, since the usual Latin for Zangi was *Sanguinus*. Nur ad-Din, the son of Zangi, at his father's death and at his own, Tyre praises specifically because he was a religious man "according to the traditions of his nation" and (the first time) "fearing God, according to the superstitious traditions of that people;" he says, too, that he was "lucky", which may hint at divine favour. He was "far-seeing and discerning" and again "far-seeing and subtle;" and he was "a just prince". In these few words there is not much to build up the concept of a king, but enough to show that William took for granted that similar standards would apply across the cultural barrier, although now he was observing from outside and far off, not, as before, intimately from inside. This appears even more clearly in the description of Nur ad-Din's general and Salah ad-Din's uncle, Shirkuh, the ultimate conqueror of Egypt:

> "a hard-working man and prompt in arms, generous beyond the means of his inheritance, zealous for glory, and highly experienced in soldiering, loved and favoured by the soldiers by means of his munificence . . . He was a man now getting on in age, insignificant in stature, even squat and somewhat corpulent . . . and, by the support of his merits, he was raised up from a low status to that of prince . . . extremely patient in his work, he would bear thirst and hunger unmoved, beyond what his age can normally sustain."

Here we have again prowess and largesse, and the natural nobility which a man can achieve—like William the Marshal, later, in the West—by his own exertions.

The most complex legend is that of Saladin, whom William called at his accession to power "a man of acute genius, prompt in arms, and liberal above average;" the two familiar qualities, at once knightly and royal, and the additional realistic assessment that recognizes efficiency. Salah ad-Din's own biographer summarized his virtues under the headings of love of justice, generosity, courage (or prowess), zeal for the religious struggle, his patience before God, his kindness and his affability and courtesy, and almost conventionality, in the modern sense. These are all virtues parallel to those which earlier Latin writers had liked to see in their own kings, and they are close to the virtues which the Latins themselves recognized in this Muslim character of singular integrity. His impact on Western literature was quick. His celebrated letter to the Emperor Frederick emphasizes the power of the Muslims, and their numbers and their interior lines of communication, and what may be a reference to the Dar al-Islam, *residuum regnum Saracenorum*. The "caliph of Baghdad, whom God preserve" will come to his aid. Here Saladin is still a mouthpiece of Islam in general, and this was only the beginning of his reputation as the great conqueror. For English contemporaries Richard enters the life of Saladin as his peer. With this is the subordinate legend of al-Adil Sayf ad-Din, "*vir eximiae liberalitatis*," and Richard's personal friend; but, once any of the accounts of the Third Crusade get under way, they are naturally dominated by the figure of Salah. The name of Saladin resounded from his victories. The tenth levied by Henry II of England for the support of

Jerusalem became known as the Saladin tithe. In the *Gesta Regis Ricardi* Salah is accused of killing prisoners, but this is to justify Richard's own murder of the hostages. Exchange of presents is a shared convention, courtly, but not only courtly. It seems to be offered as counterpoint to the exchange of murders. If the killing of the Arab prisoners is represented as a political demonstration in front of Saladin, their disembowelling for the coins they had swallowed, now a usual practice, and the drying of their gall for medical purposes, are offered without comment. An Italian condemned Richard outright for killing "contrary to divine and human law" prisoners who should have been made slaves. In the English sources Saladin lacks the *liberalitas* usually attributed to him, perhaps to obscure the real courtly defects of Richard. Saladin is early seen as punctilious, but when the Turks want to kill the pilgrims, the case for honourably observing the treaties has to be argued before him, and it is characteristic of the English chroniclers to report that the custody of the Christians is then given to al-Adil. A later French romanticized history gave much space to Richard's many adventures, but reserved to Saladin an incognito visit to test the charity of the Acre Hospital, which he then endowed with Egyptian rents.

The authentic legend of Saladin's greatness of heart was local, and largely a memory of his generous treatment of the Christians after the capture of Jerusalem. Whereas propaganda in and for Europe concentrated on the destruction of the churches and their crosses, local Christian history remembered the ransoming of the poor of the city, first by al-Adil, who begged a thousand slaves as his booty and freed them, then by the Patriarch and Balian d'Ibelin, and finally by Salah himself. The release of the widows and unprotected women, gentry, not poor people—and even of their husbands and fathers, with gifts of money for the widows, was recognized as *une grant courtoisie*. The Sultan had already received the surrender of the Countess of Tripoli, and sent her away freely and with every honour. In Alexandria, the Arab governor protected Christian refugees from the rapacity of Italian merchants "in order to keep faith with Saladin, and for God." Famous everywhere was the scene in Saladin's tent after the Horns of Hattin, a battle lost by thirst. The Sultan gave King Guy cold water, and he passed it on, after drinking, to Raynald of Chatillon, who had broken the sworn truces. The Sultan insisted that the King, not he, gave the drink; he wanted to preserve his freedom from obligation. The moment passed into European folklore; as Salimbene put it succinctly: Raynald the criminal was beheaded with Saladin's sword. This action seems to have had general European approval. It was so familiar that Joinville hopefully quoted Saladin as his authority when he sent to remonstrate with a group of Arabs who were killing Franks they had earlier fed. Joinville also quoted Saladin for the dictum that a bad Christian will never become a good Muslim, and even vice versa. Finally Salah ad-Din passed into European legend as the satirical critic of European morals, and even as the good man who sought to test the truth of Christianity by its Christian practice, and found it wanting. This was a favourite device of moralists, but, as he became a figure of Christian homiletic, he dropped out of sight as a model of the *courtois* king, until Sir Walter Scott restored him.

Among the most interesting assessments of a Muslim ruler to compare are those which Ibn an-Nafis and William of Tripoli make of Baybars al-Bunduqdari. Baybars, one of the greatest of the Bahri Mamelukes in the estimation of both writers, passes quite outside the chivalric categories. He was a practical soldier and ruler who could not afford and had no desire to cultivate personal qualities beyond the severest necessities. Both authors are scholars, Ibn an-Nafis a practising court physician of considerable intellectual range, William of Tripoli a religious of sometimes eccentric views but real originality. Baybars is described by his doctor under the guise of the ideal ruler, in the most practical terms: courageous, cruel and merciless are his first qualities; tough, harsh, active, not sleeping long, or eating heavily or greatly given to sexual intercourse, disliking tasteless food and fond of fruit. He is above all active in fighting, and always on the move because of it. In this account, of the chivalric qualities only prowess survives. Some of Ibn an-Nafis' judgements of a just society must also echo conditions under Baybars, the necessity for increasing the army and therefore for increasing taxes to support it; the necessity for industry in a society which can exempt only the sick from useful effort for the common advantage; the need for order in family as well as state. The writer is conscious in particular of two weaknesses in the practice of the Muslim community, transgression of the prohibition of wine, and an increase in homosexuality, which is wrong (he says) in male or female, because it inhibits progeny, and in men it is characteristic of those who are evil and dissolute. He speaks of the punishment appropriate to fornication and adultery and drinking wine. Some of these points find an echo in the attitude of William of Tripoli, whom one would have expected only to see Baybars as a great conqueror, on whose good-will, he did indeed point out, the poor remnants of the Latin kingdom must depend. Tripoli writes of Baybars's drastic punishments and executions, of his severity and secrecy and the rapidity of his movements. "He detests and hates wine and prostitutes," says Tripoli, because these "make strong men silly and effeminate them," and so for five years past "no brothel with its prostitutes has been found in the land which is subject to him, and no one dares to drink wine, except secretly." He prefers a few soldiers "chaste and sober" to many funded on the profits from taxing wine and prostitution—though in fact Baybars greatly increased the army, and found ample means to raise unpopular taxes. He approves marriage, says Tripoli, and has four wives, of whom the fourth, a Christian, he takes about with him everywhere. "He disapproves of having concubines, and condemns the sin against nature." He despised the Christians of his own day because they were faithless and vicious, weak and contemptible and unlike their own ancestors. Tripoli, in many respects unique among Christian writers, can use the word 'cruelty' of the execution of a Muslim, and not just a Muslim, but a religious Muslim, even a Muslim of false religion, judged by Muslim standards, and a persecutor of Christians and Jews. This picture of Baybars, tough and cruel, exacting to himself and his people, strict about sexual matters and the drinking of wine and public decency generally, corresponds closely to the more intimate picture which his own Arab physician draws. An intimate Muslim image and an external Christian image of the same man could so closely coincide only within a common framework of opinion.

Nothing so explicit occurs in the little book *On the Recovery of the Holy Land* written by Fidenzio of Padua a little later, but this too has some interesting aspects. Unfortunately it is not clear whom he means by 'the Sultan'. Sometimes he says 'Bendocdar'— i.e. Baybars—and sometimes just *soldanus*. He may mean Baybars, who had not been so very long dead when Fidenzio wrote, but he refers to him as Sultan at the capture of Tripoli, and this was in fact twelve years after his death, and the Sultan then was Qalaun. We do not know if the mistake is the reference to the town captured, as Tripoli, or to the Sultan as Baybars; probably he means

Qalaun. His references to "the Sultan" are part of his description of the Arab enemy state in general, and this helps define his image of the ruler. 'Saracens' despise the Christians for being unwarlike, not only those of Oriental rite, who might have little reason to care, but also Latins, who "dare not fight manfully . . . but rather basely and contemptibly turn their backs;" many in a group let a single Saracen kill them, and the Sultan could only comment on their inconsistency at the siege of Tripoli: "You are extremely silly and short-sighted, because you do not know when to fight, and you do not know when to make peace, and you do not know the right time to run away." One sultan had said to the Christians that whereas he was a serpent with a single head, whose tails followed, they were a serpent with many heads, and scarcely a tail to follow them all. Much of what Fidenzio says is current clerical doctrine about Muslims, rather than actual observation: cruelty especially is for him, in the traditional way, a quality that can only be exercised against Christians, and the usual cruelties on both sides are specifically levied as accusations against Muslims alone. Most of what is said of the sexual morals of the Arabs is similarly an expression of Christian doctrine, an attack on *sharia* law which we must assess as theoretical. Fidenzio accuses Baybars of a breach of faith in killing the Templar defenders of Safet, though what happened exactly is obscure. He calls the capture of Jaffa a similar breach of truce, but goes on to tell a story with a different moral. Some of the defenders could not afford the extortionate rates demanded by Christian ship-owners to evacuate them. Baybars "although he was an unbeliever and evil, must have had a certain piety, and loved to do justice on others, saying, 'Curse these people, they are the worst sort, because, being Christians, they want to cut other Christians off.' " He sent the victims safely overland by camel. Again, a Jaffa mother complained to Baybars that one of his amirs had raped her beautiful daughter. The Sultan asked if she knew his name, and, finding that she did not, arranged an identity parade; the mother recognized the culprit, and the sultan had him beheaded publicly on the spot. Fidenzio is a heartily hostile witness, but in Arab or Frank he admires toughness and, behind the 'doctrinal' accusations of depravity and cruelty, recognizes a single standard of decency and law. Fidenzio describes his perfect leader, stressing that there must be a single head; he is not drawn from an actual figure, but from abstract ideals. He should be powerful—held in reverence and fear by his followers—and decent—not voluptuous, or gluttonous or vicious; he should be outstanding in wisdom, and impeccable in his justice. He must be a man of courage and spirit—like the Maccabees, adding wisdom to these, like Solomon. He must be generous, as Aristotle recommended to Alexander (in the *Secreta*). He must watch over the people of God tirelessly. He must be gentle, so as to be able to converse pacifically with men; it is the meek who will inherit the earth; he will not be rancorous or angry, but will maintain equanimity. He will be stable and firm in the good. Thus the practical ideal, the captain, statesman and war-leader, retains some of the chivalric virtues, indomitability and prowess, of course, and also largesse. The standard is certainly still close to the Arab standard. These qualities seem to be compounded out of the virtues of the successful Muslim leaders or a negative of the faults and failures of contemporary Christians.

The difference between ordinary life in Arab and in Frankish society, then, was probably less than the difference which develops in a single country today in the course of twenty years. If we admit that between Arab and Frankish courts there were differences of culture, it was not in the wider sociological sense, but in the narrower sense of the precise intellectual content and form of their thinking. They were divided in language, in literature, and in religion; in the first two cases there was all but total separation. In the case of religion, it was less that the two beliefs were different than that each set up a barrier of intolerance, which effectively prevented the conscious passage of most ideas. The attitudes of secular life and in particular the practical ideals of government offer the chief exception, because they derived from the way men lived, governed, and fought, in much the same conditions. Even when the style and methods of fighting were different, Joinville took it for granted that the concept of honour was the same; God would protect Arabs, too, from "*vilain reproche*". Ernoul took for granted Arab dubbing of knights, a shared institution. Arab heraldry was aristocratic, like its European counterpart, but it was less formalized and regulated. Yet it was not perceived by Europeans to be different, as Joinville again bears witness. Nor was there any great technological gap to parallel the intellectual chasm. Admittedly, the Arab World always seemed remote. Professional troubadours included in their repertory the Old Man of the Mountain—the Sheikh al-Jebel of the Assassins—between Charlemagne and the Fisher King. Yet in what they thought about their rulers and in assessing how their rulers should act, and in the standards by which they judged them, certainly Arabs and Europeans at this date thought and felt in parallel. There is room for a much more detailed study, but even the most superficial examination reveals a clear broad area of agreement.

Chapter 8

Adaptation and development in the Latin East

1. The link with the Arab World

After the passage which begins, "We who were Westerners have now become Orientals" (already quoted), Fulcher approaches the end of his story:

> "Now we have forgotten the places of our birth; for many of us now they are unknown, not even mentioned. One man possesses his own homes and estates, as if by hereditary right from his father; the next, in fact, has married not merely a compatriot, but a Syrian or Armenian, or sometimes a Muslim who has obtained the grace of baptism. A third is living with a daughter-in-law or son-in-law, and a stepson, if not a stepfather; nor is he without grandson or great-grandson. This man has got hold of vineyards, that one of tillage. Different languages are used together, whether correctly or colloquially."

There seems to be nothing here beyond the intrusion of alien elements in a population which had absorbed innumerable intrusions throughout the millennia. It is always taken for granted that the Latins retained their identity only because they were constantly reinforced from Europe; possibly the existence of an independent state was more important; certainly no Latin community survived after the last government fell at Acre in 1290. Such identity as the literate of the Latin states possessed was clerical, in Latin, and aristocratic, administrative and legal, often in French. It is this narrow, and in a sense fictional, identity, that we have here to consider, if we want to measure the tenuous link with the Arab World.

Even before the 'pilgrims' captured Jerusalem in 1099, they had begun to form easier relationships with the petty courts of Muslim Syria than with the more exigent power of Byzantium. An early sign of this comes in the surrender of the citadel of Antioch, after the defeat of Kerbogha. Ahmed ibn Marwan, the commander, seeing the defeat of the Muslims, accepted a Frankish banner, but some Lombards told him that this was not Bohemund's. "He asked them, whose is it? They said, 'The count of St Gilles'." He came up and took the banner and returned it to the count, and at that very moment the noble Bohemund arrived and gave him his own banner." Historians point out that this implies a previous agreement with Bohemund. "Not many days after, the amir was baptized (*baptizatus est ammiralius*) with those who chose to accept Christ; but the lord Bohemund caused those who wished to stick to their own religion to be escorted to Muslim territory." This also looks like the observance of a previous secret agreement. Our source here is the *Gesta*, and the author may mean to contrast the behaviour of the expedition under Raymund Pilet, which "killed those who would not accept Christianity." If so, he approved Bohemund's attitude; we know that Bohemund used this text to advertise himself and the cause of the principality of Antioch in Europe, and presumably he saw no harm in a public record of tolerance during the war.

The Count of St Gilles, before he finally set out for Jerusalem, had already dabbled, sometimes hesitantly, in the possibility of alliances with Muslims. The family of the sons of Munqidh, who held Shaizar, one of whom, Usama, is famous for his recollections in old age of Frankish behaviour, already at this early date sent a message to the count, offering a pledge in money, a promise to help pilgrims and trade in horses and food supplies. The pilgrim army found a large stock of cattle which they sold in Shaizar and Hama; the Arab garrison swore on their religion not to harm pilgrims. At Homs the king made a similar agreement, and at Tripoli the ruler offered a full treaty which the count refused, unless the ruler became a Christian. In spite of his reservations, however, it is obvious that at this very early stage, even the conscientious Count of St Gilles was becoming involved in the possibilities of taking part in Muslim politics. Even earlier, Godfrey had helped the ruler of Azaz against Ridwan, the atabeg of Mosul, in somewhat quaint circumstances, because the ruler was put up to inviting Godfrey by a Turk in his following who was in love with a prisoner, the widow of a Frankish knight. The initiative was presumably the lady's. Baldwin in his county of Edessa had already set an example of associating with Muslims by allowing Islamic worship at Saruj; he could not otherwise have held the town, but the fact is that he allowed it. The advantages of toleration were clear to the leaders by the time they captured Jerusalem; hence came Tancred's anger that his banner was not held sacred when the population was massacred in the Temple. Raymund, on the other hand, whose safe conduct to the troops in the Tower of David proved effective, gained an obvious advantage; Godfrey would not allow him to utilize it, when the garrisons at Ascalon and Arsuf offered to surrender to him alone. By the time the original expedition had achieved its purpose, the ruling class, at least, had already learned to accept the existence of Islam. So had those who were close to them; Fulcher recorded with pride the sorrow at the death of his patron, Baldwin I. "The Franks wept, the Arab Christians mourned, and so did the Muslims who saw it."

The motivation of other classes was probably more varied. We receive occasional illumination. In the difficult period between the capture of Antioch city and the defeat of Kerbogha, Christ told the visionary, Stephen, "I sent you safe and sound into the city, and there you are, greatly occupied in illicit love with Christian women, and with loose Muslim women, whence a vast stench ascends to Heaven." This was no doubt the first opportunity that ordinary men in the army had of settling in. The suggestion that only loose Muslim women (*pravae paganae mulieres*), but any Christian women, would make love may be unintentional, but may reflect the difference between citizens and camp-followers, as well as the strict seclusion of Muslims. Fulcher has a curious statement of something that happened when Kerbogha's broken army was being pursued; it implies an acceptance of Muslims as moral human beings. He says that the Frankish pursuers found women in the tents of the enemy and "did no harm to them, except that they stabbed them in their stomachs with their lances." This can only mean that they were not submitted to a fate that he literally takes to be worse than death; and surely he must mean that they as well as he would so consider it?

Yet over the first century of the Latin kingdom, we can never say that recognition of a common morality is explicit; international law was the achievement of custom and necessity. The truces were not always kept, yet each broken truce is remarked as such. Raynald de Chatillon, with his raid on the Red Sea coast and his plans to destroy Mecca, always appears more or less grotesque, and seemed so to his contemporaries. Truces which caravans would trust imply, not only a valid international law, but also popular sentiment in support of it. There are many examples; another almost equally famous is Amalric's insistence, against the will and in the teeth of the Grand Master, on the arrest of the Templar responsible for the murder of the Assassin envoy. When William of Tyre tells us that the Lord withdrew his protection from Amalric's third expedition against Egypt, it is because Amalric's motive was profit. He hoped to be bought off. He was cruel to the people of Bilbais as part of an act of blackmail. Perhaps William was not thinking more than that Amalric's motives were worldly, and nothing to do with the holy war; but even this presupposes the notion that God will punish a secular war and unnecessary bloodshed, even when the victims are infidels. William shows that God did punish the Latins; the treasures of Egypt were no longer at their disposal, Egyptian trade no longer plied across free seas. This assumption of a common humanity was never more than partly explicit. Those who seemed on good terms with the enemy, or just negotiated with him, were always liable to criticism, a Raymund of Tripoli among the lords of the country, a Richard of England or Emperor Frederick among the outsiders. Many Latins of less exalted status married into the families of Christians of the country, and some married Muslims who were willing to conform to Latin Christianity; but apart from the few descriptions of the *Pullani*, the offspring of these marriages, their history is unremembered.

From the memoirs of Usama ibn Munqidh it is evident that there was friendly intercourse between Franks and Arabs from the first, which would pass almost unguessed from our Frankish sources. The latter were too self-conscious, or too ashamed to admit it, or just too indifferent to think it worth mentioning. Much Frankish custom seemed strange or even absurd to Usama, but it is equally clear, from his text, and from common sense, that the horse, and the sports of war and hunting, ensured that there was much common ground from the beginning. As the crusading army travelled south, says Albert of Aix, all the leaders and Godfrey himself were so attracted by the beauty of the surroundings that they decided to treat themselves to the pleasures of hunting, a recreation "in which the nobility take particular delight." This was as true of the Arab princes of Syria as of the House of Lorraine. Syria's reputation would spread, until a later pope must discourage Crusaders from setting out for the East with their hawks and dogs. Franks and Arabs were divided by religion, law, language, and the awareness of different origins, not by the business of everyday life. There were variations in equipment and technique, but what gave knightly service its value was the cost of horses and equipment, and the long training and experience needed to acquire the skills of fighting on horseback.

We hear more often than might be expected of Christians who pass into the Muslim camp, though rarely of those who do so entirely of their own free choice. Chroniclers recall the fate of distinguished prisoners, but their case was exceptional in every way. Robert of St Albans, a Templar, whose reasons for leaving his order and his faith are obscure, made sufficient stir in England for chroniclers to mention the episode, and to add that he offered Salah ad-Din to capture and hand over Jerusalem. He was understood to have married into the family of the Sultan. Probably conversions to Islam occurred more often than we should suppose from the silence of the sources; there are many reasons for conversion, good and bad. Through all the history of Christian relations with Islam, at least until the imperial period, Christians would insist upon the material gains that conversion to Islam would offer, no doubt because it was polemically the best way to explain why it should occur at all. In fact we do not hear of converted Franks who rise to positions of much eminence in the Arab World, in contrast to the legends which characterized Barbary Coast conversions in the seventeenth century. From time to time we hear of the baptism of Muslims, without being told anything about their later fortunes among the Christians. It seems unlikely that they were honoured or endowed to an extent that would sufficiently reward the penalties of conversion, or that the sight of defectors would encourage the Franks to defect. On both sides, the penalty of apostasy was a total break with former coreligionists. Louis IX, we shall see below, would not speak to a converted Christian, and the underlying assumption of the story of King John's mission to the King of Morocco was contempt for the '*exlex*'.

It was generally accepted that capture in war was likely to lead to conversion, and the stories of those who refused to become Muslims leave us free to suppose that there were others who did not. In the case of Kerbogha's offer to the First Crusade, he was said to have promised to give land to those who would become Muslims, and to make foot-men knights. Clearly the latter stood to benefit most. The writer of the *Gesta* was himself a soldier, a poor knight who held, not, certainly, a proletarian view, but not that of the most privileged either. He recognized the temptation to enter as a valued professional into a new society; but the fate of those who had surrendered at Xerigordo, said to have been sold as slaves all over the Arab World, would have deterred him, if he had not been a sincere Christian. The distinction in Islamic law between the free man who embraces Islam, or submits when required, and the prisoner who had forfeited his claim to freedom when he determined to fight was apparently not yet understood. Odo of Deuil, like most Latins, hated Greeks and expressly contrasted the humanity of Turks: when two large troops of several thousand Franks of the Second Crusade were caught in retreat between two rivers and cut to pieces, the survivors found that those who were healthy were forced into service by the Greeks who beat them, but the sick and the poor were given alms by the Turks; while the Turks were liberal to the impoverished, the Greeks robbed those who still retained possessions; and three thousand young Franks rode off with the Turkish army, which had shown them kindness. "O kindness more cruel than any treason, in giving them bread they took away their faith—though it is certain that, because the Turks were content with service, they forced nobody to deny his religion."

There was a special interest in the fate of women prisoners, especially at the beginning and the end of the crusading period. To appeal to the reading public, Albert of Aix collected many tales not in his written sources. Most of his tales are distinctly lugubrious. There is the young archdeacon, Adalbero, of royal blood, who went with a lady "of much frankness and beauty" to play dice in an apple-orchard, during the siege of Antioch; they took umpires along with them, but Frankish freedom of behaviour would never be understood in the East. The party were surprised by the enemy, the young man quickly beheaded, and the woman also, after being raped. Capture was not normally fatal. Several groups of women among the ill-fated reinforcements that came out after the news of the capture of Jerusalem reached Europe were surprised by the enemy. On one occasion more than a thousand "tender and dearest wives", deserted by their husbands, "noblest women and distinguished ladies, French as well as Italian" were carried off in chains "like dumb cattle" into Corrazan, "to barbarian nations and an unknown language", whence there was no escape, except with permission. The camp echoed with the ululation of the mourning of these "charming ladies"; some were abused by illicit sexual union, and finally beheaded, and only those "with a lively countenance and a handsome appearance" were carried off. Albert had a genuine, imaginative understanding of the sorrows of the bereaved women "carried off by stern enemies to an unknown and alien land." Yet he also knew that some had quite happy experiences. There was the captured wife of a European knight, for whom one of the Turkish knights "burned with immoderate love" and whom he married. There was also the nun of Saint Mary's convent at Trier, who had been with Peter the Hermit's party, not altogether a recommendation for steady character, had been captured and subjected to "oppression by very wicked men"—"unwilling illicit copulation"; restored to the army when Nicea was recaptured, she was relieved of penance in the circumstances and absolved by the Legate. However, in some cases of rape sympathy was wasted. The nun had a Turkish lover, who sent an agent to say he could not live without her, would even become a Christian for her, and asked her to return to his "illicit and incestuous beds". She slipped away in the night, and in the morning they found her gone, "for no other reason than that she could not withstand desire."

When the last cities of the coast fell in the thirteenth century, it was taken for granted that the captives would pass into Islam, and not by compulsion so much as by inevitable attraction and absorption. Sometimes it is assumed that converts specially hate their former faith, as in a description of the fall of Acre, given by a Greek monk who was visiting the papal court; it is possible that he was jeering at Frankish loyalty. Ricoldo da Monte Croce, when he reached Baghdad at the end of his long tour into Middle Asia, claims to have talked to a nun "worthy of belief" who had been captured at Acre. According to him, it was especially the nuns who were taken as concubines, to rear up many sons, and increase the Muslim nation. It happened to lay women too, but nuns were most in demand, because, says Ricoldo, experience shows that they breed the most powerful and warlike men, from whom "leaders and sultans" are made, and those most hostile to Christians. This is a little less grotesque than it sounds. The fate of those dedicated to the service of the church naturally preoccupied him.

"Others in fact were sold and separated and given to actors, so that these might lead them round the world to the ignominy of Christians ... Why did it please (Jesus Christ) that nuns and virgins should be compelled to be actresses and wander about the world, rather than sing to God in the convent ...?"

In North Africa prisoners remained accessible; in Asia they might be lost to Europe for ever. Within Palestine in the twelfth century there was more free movement. Margaret of Beverley and "of Jerusalem", born of a pregnant pilgrim, returned alone to the country of her birth, fought against Saladin at the siege of Jerusalem, was twice enslaved and ransomed, suffered famine and robbery, was saved by the name of Mary from being executed for theft by the Arab army; and her book of psalms was returned to her by a repentant 'Parthian' robber. Her brother was a protégé of Becket's who became a Cistercian; she too renounced the world, though her rough world hardly seems enticing. This wandering literate family, freed from ties by pilgrimage, exemplifies the chances of passing between different worlds.

It seems that there was bilingual communication between Arabs and Franks, but it has left almost no record at all, and must often have been oral, though there are incidental references in most of our sources to Franks who spoke and even wrote Arabic. It seems to have been the product of natural commerce with Arabs, but not often utilized for an enduring purpose. For example, the English with Richard I were impressed by Bernard, "the King's spy", who went with two others who were natives of the country; they were dressed in "Arab clothes which came from Egypt," and "really they in no way differed from the appearance of Arabs." No one spoke the Arabic language better. For giving the King intelligence of a caravan from Cairo the three were paid a hundred silver marks. This is in contrast to the nearly complete failure to produce translations of Arabic books, even such as had the most mundane and utilitarian value.

It is really astonishing that the crusading states produced so little literary interchange, much less than the Spanish Reconquest, not more than Norman rule in Sicily. Two translations originate in the East, Stephen of Antioch's medical texts of Ali ibn al-Abbas al-Majusi, and Philip of Tripoli's widely read *Secreta Secretorum*. Yet there was no school of translation. There was anti-Islamic polemic, and a little appreciation of Muslims. Ricoldo da Monte Croce admired their practical virtues, and especially their love for one another. Yet Muslims, though quite as harmonious as Christians, do not and did not live up to this extreme and unexpected encomium. We shall soon see reason to doubt William of Tripoli's understanding of Arabs. Although William of Tyre is the most considerable original author of the Latin states his lost history of the oriental princes may well have depended even more than he admitted on hostile oriental Christian sources; judging by his extant masterpiece, we cannot expect there to have been a deep understanding of Arab culture or Muslim society. He knew contemporary politics, but we look in vain for any interest in Arabic literary or scientific achievements, or for any knowledge of Islam beyond the legends which were the currency of the ordinary man of his time. William of Tyre is a Latin author, with no real root in any other culture; he liked the Byzantines, but was unfamiliar with Greek or Greek patristic literature. As far as the evidence goes, many contemporary Englishmen knew more about Arabic scientific sources. In this he seems wholly representative of the Latin East. The East was too far from the centres of Latin literacy to develop schools in parallel with contemporary schools in the West, and so did not share European interest in Arabic sources.

There was also a false link, a 'non-link', with the Arabs in the pleasure which European writers, both in the East and in the West, took in the high flowery style which Arabic lends to any European translation. Histories sometimes gave to oriental characters an imaginary, quaint style of talk supposedly suitable for Orientals. This was not done on the scale that we remember from Galland's Arabian Nights or from the exoticism of eighteenth- and nineteenth-century fiction, but still it is perceptible. Authentic phrases also were realized. The *basmala*, "in the name of the Compassionate, the Merciful," was fairly familiar even in the west, and Matthew Paris quotes verbatim the letter from al-Kamil to the Pope which Gregory IX believed that Frederick had forged. It cites exotic titles for the Pope, as conceived from the outside: "thirteenth Apostle . . . maintainer of the adorers of the cross, judge of the Christian people, leader of the children of baptism," and the Sultan is among other things "holder of the two powers of the sword and the pen." The "letter from Saladin to the pope" of 1184 was much duller. An example from the late period is the letter from the young al-Ashraf, son of Qalaun, to the Master of the Temple, to warn him of the attack on Acre:

"The Sultan of Sultans, the King of Kings, the lord of lords, Malak al-Ashraf, the powerful, the redoubtable, the chastiser of rebels, the chastiser of Franks and Tartars and Armenians, seizer of the castles out of the hands of miscreants, lord of the two seas, servant of the two pilgrimages."

Compare with this the entirely fictitious "Balthasar, the son of the illustrious King, Sultan, King of the Babylonians, Assyrians, Samaritans . . . Elamites . . . Indians . . ." (early fourteenth-century French). Often the exotic style occurs in the accounts of, or deriving from, Crusaders who spent a limited time in the East. It is very noticeable when it occurs in the *Gesta Francorum*, a work of sober tone, but this also represents the early reaction of a writer brought up in Europe. Orderic Vital's story of Bohemund I of Antioch and his *"princesse lointaine"*, itself perhaps circulated by no other than Bohemund himself on his last tour of Europe, is a primitive example of the exotic genre. Bohemund and his knights are succoured in captivity, and freed by, and finally convert, the daughter of their captor; Bohemund bows himself more or less gracefully out of accepting her love, and marries her off to his cousin. The *dulcis amica* phraseology of this absurd piece of manufactured myth attaches it ambiguously to the literature of romance. Differences in style and idiom between Arabic and European languages have always led Europeans quite erroneously to suppose a difference in substance.

The absence of much literate appreciation of the culture of the mainland is what makes this coastal state look like a heavily garrisoned trading post, rather than a colony, even in its greatest days. We can recognize some of the ways in which its society and its ideas resembled those of the Arabs, as I did in the last chapter, but this only seems to indicate a parallel situation; we could not be sure of a positive influence. In the Latin East, concurrently with, and perhaps caused by, the refusal of the church to tolerate Islam, relations with Arabs developed along purely pragmatic lines. Effective cultural interchange presupposes a certain self-assurance which the crusading community in general lacked. We cannot say that a society which established and maintained itself in difficulty was unable to adapt itself. Yet it never achieved homogeneity.

2. Self-criticism and self-analysis

The contrast between the spirit of holy war and the often sordid society it created is a favourite theme. We cannot neglect it only because it has been overdone. Secularism and cynicism were endemic in this society. Italian merchants went about their usual business, but land-hungry knights and a new petite bourgeoisie, partly proletarian in origin, and married to women with strange customs, were disoriented by unfamiliar patterns of life which perhaps demoralized the clergy also. In the first generation, Walter the Chancellor describes how people defied the spirit of fasting with their gluttony, and, rather naïvely, the means that husbands and wives used to inflame their mutual desire. Ill-gotten wealth, he thought, favoured sexual indulgence; wives prostituted themselves incestuously (a word apparently used rather rhetorically than exactly by contemporary moralists), and men would have to pay women who solicited them in the streets to leave them in peace. The point about this (and there is more) is that public defiance of religion would not have been so easy in Europe. In the later days of this society, Joinville, a decent, sensible foreigner, needed to place his bed in his tent in Caesarea where everyone could see he was alone in it. In the middle period, Ernoul's account of the Patriarch Heraclius is famous—his mistress, Paske de Riveri, was the wife of a merchant in Nablus, whose complaisance he bought; when she was widowed, she lived openly as his wife, and appeared in state, with guards and grand dresses; and when a messenger brought him news, publicly in Council, of the birth of one of his daughters, he hushed him with "Quiet, you fool"; this lady was generally called the Patriarchess. In Ernoul's eyes, all the city, clergy and laity alike, followed the example set them, and there was scarcely an honest woman in Jerusalem. There was no objection to ascribing sins to the people of Jerusalem at this date, because it explained why God allowed Salah ad-Din to capture the city; but it is clear that Ernoul did not think that he was inventing facts, though he may have been unusually uninhibited in the circumstances from expressing them. What he saw was a secularization under cover of religious pretence. James of Vitry's attitude was much the same. Bitterly as he criticized all groups in the Kingdom, the worst are the "scribes and pharisees", and he, too, means those whose wickedness is masked by religion. He specifies both laity and clergy, men who cut the throats of their wives, wives who poison their husbands, professional poisoners, clergy who regularly frequent brothels, and masters who will not allow their slaves to become Christians, because then they could not so easily oppress them. Among each second generation of Franks, the institution of marriage was in disuse, he said. It is the job of moralists to exaggerate the evils they attack, but there is more here than the criticism of the morals of other people. There is a conviction that society was not trying to be Christian.

Secularism showed itself in other ways. William of Tyre recounts an interesting talk with Amalric. The King asked him if, apart from the teaching of the Saviour and his saints, there could be "necessary and evident proofs" of the future resurrection—as we should say, irrefutable and self-evident proofs. William, himself describing the conversation, begins by saying that what the Lord, the Apostles, the Fathers and even the Old Testament had made so clear could need no proof, but this was just the argument that the King had anticipated, and it did not answer the question. Amalric said that he believed the doctrine firmly, but asked for reasons that could be used in discussion with a man who denied and rejected Christian doctrine. William now replied more professionally, arguing heuristically. Suppose yourself the person, and we will try to find the reason—Right, said the King—Do you agree that God is just?—Yes—The just must reward good and punish evil? In this life, this does not happen, so there must be another. The King is relieved, and admits that this has banished doubt. Amalric shared the piety of his House, and his faith and doubt and sense of reassurance are rather touching; but they witness to an atmosphere which had nothing to do with the proximity of Islam, a religion which does not doubt the future life or resurrection. This conversation does suggest a society less clerical than that of western Europe, and less religious than the Arab. It is reminiscent of the supposed free-thinking of Frederick II. It owes just this much perhaps to the presence of Muslim Arabs nearby: at this date and in this place anyone might easily imagine discussing religion with an unbeliever, because people with quite different beliefs lived in the same town and ruled the surrounding countryside. In contrast the characteristic of western European thought was its homogeneity.

William of Tyre muses shortly before his death upon the causes of the danger in which the Latin Kingdom already found itself, and he places first the contrast between his contemporaries and their supposedly pious ancestor:

> "criminal descendants, concealed traitors to the Christian faith, throwing themselves wantonly into all forbidden things, like to or worse than those who said to their Lord God, 'Depart from us! We do not desire the knowledge of thy ways.' "

James of Vitry spoke of those people who would not commit themselves to Christian, Muslim or Jewish belief; and of others who did not believe in the future life, and so gave themselves up to current pleasures. William reflected upon the past eighty years and more of glorious achievement, and, citing the prophets, deplored alike people and priest, because "they have no soundness in them, and can bear neither their sins nor the remedies." Yet every historian (he argued)—Livy, Josephus—has had to describe the bad as well as the good times of his people. It happens that the moral critics have left us much better informed about the bad.

The most famous of estimates of life among the Latins of the East are those by James of Vitry, a critical Western mind who picked up what he could of knowledge of the East to which he had come to work—he was Bishop of Acre—using good Latin sources, but not making use of Arab material. He has had a decisive influence on modern Western historiography. As much as the kindly Usama, he is responsible for our image of the Crusaders as vulgar, barbaric and narrow-minded. His is the classic description of the nations of the Latin East.

The Italians—Venetians, Genoans and Pisans—he sees to be necessary as the channel of all trade, pilgrimage, the war at sea, in fact for communication; they are the most serious and careful, watching what they are doing behind a prolixity of words, and living longest because the most sparing in food and drink. He contrasts the transmontanes, German, Frankish, British and English, who are impetuous, prompt, and lavish in food and drink, in devotion to the church, to works of mercy and to fighting the enemy. The *Pullani*—indigenous Franks, usually of mixed parentage—called these North Europeans *filii Hemaudii* because of their frivolity and lack of moderation. But the *Pullani* themselves receive the hardest treatment from Vitry; and besides this he sees the whole array of oriental churches as so many pullulating curiosities beside the stability of the Latin church. He regards the various churches as nations who have adopted different forms of

Christian belief, *Suriani* (Arabic-speaking orthodox or Melkites and, in a general sense, the Christian Arabs), *Iacobitae* (including both Copts and Syrian Monophysites, and here supposing the belief a clue to the nation), Maronites, Armenians, Nestorians and even Mozarabs (whom he does not assert to be orientals of course), Essenes and Samaritans. Yet although these peoples are seen as nations, they are defined ecclesiologically, by their beliefs (each his distinguishing heresy), their church customs, their church histories and sometimes their prophesied futures. For him, what matters, of course, is to approximate to the Latin rite (as much as to the Nicene belief). He does not for that reason spare the Latin clergy who substitute for 'feed my sheep', 'shear my sheep'.

Sometimes Arabs, 'Saracens', figure as a frame of reference in the background; thus the 'Syrians' use Arabic ('Saracenic'); again, we are told that the Arabs despise the Samaritans even more than the Christians do. Vitry realizes that the *Suriani* are Byzantine in rite, but he sees them essentially as a subject race who have served so long a string of masters, Greeks, Romans, 'Latins and Barbarians'—Berbers?—Christians and Arabs. They are occupied in "the practice of agriculture and other baser necessities," they are unwarlike and effeminate, except for a few archers, and, in the circumstances not surprisingly, they are disloyal to the Latins, "double-faced, cunning as foxes, just like Greeks, liars and inconsistent, friends of fortune, traitors," "traitors and really corrupt;" they are easily turned by rewards, have one thing in the mouth and another in the heart, and for quite a small sum will act as spies for the Arabs. They keep their women shut up at home, like Arabs, and they veil them, lest they be seen involuntarily. They pride themselves on their beards as symbols of virility, and despise the clean-shaven Latins. Vitry inevitably assimilates the 'Syrians' rather to Greeks than to Arabs; since 'Arab' is 'Saracen', the notion of a Christian Arab is inconceivable; ecclesiologically, he is right; yet he sees the close acculturation to the Arab World, and realizes that the sympathies of the Syrians are rarely, if at all, with the Latins. In spite of everything, shared Christianity was a link, but he grossly overestimates its strength and surprises himself when the link breaks. We can really sum up all he says in one of his phrases: "they are more than half on the side of the Saracens", or, more freely, "being Arabs, they are more than half on the side of their Muslim fellows."

Vitry's most famous description is deservedly his description of the second or third generation of Latins, the *Pullani*; and his distaste for them perhaps measures an unconscious acceptance that the *Suriani*, after all, have never really been on the Latin side at all. The *Pullani*, however, delatinized Latins, de-Europeanized colonists, are really cultural defectors, people who want to enjoy themselves where they are in an appropriate way, and on reasonable terms with all who have lived there already. His most famous comment is that they were fitter for the bath— the public bath—than for battle, an antithesis that has amused all but the most Frankophile historians. Vitry says, too, that they do not trust their wives to go to church above once a year, keeping them secluded under strict guard, but let them go to the bath three times a week, under suitable supervision. He does not like it that the men are soft and effeminate and brought up on pleasures; that they wear clothes as soft as women's, and in war are despised as women by Arabs, who had trembled before their fathers, although they were few. They are given up to debauch, lust and idleness. The more strictly their women are guarded, the more they manage by a thousand devices to escape. "Beyond measure and beyond belief they are taught fortune-telling and sorceries and numberless abominations by Syrian and Muslim Arab women." This was unacceptable cultural integration. They also corrupt and overcharge the pilgrims who come by way of devotion to the Holy Land. There are some points to notice. We need not take the homiletics too literally; corrupting and overcharging tourists, religious or secular, may fairly be considered universal. The main point of Vitry's complaint is surely the *Pullani* preference for alien pleasures over fighting—for the baths and the soft clothing; lusts and magical practices flourished equally in the West. It comes out clearly that it is the *Pullani* lack of political commitment that Vitry hates. These people, he says, are apt to waste their combative energy in internecine quarrels, and even to find common interests with the Arabs, "entering into alliance with the Muslim Arabs and rejoicing in the peace of the enemies of Christ." Vitry is thinking primarily of townsmen; it is the *Suriani* who are cultivators and country spies. He is thinking, too, of ordinary people; he says nothing of the great lords who hunted and hawked and drew the rents like Arab landowners, but who could be counted on for the defence of the realm in which they were privileged.

It is possible to look at the integration of the Latin communities in their last days. What sort of society was the final product of the Latin East? When only a few isolated coastal cities remained in European hands, and obviously on sufferance, they served some purpose still as ports for intercontinental trade. Can we say that these partly isolated communities were in any way an adaptation to, or, more, an integration into, their surroundings?

Fidenzio of Padua, a Franciscan writing in the last days of the Kingdom of Acre, divides the Christian people simply into *Latini* and *Suriani*. The Latins, according to him, are still a very mixed bunch, much as they had been at first conquest: "divided by their different languages and different customs," coming from different parts of Europe, and quite often promptly returning to them. Many of them are poor and unarmed, and would be useless in war; they often get themselves killed through their lack of caution anyway. Those who come with great fervour to the Holy Land "return with greater fervour to their own home." Those who promise great things do little or nothing,

> "and carnal things happen, and what really is wrong, they do great harm to the Christians because they go up to Jerusalem in spite of the general sentence of excommunication, and pay a lot of money to the Muslim Arabs, which the latter use to fight the Christians."

Then there are those still worse Latins who sell the Muslims iron, arms, wood and other contraband of war used to kill Christians. Finally there are the "many Christians among the Latins" who cross to the Holy Land only to join the Muslims for love of riches and carnal desire, give up their Christian faith and fight against their old co-religionists. In brief, says Fidenzio, of those who cross the seas, many do more harm than good.

Then he tells us that the *Suriani* originated in the Holy Land and were converted to the Christian faith by the Apostles and other saints. For the most part they dress like the infidels; they are divided into Greek Orthodox and Monophysite—he means, therefore, all the oriental churches known to him—and are divided among themselves in belief, are not fond of each other, but rather quarrel. Speaking generally, they are not warlike, and do little for the defence of the Holy Land. Taken all together, the Christians (even the Latins) are a womanish lot, and sometimes many run away from just a few Arabs. The Arabs despise them, and take their cities and villages; they were rich, and are now poor. Fidenzio's picture is clear enough of the Latins, and, like Vitry, he feels that the *Suriani* really belong with the Saracens, but he cannot bring himself to admit that religious allegiance is not necessarily the primary sociological classification. It is true that with Fidenzio we have a crusade propagandist who wants to make out that the position of the Christians, and in particular of the Latins, is desperate; but the event showed that it was desperate, and we need not doubt his analysis. Neither he nor Vitry lacks scientific method.

We only get an idea, and then hardly more than a hint, of an acceptable multi-religious society, in William of Tripoli, writing probably just a little earlier (1273). Elsewhere I quoted his favourable estimate of the Mameluke Sultan Baybars. Here it is relevant that the great Sultan seemed rather the defender than the persecutor of subject Christians to this attractive, eccentric Dominican writer. He also argues that the Sultan could easily complete his conquests by capturing the coastal cities; God restrains, not his faculty for doing so, but his will. On the other hand, it is known (he writes) that Baybars's great ambition is to capture Acre, "head and refuge and power of the Christians," and some suppose, as a Muslim told some Christians, that the sultan's plan is to pretend friendship for the Christians, and to lull Acre into such sense of confidence as to create the opportunity for its capture. At a time when in fact all Christian hopes in Asia were about to come to nothing, Tripoli's attitude was conditioned by his expectation of the immediate collapse of Islam.

The learned Muslim astrologers had themselves foretold it. He gives one Arab legend after another to show that Muslims should expect the quick extinction of their faith, and he himself is one of the few mediaeval writers to emphasize the points in common between the two faiths. (He is a principal source of the passage on Islam in Mandeville.) He believed that he was able to show Muslims that Christian belief was the perfection of their own doctrine of Christ, the completion and integration of faith in the single precept "which is the love of God and one's neighbour, or true friendship, which alone fulfils all the precepts of God." And so, he claimed, he baptized more than a thousand, "without arguments of philosophy or military arms." This is not credible, and his claim that he impressed educated Muslims is barely more so. His actual arguments are little improvement upon those of other polemists. Yet he was a preacher before he was a polemist. We might dismiss him as a crank, if his arguments did not seem to verge on, while never quite achieving, a sympathetic understanding of Islam. His claim to have baptized so many is inexplicable. (Could mothers perhaps have been seeking magical protection from the evil eye for their babies?) His desire to do so without recourse to arms is also unique, and much more attractive than the usual attitude. It is only possible to say that Tripoli seems, more than any other writer over perhaps the first millennium of Islam, to be able to envisage some kind of coexistence, and to see, however dimly, that in shared beliefs, in central ideas though not in peripheral practices, Christians and Muslims already coexist. In him there is no reflection of the analysis into Latins, Christian Arabs ('Suriani') and Muslim Arabs ('Saracens') characteristic of the crusading intelligentsia.

The end of the Latin colony, the destruction of Acre, reflects the failure to adapt. The last Latin possessions were treated according to the law of *jihad*; the army of Islam was resisted and those who would not submit were subject to death or enslavement. Crusade was destroyed by counter-crusade. The future would not lie with soldiers, nor with the church in its militant aspect. The Templar of Tyre describes the scene in Acre, lit by the fires of burning buildings, the townswomen (*"les dames & les bourgoizes & damoizelles . . . & autre menue gens"*) running and crying in the streets, mothers separated haphazard from their children as they were caught by the troops that had fought their way in—a mother killed, or the child at another mother's breast, or a pregnant woman. Families that were not separated by actual force were separated by their own fear in flight. Some took refuge in the Temple, which held out another ten days. During a parley, some of the Sultan's army attacked the women and were all killed by the defenders. The end of it is described by Ricoldo da Monte Croce, who got his news from a captured nun, who, like him, had reached Baghdad; his natural concern was to find if any of his own Dominican brethren had been enslaved instead of killed. Their house was near the quay and they might have got away, but stayed with the Franciscans who had taken refuge with them, and were all killed in the church. Ricoldo found a torn and bloody Dominican habit in the Baghdad market.

This drama, *mutatis mutandis*, makes a pair with the capture of Jerusalem by the Crusaders; these were the first act and the last in a play of irreconcilables. The determination to retain a Latin identity took the form of an inveterate hostility which made any sort of accommodation impossible. Any communication between the religions was personal and temporary. Latins and Europeans were rulers whose culture had never learned submission. We must be clear that religious hostility was fully mutual between Christians and Muslims. On many occasions Arabs refused to fight side by side with the Frankish allies of their rulers. The horror expressed by Christian writers at the removal of the cross from the Temple in Jerusalem, and greater horror at Frederick II's toleration of it, represents very fairly how unreasonable this attitude was. Turn about, churches were converted into mosques and mosques into churches. Worse than this was the deliberate defilement. There are many complaints, in almost standard form, of the Muslim abuse of Christian images, the cross especially. Ricoldo in the letters just quoted gives a number of examples of churches defiled; though some of his examples may represent only lack of respect for disused churches, other examples seem deliberate. On the other side one example will do. At the brief capture of Damascus in 1260 the Prince of Antioch had Mass sung in the Mosque of the Umayyads, correctly called a former Greek church; the other mosques he had defiled by donkeys, wine was scattered on the walls, with grease of fresh pork, and salt, and the excrement of his men. There was no will to toleration among ordinary men, still less among clergy; even had it been possible to find an accommodation which the Muslims could accept, the will to do so was lacking. The nearer future would lie with the merchants, in trading settlements negotiated with the Arab authorities. Later there would be a future for European 'experts', but until the seventeenth century the European residents in Arab countries were usually either prisoners in process of absorption, or temporary residents on sufferance. There was certainly a further absorption of Europeans who turned freely to Islam, but they have left only a few traces.

3. The Arab World through Latin eyes

The Franks had many faults, but the picture of crude barbarians, only partly civilized by their brief stay in the East, is over-simplified. Of the early history of Islam, like other Europeans, they were abysmally ignorant, but this was a deliberate choice. Their knowledge of contemporary Arab politics was usually erratic; this was even true of William of Tyre. Their demography of the Arab World was vague, though it began at an early stage. The *Gesta* and other early works began to pick out the Turks, as an enemy of special repute, and soon other identifications were made. One Egyptian army was described as made up of Arab horsemen, Nubian foot—*tam Arabes equites quam Aethiopes pediates*—and the Turkish archers from Damascus. In spite of the value of military intelligence, accounts of national, social and cultural groupings in the Arab World remained vague; perhaps only the Bedouin Arabs were clearly distinguished. In spite of this we owe to the Crusaders some good geographical accounts, and some lively pictures of life among the Arabs, unhappily always very incomplete. Their ignorance came from that indifference which characterizes others besides themselves, and when a subject caught their imagination, they would follow it up with real interest.

In his description of Egypt, William of Tyre's first thought is that Cairo, "called Masr in Arabic," is the finest place in the country, a "noble and outstanding metropolis;" his next is to identify its history. He does so, a little doubtfully, but correctly enough, as the continuation of ancient Memphis, of which the ruins might then still be seen, and were still impressive; the local farmers identified the site, and William assumes that at some time the population must have been transferred. He realizes that the ancient Babylon was somewhere different, and is not clear how the name came to be applied to the Cairo site. The sequence of Roman Babylon and Arab Fustat he does not know, but describes the foundation of Cairo proper in 361 Hijrah. He takes some care also to describe the physical and economic geography, the narrow river cultivation of Upper Egypt and the wealth of produce of the Delta.

In his description of the Cairo embassy of Hugh of Caesarea at the end of Amalric's second Egyptian expedition, there are hints of provincialism, but these may belong to the story as Hugh related it to William, rather than to that which William relates to us. William tells us that he is describing the Cairene setting because it is different from, and because it is unknown to, his own world. He knows that we will admire the ostentation of the "custom of the house of the prince," the "state and magnificence, the vastness of wealth and variety of glory." Hugh, with his fellow-envoy, Walter of Fulcher, a Templar, at the head of the embassy, was conducted to the Qasr by the Sultan—the khalifa's

vizir—through narrow streets, by the light of torches, and preceded by a large body of swordsmen. They passed a first and
second guard-house, and then came out into a larger court where
the daylight reached. Now their eyes were held by marble columns
and fountains filled with limpid water, the gilded ceilings and
finely worked window screens, and the polychrome rows of the
pavements. There were Sudanese soldiers in formation, there were
unknown birds singing, and such animals as only the wanton hand
of a painter could devise, or the poet, licensed to lie, could imagine
in his dreams of the night. In this description we are nearer to the
spirit of Lamartine at Bait ad-Din than to that of Caractacus in
Rome.

The humour is stressed by the comedy that follows. The vizir
prostrates himself three times, uttering such devotion as no
mortal should receive. Suddenly the curtains, studded with
jewels, are drawn back to reveal the Caliph on his throne and surrounded by his domestics and his eunuchs; he permits the vizir to
kiss his feet. The treaty agreed is read to the Caliph, who signifies
his assent. Now comes the joke. The ambassadors insist on shaking
the Caliph's hand upon the bargain. Horror all around is succeeded
by renewed horror when Hugh rejects the Caliph's reluctant but
still gloved hand, and insists that a prince's hand upon a bargain
must be a bare hand. He wins his point after brief caliphal hesitation. That is all. "As Lord Hugh reported it to us, he was a youth
with the first down of puberty, tall in body, with a pleasant face,
extremely generous, having unnumbered wives." Presumably the
last quality was hearsay. It is clear that William is unimpressed
by the last days of the Fatimids. He is poking a little gentle fun at
the young Lord Hugh of Caesarea; certainly he is indulging a
taste for the exotic. He himself was familiar with the palaces of
Byzantium, and most travelled men of rank will have known the
great buildings of the Mediterranean of the twelfth century. It
would be a mistake to understand barbaric awe on the part of
Latins who in fact were accustomed to splendour.

Joinville, who saw the extinction of the Ayyubids as William of
Tyre had recorded their rise, has always, and rightly, been judged
exceptional. He was frank and unreserved and no more sophisticated than Hugh of Caesarea; he had endless common sense
instead; his narrative is always personal. Perhaps because his
interest is in day-to-day events, he recognizes and accepts the
ordinary humanity of the Egyptians, apparently without realizing

that it was unusual to do so. Places and strategy have little interest for him, the possible uses of Damietta, for example, either strategically or as a kind of free port; people and their doings make up his recollections. He has no familiarity with the Levantine background. He appreciates the frequent kindness done by 'sarrazins', just as he is often frightened by their threats and severities. He owed his life to the Arab who came from the lands held from the Western Emperor, and who talked French; he described alike the killings of the sick prisoners and the humanity of the old Arab knight who used to carry the wounded Raoul de Wanou to the "*chambres privées*". Some conversations were in French, some through professional interpreters, some through Franks of the East, like Baldwin d'Ibelin, "*qui savoit bien le sarrazinnois*". The assassination of the Sultan, Turan-Shah, is told in circumstantial detail which is totally matter-of-fact. There is no exoticism here, though there is often a dramatic heightening of the situation; for example, when the last-moment discussion about whether to kill the Franks after all is taking place. The amir who is in favour of doing so reads the law which prescribes loyalty to the Sultan, then "turns the page" and reads the commandment to "kill the enemy of religion." This, of course, is hearsay. Joinville was not priggish in his personal relations. When the well-dressed, handsome Arab, bearing gifts for the King, who spoke French so well, turned out to be a convert from Christianity, Louis refused to speak to him any longer, but Joinville remonstrated with him at length. The convert, not Joinville, broke the acquaintance. Joinville contrasts with all the other writers, in his lack of interest in the different cultural background of the Arabs, and equally in taking them as he found them. He talked with Arabs and knew them with all the intimacy of a soldier, an enemy and a prisoner, but he knew little of their way of life and nothing at all of the society in which both they and Christians, not only Eastern but also Latin, lived together.

Roughly contemporary with William of Tyre is the statement of Gerard of Strasburg, Frederick I's ambassador to Salah ad-Din. Part of this is second-hand, as when he describes the androgynous, civilized, warlike and hospitable inhabitants of Corsica; in contrast is the exact description of Malta as Muslim Arab, i.e. 'Saracen', under the rule of the King of Sicily, and similarly of Pantellaria. Coming to the North African coast, the writer uses the word *Arabitus*, to denote a Bedouin (as until lately a town Arab might do) and then comes to his personal experience on entering the port of Alexandria. There is a strong implication of the Mediterranean as one area with a variety of inhabitants. The ruins of Alexandria gave primarily the impression of a city once much greater. It impressed by its movement of trade, the passage of many people, and the freedom of worship for every religion. Gerard, like William, cared about the historical identification of Cairo; there had been three Babylons: the Babylon where Nebuchadnezzar reigned, and the deserted Babylon on the Nile where Pharaoh reigned, and the new Babylon on the Nile, populous and inhabited with merchants who pass on the produce of "India" to Alexandria. The Nile is greater than the Rhine. There is a good supply of grain and vegetables. Not far is Cairo, the military city, also important, the seat of the king and the chief generals, its buildings "not less admirable than sumptuous," surrounded by a closed wall and by beautiful clearings. As of Alexandria, Gerard notes that in Cairo Muslim Arabs, Christians and Jews are all living together, each 'nation' practising its own religion, and there are many churches. There is a balsam orchard watered by a spring, where the Holy Family rested, and where Saracens as well as Christians come to honour the Virgin, and to take the water of the spring, especially at Epiphany. Both religions also honour the palm tree where she rested, and other places associated with the Holy Family. Gerard speaks of the Pyramids—the two marble mountains, a strong bowshot apart and two bowshots high, squared and built by skill, admirable work; he also describes the crocodiles, and the wealth of birds and the fruits of the earth. He adds that there are no metals, and that the horses are only just good enough.

There is little in his account which is not straightforward reporting, with a natural interest in economic factors. The chief European interest apart from the Crusade was in trade. A practical attention to things seen here replaces the exotic. The point of sociological interest to Gerard is the freedom of worship, or, more exactly, the freedom of 'nations' to live side by side with their own customs. Gerard's references to Islam as a religion are the usual mixture of fact, misinterpretation and error. His account from Damascus ("most noble city") of the Assassins is interesting for its lack of any reference to their religion—except to say they have none—but there is a full and fanciful account of their organization as a secret society which might have been picked up from any hostile source, Muslim or Christian. Gerard concludes with the commonplace piety of the Crusades: the Lord in his justice allows to some the reward of eternal life, but to the impious the rewards of this. The best regions, abounding in corn and oil, gold, silver, jewels, silk clothing, aromatic pigments and balsams, and all that the eye can desire, are in the hands of the reprobate. At this date the wealth of developed natural resources was still in the Levant and eastwards, rather than in northern Europe, but it was taken for granted that the cultural differences, often noted with interest, were comprised within a geographical unit.

The wordly success of the ungodly became a problem nearly unbearable, when gradually the Latin kingdom was eroded and finally obliterated. For some this posed an acutely emotional problem in theology. This was never expressed with more pain or puzzlement or vain struggle to understand than by Ricoldo da Monte Croce, in his Baghdad letters, which I have quoted earlier. In his *Itinerarius*, written to describe the same visit, we find also one of the most interesting descriptions of good natural relations, and even spontaneous admiration of Muslim ways. Ricoldo is in one sense the last writer of the Arab Crusades; it was the accident of his journey eastwards that saved him from death at Acre. We might also say that he was also the Crusader who knew most about the Arabs. He describes the reception he received in Baghdad in a passage which has deservedly become famous:

> "We therefore report certain Muslim works of perfection thus briefly, rather to shame the Christians than to praise the Muslims. For who will not be astonished if he carefully considers how great among these same Muslims is the attention to study, the devotion in prayer, pity for the poor, reverence for the name of God and the prophets and the holy places, their serious ways, their kindness to strangers, and their concord and love towards each other."

Ricoldo is indeed writing to shame the Christians, just as he says; this is not just an excuse for repeating something favourable about the enemy, it is part of a known genre in homiletics, the satirical contrast of Christian with Muslim behaviour. Yet he is also speaking from actual experience; and he is the author of a document which for long remained the major anti-Islamic polemic of western Europe. It is true that it is largely adapted from a Spanish original; but much of it is tendentious and aggressive enough to make the testimony I am citing particularly impressive, as not being the product of the author's natural inclination.

Writing at the same time as he was composing his letters of lament for the fall of Acre, already quoted, he says that "they really received us as if we were angels of God, in their schools and centres of study and their monasteries and their churches or synagogues." In some passages Ricoldo takes it for granted that European and Muslim Arabs share a culture, because the differences presuppose that much is held in common, and he does so even in the field of religion itself. For example:

"They have in Baghdad many places devoted to study and contemplation alone, in the manner of our great monasteries, and those who come are provided out of the common store, that is, with bread and water, and they are happy to apply themselves to contemplation and study, in the greatest poverty."

Again, "their care in prayer is such, and such their devotion, that I was amazed." As for their concern for the poor, they are "almsgiving in the extreme"; not only do they give the mandatory Quranic tenth (*zakat*); not only are they "required to give a fifth of what they acquire by violence of arms," but in addition they make great gifts and legacies to the *awqaf* (*gazophilacium*); they redeem Muslim prisoners of the Christians, and even redeem and release Christian slaves. They also free birds, if they cannot afford to free human slaves. Again,

"it is especially their practice to do or say or write nothing worthwhile without starting, 'In the name of the Lord . . .' When the name of the Lord crops up in reading or writing, they never dare just to name Him, but do so always with a word of praise, like 'God, may he be praised' or some such."

Among the concepts most difficult to define at this date are *affabilitas* and *urbanitas*, both of which Ricoldo attributes to his hosts; he means kindness, generosity of spirit, sophistication, the proper way a gentleman should behave. The Dominicans were received by the notables and the learned of Baghdad freely and easily. Ricoldo puts down the expression of praises of Christ, whenever he was mentioned, to the sense of hospitability, rather than to Muslim reverence for the Masih of the Quran. He explains how put out their hosts were when they would not eat with them, and adds how strong is the bond of the host to the guest, especially among "the Arabs, who are noble among the other Saracens." Sometimes when we read what Ricoldo writes about the severity of Arab manners we are only half convinced; he exaggerates the "gravity of the ways," all the Arabs like monks, even the little boys. We can believe that they were serious, but not (as he claims) that there was no singing that was not religious. Probably Ricoldo could not recognize secular Arab music as such. It is hard to believe that it was not a mistake to think that no Arab ever mocked or detracted or blamed another. Nor do we easily believe that instances of reluctance to fight, or of forgiveness, are as typical as he thinks; there was a little exaggeration, precisely to shame Christians. The rest carries conviction. Yet he goes straight on to attack Islam, as a religion, according to the basic plan of his own great—but quite derivative—polemic against the Quran. The contrast with his more spontaneous observation of fact, and even overstatement of facts observed, is inescapable. Ricoldo had an exceptional advantage in his experience in Baghdad; yet he remains representative of a culture which combined accept-ance of attitudes largely shared, with the incessant commination of Islam and its Prophet.

In spite of the easy doctrine that Muslim success was chastize-ment of Christian sins, the uninterrupted triumph of the Muslims in the second half of the thirteenth century produced a crisis of conscience for Ricoldo and probably for many others. Gerard of Strasburg had been concerned about the wealth of the Arab homelands at a time of Crusading success. Now Ricoldo was more acutely worried that the Muslims should have the most fertile parts of the world (or so it seemed), and the Christians be given the second-best parts. Less serious-minded or less disinterested writers slipped easily into a slightly cynical pacifism. An imaginary correspondence of the Sultan with Pope Clement V, probably written in France at the beginning of the fourteenth century, harps greatly on the power and wealth of the Arabs.

"As we have gold and silver and choice statues and most precious jewels in superabundance, thirsting for nothing, except the blood of Christians: Come quickly, if you want, with your people . . ."

It recommends the Pope not to expose his children to danger or to cut off the innocent. Even in extremity, crusading leaders were divided and their men disillusioned. Europe had naturally lost its taste for crusading which seemed to serve no useful purpose, either secular or religious. The mediaevals retained a clear impression of the greater wealth and power of the Arab states which history would in fact reverse. The period of crusading initiative ended with a sense of uncertainty in a mood of self-questioning. To that extent we may compare the moral condition of twentieth-century Europe in the phase of decolonization. In both cases, however, commercial interests continued to expand after the retreat or defeat of armies.

4. Merchants, mercenaries and others

The characteristic thirteenth-century interest in the further East was both anti-Muslim and anti-Arab. It was centred on the Mongols, and found its most practical expression in the travellers, John of Plano Carpini, William of Rubruck, Marco Polo; this was reflected in the public interest, in, for example, its popularization by Vincent of Beauvais; it held out the hope of direct trade with the sources of wealth which originated beyond the Arab World; and it represents the dream of a world from which the Arabs had been eradicated, or in which at least they might be much reduced, or perhaps would be dominated by Christian rulers. Till then the world had meant the two divisions of the Mediterranean. The impact of the Mongols was especially in the realization of worlds beyond, and in the hope of an escape from the old polarization. When the Mongols were converted to Islam and the Arab World was again stabilized under Mameluke rule, the great trading interests of Italy and the western Mediterranean must settle down to the humdrum business of dealing again with the Arabs, more than ever the great source of luxury imports. Men were conscious of the wealth of the East; the actual active trade in the Levant was the visible proof of it, not only for the traveller, but for the merchant and the consumer on European shores. As crusade died away into a condition almost perpetually balanced between peace and war—at least until the defensive war against the Ottomans—pilgrims no longer constituted armies, the only European soldiers were in Arab employment, and merchant communities took the place of the crusading feudatories; or, more exactly, the merchant communities and the groups of mercenary soldiers found a new relation with the Arab World, as tolerated aliens. Missionaries were not motivated in quite the same way as merchants, but there was a common economic basis; the more settled missions were linked to trade routes and busy centres, and often had the character of a chaplaincy service.

Europeans as Crusaders had been a disruptive force, but their adaptability and persistence made them effective and loyal mercenaries. In 1227, al-Muazzam Sharaf ad-Din, Sultan of Damascus and brother to al-Kamil, who leased Jerusalem to Frederick II, died, leaving

> "children who were small. Sharaf ad-Din ('Coradix'), before he died, left his land and children in trust to a knight who was born in Spain and who had been a brother in the order of the Temple. He left them in trust to him because, since he had left the Christians and come to him, he had served him loyally; and also because the knight never wanted to become a Muslim, and he stuck to his religion, except that he would fight against the Christians. And because of the loyalty that al-Muazzam saw in him, that he held and kept his religion, he knew well that he would loyally care for his land and his children. That is why he left them in trust to him, and would not do so to Arabs. He well knew that they would give them up to the Sultan of Cairo."

This picture is not quite accurate; al-Muazzam's son an-Nasir Salah ad-Din was a young man, who succeeded his father, and for a while resisted spoliation by his two uncles. Nevertheless, the picture of the loyal Christian knight in Arab service is interesting. This seems to have been a pattern of employment, especially in North Africa, over a very long time.

The great trading interests, the Italian cities, Marseilles, Catalonia, all had consulates in the cities of the North African coast. A number of the treaties on which they were based have been printed; de Mas Latrie's collection of documents about Frankish communities in North Africa includes both papal letters and bulls, and treaties between European and Arab communities. In many cases, both the Latin and the Arabic versions exist; the treaty between Frederick II and Abu Zakariya in Tunis survived only in the Arabic, in Spain. De Mas Latrie's main collection includes over 150 treaties covering the period from the second quarter of the twelfth century to the early sixteenth. The European contracting parties include Aragon, the Sicilies, Venice, Genoa, Pisa, France, Majorca. This trade had to function under difficulty. As warfare was gradually reduced, papal prohibitions, based on a theoretical war footing, took its place. Whatever the customs imposed by the Arab authorities, Christian taxes were a worse burden. Most goods, and all war goods, must be subject to boycott in time of war; carriage was forbidden by the Holy See, and exemptions had to be bought. In spite of this, trade seems to have flourished. It was largely a trade in luxury goods, spices, drugs, dyes, *mumia* (mummy dust), gold and silver thread, porcelain, sugar; there was exchange of textiles, silk and cotton for wool and linen. The trade in slaves continued to flourish, both in females and in males, who were wanted for the armies. All the goods were expensive and paid the carrier to take risks. The treaties conceded reciprocal rights; thus, in a treaty between Pisa and Tunis of 1397, the Tunisian subject has the same rights to security of property and person in Pisa and its dependencies as Pisans in the territories of the King of Ifriqiya.

The type of commercial community that these treaties set up survived in an attenuated form into the middle of the twentieth century; and it was not much earlier that consular or other foreign jurisdictions disappeared, after having developed from a freely negotiated treaty right into a colonial imposition. Although there is not much evidence from the treaties about the sort of life the traders led, it is evident that they lived largely cut off from the local communities, keeping themselves apart in their *fondacos*, from *funduq*, now used in Arabic for a hotel. They had their own chaplains, whose tenure was a benefice. Each *funduq* was a self-supporting community, a kind of free zone. Thus James I of Aragon on 3 May 1261 rented out the *funduqs* at Tunis for 5,500 silver bezants for two years, "the new and the old *funduq*" with their surroundings, the consulate, the market-stalls, courts, offices, oven and tavern with all their fittings and equipment. The next day he confirmed the consul's grant of two of the shops to the chaplain, for the upkeep of the altar of Saint Mary in the chapel of the royal *funduq*, one to live in, and one to store his supplies and use as he pleased; the chaplaincy was granted for life. For the most part these treaties represent no more fruitful cultural exchange than mutual financial advantage, though an early written confirmation of an oral agreement, dated July 1157 by Abu Abdalla ibn Abd al-Aziz of Tunis, to the Archbishop and peoples of Pisa, begins in the Latin version with an elaboration of the *basmala*, "In the name of God the Compassionate and Merciful, thanks be to God the almighty, who is the support of all the world . . ." In any case, these treaty-based communities provided a pattern of commercial interchange that would continue through centuries; they formed an enduring background to the spasmodic exchange of ideas.

In contrast is the clerical propaganda in favour of papal restrictions on trade with the enemy. William of Adam reverses the attitudes of men of business. He justifies the boycott which they resented and infringed. He is writing at the time of the Sultan Qalaun, in whose reign the last relic of the Latin kingdom was all but destroyed by the capture of Acre. He is attacking the business in slaves. This was a distasteful trade which great poverty may have excused in the parents who sold their children of either sex—they were Greeks, Bulgars, Hungarians and others, as well as pagans, including Tatars, from Asia, and many may have thought to give their children a better chance by doing so. Profit alone motivated the Christian merchants who transported them to Egypt. William of Adam has a lurid picture of Egypt, often ludicrous; he says that the land of Egypt eats up its inhabitants, who waste away through abortion, so that it would soon be depopulated, if it were not replenished from abroad. He did not understand that a large and flourishing population demands more workers, and so he assumed a land in decay. Those who saw Egypt, of course, did not fall into this mistake.

He feared for the corruption of the boys. He said that the people of Egypt, being given to the pleasures of the flesh, were unsuited to military life, and must therefore recruit their armies from abroad. Mameluke power was indeed foreign and military, but the vacuum it filled was not created by the luxury of the Egyptian farmers who toiled to produce the harvests. Together with the need to recruit the armies, William of Adam places another motive, the demand for sexual indulgence, in the Egypt of his imagination. The merchants take suitable boys, and fatten them up, and wash them often in all kinds of baths, and dress them in soft garments, so that they are "plumper and pinker and more delightful," and so sell them as male prostitutes on a market where a man and an effeminate may live as man and wife. There is a certain cultural difference here, and one which came increasingly to the fore in the European mind for centuries; where homosexuality was rejected in Europe with an excess of horror, it was treated in the Muslim world as only one among many sexual irregularities. The degree of toleration produced a strong reaction among Europeans, who made it a capital offence, and they exaggerated the facts. The actual extent of homosexual practice in Europe at this date we cannot possibly guess, because of the strength of the prohibitions; obviously it was harder to practise, but there is no real basis for comparison. Obviously, too, any degree of toleration in the circumstances looked like encouragement, and we must allow a good deal to an over-heated clerical imagination. This is in itself a part of the failure of cultural interchange; Qalaun was the contemporary of Ibn-Nafis who, like William of Adam, reproved homosexuality as contrary to reason as well as religion. It is clear that the argument is here primarily an attempt to win support for the boycott against the Arabs. Slave-boys employed as catamites are offensive to sentiment, at most times and in most places; and in case of war, there was real danger in the recruitment of the élite Mameluke force. In case of war Egypt would also, as always, be vulnerable through its shortage of wood. It is obvious which was the more profitable line of attack. To argue about wood was an unpopular cause, uninteresting at best, and any attack on the import and export of commodities aroused opposition in the trading cities of Italy and elsewhere. Allegations about grossly exploited children were much more likely to win support, and that is why this was stressed. Yet it would have been ineffective if there had not been a real area of cultural difference.

Papal letters to North Africa were mostly concerned with the maintenance there of a clergy. In the eleventh century Leo X and Gregory VII were still concerned to support the existing hierarchy. A century later Innocent III was writing to recommend Religious whose work was the ransom of prisoners. The thirteenth-century popes are concerned to maintain Christian discipline among the many Latins in the service of Arab rulers. They adopt a religiously neutral form of address; thus Gregory IX to the King of Morocco: "to the noble amiramolinus, that he may know the way of truth and remain in it faithfully for ever;" 'amiramolinus' we have met before, here probably supposed to be a proper name; Honorius IV gives dispensations to friars to adapt their rule to the life around them, and Gregory threatens the ruler that he must treat the Christians well, or they will be forbidden to serve him. Innocent IV tries to persuade the Moroccans to hand over fortified places to the Christians; there is a faint hope of crusade in the remoter distance, but on the whole the note is realistic. In 1290 Nicolas IV writes to the noblemen, barons, notables, knights and all mercenary Christians serving in Morocco, Tunis and Tlemcen; they are to watch their manner of life, and ensure that the Christian religion is honoured both by Christians and by Muslims, and must obey the bishop the Pope has sent. Besides the merchants and mercenaries, there were Christian prisoners. Salimbene describes one friar's mission to Egypt. Salimbene had himself cured him of an illness of which he lay dying; then he went to North Africa at the time of Louis IX's last crusade. In 1279 the community of Christian prisoners in Egypt sent to the Pope to ask him "for the love of God to send them a good, competent priest, to whom they could confess their sins with confidence." The Pope entrusted the business to the Minister-General, who nominated this same priest, who was evidently reluctant, and went on obedience only. He managed to extract permission to return for the next chapter-general, and then to be sent back to his own province at Bone. He did everything commendably. "He did and caused to be done many good things to those Christians" and "he reported how the Arabs had the Christians in chains, and made them dig the pits of their castles and carry earth in baskets; and that each Christian was only given three small loaves a day." He saw the unicorn, and balsam vineyards, and brought back wonders to show the brothers, manna in a glass jar, water from the fountain of Saint Mary, without which the balsam will not fruit, and balsam wood and many other unknown things. Several aspects of this strike us. One is the professionalism which obtained among the Franciscans, posting to one Arab country a brother who already had experience of another. Another is the relatively casual attitude to the Christian prisoners, compared with the interest shown in the balsam, and even the unicorn.

A few missionaries continued for some time to maintain the crusading spirit and nearly to re-enact the experiences of Cordova five centuries earlier. Lull himself, the greatest eccentric of his age, tried twice to achieve martyrdom by attacking the Prophet in North Africa, but was shipped off by the cadi, after a short imprisonment; he finally achieved a kind of martyrdom by provoking a street crowd in Bujaya. The Franciscan missionary records show that in Asia similarly, in the fourteenth century, to attack the Prophet and to preach Christ were still confused, resulting sometimes in provoked martyrdoms. A report dated from Trebizond in May 1314 from the Minister-General in the East to the procurator of the order in Rome gives just such a case, involving four men. There were similar cases, but the fact that the order was able to maintain quasi-permanent establishments for a time shows that there was often greater prudence. Missionaries, both Catholic and, in due course, Protestant, learned discretion, and gave up attacking the Prophet, at least until, as colonial rulers, they could do so with impunity. The records of the Carmelites in Basra in the seventeenth century show in intimate detail how it was possible —though not easy—to do semi-consular, semi-chaplaincy duties without causing offence; but though for later periods much material is available, we lack sufficiently detailed accounts for the Middle Ages.

Nevertheless there is abundant evidence that Latin communities lived successfully in their *fondacos* and other communities. The pilgrim trade continued, although it was necessary to purchase exemption from the prohibitions of everything deemed to be in *dispendium Terrae Sanctae*. We may take one pilgrim account of the fourteenth century as an example, that of the Irishman, Simon of Semeon. Simon and his companion, Hugh the Illuminator, who was destined to die en route in Cairo, set out from Ireland in 1323. More than thirty years had passed since there was a Latin State on the Asian coast. The Ottoman advance had not yet roused old European fears. No great change of attitude, however, contrasts with that of earlier writers of the Latin Kingdom. It is evident that Simon's information is sound and that he is drawing on well-selected local knowledge among Latin residents. We are struck by his interest in administrative matters, and in ordinary as well as ecclesiastical business. His approach to Egypt, his first Arab and first Muslim country, is altogether practical; he sees normality. He does not pick a quarrel over religion; he does not think that much credit is due to Islam, but where he sees that it is, he is prepared to give it.

These characteristics are typified by his short experience of Alexandria. The system of port control over debarkation and unloading seriously interest him, and he is fascinated by the Mameluke system of pigeon post, by which authority can be sought from Cairo to admit a traveller to Egypt, and by which the Sultan knows almost daily what is happening throughout his kingdom. Simon abuses the Prophet, while admitting that Muslims keep their mosques clean and with reverence. When they are abused themselves by passers-by, the two Irishmen take it quietly. The 'amir of the port' comes at the fixed time with armed supporters, and explains the need for trade to the crowd. However, the two Irish Franciscans are recognized as Religious. Some of the converts to Islam—and he says there are many, though with the lips and not the heart—say they are spies, to gain credit for themselves. The two reply, "If Muhammad is true prophet and lord, keep peace with him and maintain his praise" but say that they serve another lord, "eternally generated Son of God, born of the Virgin Mary, and are not spies, but His sons by adoption." This is meant for a conciliatory speech, and may have been even more so in fact than in memory. The two are sent to the Marseilles *fondaco* (they came on a Marseilles boat) and Simon explains to the reader the system of consuls, who at once control and protect the interests of the merchants of their nations. He takes occasion to say that poor pilgrims are not welcome because they bring in so little money; but this may be said to justify himself in the light of the papal prohibition of pilgrimage (except by licence), because it helps the enemy with needed cash. Because they were poor, their order to depart from Alexandria took fifteen days to come through, though many people today must wait longer to get an entry visa to a foreign country.

In one place, Simon calls his sources of information "worthy of belief"; he knows a good deal about the Arabs of Egypt through sources unfriendly, but not always ignorant. If, as is likely, they were Latins, they knew more than their crusading predecessors. He himself was only three months in Cairo (September to December). His description of the Delta and of irrigation cultivation cannot be only the result of direct observation; it probably combines what he saw in transit with the product of intelligent questioning. He was impressed by the vegetable and animal wealth of Egypt, and quite simply by its beauty, though this was an aesthetic judgement closely allied to an appreciation of economic value. Simon cannot find enough words. "Now this land is the noblest and most handsome of all the lands on the earth, because of its great beauty and fertility, great beauty and amenity, great richness and wealth," full and flat, and strong and firm. Synonyms fail him, as they do the translator. Not that he was uncritical; but he was impressed by many crops, including those which were unusual in the north, like oranges, and others like sugar-cane and sycamore fig which were less well known in Europe. He notes that apples and pears will not fruit. He admires the abundance of plants and the perfection of the sweet-smelling roses. He thinks well of the cattle for size, and admires sheep and goats with an appreciatively critical eye. Horses and donkeys are small and lively and like Irish ones. He has less detail, naturally, on the camel. He interrupts this survey to note the absence of wood, other than fruit-trees, and to deplore the bad Christians who import it. Birds "especially abound, doves, poultry and water birds, and many other kinds of the noblest birds." The farmers he does not like at all, finds them "base", living at the same level as their animals, their houses made of sun-dried mud and straw, and quite indefensible; for protection they depend on the army of the Sultan, the flooding of the Nile, and the desert. It is hard to believe Simon was unfamiliar with equally poor conditions in Ireland, but not perhaps with such peaceful farmers.

He concedes the distant beauty of Alexandria, but he finds both Alexandria and Cairo streets narrow, winding, dark, dusty and full of all kinds of filth, and quite unpaved. Presumably he is judging by Irish standards again. In Cairo it is difficult to get from one part to another, and important people do not go on foot. Large numbers of asses stand around to be hired, apparently like taxis. There are no cars or vehicles in Egypt or India (apparently meaning the East in general), as in Western countries, but there is an infinite number of camels. Cairo is twice as big as Paris in extent, and four times as great in population, and if one said more it would not exceed the truth. Apart from the churches, which are well built, well ornamented and well kept, the houses are much meaner than those of Paris, mostly made of mud in the lower part and palm branches, or canes or light woods and mud above. He respects the official quarters of the Sultan, in contrast to his opinion of the rest of Cairo. The *castrum* is "huge and fine, very suitably built and adorned with furnishings of war, with palaces, workshops and other impressive government offices." He and his friend observed the duties of a tourist and pilgrim; near the *castrum* they saw the elephants and a giraffe. Simon gives a good description of the Giza Pyramids, supposing them to be the granaries of Joseph, as was the tradition. An obelisk he considers finer than the one in Rome. He thinks that Babylon is *castrum Pharaonis*, and he describes the building of the City of the Dead which to this day contains so many splendid Mameluke monuments. The church (now Abu Sergah) where the Holy Family was believed to have sheltered, had just been handed over to the Latins, who called it "Our Lady of the Cave"; the Marseilles consul had gained the concession. On the other side of Cairo, the Virgin's Tree continued to be the object of devotion to all Christians, European or Coptic, and, in spite of recent anti-Christian discrimination, Muslims also still came.

In Alexandria he noted that "Saracens, Christians, Greeks,

Schismatics (Copts) and perfidious Jews" dress all much alike; only the Franks—Europeans—were dressed distinctly. The usual Muslim Arab style, however, in different weaves of linen or cotton for the common people, in silk or gold thread for the rich, resembled the Franciscan habit, except for the hood; in its place is the turban or *imma*. Europeans call the Copts and Greeks "Christians of the belt" because they go belted. Women are strictly enclosed, and greater strictness is a sign of nobility. They wear armlets and anklets of gold or silver, in which extracts from the Quran are kept; Jewish and Coptic women are similarly dressed and adorned, but the Copts can be recognized by their use of black antimony. He noticed also the use of nose-rings, and stains to colour hands and feet. Veiled women see with difficulty through fine cotton. Observations like this lead Simon to Quranic quotation (in this case XXIV:31, in Ketton's paraphase *azoara* XXXIII/XXXIV).

Simon reprehends a slave-market where "Indians, Copts (*schismatici*) and Nubians" are exposed for sale like animals; in the constant fighting against Bedouins and Nubians, prisoners are regularly made and can find release only by being ransomed or being sold—"men, women, sucklings, youths, greybeards." Simon believes that the tribal markings on the cheeks of the Sudanese were burned in to purge them from sin. He says (probably referring still to the Sudanese) that those who are converted from Christianity to Islam are 'worse' than the Muslims; the Mamelukes of the camp on Roda are also badly behaved. The chief absurdity is the tale about the cheek markings. He says that the old wives' tales about Christian slaves who are yoked like animals are not to be believed. Christian captives are well treated, craftsmen especially, such as masons and carpenters, attached to the sultan, but all, including women and children, are humanely treated (*satis humaniter*) and supplied with money and bread. He brings up the now usual accusation of widespread or even universal sodomy, and even frequent bestiality, but does not claim to be an eyewitness of these irregularities. The Sultan pays three thousand dirhams for every live gerfalcon, and half that amount for one that has died on the way, while being brought to him; they are supplied with the food they need; this has always been the custom of his predecessors, and will be that of his successors. Simon considers the military exercises in the *maidan* playful and effeminate in comparison with European tournaments. He condemns as uncivilized the Sultan's custom of eating in public in the city with many people sitting around, without a proper table, "dispensing with all elegance." He respects the fact that all, noble and base, young and old, and travellers of every religion and condition, are subject without exception to the same "elevated justice" with its severe penalties.

All these observations are interspersed with quotations from Ketton's Quran and phrases abusing the Prophet which, taken by themselves, we might call hysterical. Taken in their context, they still seem comminatory, almost liturgically so, but they become formal almost to the point of unreality. Simon is and means to stay a good papalist, but, theology subtracted, Simon has observed and enquired over a wide field of interests. He reflects the attitude of well-established informants, but he himself is quick to notice differences with Europe and to make comparisons. There is no suggestion that he has found a totally alien civilization, though no doubt Cairo is further from Clonmel than Paris is. This narrative of the early fourteenth century looks back over some eight centuries to one common Mediterranean world. In many ways it also looks forward to travellers' tales of much later date, into the mercantile era and even after.

Despite individual differences, the overall impression the travellers give is always much the same, admiring the wealth of the country, especially Egypt, closing their minds to the people. The Augustinian, James of Verona, passed through Cairo on pilgrimage with a companion, ten years after Simon. He too admired the "fertile and productive" Delta, its incomparable sugars, its "noble fruits", limes and apples of paradise. To Alexandria came "ships from all the regions of the world, carrying all things delightful to the human body;" everything was sent up to Cairo, a city "filled with all good things." He noted the "sweetest waters" of the Nile, *grande et admirabile*. Prayers which he believed unavailing were offered in "very beautiful" mosques of Cairo; in the City of the Dead he particularly liked the tombs of the great, with their ornament of marbles, porphyries and alabaster. There was talk of a crusade (*rumores passagii*), and the Latins feared to be taken up as spies. The two travellers slipped away to Damietta. From visitors' accounts it is possible to reconstruct something of the life of the Latin residents, and still more of the conscious impact of Arab material culture on passing Europeans.

Western merchant interests in the Arab World never changed

radically. Their relative importance ultimately decreased, because of developments in different parts of the world, though European interests in India increased the actual volume of European travel through the Levant and other Arab lands. In this sense the pattern after 1290 remained unchanged until the imperial age, and even then there was continuity. Throughout the Middle Ages, the development of trade is certainly more important than the history of such military exploits as those of Chaucer's knight; but neither trade nor war contributed seriously to communication between the Arab and European cultures. As long as the Mediterranean remained the principal sea route of Europe, a realization of unity survived, but it was rarely articulate, and there was little useful exchange of ideas, even at the practical level.

Chapter 9

The Arabs, Islam and European theology

1. The conflict

The venomous attacks on Islam by the Christians of mediaeval Europe seem the more strange that Islam and Christianity are so alike; but two groups who hold the same mutually exclusive theory inevitably exclude each other. Different explanations of this irrational virulence have been put forward, but none is needed. Societies are more often suspicious of each other than not, and, as in our own day, are liable to express their feelings in ideological terms. We can identify their hatred, if we like, as a biological or zoological function, such as occurs also among rats and other animals.

Europeans picked on the most easily understood areas of difference and exaggerated them. Their preconceptions dulled their apprehension of Arab life and grossly distorted the facts of the Prophet's life and of the Arabia of his day. They made inequitable comparisons. They criticized the Prophet for making war against the unbelievers in Mecca and the Jews in Medina who had attacked him; Jesus had fought no war. Yet so slight was the resulting difference between the two religions that their laws of holy war approximated in great detail, and Muslims tolerated Christians more willingly and persistently than Christians did Muslims. To take another example, the two laws of marriage and concubinage were quite different, and Christianity since its early days had stressed the value of total sexual continence in a way that was foreign to Islam. Europeans did sometimes appreciate that their practice was much the same as the practice of their Muslim neighbours, but they preferred their own more exacting laws (whether observed or not), and were prepared to judge, not practice against practice, but theory against theory, and even, often, their own theory against Muslim practice. As far as public behaviour is concerned we can be sure that the Arab World exacted a much greater degree of public decorum in relation to women, and often a less degree of decorum in relation to homo-sexuality, than did contemporary Europe, but there is no reason to suppose that there was any significant difference in sexual practice of all kinds, although this is quite unassessable on the evidence available.

Above all, Christians would not accept that the Quran was truly revealed. Even those who admired some Muslims or those who recognized the practice of virtue among them were unable to recognize the greatness of the Prophet. His true character was only vaguely reflected in their writings, though a little more frequently as time passed. For the most part he was subjected to gross abuse which, however shocking in itself, we must understand as rooted in folk-lore. The Quran was seen as the product of the events of the life of the Prophet, but rather as a deliberate contrivance than as God's revelation in response to particular needs. The resemblance of the Quran to the Christian Scriptures was seen as a plagiarism, where Muslims see the Scriptures as a corruption of revelation which is intact only in the Quran. Christians never recognized that the methodology of their interpretation of the Quran and of the Prophet's life could be transposed for use against the Christian Scriptures, Christian heroes and Christ himself, as has since happened. Some of the more scholarly polemists used the text of the Quran despite itself as a witness to Christian doctrine. The hub of all debate was the unity of God. Responsible writers based their arguments on the Trinity, which it was then fashionable to 'prove' on Augustinian principles. From the proposition that the unity of God presupposes the Trinity of Persons it seemed to follow that, if there were no Trinity, there could be no unity. Both Muslims and Christians were doubtful of the true monotheism of the other. This may partly explain the invention, surely malicious, that Muslims worship idols.

Yet even gross caricatures of Islam had a faint whiff of fact that lent them a kind of credibility. Where were the sources? The manuscript that Eulogio found in Pamplona was already old, but seemed to him to confirm his existing ideas. Most written material can be traced to Spain, either as source or as channel, but it must have been reinforced by local oral tradition, and stories originating in the East must also spring from local Christian sources. Minorities naturally cherish scurrilous derision of their masters.

Scholars travelled between the North and Spain, and Spanish Jews travelled to England and further; but returning pilgrims, and mercenary and free-lance soldiers from Spain and the East, are the most likely vehicles. It is possible to recognize in the twelfth-century surge of misinformation a long submerged fund of satire against Islam suddenly released by Christian victories.

2. Legendary treatment of Islam

Accounts of Islam that appeared early in northern Europe, as Southern pointed out, were most divorced from reality, and most remote from any contact with Islam. This argument can be taken too far, however; the ninth-century (or earlier) Pamplona account must come from Spain; we can recognize a distinction between untrue accounts which are deliberate, probably malicious, misrepresentations; and those which are totally absurd, based on pure fantasy. The earliest Northern lives of Muhammad are by writers whose lives were spent mostly in the eleventh century, and who survived into the early decades of the twelfth, Guibert of Nogent, Hugh of Fleury, and Sigebert of Gembloux. These were Benedictine writers of the age of the Gregorian reform; they are consciously clerical, humanist and insular. They can have known only the first generation of Crusaders. To their work should be added the poems by Walter of Compiègne, Alexandre du Pont and Embrico of Mainz (attributed to Hildebert of Lavardin). The chroniclers were more serious than the poets. Hugh of Fleury was a relative of William I of England who became Abbot of St Augustine's, Canterbury, and ruled from *c.* 1091 to 1124. He is the first writer to make use of a popular and very inaccurate account of the life of the Prophet which has some distant echoes of fact. It was repeated by a number of later writers, especially English chroniclers, but including the great thirteenth-century encyclopaedist, Vincent of Beauvais. The chief point of interest about this story is that it describes the marriage of the Prophet to Khadija, the 'lady' of Corozan. Khurasan was always considered by Arabs to be the key province of the Abbasid caliphate; whoever controlled it controlled the caliphate. The word is used by early crusading writers, in particular the author of the *Gesta Francorum*, whose usage is likely to be representative of the habits of 1096. In the *Gesta*, 'Corozan' seems to refer to the whole Abbasid caliphate, in a vague way; in this story of the Prophet, however, it is seen definitely as a province. Khurasan actually has nothing whatever to do with the Arabia of the Prophet, of course, but the use of the term at all suggests a crusading origin for the story. The story also says that Muhammad travelled to Egypt and Palestine. This had a real Islamic source. This story shows no other sign of historical or geographical perspective. Sigebert of Gembloux, a supporter of Henry IV and opponent of Popes Gregory VII and Pascal II, included a similar account in his great chronicle, but it does not refer to the locality 'Corozan'. Sigebert and Hugh both conceive the country of Muhammad's birth in feudal terms; they stress the idea that he was "poor and an orphan" but seem to assume that this must mean that he was of low birth. His teaching, thought Sigebert, was the means by which "he arrived at the kingship." This may as likely be of Spanish as of Crusading origin; Eulogio's manuscript said *"pusillus"*.

It is particularly remarkable that Guibert of Nogent is vaguer about the setting of Muhammad's life than Sigebert and Hugh, whose dating is accurate, because they make use of Anastasius the Librarian, the Greek scholar of the ninth century; as Hugh of Fleury complained, "he said little, but he did indicate clearly in what times Muhammad lived." The "said little" is significant; writers wanted colour and sensation. Guibert of Nogent certainly collected information from returned pilgrims, and says that he has never seen a written account of Muhammad's life, but gives "the popular opinion" of him. He calls him, with some doubts, '*mathomus*', which in fact suggests a written source, which explains the substitution of *t* for *c*. He adds that, as he caused so much harm, it does not matter whether the evil things he says about him are true or false. We shall see below that he quite frankly admits to "joking", perhaps practical joking. His is one of the earliest examples of the tale which supposes that the Quran was a book of the law which appeared by a false miracle on the horns of a cow (or bull or ox). This sort of thing exemplifies the shifts to which the Christians were put to explain how the Prophet could have been accepted by the people, and is indeed a sort of back-handed compliment, a grudging admission of his charismatic power. It is interesting that this story should have appeared at this time; it also appears with the somewhat later story of a dove trained to whisper in the Prophet's ear, in a *libellus in partibus transmarinis* given a wide circulation by Vincent of Beauvais, who claimed that it originated in Syria.

The poets, Walter and the Frenchman Du Pont, and Embrico, take the process of mythologizing even further. We pass entirely into a world of fantasy. They all have the legend of the cow or calf or bull. The poems do not perhaps intend to be taken seriously. They are humanistic exercises, but Du Pont's French legend of Muhammad stresses an aristocratic concept which must relate to a vernacular and courtly audience. He makes it a reproach to the Prophet that he raised his status by marriage to Khadija. The idea that the Prophet was 'base-born' is of course quite wrong, and the special emphasis that Du Pont gives it is characteristic of an age when—in Europe—great fortunes were made by marriage and doubtless also resented. Khadija's able steward persuaded her into marriage with arguments that reflect the later Western satire on marriage. As a general tendency, the same theme is present in all these earlier writers, who have many things in common, though not enough to indicate a specific common source.

Some of the 'popular' ideas of Muhammad were taken up by writers who possessed a much closer knowledge of Islam, and in some cases a knowledge of Arabic. Walter and Du Pont speak of Muhammad as "rhetorician, arithmetician, dialectician, geometrician, musician, astrologer and grammarian;" that is, they apply the Western tradition of the quadrivium and trivium to Muhammad, as though he had been brought up in the cathedral schools of the West. The 'Corozan' story of Hugh of Fleury spoke of the Prophet as *'magus perfectissimus'*. We have seen that such notions reflect respect for Islamic science, and are, again, a backhanded compliment, to explain away the success of Islam without accepting it as true. Later, these ideas were taken up by writers who had a real knowledge. Mark of Toledo early in the thirteenth century, translator of the Quran and of Ibn Tumart, spoke of the Prophet as having become as skilled in the mathematical arts as was possible in those distant regions. The *Cronica de Espana* calls him very learned in the magical arts, and one of the most learned in Arabia and Spain. In the meantime an example of the *nur muhammadi* literature had been translated from the Arabic, *De Generatione Machumet*, and this is likely to have been available in Toledo. Contrary to its intention, it will have given colour to the magical implication of the 'Corozan' tale. Thus stories of popular origin came to find acceptance among those who should have known better.

The theme of relaxed sexual morals is well represented in

twelfth-century writers. The idea was part of the Spanish
Christian tradition, as well as that of the Christians of the East.
It does not occur in the 'Corozan' story, but Guibert has it: "he
removed the restraints on all shamefulness for his followers."
Writers in the later twelfth century whose information did not
derive from more scholarly writers show the same tendency; after
quoting the 'Corozan' story, Gerald of Wales added that Islam
taught whatever would best please man, and explained that "as
many wives and concubines as he can sustain" were allowed by the
law, Orientals being libidinous, "strongly influenced and compelled to it by the heat of the region." Alan of Lille claims that
Muslims assert polygamy because the whole of their lives is spent
in sexual desire. In the poems of the earlier part of the century,
however, this is taken to even more absurd lengths. "You dissolve
marriage and corrupt virginity," say Walter and Du Pont, and the
latter gave the vernacular public the idea that every Muslim was
allowed ten wives and every Muslim woman ten husbands. Here
the bias against the moral system of Islam has reached the opposite
pole from the fact; but this was not serious; it was offered for the
public amusement. In the real world such an arrangement would
be arithmetically difficult; this is an orgiastic fantasy of the
author's. The attitude of the poets is thoroughly frivolous; that
of the clerical writers is not much more responsible, although its
purpose is didactic.

It may well be that frivolity is also the explanation of the themes
of the *chansons de geste* which also date from the first part of the
twelfth century, including the assumption that Muslims worship
a variety of idols. Even Guibert, vague and abusive and content to
rely openly on popular opinion, knew better than this. After a
rather crude joke, he says,

> "But joking apart—which is done to deride the followers (of the
> Prophet)—it must be quietly admitted that they do not consider
> him to be God, as some people think, but a just man, and that he is
> the protector through whom the divine law is passed down."

In the 'Corozan' story the Prophet is thought to have called himself
the Messiah, and though this is quite wrong, it is less absurd than
the gods Apollin and Tervagant and Mahom. Apart from some
slurs against the pagan origins of the Kabah in Mecca, which
their authors would have omitted if they had known the advice of
Gregory the Great to Augustine about the consecration of pagan

temples, the tradition of the idols worshipped by Saracens is effectively confined to the *chansons de geste*, and some other and later romances. An immense idol of Mahomet figures in the Chronicle of the false Turpinus; but this audacious fiction has notorious affinities with *Roland* and the Charlemagne cycle. The *Gesta Francorum* speaks of gods, and of oaths taken by Muhammad as a god, and this antedates the *chansons*; but it is not at all clear that the author shares the characteristic belief of the *chansons* about the gods Apollin, and the rest. This may well be a late elaboration.

The picture of Islam in the *Chanson d'Antioche* and its fantastic continuation, of *Jerusalem* is very close to that of the Charlemagne cycle. Some lines in the *Couronnement de Louis* describe quite clearly one of the more unpleasant stories about the Prophet which may have derived equally from Spain or the East, and it has even one line which is in touch with reality, "he was a prophet of almighty Jesus." In the rest of the poem Mahomet, together with Cahu, is addressed as a god. This single line is put in the mouth of the Christian, William of Orange, and it may be in the mind of the author that Muhammad was really the man William describes, though worshipped as a god by the Muslims. How seriously are we to take the pagan system of the Charlemagne cycle and the crusading *chansons*? On the face of it we have here the frivolity of the ordinary man, who is not interested in the abstract pursuit of truth. It is obvious that Chaucer did not take this sort of thing seriously, when he put the oath "by Termagaunt" into the mouth of Olifaunt in his burlesque *Sir Topaz*, yet the tradition survived Chaucer and appears solemnly in fifteenth-century poems. We know that these ideas belong to a fairly clear literary tradition in the vernaculars, and that they are in contrast to the clerical tradition which, however defective, aimed generally at producing convincing information.

It is generally assumed that with the appearance of crusading and Reconquista literature we have revealed to us for the first time the common layman's picture of Islam, but in the nature of the hypothesis there is no proof of this. There must have been some belief that Muslims were pagan and polytheist, but we cannot be sure of more than that. These absurd gods and idols appear at just the time when more writers were beginning to write about Islam in a different way; though their stories are also often legendary, they are the perversion, or the dim reflection, of actual facts.

It is just as likely as not that the fabrication of Apollin and company occurred in the twelfth century and that it was deliberate. The Eastern *chansons* may represent a positive rejection of the attitude of learned men to Islam, a kind of protest against the management of the crusade; and the Western cycle may equally reflect a layman's world in protest against the theological approach. On the other hand, their scheme of pagan gods suits their poetic plan much better than the clerical polemic could ever have done. The final image of the 'pagans' with which the *chansons* leave us has a certain grandeur, and is a good deal less unpleasant than the image of Muhammad which the clerics convey. It may be an elaborate protest against taking the whole thing seriously at all.

3. Serious polemic

The popular stories and poems of the earlier twelfth century thus treated crusade—the *chansons* are wholly about the holy war—sexuality and the Quranic revelation of the unity of God, all in a thoroughly frivolous manner. They are serious only about incidentals, like honour or status. The usual clerical approach, especially from the middle of the century, was not like this. There were a number of serious attempts to show the truth about Islam, and these necessitated its 'disproof'. Although—or because—they were serious, these writers for the most part felt committed to the stories that had been irresponsibly created by their frivolous predecessors. As they turned up more and more genuine information about Islam, they regretted the legendary, or 'Christian' or 'true' version of events, which seemed less and less probable. However, the 'Christian' version was, however remotely, a reflection or distortion of the actual facts, and it was therefore just possible logically to suppose that the actual facts were distortion, and the 'Christian' version the true one after all.

A Jewish element was contributed by Pedro de Alfonso (his godfather at his baptism in 1106 was Alfonso VI of Castile). Among his dialogues against Judaism, one against Islam introduced to the Latins a polemic tripartite test of a prophet, by "probity of life, the presentation of true miracles and the constant truth of all his sayings," together with much accurate and some erroneous information about Arab ritual and customs. Then, in 1142, Peter the Venerable, Abbot of Cluny, who was travelling in Spain at the invitation of Alfonso VII (of Castile) paid two translators to turn from scientific to religious texts. Three of their translations are of little importance, but that of the Quran by Robert of Ketton, though a paraphrase containing many ellipses, was the most widely read version in any European language till the seventeenth century. Equally important was the translation by, probably, a Mozarab, of the *Risala* or *Apology* of al-Kindi (not the Arab philosopher, but a pseudonymous Christian), the Latin of which the Abbot's secretary corrected. Its scurrilous interpretations of the Prophet's actions and its Trinitarian arguments fell perfectly into the polemic pattern, to which it gave a new verisimilitude, because the author was familiar with the actual facts that he distorted. This book circulated widely in an abbreviated form in the *Speculum* of Vincent of Beauvais; a text incorporated by Matthew Paris in the St Albans Chronicle and used also by James of Vitry looks like a still shorter abbreviation, but may spring from the living tradition of the Christian East. Translation supported polemic. There was a short tract, apparently intended to give St Bernard background information for preaching the crusade; he probably made no use of it. There was a treatise by Abbot Peter himself, a sincere, but not very successful, attempt to approach religious difference with imagination and sympathy. It read unambiguously as a direct appeal to Muslims, but neither Peter nor Alfonso nor anyone else seems to have thought of putting it into Arabic. Finally, there were a number of headings sent to the Abbot by his secretary (who had remained in Spain) as a plan for his treatise. They were largely ignored, but in themselves they constitute a summary of most of the points that recur in this literature.

The complex relations of all the Spanish sources were brilliantly studied by M. T. d'Alverny. Early in the thirteenth century, Mark of Toledo made a better translation of the Quran, which was negligible in its influence, as was his version of the praises of God by the Almohad leader, Ibn Tumart. He also translated Galen from Arabic, and perhaps the *Opposition to the Fuqaha* (*contrarietas elfolica*), ostensibly the work of a convert from Islam, more probably by a Mozarab. Later in the century this work was the chief source of the great polemic *Refutation of the Quran* by Ricoldo da Monte Croce which was influential as late as the end of the seventeenth century; of Ricoldo's shorter but more individual work I say more later on. Mark's motive, like Peter the Venerable's, derived from the belief that more accurate information would make refutation more effective. The same motivation brought into being two formidable works of mediaeval Islamic scholarship, the *Fourfold Condemnation*, by the Dominican, Ramon Marti, or by an author of the same milieu, and a much longer work at the end of the century, *On the Muhammedan Sect*, attributed to the Mercedarian, St Peter Pascual. The first of these used a variety of well-chosen Islamic sources, including al-Bukhari, and Ibn Ishaq's *sira rasul Allah*; the second made extensive use of the *sira*, but did so in a vain search for corroboration of all the most absurd Christian legends. Considered as scholarship, the weakness of all this work was its polemic intention. The *Fourfold Condemnation* is superior only in its more straightforward use of the material, which is selected polemically, but not forced beyond its obvious meaning. The *Cronica de Espana* and the *Historia Arabum* of Roderick of Toledo used authentic Muslim material that is over-laid, in the former especially, by legendary matter.

At the eastern end of the Mediterranean, the study of Islam was more primitive. Sophisticated writers like James of Vitry depended on oral sources. The later days of the Latin states produced one original writer in William of Tripoli. His story of the progress of Islam from the childhood of the Prophet through the expansion of the Arabs into Spain and Provence, breaking off at that point and beginning again with the invasion of Egypt by Louis IX, is a curious mixture of fact and of Muslim and Christian legend. The historical perspective suggests a strong Western admixture in the Christian element, which is primarily East Latin. I earlier quoted William's praise of Baybars; he stressed those aspects of Islam which come closest to Christian faith. He cited "Oriental chronicles", the Prophet's "imitators", and Arab "masters", but his work does not seem to be based on authentic documents. Mandeville derives from him. It is a pity that we do not know more about the studies that resulted in a knowledge of Islam which was often sympathetic.

The quality of the knowledge that the Spaniards acquired of Islam and therefore of Arab culture can be exemplified by brief quotation.

> "Muhammad proclaimed a fast of the thirty days at a prefixed time, and he who did not fast at the fixed time for some reason should redeem the obligation of his fast by alms, if he was rich, and if in fact he was poor, by fasting at another time. He taught them to

pray at the place of worship, or else at home, five times a day; but, before they entered the temple, he ordered them to be washed in water."

This is Mark of Toledo; and if it is not quite accurate—and he continues in the same strain for some length—it is clearly an attempt to state facts non-committally, which is in sharp contrast to his story of the Prophet's life. Here is a quotation of the *sira rasul Allah* from the *Fourfold Condemnation*. Some Arabs send to the Prophet and ask him for a miracle.

> " 'You know that there are no men who have a more confined city than we, or who have less water or less food, or a more confined life than we; if, as you say, you are a prophet and messenger of God, ask the Lord your God, who sent you, on our behalf, to move those mountains, which hem us in, away from us, and to widen our land, and to cause rivers to flow here like the rivers of the Eastern land; and to resurrect one of our ancestors for us, and let it be Qusayy, because he was a true shaikh, and we will ask him whether what you say is true or false.' . . . Muhammad answered them, 'I am not sent to you to work miracles.' Then they said to him again . . . 'Ask your God to give you palaces and treasures of gold and silver . . . For you go into the market and earn your living as we earn ours. So that we should know what merit and dignity you have with your God, if you are sent to warn us, as you say.' Muhammad answered, 'I shall not do that, nor I am one who asks the Lord his God to do such a thing, and I am not sent to you for that; but God sent me to proclaim and to warn.' "

Had all the writings of the period been like this, readers at that time would have had a good picture of the Prophet and of the Arab background.

This did not happen. What sort of picture of the Prophet's Hijaz does emerge? If we ignore the earliest and silliest of the legends, but take into account absurdities surviving from the past, but still credited, we receive a very mixed impression. The 'Corozan' tale, which continued to be popular, began by saying that Muhammad, the prince of the Arabs, was of the race of Ismail, son of Abraham. Brunetto Latini tells us that Abraham circumcised Isaac eight days after birth, and Ismail at the same time, when he was thirteen; for that reason the Arabs, the descendants of Ismail, he says, have always done so at that age. Occasionally the whole genealogy of Muhammad was given. The fact that the word *Saracen* was wrongly supposed to be used by the Arabs themselves, to imply a claim to descent from Sara, is relevant here. The Paris theologian, William of Auvergne, saw in the life of Muhammad and the rise of the Arabs the fulfilment of the divine purpose: "I will make the son also of the bondwoman a great nation." William of Tripoli, whose little history of Arab aggression entirely omits those periods when Europeans attacked the Arabs, saw the fulfilment of another prophecy about Ismail, "and he shall pitch his tents against all his brethren." "Let him understand who reads," says Tripoli, "whether this prophecy is fulfilled in Muhammad, since it seems that in none of the children of Ismail has there been found one so wild and powerful to pitch his tents against all." The general notion that the Arabs were ferocious people who sprang from the background of Ismail, and over-whelmed the world, is one of many misconceptions of the day which have survived with some force into our own time.

Because writers were opposed to Islam, they sometimes show sympathy with the Meccans. Some know that the Meccans were merchants; it was understood that Arabia was a place from which it was possible to travel to Egypt or Syria, and Muhammad as a young man was believed to have travelled as a merchant on behalf of the wealthy Khadija. Roderick tells the story, deriving from Ibn Ishaq, of the rebuilding of the Kabah (before the announcement of the Prophet's mission); in this the elders of the Quraysh appear as a council of city fathers, at least implying an understanding of civic life in Mecca. He also remarked in passing that Mecca in the days before Islam owed its importance to its many idols. A little less correctly, Pedro de Alfonso had said that the inhabitants of Arabia were "for the most part soldiers and farmers, and almost all idolators, except for some who held the Mosaic law according to the Samaritan heresy, and others who were Christians—Nestorians, or Jacobites." It was often said that the people of Arabia were "rough and untaught," "Arabs, *villani*, uneducated people." The reason for this untrue description of a people who enjoyed a complex literature is doubtless apologetic, to show that they were likely to be deceived; but it may obscurely reflect the implications of descent from Ismail, the townsman's view of the Bedouin. Lull told his son that,

> "Yathrib and Mecca and all that province were full of people who
> believed in idols, and who adored the sun and the moon and the
> beasts and the birds, and had no knowledge of God, and had no
> King, and were people of little discretion and little understanding."

He seems here to be applying some standard account of animistic religion of which there is no evidence, but he added, more historically, that this uncivilized people had no belief in a life after death, and he realized that Muhammad's preaching was essentially of Judgement and the heavenly reward. Many accounts emphasized the paganism of the Arabs in Muhammad's youth: "and there, in the course of many disagreements, by preaching that one God only should be adored, he very often quarrelled with those who were of the race of the Quraysh and adored idols."

There was some idea that Arabia had been a Christian country, but this was not usual. Roderick thought that Arabia and Africa were torn between the Catholic faith, the Arian heresy, the Jewish perfidy and idolatry. The substance of so many of the legends about Christian or Jewish influences at the time of the Prophet was that Arabia was an area subject to outside influence because it was unruly and under no government and on the edge of the known world. Latins were not always, but often, well informed about the history of the various Christian heresies, and their chronology makes Islam the culmination and often the sum of all the heresies, an argument sometimes worked out in detail. In consequence their picture of Arabia seems to be set less in the material world than in an abstract world of dogmatic history. Described as poor, or uneducated, or idolators, they might as well be Europeans as yet unconverted to Christianity, and there is no reason to suppose that they were thought of otherwise. There may be some European memory of the shock caused by the eruption of the Arabs in the seventh century. The 'Saracens' whom Muhammad converted were apparently not the 'Arabs' who transmitted Aristotle to the Latin West. Neither did they correspond to the Moors and Berbers whom the Christians of Spain were defeating, or the armies who drove the Crusaders out of Syria. These were three aspects under which the Arabs were known to mediaeval Europe, and there seems to be little relation between them. That they represented one continuous culture would be incredible to someone who knew nothing at all of the subject, except through the mediaeval sources.

In saying this, we must make a reservation. The dissociation of the Arabs as a source of scientific learning from the Arabs as 'Saracens' was virtually complete. Contemporary Saracens and Saracens of the time of the Prophet, however, were connected. The rise of Islam was associated with the nature of its teaching, the

history of the Muslims in later times with their history in the time
of the Prophet. The interpretation of all the events of the Prophet's
life at Medina in terms of private vengeance was derived from the
Risala and kindred sources; translated into Latin, and into the
terms of a wholly different society, they acquired more the look of
political assassination than perhaps even he intended. The duty of
jihad laid down in the Quran gave religion the air of having
endorsed aggression; in the Latin concept, the religion was the
product of the war, not the war of the religion. Every contemporary Muslim, just by being Muslim, appeared a kind of aggressor.
It was possible to justify any of the horrors of warfare by remembering the early days of Islam with indignation. A wicked Muslim
was thought to act out of the nature of his creed; a wicked
Christian could always be found an excuse. All the sins of the
Christians, generally the same sins as the Muslims', were either
to be explained away, or at least condemned as contrary to
Christian discipline. There is even no special association of astrology, still less of magic, much of which was translated from the
Arabic, with Islam, except in the assertion of the 'Corozan' story
that Muhammad was a *magus*. Muslim philosophers were generally
dissociated from religious controversy. The greatest exception to
this rule is discussion of a future life. Even there, for example,
Roger Bacon in England and Ramon Marti in Spain, at about the
same time, were quoting al-Farabi, al-Ghazali and Ibn Sina, as
they supposed, against Islamic doctrine. William of Tripoli
thought that the Muslim doctors were turning to Christianity
because they could not accept their own teaching on Paradise.

Ricoldo's account of his journey illustrates a special polemic
pattern. It was uncharacteristic of almost all of Ricoldo's work that
he should have written so enthusiastically, almost too enthusiastically to be convincing, of the Arab scholars of Baghdad. His
passages of generous praise are followed immediately by a summary of his narrow polemic—"the Muslim religion is wide (i.e.
easy), confused, hidden, most deceitful, irrational and violent."
"Confused", because "it cannot be reduced to order," a point
which seems personal, reflecting a failure to discuss profitably,
perhaps; and because it is "confused in its confusion," as to say,
"Do not do such and such, because it is forbidden by God; and if
you do it, God is merciful and compassionate, and knows that
you are weak." Islam is "hidden" in that it is hard to know what it
really says; for instance, the prohibition of usury and fornication is

accompanied by legal means of evading the law. These are points unintelligible to Muslims because of that very cultural barrier which forced Ricoldo to understand Islam so ill.

A comparison of Ricoldo's fields of interest would reveal much to a careful analysis. He passes through Samarra like a tourist; it has so many ruins that it is like another Rome, *quasi altera Roma*. The followers of Ali keep a fine mule ready saddled for "a certain son of Ali who is six hundred years dead" (the hidden *imam*). In contrast to this he is very interested in the Mongols, in their sociology and from the point of view of comparative religion. As with the Sunni Muslims of Baghdad, he is willing to give credit to the chief men of a "false" religion. They have "high priests of idols" who "are men from India, really learned and well organized and really serious in their ways. They know the magic skills jointly, and support themselves by the advice and help of demons; they exhibit many illusions, and foretell some things in the future." There is no obvious pattern in his praise and dispraise. The Mongols were of interest as potential Christian converts, but this was not true of the Muslims; on the other hand the Shia, treated so cursorily, are not less easily converted than Sunnis. In the case of the Christians, all belonging to separate churches, the case is different. Here the nature of his interest is immediately apparent, and here we find no anthropology, and no tourism, and certainly no extravagant appreciation of the virtues of an alien culture.

Of the 'Jacobins' (Monophysites of Syrian rite) he said,

> "We answered them, that we came for their salvation, and, taking up the word, we commended the works of perfection which they displayed, such as so long and so strict a fast and the greatest abstinence, and the great length and devotion of their prayer, and we adjured them by the blood of the Crucified, which they specially venerate, lest with so much labour they should yet descend into hell through their infidelity" (i.e. heresy).

How the visiting Dominicans preached the two natures of Christ to the monks and the Patriarch and the people follows at length. Characteristic of the mediaeval Latins were both the enthusiasm poured out on separated brethren, and also the belief that they must be damned, despite their fasts and prayers, if they stick to the doctrine of the single nature. Ricoldo sympathizes with the Monophysites when the Nestorians persecute them. The Nestorians (Assyrians or Chaldeans) he naturally finds less to his taste.

"Their position about Christ, if it be minutely examined, empties the whole mystery out of the Incarnation, and they assert the same about Christ as the Muslims do. Whence also I found among old and authentic histories, which the Muslims had, that these very Nestorians were the friends and allies of Muhammad."

This, I am afraid, is highly inaccurate, and the old authentic histories must be also. It is regrettable also that Ricoldo said that the Patriarch flew in the wink of an eye from Baghdad to Mecca, "where Muhammad is buried." All Ricoldo's polemic and his vaunted discussions with the Arab scholars of Baghdad were based thus substantially on misinformation. We sympathize with the unfortunate Assyrians who offered the Dominicans a church and a good site and other necessaries, on condition they stop preaching; these Europeans replied that they had not come for palaces or churches, but just in order to preach. The triumphs Ricoldo records are doubtless concessions for the sake of peace; Ricoldo was really unhappy at these little deviations, and he speaks with relief (elsewhere) of the Greeks who are near the Latins in language, behaviour, rite and creed. This measures how far he had travelled beyond the experience of other and earlier Crusaders who distrusted, as they were distrusted by, the Greeks. Yet his attitude is illustrative. In an age when the phrases of the creed could seem to determine the fate of every individual of the church which found itself in error, it is obvious that orthodoxy—Latin orthodoxy—was the expression of something more than a theological controversy. Unity in every detail of belief expressed the unity of the people.

Yet Ricoldo's work, taken as a whole, constitutes a remarkable concentration of the facts that the thirteenth-century mediaevals were able to learn about Islam. Moreover, he illustrates with particular accuracy the reasons that lay behind the European urge to condemn and condemn; condemnations of Islam are only an aspect of other condemnations, of the oriental churches, as well as of the great heresies which sprang up in, or invaded, Europe, and even of each individual intellectual eccentricity. It is in the context of European thirst for orthodoxy that we must see the passion for identifying the heresies that Islam resembled (or might be supposed to derive from), and for specifying minutely each separate count on which Islam must be detested. So much theological literature is boring because it is so constantly reiterated, perhaps for reassurance. All the straining after orthodoxy is,

The Arabs and mediaeval Europe

in a way, a search for reassurance. Occasionally a Muslim author is used to drive home a point against Islam; Ibn Sina is often quoted against what the Muslim idea of Heaven was supposed to be. The bounds of orthodoxy were rarely relaxed to admit even so distinguished a thinker, and not even in the cause of orthodoxy. The experience of the fourteenth-century English monk and scholastic, Uthred of Boldon, is exceptional only in what he said, not in its condemnation. A number of interesting propositions of Bolden's were censured, among them the assertion that Muslims (also Jews and pagans) who are quite ignorant of Christianity may be saved, if they avoid sin, by the operation of a "common law"; he thought it possible that those who did not "believe" the faith of Christ might nevertheless "possess" it.

The argument brought forward against Islam by even the most learned and intellectual men of the thirteenth century would have left Muslims very little impressed. The abuse of the Prophet, of course, would have angered them, and when they heard it, it did; but nothing that was said could conceivably have touched their faith in the sense of introducing a doubt into their minds. Christian writers never got at the roots of Islam. Not even their subtlest arguments, that which was supposed to 'prove' the Trinity, or those that were based on Scriptures which Muslims do not accept, or on an interpretation of the Quran which Muslims would deride, could in practice be used as ostensibly they were intended, to convince Muslims, or to defeat them in debate. Only one conclusion is possible, as I have argued in greater detail elsewhere. They were intended for internal consumption, and were the better for that if they could be presented as having successfully silenced Muslims in debates which can rarely have happened at all, and never profitably.

It is the curious fact that Islam was not associated seriously with the great heretical movements, or with alleged heretical conspiracy. No one pretended that Albigensians—or Waldensians—were associated with Islam. The Shepherds' Crusades associated themselves with Islam, but most of the heresies of mediaeval Europe, even those which from the late eleventh century onwards were essentially popular and revolutionary, seem to have had no precise connotation of Muslim ideas. The most that was alleged was that Arab rulers had plotted some of the movements; no one ever associated even a pretended Muslim idea with a pretended heretical notion. Not even in the suppression of the Templars, so closely connected with Islam throughout their history, and as certainly as possible a fabrication, was there any emphasis on a positive Muslim influence, as would have been easy and obvious. Islam was accused of violence and sexual antinomianism; yet those sects that were violent and antinomian were not made out to be influenced by Islam. The fact is that Islam was never believed to be a dangerously attractive proposition. If the ideas condemned in Paris in 1277 had been 'Averroist', as Renan claimed, Islam and Christendom would have shared a heresy. This was hardly the case, and yet the two religions shared so much more than Europeans thought they did; common ground was rarely recognized, and, when it was, it gave little pleasure. Muslim devotion to Jesus and his mother was often welcomed as "poison mixed with honey". At most, approval was grudging. Muhammad, said the theologian, William of Auvergne, "forbade sodomitical filth, and ordered some worthy things, and prohibited some unworthy ones." The real emphasis was on disagreement, but it was theoretical and rarefied and had little to do with real life.

If no one really thought Islamic doctrine infectious, and if no one would ever usefully engage in controversy with a Muslim in free and equal conditions, why did the accuracy of anti-Islamic polemic improve so radically? It became more plausible, but we cannot now believe that it was intended to convince. Partly we can explain the new scholarship simply on the grounds that the human mind worries away until something that it can accept as true has emerged; but that presupposes at least a continuing interest, which itself requires explanation. An explanation might be that this material was meant to fortify the faith of Christians remaining under Muslim rule, and in Spain it may have had some such effect. Yet this is only a marginal advantage; those Mozarabs who had retained their faith in hopeless times were not likely to falter when Christian armies were in the ascendant. Another answer possible is that all this was war propaganda, and it doubtless did have some use in encouraging the armies; but the more abusive stories will have been of most use, and the more scholarly of least, for this purpose. The spurts of writing about Islam often followed the Christian offensives; they did not necessarily accompany or precede them. The Crusaders of 1096 did not go to the east with accounts of the Prophet tucked into their chain-mail; we know that they had even vaguer notions of Islam when they went than when they returned—though they returned with ideas more abusive than those with which they went—and the evidence is that they were simply not interested. What did inspire them was the notion that Arabs or Turks were attacking them, and attacking God, but just how they were attacking God they did not care; God is always on 'our' side.

Only professional apologists were interested in Islam; even writers who felt some interest in Islam for its own sake were never free of the obsessively apologetic approach. In this sense the view they expressed was Christian rather than European; but we could carry this distinction too far. It is necessarily the accepted orthodoxy which expresses the sense of identity and the cohesion of a society. No non-conforming element, by definition, can do this. The desire to conform, and to make others conform, which results from the biological urge to belong consciously to a group also implies the consciousness that alien groups do not conform. The function served by the literature about Islam was just this, to establish that Muslim Arabs were different from Christian Europeans. This was expressed primarily in theological terms, because that is how the conformity of Europe was expressed. In a period when Europe was in a mood of aggression and expansion, its surplus energy created an attitude to its Arab and Arabic-speaking neighbours which was based, not on what the Arabs were like, but on what, for theological reasons, they ought to be like.

4. The holy war

The use of force was essentially an evasion of speculation. If imaginary debates were good internal propaganda, force was the escape from debating reality. Louis IX, as seen by Joinville, was sensible, and sensitive, in his thoughts about religious doubt, but he thought that dispute was dangerous for anyone who was not *"tres-bons clers"*; the sword in the enemy's stomach was the only sure defence. We know that the learned themselves were of much the same opinion.

Joachim of Flora was admittedly eccentric, but he had a clear historical perspective, and the ability both to present current ideas and to sum up for himself. His overall pattern is his recognition of a series of different ages. The Beast of the Apocalypse "directed the Jews against the Apostles in war, and the pagans against the martyrs, the Arians against the Catholics; most recently, he appointed the sect of Muslims, more monstrous than the others, against the hermits." The choice of hermits is not as odd as it may look, because they represent the perfection of Christian life; perhaps Joachim realized what so few did, that ordinary Christian practice was hardly different from the imaginary violence and sexuality that the Christian moralists attacked. When he is speaking of the "desolation" of the churches he says that it reaches from Syria and Phoenicia through Palestine and Egypt, Africa, Mauretania and the islands of the sea, where "the name of Christ is effaced;" and the doctrine of Muhammad "is preached as of a great Prophet of the Lord and a herald of the Most High." To this onslaught Europe has replied. Joachim recognizes the signs of Christian military revival only with Urban's preaching. "Truly after that so much boldness was given to the Christians;" it was as if the Muslims were annihilated.

> "To concentrate much in one piece; the Muslims in Egypt paid tribute to the Christians who attacked the parts overseas, and those who possessed Asia to the conquerors of Constantinople; Africa and the cities captured by the King of Sicily had Christian colonists. The Kings of Spain often triumphed over their enemies."

These passages give us the whole picture of the successful war of 'recovery' of lands once Christian. We should keep in mind the historical perspective of persuasion and recovery into which the law was fitted and which justified it. Writers were conscious, and right into the Ottoman period remained conscious, of the long detailed history of Europe's wars against the Arab World.

In this process of providential intervention—the intervention by the Beast—we may ourselves situate a number of factors which existed long before the law of Crusade was formed, and which went to its making. The effective excommunication of Jews from sharing any common life with Christians was certainly not the influence of the idea of *jihad*; it was laid down by councils of the sixth century, although they were repeated in the Carolingian period. Gregory of Tours reflects the pre-Islamic treatment of European Jews in his history, and he illustrates also another strand in the final pattern, the conviction that God must always give the physical victory to the Catholics; in his time, of course, that meant, over the Arians, but it was an idea that survived a considerable experience of crusading until it had to be modified to take into account the increasing number of failures. It was this spirit which inspired the martyrs of Cordova to fight their war to an uncompromising finish, in the only way open to them; however idiotic they may seem, we must respect their logic as well as their courage. In the directly formative line there were the decisions of Leo IV and John VIII, who failed to rouse European morale, as their successor managed to do over two hundred years later; but who tried to instil into men, not only the fighting spirit, but confidence that if they died for their faith God would take their sacrifice into account. Lastly, there is Urban himself; whatever it was that he said, he gave the final impetus to the justification of aggression. His idea was revolutionary in that he knew the moment to set ancient ideas in motion.

There was in fact a different and much less prominent line of Christian thought. It can be illustrated only twenty years before Urban preached, and when already ideas of crusade were being canvassed. That was a moment of equilibrium. Christians had begun to be successful, in Sicily and in Spain, but the idea of attacking the East was still tentative, and the extermination of Muslims in Sicily and Spain was still unthought of. It was reasonable to expect the equilibrium to last longer than it did, and this is what seems to be in the mind of Gregory VII. At the culmination of the movement for church reform, he showed little spirit for crusade, although the notion was discussed in his pontificate. When he wrote to the rulers of Spain in 1077 to ensure that the Spanish church conform to the Roman ritual, he referred to the period when the kingdom had been overrun by "Saracens and pagans" in no very severe terms; his anxiety was all lest the Mozarab rite should be maintained. He wrote to the Christians of Hippo—this probably means Bijaya—in 1076 recalling them to the Roman obedience, and recommending them to set an example of faith and charity among themselves, and to incite the "peoples of the Arabs who are around you" to emulate rather than hold them in contempt. These Christians had elected an archbishop, Servandus, and sent him to the Pope to be consecrated, with a recommendation from the Hammadid king, an-Nasir. Gregory wrote to Nasir, addressed in terms of classical geography as king of Mauretania Sitifensis, "health and apostolic benediction." He addressed him as "your nobility" and said that he had consecrated Servandus, as Nasir had asked; and he thanked him for presents he had sent and for freeing Christian prisoners.

"This goodness God, Creator of all things, without whom we can do nothing good or even imagine it, inspired in your heart; he who illuminates every man coming into this world illuminated your mind in this. For almighty God, who wishes that all men should be saved and none lost, approves nothing in us so much as that man after loving himself should love his fellow, and that what he does not want done to himself he should not do to others. You and we owe this charity to ourselves especially because we believe in and confess one God, admittedly in a different way, and daily praise and venerate him, the creator of the worlds and ruler of this world."

Gregory seems sometimes to quote and sometimes to paraphrase the Bible, but in the phrase "creator of the worlds and ruler of this world" there seems even to be an echo of the *fatiha*. He ends by stressing his sincerity and wishing Nasir health and honour in this life and the next, saying that "we ask with heart and mouth that after the long space of this life that same God will lead you into the bosom of blessedness of the most holy patriarch Abraham." This last phrase implies a fine appraisal of the point where the two religions most easily come together, and the whole letter is based on an assumption of common ground.

This was not the direction that history was to take. Gregory's attitude, of which we have only these few clear indications, is unparalleled almost until modern times, but this is doubtless because the whole picture was changed by the success of the First Crusade. Even when the Crusades had manifestly failed, it was impossible to return to the moment that just preceded their preaching. Once the Muslims were denominated the enemies of God, further seeking for common ground was useless. It is useful here to consider in a little more detail the question of 'martyrdom' and 'indulgence'. We saw that the talk of martyrdom was essentially popular; despite Guibert, there is no clear statement that those who die in battle are martyrs by any reputable theologian. The official councils, and in particular Lateran IV, simply promised a plenary indulgence to those who fought in person on the Crusade, or who financed others to do so, and the equivalence of these two operations is itself a dismissal of the suggestion of martyrdom. The indulgence had first been developed in the course of the eleventh century; it was not a substitute for confession, also enjoined by the Lateran Council, but it was anti-sacerdotal in its effect, because (in that, at least, like martyrdom) it was gained without reference to a priest; it was a substitute for penance, traditionally hard, and was given for a good work, offerings, pilgrimages, and so on. The first plenary indulgence was offered by Urban for the Crusade, or so it came to be generally believed; previous indulgences were for a period of days. The Crusade remained till the fourteenth century the only form of 'plenary indulgence', though more and more works came to qualify for limited indulgences. The important point is that it was gained equally for fighting, and for enabling someone else (by paying money) to fight instead; it excluded martyrdom on the grounds that both exercises earned the same reward. This may seem a nice point in Catholic theology to some readers, but its effect is to make death on crusade into something less than martyrdom strictly understood, a meritorious work like other good works. St Bernard made this clear when he was preaching the Second Crusade; it was given to those who made their confession with contrite heart, an exercise which a true martyrdom would render superfluous. It was this that made it possible to turn crusading into a cheap purchase of penance which might be remitted on payment of a kind of tax.

European sentiment by the middle of the twelfth century had already begun to harden into a more legalistic concept, and was not modified by contact with Arabs, or by necessities of war, as it was in the Latin states themselves. "This we altogether forbid," preached St Bernard, "that for any reason they should enter into an alliance with (the Muslims), neither for money nor for tribute, until with the help of God either their religion or their nation has been destroyed." St Bernard's 'Book of praise of the New Army, to the Knights of the Temple' illustrates the thinking of the churchmen of the day. The soldier of Christ, he asserts,

"carries a sword not without reason; for he is the minister of Christ for the punishment of evil-doers, as well as for the praise of good men. Clearly when he kills a malefactor he is not a homicide but as I should say a malicide, and he is simply considered the avenger of Christ on those who do evil and the protector of Christians. But when he himself is killed he is known not to perish but to survive. Therefore the death which he proposes is for the profit of Christ, and that which he receives, for his own. The Christian glories in the death of the non-Christian, because Christ is glorified; in the death of the Christian the liberality of the King appears, as the soldier is led to his sword . . . Not indeed that even non-Christians ought to be killed if there were some other way to prevent them

from molesting or oppressing the faithful; but now it is better that
they should be killed than that the rod of sinners should certainly
be left over the fate of the just: lest perchance the just reach out
their hands to iniquity."

Not only, therefore, is Christ glorified in the death of the infidel,
but killing is justified if only because the Christians may begin to
pick up the ways of the Arabs.

St Bernard's usual eloquence had less effect upon the fortunes
of the crusade than upon affairs in Europe. The clearest statements
of crusading theory come in fact in the thirteenth century, when
the crusades as an eastward movement of the western Europeans
were already exhausted. Humbert of the Romans was a back-room
expert who summarized the theory as it stood in the thirteenth
century; he made a collection of his crusading sermons, and his
reputation in this field stood so high that he wrote his *Threefold
Work* to brief the Fathers at the Council of Lyons in 1274. A just
war must cause the innocent to suffer, as so often happened in
Europe to poor farmers, and hospitals and leper-colonies; but, he
argued, the Muslim nation was culpable in the highest degree.
There must be a sufficient cause to justify war, nothing like
injured pride, or avarice, or vainglory; but the army of God
fought for something better than even a material right, it fought
for the faith. A just war must be fought on adequate authority;
but the Crusade was fought on the authority of God, and so it was
a just war in the highest degree. The church wields two swords,
against heretics and against rebels; but Muslims destroyed the
body like the latter and the soul like the former. However, it was
permissible to allow Muslims in Christian territory to remain
alive, because they could do no harm, they might be useful, and
they might even be converted. When it was objected that it might
happen that innocent Christians suffered more than guilty
Muslims, Humbert pointed out that this was not so, and instanced
the splendid occasion when the blood of the Arabs came up to the
horses' knees, at the capture of Jerusalem in 1099; he ignored the
more recent history of the Latin states. The doctrine of the just
war received a horrible impetus from the Crusade. Apparently
some objectors contrasted the behaviour of Christ and the Apostles
with this shedding of blood, but Humbert pointed out that conditions had changed: Christians then had had no power and so been
compelled to proceed by humility; now it was quite different;
then they had miracles, now they had arms. In any case, who was

willing to see the Christians perish as a result of non-resistance? Humbert was not evangelical; he was certainly realistic.

There was considerable criticism of crusade, often expressed— both by radicals and by conservatives—as a demand for reform and for a new lay initiative, and it was the practical reply which was effective—who was willing to see the Christian perish? It would not be long before both crusade and indulgence came into disrepute, and would do increasingly. The historical perspective changed as the momentum of 'recovery' died away. Crusading remained an active fantasy, long after it was clear that it would never again be more than an excuse for profitable raiding. When there was a revival of serious crusade in the Balkans at the end of the fourteenth century, the reason was genuinely defensive, and resistance to the Ottoman Turkish advance came well within the principle "who is willing to see the Christian perish?"

5. Toleration of Muslim communities

We saw that no European was ever suspected of crypto-Islam, no heretic of Muslim influence. This, of course, excepts the Moriscos. Although theoretically Islam was identified as the sum of ancient heresies, it was never actually treated as a heresy until the sixteenth-century Inquisition was able to lay its hands on baptized Moriscos. No unbaptized person was ever in theory subject to the jurisdiction of the Christian courts. European converts to Islam presented no problem. Either they would stay Muslims, or they would return to Europe, if they could and wanted to, and say they had been forced to conform, or just say nothing at all. The villages and town populations in the areas conquered by the Europeans were gradually eradicated, but Muslims were treated better than heretics; they were never all burned quickly, like the Albigensians. They were eliminated by a steady pressure, aided by frequent riots and massacres and occasional warfare, but surviving in Spain until the expulsions and oppression that culminated in 1609. There is a closer resemblance between the fate of the Jews and that of the Muslims, and in canon law their situation was practically the same. Nevertheless, the Jews were welcome in Europe more often than the Muslims, if not all the time, or in all areas.

We have seen something of the scholastic argument about holy war. This had its logical sequel in the assessment of the status of Muslims within Christendom. Many Dominicans play a major part in the story of mediaeval controversy with Islam, and another, Robert Holcot, an Englishman who died in 1349, has an unhappy contribution at this point. He carefully distinguished pagans, Jews, Muslims, idolators and heretics. Muslims who submitted to the church might be allowed to live as hewers of wood and drawers of water, in the hope of their conversion, and on condition that there was no "insult to the Creator". We shall hear more of *contumelia Creatoris*, a technical term which included public worship other than Catholic. Muslims who did not submit were rebels, persecutors and heretics, and might, and sometimes should, be killed, and their property given to the faithful. It was necessary to leave a few Jews alive, in order not to prevent the fulfilment of the prophecy that a remnant would be converted in the last days, but this did not apply to Muslims who had unjustly occupied the lands promised to the seed of Abraham (i.e. not the Jews) and other Christian territory; moreover, when Christian missionaries go to Muslim countries and attack Islam they are killed. All property belongs to the just, who may take it from the unjust; the mystical Body of Christ, the redeemed human race, may cut off a putrid member; and in any case—the justification of terrorism— it is right to induce a healthy attitude by fear. In all these arguments Europe is already approaching the position which would produce the treatment of Moors and Jews in Spain in the sixteenth century, though, to be fair, it reminds us also of the knightly attitude of the twelfth century; in *Roland*, the pagans are offered no alternative to death or baptism. Holcot offers very little better. Indeed, the whole argument is not only unpleasant; it has also an air of unreality about it. It can be argued that the Christian position now approximated very closely to that of the Muslims in the law of *jihad*; but in fact it did not have the protection of an unalterable law. Christians within Dar al-Islam could always appeal to the Quran, although the law was sometimes abused; within Christendom there was no final protection for the unconverted Muslim, and none at all, of course, for the converted Muslim, as the history of the Inquisition was to show. The first of the Decretals of Gregory IX which affect 'Saracens' dates from rather earlier, from the Lateran Councils of 1179 and 1216. Christians who take service in the houses of Jews or Saracens, or take care of their children, are excommunicated; those who despoil them of their property, after they receive baptism, and Christian princes who permit this, are also excommunicated; that is, those who did not become Christian had no protection in canon law. Those who took prohibited merchandise to the Arabs, and those who sailed as masters in their ships ("galleys and piratical ships"), were excommunicated; to encourage enforcement, Christian princes were ordered to confiscate their property when they arrived in their ports. Those who go to Alexandria to recover their fellow-citizens held in captivity are allowed to do so, provided they do not take goods with them, or money, beyond what has been agreed under the articles of redemption; there is a special excommunication for those who carry goods or send them by others, for profit, except in time of peace, and this includes those who arrive during a truce. It was also forbidden to carry any merchandise at all, directly or indirectly, in time of war, or to have any other dealings with the Arabs at such times. Those Religious or clerics who want to preach Christianity to 'pagans' (probably meaning any non-Christians, other than Jews) are indulgenced to take any food (so far as allowed by the laws of fasting) that they are offered, and are given the right to preach without interference from the Ordinary.

There is an interesting commentary by the fourteenth-century canonist John of Andrew, which adds considerably to the sense in which the courts construed the canons; his remarks may be taken to represent more than a century of interpretation. No one under this canon can take public office of any kind or, of course, hire a servant in the market. The main purpose is to cut Christians off from unbelievers. John accepts that, overseas, those who sell war goods to the Arabs are "superior in malice" to them, and so are those who take service with them, to command their galleys and ships. The excommunications must be published in all the maritime cities, and offenders who are caught should be enslaved. Those who sell even their own arms to them should be beheaded. A good indication of the practical effect of these excommunications is given by the question, what is the good of a second excommunication, since once out of the church is out of the church; but John argues that it is sensible to bind a man with more than one chain. What about those whose agreement to redeem a prisoner involved war goods? John thinks that the exemption covers them, but thinks it better to refer the case to the Pope, lest there be some trick in it. There is something a little less than single-minded; the rules of modern warfare are more ruthless. On the permission conceded to those who go to convert Arabs resident in Europe,

John says that they can stay to eat with them, following the example of the Lord (who ate with sinners) but that the principle, namely that they should not become polluted, remained. Why was it permitted to eat with Muslims and not with Jews? Because the Jews distinguish between the kinds of meat Christians eat, and Christians must not seem to be inferior in anything; and now both Jews and Muslims distinguish, so that although the canon does not say so, it is no longer permissible to eat in their houses or have them to eat in ours. This last opinion is based on a number of mistakes, but the principles underlying it are only too clear.

In the Gregorian Decretals there is another group of canons issued by Innocent III. The first of this group orders Muslims and Jews of either sex to wear distinctive clothing, so that they may always be distinguished from Christians, and forbids them to go out on Good Fridays, Passion Sunday or other days of lamentation, lest they presume to insult the Creator. '*In contumelia Creatoris*' generally amounts to 'anything that might provoke a Christian public'. The reason for the distinctive clothing was apparently the occurrence of the 'mistake' of Christians marrying Muslims or Jews; the word used is *commixtio*, which may include illegitimate loves, but the commentator perhaps means matrimony. This had not occurred everywhere; in some places the distinction in dress already obtained; the canon expressly concerns only some 'provinces'. It is hard to imagine any provinces where a believing Muslim or a believing Jew was not known, or, indeed, any situation where Muslim or Jewish families would permit such marriages. Marriages were not made at individual choice, and the only *commixtio* which distinctive clothing could prevent would be the casual one. The commentator further justifies the law on the ground that different classes of people are normally distinguished by their dress, novices from professed monks, prostitutes from matrons, men from women. This seems nearer to the real reason, which must have been to enforce the separation of the communities. Another canon with the same purpose condemns the appointment of Jews to public office; it assumes that they will use this to harass Christians, and requires that what they gain by it shall be given to the (Christian) poor, and that they should be dismissed "with shame from the office they have irreverently assumed;" apparently as an afterthought, this canon, one of Toledo applied to the universal church, is extended to Muslims. Another of Gregory IX's warns the King of Portugal not to appoint Muslims or Jews to office, and if he does farm out revenues to them, he must see that royal officers protect the clergy.

The laws we have just discussed are representative of the thirteenth century. They received considerable fortification early in the fourteenth. One of the oddest is a canon of Clement V's promulgated at the Council of Vienne. This orders Christian princes to forbid Muslims in their territories, whether living apart in their own areas, or mixed with Christians, from calling to prayer from the minarets, or from going on pilgrimage. The interesting points are the reasons actually stated in the text of the canon: "Our faith is not a little disparaged by these things and scandal is generated in the hearts of the faithful." Even more curious are the descriptions of the actual offences. The call to prayer is made by "priests commonly called Zabazala" in the mosques "where the same Saracens come together" (*jamia*) and "adore" Muhammad; "at certain hours, from some lofty place they call on and extol the name of the same Muhammad in a loud voice with Christians and Saracens listening, and they publicly proclaim certain words in his honour from that place." There are truthful elements here, embedded in ignorance. The Pope pretends that the Prophet is adored in the mosque, but only says that he is extolled by the *muezzin*. On the pilgrimage he speaks with complete ignorance; it is almost as though he thinks the pilgrimage is itself within Christian territory; he says that there is a place where a certain Saracen was buried, and whom Muslims venerate in their cult. "A great multitude of Saracens from the same parts and from others come together there." The reason for this vagueness is difficult to interpret. All these things are "an affront to the divine name and a reproach to the Christian faith." It is not even clear that the Pope knew whether the *hajj* was made within Christian territory or beyond it. We might almost suppose that he was speaking of the local cult of some Muslim saint, but the commentary makes it clear that the "certain Saracen" means Muhammad, and the "place", Mecca. However we judge the historical and geographical knowledge of the Curia, it comes out unambiguously that the affront to God lies in permitting the public practice of Islam.

The commentary is as interesting as the canon itself. It credits the ancient story expressly attributed to "ecclesiastical histories", that Islam was the creation of a dissident Roman cleric who taught the Prophet, doubtless a distant echo of Waraqa. According to the commentary, however, this decision of the Curia was given in response to a very leading question; on the hypothesis that there are some Christian princes who out of avarice accept taxes from Arabs and Jews, to allow them "to be and to dwell," either by themselves, divided from Christians, or else mixed with the Christians in the same city and the same quarter, and there invoke Muhammad from their mosques; and that they go on pilgrimage to the shrine of someone whom their law holds holy; and that grave scandal is caused to the faithful; in that case, "we ask you, holy father, whether such princes should reap the benefit?" Thus this is a legal decision made in legal form, not an administrative regulation, and so are many canons; the ignorance of the canon derives from the question, which doubtless was so worded as to elicit the answer that was given. It is tempting to hypothesize constructive malice. While accepting the principle, the commentary objects to the word 'Zabazala'. The writer has talked to John, the treasurer of the King of France, who was a prisoner of the Arabs for four years, and who is confused about some points himself, but does introduce some accurate information about the prayer. He considers that the *fuqaha* and the *hajjis* are two kind of 'priest'; but he rather pointedly corrects the canon by saying that the *muezzin* is a 'minister'. He points out that the morning prayer is *salat as-subh*, and suggests that the word Zabazala may be a corruption of this. This is intelligent scholarship, and naturally it does not extend to any question of principle.

The *extravagantes* contain two more canons of Clement V. One only forbids the usual sale of war goods to Granada; it is interesting that it states that for Muslims to inhabit Granada at all is "an insult to the Creator"; and also that it appears from the commentary that some attempt was made to use it to justify evasion of the standing prohibitions, against the plain sense of the text. The second is yet another of the many papal repetitions of the excommunication for trading to Alexandria and elsewhere in war goods, and goods generally. It uses stronger condemnation than ever; the Saracens are a horrible and perfidious nation, and in addition to the existing excommunications, the traders are declared "perpetually infamous", incompetent to make wills, for the benefit of either chosen heirs or relations, and, of course, inadmissible to any public office.

The purpose of all these canons was primarily to insulate Christians from every means of communication with the Arab communities left on Christian soil, and from the outer Arab World. The only exception was for the preachers who in fact were sent by the Pope to put pressure on the remaining Muslims to become Christian. The prohibition of the call to prayer and of the pilgrimage seems to be simply oppressive, but it seems likely that the ostensible reason was at least partly the true one, and the same as in the case of preventing Jews and Muslims from going out on Good Friday, that the popes wished to avoid the provocation of the general public. It is clear that they sympathized with the public, and thought it perfectly reasonable to blame a Muslim on a Good Friday, or to be outraged by the voice of the *muezzin*. By forbidding public practice of non-Christian religions a further step towards isolating the Muslims was effectively taken.

In the course of time the Christian church developed a set of rules which covered all the likely relationships between Europeans and Arabs. We can even see the way the rules were applied to Christians living in Muslim territory from the instructions sent to missionaries by the Dominican canonist of the thirteenth century, Raymund of Penaforte. What was forbidden was trade "to the prejudice of the Holy Land;" that was why armaments at any time and other goods in time of formal war were forbidden; the excommunication was automatic. If a man traded in forbidden goods in ignorance of the law, and, having been warned, recovered them, he was still excommunicate, but he might be absolved. A man in grave economic need who was involved in the trade even indirectly was a more serious case, but he might be treated leniently. The canons did not take into account the case of a man who bound a Christian to a Muslim employer, or who sold Christian slaves to Muslims, but he was in mortal sin. Another case that the law ignored was that of the relations or spouse of someone who became Muslim. Especially the parents, Raymund allowed, might continue to live with such a one, whether to reconvert him, or because they were dependent on him, or even, according to one manuscript, out of charity. Spouses in this situation might continue to live together, provided there was no "insult to the Creator", a phrase, as we have seen, that might mean almost anything. Since Jews "attacked" Christianity by their rules of forbidden foods, and Muslims in this matter "judaized"; since it was an insult to the Creator for Jews or Muslims to go out of doors on a day of lamentation, or for Muslims to rule themselves in Granada, it is difficult to see how the Muslim spouse could avoid being in this condition; we must hope that the canonists did not enquire too closely.

We are not concerned with the effectiveness of the decrees. So far as trading was concerned, the rules were tightened after the disappearance of an Eastern Latin state, with the fall of Acre in 1291; but, as had earlier happened with crusading vows, a system of exemptions developed. Both trade and the right to go on pilgrimage were subject to licence, and this provided a useful source of revenue to the Holy See. At the other pole, the Christian rule over Spanish Muslims varied from place to place and time to time. In Portugal canon law had the priority over royal law, because the Pope was the suzerain. Granting the variations in the application of the law of the church, depending in Christian countries on the strength of the monarchy, and in the Levantine and Egyptian trade on the ability of the popes to enforce their law, and on the business of licences, we can still recognize in the collections of canons a body of law which closely resembled the Muslim law of *jihad*, or holy war. With the Muslims, too, the actual application of the law and its occasional breach depended on times and circumstances, and there was not perfect stability.

Considering the law itself, the two concepts had come very close indeed. The essence of the Muslim concept was that *jihad* was not only a physical war, but a spiritual one; and it might be waged against bad Muslims who ceased to deserve the name or the right, and finally against rebels. So in Christendom, the Crusade came to be applied to heretics, and then to Emperors whose policies did not agree with the policies of the popes, and to any rebel. 'Crusades' has finally come to mean any active good work undertaken on principle. The basic choice offered to the non-Muslim who is engaged in *jihad* is to become Muslim, to fight, or, if he is Christian, to accept the position of a tributary, that is, one who may practise his religion with some limitations on its public celebration, who enjoys the protection of the government, but who does not enjoy the full rights of the citizen. He cannot witness against a Muslim. Almost exactly this system was already employed in reverse in Spain from early in the twelfth century, with the capitulations of Tudela and Saragossa, and a little later Tortosa. Canon law in this way only followed the practice of the Spanish rulers, and sought to regulate it. The great difference between Christian canon law and Muslim *sharia* law (not *qanun*, which does not correspond to canon law) was that the former could always be reversed, although it represented the church in a formal sense; the latter was based on an irrevocable revelation. The Christians within Islam had only a limited freedom, but they did have the freedom of worship, and they survived. They were generally forbidden bells, as Muslims were the *muezzin*, but they were not subject to the same relentless pressure. Muslims of Italy early succumbed to the pressures on minorities; the Muslims of Spain finally were ejected, or forcibly converted; once converted, they were subject to the Inquisition. The Arabs of Europe could not survive as a separate culture or community, in the way that Christians did in the Arab World. Knowing what lay in store, we can recognize the decisive difference between Islamic law and Christian law in the early fourteenth century, despite their consistent similarity.

This close similarity leads naturally to the question, was canon law, most of which postdates *sharia* law by many centuries, directly under its influence? There is no evidence for this at all, and some against it. The isolation of Jews preceded Islam, and everything later followed in the same line. The assumption must be that societies with a similar problem in a similar situation produce a similar solution. This could only be true if the similarity of situation (ideas, society, history) were very close, but this was the case. We cannot exclude the influence of example; we can be reasonably sure there was no documentary influence.

The traditional contrast between peaceful Christian origins and the warlike rise of Islam was clearly meaningless, when the rules and the behaviour of the two societies so nearly approximated. Humbert of Romans was honest enough when he said that Christians should use force when they had it, and leave humanity for when they did not. When Peter the Venerable called on Muslims to emulate Christian toleration of the Jews, did he remember how the Arabs—or the Jews either—were treated during the First Crusade? The fact is that as Europe came to care more and more for orthodoxy and uniformity, it successfully shut off outside influence. One result was that it generated tremendous power of internal revolution, and future change was very little the product of thoughts borrowed from other cultures.

Chapter 10

Arabic scientific literature in Europe

1. The rediscovery of the ancient world

Paul Tannery said of geometry of the eleventh century in Europe: "This is not a chapter in the history of science; it is a study in ignorance." Its level, he said, was equivalent to that in Greece before Pythagoras. Scholars like Raimbaud of Cologne discussed the implications of the terms 'acute' and 'obtuse' angle. Arithmetic was not in such a bad way, and the use of the abacus was associated with Gerbert of Aurillac, Pope Sylvester II. The revival of scientific learning is sometimes dated from his studies in Spain at the end of the tenth century. His writings on arithmetic and logic are his chief claim to honour; he can hardly be blamed for his myth, which was apparently not of his own creating. All the same, Europe was slow to adopt the algorism (from al-Khwarizmi), or decimal numeration; it was long a matter of academic knowledge rather than of practical use to men of business. In general, scientific studies had added little to the *Etymologies* of Isidore and the works of Bede. It was this gap in the European apparatus of learning that translation from Arabic in the twelfth century would fill. Medical knowledge at the beginning of that century was not in such a bad way, thanks to the work of Constantine the African at Monte Cassino, and associated with Salerno, which put Arab sources into a Latin form; and his influence was carried on into the twelfth century by his pupil, John Afflacius (al-Fasi?), whose history was apparently similar to Constantine's. The Salernitan experience included anatomical experimentation with pigs, which it did not owe to Arab links, but it foreshadowed twelfth-century attitudes, although it did not meet the high standards of translation that came to prevail. The explosion of scientific translation was the product, in practice, of military success. The opening of much of Mediterranean culture to the people of the north of Europe was the result of the European conquest of southern Italy and Sicily, and of Toledo and other smaller centres in Spain. In the central area, the influence was more Greek than Arabic; in the west it was naturally exclusively Arabic.

The feeling of the age was expressed largely in the work of translation. Constantine's texts were criticized and replaced by Stephen, a translator who in Antioch in 1127 completed a version of the *Liber Regalis*, the great medical epitome of Ali ibn al-Abbas al-Majusi. This was explicitly a correction of the partial versions put out by Constantine; Stephen objected to Constantine's work, because it was unfaithful to the original text, and was presented as if it were the original. Stephen preached the importance of trans-ferring knowledge from Arabic into Latin, and he realized, and supplied, the need for a medical glossary of Greek, Latin and Arabic technical terms. He exemplifies the newly felt need for exact translation, together with a sense of obligation to the sources which was relatively rare in the Middle Ages; and he also expresses the new enthusiasm for 'philosophy'. He had learned Arabic in order to advance from "the naked beginnings of philosophy," and he proposed, if the favour of God should permit, to go on from his study of the things of the body to "things far higher, extending to the excellence of the soul," more specifically, "more famous things which the Arabic language contains, the hidden secrets of philosophy." Perhaps he was thinking of works by Ibn Sina, to which his medical interests might have led him. In any case, no other translation by him is known (unless he is the unknown Stephen quoted below), so that we must presume that God's favour was not after all extended to his project. 'Philosophy' as it was then used had the sense of moral and natural philosophy, often including magic as well. At the beginning of the twelfth century philosophy was coming to mean that body of learning which was neither Patristic nor humanist, which had reached the Arabs from Hellenistic writers, and to which they had added. For Stephen and for most of the translators from Arabic the idea of Greek sources at this date was secondary, and the impact of Byzantium was much less than that of the Arabs, especially in Spain. Stephen called himself "the disciple of philosophy" and we have the impression of a school of young writers who were radically changing accepted standards, mostly in Spain, although in fact there was no school, no group, no esoteric association, only an open society of spon-taneous 'philosophers'.

Adelard of Bath was one of many Englishmen of the century who were remarkable for their scientific and Arabic interests; Adelard was Stephen's contemporary, and more than hints at the same intellectual excitement. He was a Mediterranean traveller, who knew Magna Graecia (Southern Italy certainly, and Sicily probably), and also the Latin states of the Levant. Adelard found in Virgil the appropriate text, *felix qui potuit rerum cognoscere causas.* His Platonic *De Eodem et Diverso* expresses the contempt characteristic of twelfth-century scientists for Northern teaching (with its emphasis both theological and, at that date, humanistic)—"What the schools of France are ignorant of, those over the Alps preserve; what you do not learn among the Latins, eloquent Greece will teach;" it is dedicated to the Bishop of Syracuse. This work shows no sign of Adelard's later interest in the Arabs, and no sign of Arab influence. In his more important *Questions on Natural Science* the Arabs have taken the place of the Greeks as his mentors, although there is no actual citation from Arabic. There is one acknowledgement of an oral source; he remarks, on the physiology of nerves and veins, "I heard an old man in Tarsus of Cilicia discussing these and many other things." What then is his relation to the Arabs at this stage of his life? Adelard wants to discuss and explain a wide variety of 'philosophical' or 'scientific' problems, but these are subsidiary to a basic problem of method and of theology; he argues that it in no way detracts from theology to seek an explanation, or *ratio*, in physical things of all kinds; all subsist in God, but, so far as reason extends, we should listen to it. Adelard writes in the form of a dialogue with his nephew, who is rather aggressive in manner, and he may be considered a fictional device, whether in fact he existed or not. It is curious that when Adelard is rejecting a generation which refuses the ideas of the "moderns" he should choose a youthful opponent, but the nephew represents those who stay at home, and "this generation" includes young men who resist the ideas of the travellers. In a straight comparison between ancients and moderns he said "neither did the former know everything, nor are the latter ignorant of everything." In any case, Adelard imputes the new ideas to the Arabs.

The nephew begins by asking for "something new in the way of Arabic studies." Adelard tells his nephew that he does not want anyone to think that he is propounding something as his own opinion, when he is really offering the "judgement of the Arabic schools"—"I have known what happens to true teachers among the ordinary people." He uses *Arabicus*, as a noun, perhaps to designate the culture, rather than *Arabs*, meant for the nation, or *Saracenus*, perhaps for the believer. "That is why I am putting the case of the Arabs, not my own." A little later Adelard closes one passage of discussion by saying that he will go on to something more difficult, because what he has just said is obvious to the "bleary-eyed and the shaven." He is quoting an old Roman proverb, meaning the idle gossips of the chemists' and barbers' shops. The nephew replies aggressively:

> "That really is clear to no one but the bleary-eyed and the shaven. Haven't those Saracens deceived you with subtle trifles? You shall never trick me into concealing your bogus and unintelligible reasons disguised by subtle untruth. What you are doing must be exposed. You argue something intelligible neither to me nor to you, in order that I shall get fed up and concede untruths to you. You do not know who you are talking to—but let us put it to the test."

This tirade must surely reflect reactions actually experienced by Adelard in using his foreign methods of study. Just a little later he says,

> "from the Arabic masters I have learned one thing, led by reason, while you are caught by the image of authority, and led by another halter. For what is an authority to be called, but a halter? As the brute beasts, indeed, are led anywhere by the halter, and have no idea by what they are led or why, but only follow the rope that holds them, so the authority of writers leads not a few of you into danger, tied and bound by brutish credulity."

Adelard's thought is Platonic and Hellenistic, not identifiably Arabic at any point in these writings. It seems that his remarks must be related to techniques of promiscuous enquiry. The exact connotation of *the Arabs* must be guessed from other works.

In contrast to the *De Eodem*, with no reference to Arabs, and the *Quaestiones*, with references but no Arab sources, is the group of his actual translations from the Arabic, which present something of a biographical problem. In his *Ezich Alkauresmi*, from Mas-lama's Cordovan adaptation of al-Khwarismi's astronomical tables, he wrote, "we study for the advantage of the Latins"; in his study of the astrolabe, *De Opere Astrolapsus*, he makes wide use of Arabic terms, and in the dedication to the young Henry (probably of Anjou) he writes, "not only may you examine things contained in the Latin writers, in order to understand them, but you may also aspire to understand the opinions of the Arabs about the sphere and the circles and motions of the stars." All work on tables and calendars taken from the Arabic involved, of course, an understanding of the Hijra year. Adelard also translated the Arabic Euclid, probably the *ysagoga Alchorismi* (arithmetic, geometry, music and astronomy) and the *ysagoga minor*, *al-mudhkal as-saghir*, Abu Mashar Jafar's lesser astrology, necessary, says Adelard, for "higher knowledge of philosophy" and, as Lemay has shown, a vehicle of Aristotelianism.

Adelard's work of translation is like other similar work of the time. The puzzle of the 'Arabism' of the *Quaestiones* remains. Their contents, the experimental science, can be quickly illustrated. For example, there is a short discussion of why grown men do not take milk at the breast; then, "as we have begun to talk about human nature," the nephew asks why "if a leprous man goes into a healthy woman, it is the man who first has relations with her afterwards, and not the woman herself, who catches the disease." Adelard explains that because the female nature is "cold and wet", and the male hot and dry, part of the semen remains, and the next hot and dry contact contracts the disease "by likeness". The nephew asks how the female nature can be thought frigid, because women are more wanton than men; "more wanton, of course," Adelard explains; but the cause of their desire is not frigidity, but humidity; they suffer from ill-digested blood, because of their frigidity, and desire to be purged by coition, the semen being "blood changed to whiteness". The woman's cold nature wants association with the heat of the male. "Serpents even enter the mouths of sleeping women because of the frigidity of their nature." There seems nothing specifically Arab, and nothing likely to have resulted from observation or experiment here; we do not really believe in the transmission of leprous infection by the means described, nor do we credit the snakes that enter the mouths of the sleeping women. We do note the 'scientific' impartiality with which moralizing is avoided; as Adelard says elsewhere (of a running nose)—"nothing natural is unclean or improper." At the beginning of the same book, Adelard reminds his nephew that seven years earlier, at Laon, Adelard had dismissed his students, including the nephew, and they had agreed between them that, while the one would pursue his Arabic studies, the other would acquire "the changeableness of French ideas." There was some association in Adelard's mind between the use of reason in the Arab World and professionalism; France seemed to him, not only ignorant, but amateur. On the other hand, the nephew is allowed to make one good point against him; Adelard must not quote Arab authorities any more than the nephew Latin ones; reason alone must judge between them. It is not possible to define exactly what the "opinions of the Arabs" meant to Adelard, but it is at least clear that he felt he was bringing something new and important to Europe, and that he was impatient, even contemptuous, of the purely indigenous developments of the north, literary, humanistic, theological.

In this he was representative of the movement for translation among the men of scientific interest who sought their material in Spain and in Arabic. Hugh of Santalla was an independent translator, like Adelard, though less distinguished; his work is dedicated to the first bishop of Tarazona after its conquest by Alfonso VII, and he makes it clear that he was executing a conscious policy of literary Reconquista, taking over the useful learning of the conquered Moors. This policy was the bishop's; in the introduction to al-Biruni's commentary on the Khwarismian tables, Hugh refers to the discovery of a text in the most secret parts of a library, a success earned by the bishop's "insatiable longing for philosophizing." Hugh will not use the method of dialogue "as the Arabs are accustomed to do," lest by following too closely the 'ancients' he seem to dissent from the moderns. He refers to his translation of the *Centiloquium*, a summary of Ptolemy's astrology (the *Quadripartitum*); he speaks of the "hidden things" of its wisdom (*tante sapiencie archana*); and in a translation of a short piece on divination by bones (spatulamancy) he speaks again of "the hidden things of such antiquity." He tells too how the old manuscript he is translating was found by Ablaudius the Babylonian among other old manuscripts in Athens, and how the author was called *Anunbarhis* among the Chaldeans, and Hermes among the Greeks. 'Anunbarhis' may possibly represent the Egyptian Anubis or, more likely, the Greco-Egyptian hybrid, Hermanubis, a guardian of the underworld, and there may be some confusion with 'Hermes Trismegistos', the Ptolemaic form of the Egyptian Thot, though the Hermetic corpus does not include spatulamancy. Hugh finds 'Indians' in Egypt; and counts Abu Mashar among them. The three qualities, the sense of revealing the *arcana*, the sense of bringing back lost antiquity, and an inextricable confusion of

Arabs (counted among the ancients), Greeks, Egyptians and Chaldeans, are characteristic of the translating movement. So is the "unsatisfied longing to philosophize" of which Hugh speaks, in his own case as well as that of his patron.

One side of this complex of attitudes is well illustrated by an unknown translator named Stephen, part of whose text is printed by Haskins. Looked at from the point of view of the new science, opposition was simply obscurantist. The writer refers to the subtle and hidden things of astronomy; again, he means, not occult arts, but an arcane science (including judicial astrology) which he wants to reveal to the literate public. He sees Aristotle—then known by only some of his works, and also by works that were not his—as one in a line of scientific transmission: "he took many things from his predecessors, but all from God, except those which were obscured by error or untruth." The inspiration of pagan philosophers by God was important to many of the translators, as we shall see again and again, and was part of their insistence on the recovery of lost knowledge.

> "But these things come about because, if there were not so great a crowd of disparagers, the Latin world (*Latinitas*) would have had more daring writers, and a more fruitful crop of philosophy would have sprung up among us. But, since there were many hosts of detractors, and few who were kindly disposed, so certainly those rather rare writers of the arts were more frightened by the fierceness of the many, than encouraged by the kindly zeal of the few."

There is a gloomy attitude of personal despair in which the fear that Europe will not be restored to its ancient learning predominates. This fear at least would not be realized, though the uses to which knowledge would be put might have justified the writer's pessimism. "Europe, which could have had nearly the fullness of the arts, is lower than the other nations."

Vagueness about the 'ancients'—who or when they were—was common. Raymund of Marseilles, writing in 1140, said, "we have known many of the Indians or Chaldeans, and of the Arabs, to be very good at astrology." In fact he owed all he knew of astronomy, or astrology, directly to the Arabs, and indirectly, no doubt, to the Chaldeans; he knows that the Arabs will enrich Europe: "If God, as we hope, approves," he remarks, after explaining how the philosophers understand the planets to exercise their influence, "we strive to compose in honour of Christ Jesus . . . and for the common advantage of the Latin world." Yet he considers the danger that science may affect religion. He will date his calendar

> "not with years from the creation of the world, or years of the Greeks, or of Yezdigird (Zoroastrian) or of the Arabs or of others, but with years of the incarnation of our Lord Jesus Christ, so that whatever is said here shall be found to be, not heretical or foreign to the true faith, but Catholic . . ."

The association of heretical and foreign does not obscure Raymund's idea of the universality of scientific knowledge. He cites the support of the most learned, "although they are of the Gentiles," i.e. Arabs and classical Greeks. A man who "is ignorant of the wonders of the heavens" is not really a rational being. In the poem with which he prefaces his work, he speaks of the study of the stars among the Ethiopians, burned black by the sun, and among the Assyrians, who in his mind merge with the Persian magi, but whose writings about the stars he knows were important. The Arabs are the third in this grouping of learned nations.

Arab science and Islam were always dissociated. The proponents of the new science were never accused of crypto-Islam. Two translators who were involved with both subjects were Hermann of Carinthia and Robert of Ketton, two friends who were among those employed by Peter the Venerable on translating his Quranic material; Ketton contributed the Quran itself, Hermann two of the least useful of the legendary pieces. They wrote affectionate prefaces to each other (*mi Rodberte, mi Hermanne*). Both found Arabic, as a language at least, unsympathetic. Ketton complained of its prolixity, and he admitted to altering the sense of the Quran itself, as he thought, to make it more easily intelligible to Latin readers, so that his own translation certainly is both prolix and frequently unintelligible as well as inaccurate. Hermann's translation of Abu Mashar, the *maius introductorium*, abbreviates the source, in contrast to John of Seville's roughly contemporary literal translation; the contrast is worked out in detail in Lemay's careful study. Hermann prefers the arrangement of Latin works to that which is customary in Arabic, and he is fond of humanistic and classical references; he and Robert worked late and alone on their difficult Arabic sources, spurred on by the "highest goddess" Minerva, Queen of holy powers, *regina numinum*, who touched the crown of Hermann's head. Yet, though strongly attached to their own culture, both devoted their working lives to the translation of

Arabic science and divination into Latin. Ketton speaks of the inadequate knowledge of the Latins in the field of astronomy, and Hermann refers nostalgically to their joint efforts to extract the "innermost treasures of the Arabs". Their realization of the inadequacy of Latin sources impresses us more for being reluctant.

Hermann's work gives some special clues to how he regarded "the Arabs". In his *De Essentiis*, an original work based on his Arabic reading, he refers to the Prophet as "Agarene" and not as "Arab". Then he uses one of the old Spanish polemic themes, that the Quranic identification of the Messiah Jesus as "spirit and word of God" necessarily implies the Trinity because there is no division in God—"written in these words in the Arabic language, *roh alla vua kalimatu.*" If *vua* is taken as a bad copy of *wa*, this is an accurate summary. "Agarene", therefore, means "Muslim" here, but we form an impression that the "Agarene" is known accidentally through Arabic, just as also, say, Aristotle is (for Hermann) known only through Arabic. Hermann also speaks of the failure of the Fathers to realize how the unbelievers had foretold the virgin birth. On this point he does not cite the Quran, which witnesses to it unequivocally; but he does quote "Hermes and Astalius" and Abu Mashar, as having done so in Persian and Arabic. It is certain that he had no clear idea of which nations spoke which languages, or when individual authors flourished. He elsewhere calls "Hermes", the Hellenized Egyptian Thot, "Persian". Arabs and Hellenes, Persians, Indians, Chaldeans, Egyptians, he confuses hopelessly. In another passage he distributes the nations to the planets, and asserts that experience confirms this, the Arabs celebrate Friday and are placed under Mars and Venus, whose warlike and erotic qualities they reflect; so the Jews, under Saturn, with Saturday, exhibit melancholy, fraudulence, villainy (or lewdness?—*nequitia*), jealousy, unbelief, pertinacity; and the Christians and Romans under Jupiter and the sun, Sunday, enjoy liberality, honesty and victory from the sun, and peace, equity and humanity from Jupiter. The idea would be more elaborately worked out by William of Auvergne in his *De Legibus* and taken up by other later writers. Hermann explains that the astrologers "place all the nation of Muhammad under the reign of the Arabs," but all their subjects of Christian faith he classifies as "Romans" and says that the Arabic language confirms this by calling Christians indiscriminately "Romans" or "Nazarenes". For Hermann, "Arabs" exclude Christians, and include, but are not necessarily coterminous with, Muslims. The Greek pagans are perhaps absorbed by the Arabs; yet he is quite clear that Persians are different though he does not know who they are.

Certain themes recur. Hugh of Santalla spoke of the men of former ages with regret, the *antiqui* and the *prisci*, and Adelard began his first book (*De Eodem*) by remarking the fluency of the ancients and the inarticulateness of the moderns. Dominic Gundisalvo, in his *De Scientiis*, based on al-Farabi, wrote,

> "As there were once many philosophers, yet among them all only he who was believed to embrace a knowledge of all things with certainty was called simply wise. Now, however, the world is getting old, and no one is to be called, I do not say wise, but, what is less, a philosopher."

He announces his *De Divisione Philosophiae*, also much influenced by al-Farabi, with the same sentiment: "Happy that earlier age which produced so many wise men, who shone in the shadow of the world like stars." Now men are taken up with worldly cares, he says, busy with eloquence or moved by ambition, and the study of wisdom has become feeble. His sources do really cover the ancient inheritance and its modern continuation, the Greek, Jewish and Arab worlds, Aristotle, Euclid, Boethius, the Psalms, Ishaq al-Israili (Isaac Judaeus), Isidor's *Etymologies*, Ibn Sina, al-Ghazali and al-Kindi. This inclusiveness marks the beginning of a scientific culture which would be characteristic of the later twelfth and the thirteenth centuries.

The greatest of the translators died in 1187 at the age of seventy-three. Gerard of Cremona's devoted pupils prepared a list of his translations and a short biographical note in his memory. The list consists of seventy-one titles, and sixteen more have been identified. It classifies them under the headings, *dialectica, astrologia* (including astronomy, of course), philosophy and medicine. The note explains that Gerard was originally attracted to Toledo, the site of his life's work, by his passion for the study of medicine, and for the *Almagest* of Claudius Ptolemy. There he found a mass of books in Arabic, and he pitied the Latins to whom they were inaccessible because they simply could not read them. He learned Arabic thoroughly, says the note, and now joined a love of translation to his love of science; to the very end of his life, we are told, he did not stop translating. His achievement must not be underrated because he was prolific. Besides the *Almagest* and other

Hellenistic works brought into Latin from their Arabic versions, it includes al-Kindi, al-Farghani, Thabit ibn Qurra, Ali ibn Ridwan, ar-Razi, and, above all, the Qanun (*Canon*) of Ibn Sina. Gerard is a sympathetic figure. He said that he was born under the royal sign, under the domination of the sun, and when his students challenged him, asking where his kingdom was, he replied, "In my soul, for I have not served any mortal man." This was as proud a boast in the days of feudal lordship as it would be in the rat-race of today. It measures his sense of his vocation and of the revolutionary achievement of this movement of thought.

This last story we owe to Daniel of Morley, one of the Englishmen who stand at the beginning of the English mediaeval scientific tradition and who at the end of the twelfth century formed so strong a link between Spain and England. Daniel, like Gerard his teacher, had been disgusted by the schools of Paris, where the seats of learning were occupied by "animals", and he went on to Toledo to hear "the wisest philosophers in the world." Then he came home to England to pass on their teaching, which was the *doctrina Arabum*. This revulsion from humanistic and theological studies seems to be characteristic of the scientific movement based on translation from Arabic. Daniel says that Christians have now been mystically liberated from "Egypt", i.e. from the non-Christian world, and "with the command and help of the Lord, let us borrow wisdom and eloquence from the philosophers of the nations (i.e. non-Christian nations of all ages), and so let us spoil them in their unbelief, that we in our faith may be enriched by their spoils." In all these writers there is a great variety of attitude and a widespread individualism, but they continue to reflect the main themes, revelation of the "ancient philosophy", or science of the Hellenistic world, combined with resentment at the resistance of Europeans who were not interested.

These were of two kinds, the cultivated and the philistines. The twelfth-century humanists show little or no sign of being influenced by translations from Arabic. John of Salisbury, the best Latinist of the twelfth century, hardly refers to Arabic sources, even when he is discussing astrology. In his *Metalogicon* he twice mentions the Arabs, once to classify them linguistically with Scythians, and once, more realistically, to admit that there is not much geometry except in Spain and Africa; the peoples there, and the Egyptians, and a few of the peoples of Arabia, he says, practise it for the sake of astronomy. Lemay has made out a clear case for the influence of Abu Mashar's Aristotelianism on Bernard Sylvester, but no debt to Arabic is acknowledged; the *De Universitate Mundi* mentions Arabs only in purely classical terms, dealers in gum arabic.

> *Sic liquor heliadum, sic cedria, sic quoque gummu,*
> *Quod transmittit Arabs, quod terebinthus habet.*

The Euphrates recalls Babylon, and Damascus, the Abana; the Tigris, the defeat of Crassus; in a summary of learning, Rome and Athens are grouped with Chaldeans, who are sited on the Indus; Aristotle, the Platonists and the Pythagoreans are added. The great logician Abelard was unaware even of much of Aristotle, and knew nothing apparently from Arabic sources. His persecutor, St Bernard, never seems to have realized what contribution translators would make to speculative thought, and he left them in peace. At the unlettered end of the spectrum, the monks of Bury St Edmunds were delighted when the Abbot spoke slightingly of their more literate colleagues; it seemed to vindicate their ignorance. "Now our philosophers can have their philosophies; now it is clear what use their philosophy is." A somewhat higher level of philistinism just insisted on pragmatic advantage, as witness the lament from the translation of Ibn Butlan: "From the sciences men want nothing but practical help; argument and definitions they do not want." The European temper was in many ways opposed to pure science. Different levels of hostility or indifference or lack of interest form the background to the determination and dedication of the translators who saw the practical advantages in any increase in knowledge.

2. The thirteenth-century use of Arab sources

Important translations were made in the thirteenth century. Greek writers still passed into Latin through their Arabic form; Michael Scot's version of Aristotle's various works on animals, brought compendiously into one, *De Animalibus*, is a case in point. The translation of the work of Ibn Rushd (Averroes) was important for the West, though perhaps more as a vehicle for the thought of Aristotle than for an 'Averroism' which was partly at least a nineteenth-century myth. Translation was no longer, itself, and by virtue of happening at all, a kind of revolutionary speculation. There was no opposition to translation. Humanism was dying, and theology was becoming more systematically speculative. Peter Lombard set the direction of European thinking, and his genius was indigenous. The most important development was that new knowledge was absorbed. Arabic thought was a major influence, but it was now an influence rather than a source. In many ways the historical distinction between different ages and different peoples was better understood. Writers were less excited by their material and better able to control it and make use of it.

It would be quite impossible to list the Greek and Arabic sources made available to Europeans in these two centuries; the information is accessible in detail; but it is worth looking briefly at some of the main acquisitions of European literature by the beginning of the century. If we take the Greek first, we usually think of Aristotle as the major gain. It seemed so at the time only to a certain section of the educated world. For us, and in the light of later history, Aristotle seems the formative discovery of the age. For the logicians, for the metaphysicians of a slightly later date of the theological faculties, for the moral philosophers of the Arts faculties, the same judgement would have been contemporaneously valid. For the scientists Aristotle was only one source among many, and for the political scientists pseudo-Aristotle was as important as Aristotle. Astronomy, cosmogony and geography were known from the *Mathematiki Syntaxis* (*Almagest*) and the *Geographiki yphegesis* of Claudius Ptolemy, medicine from Galen and, more remotely, the Hippocratic corpus. The Hermetic corpus also enjoyed great fame, as the work of one of the philosophers of antiquity, and the *Asclepius* was known in the Latin translation of Roman date in which it has come down to us; nevertheless, it exercised little influence, and its admirable monotheism and devotional purity had little to offer comparable to the Areopagite texts. Even they appealed only to a limited number. "Hermes" has his place among "the ancients", and is relevant to mediaeval awareness of the great Arab philosophers, in the sense that he appeared approximately as one with them. By the early thirteenth century, translation from the Greek was as common as, or commoner than, translation from Arabic, but it remained true that some Greek works would always be known from the Arabic, and that the original impetus for translations came from Spain, from individuals, but especially from the schools of Toledo. We could exaggerate this point. The Norman conquest of Magna Graecia, of Sicily and Apulia, would certainly have resulted in much the same movement of translation, but with the Greek almost certainly predominating. If from the final account, we were to subtract one individual, Gerard of Cremona, the balance of Arabic over Greek translations would in any case not seem overwhelming. In the twelfth century, we saw that all those who wanted scientific knowledge went to Spain, and Adelard actually deserted the Greek for the Arabic linguistic area. This could not have continued into the thirteenth century.

Of the Arabs, we can deal first with the last to write and to be translated, Ibn Rushd. He was inseparable from the texts of Aristotle which he introduced and commented on; he was a Jowett of his age. He was hardly even an 'Averroist', certainly not in his thirteenth-century influence on Europe. The fluent blend of cultures is best seen perhaps in the *Secreta Secretorum* (it should be *Secretum, sirr al-asrar*), the compendium attributed to Aristotle as his advice to his old pupil, Alexander the Great. In an elaborate introduction, the thirteenth-century translator, Philip of Tripoli, blends the Old Testament virtues which he attributes to his patron, in a homiletic and yet courtly style, with talk of "this most precious pearl of philosophy," of the science "which no one in his right mind would resist," and of the difficulties which arise because the "Arabic way of speaking is one thing and the Latin another." The book thus introduced is a pocket edition of all the subjects that most interested the Middle Ages; there are fairly lengthy discussions of different branches of science, medicine, the regimen of health, the calendar, astrology, the duties of kings, the qualities of justice and the rules of good government. This was really popular among the educated of Europe; over two hundred manuscripts are known. It is a translation of an Arabic treatise, itself the elaboration of a simpler form, adapted in its turn from a translation by Yuhanna ibn al-Batriq from a presumed Syriac original; it is possible to pick out Greek and Persian contributions to the Arabic and Syriac elements. The foundation is pagan, the superstructure has been altered from Christian to Muslim and back to Christian again; it received a number of Latin corrections, and was re-edited by Roger Bacon. It must be one of the most completely intercultural products of the world.

The classic Arabic authors translated were al-Farghani, al-Farabi, al-Khwarismi, al-Kindi, al-Ghazali, and among translators of pagan or Christian origin Thabit ibn Qurra, al-Battani, Qusta ibn Luqa al-Balabakki; the great medical writers translated included Ali ibn al-Abbas al-Majusi (Haly Abbas), Ibn Butlan, Ali ibn Ridwan and, of course, the two greatest of all, philosophers as much as medical writers, ar-Razi, and, the most important, Ibn Sina (Avicenna); more modern writers included az-Zarqali, Ibn Tufayl, Ibn Bajja, al-Bitruji, and Jabir ibn Aflah, and, among many Jews of Arabic culture, Ibn Jabirol and Musa ibn Maymun (Maimonides) in particular. This, of course, is nothing like an exhaustive list. Natural philosophy, especially physics, extended naturally into metaphysical and moral philosophy, so that there was a distinct influence beyond the strictly scientific; Ibn Sina, unique in his own right, was also unique in his influence on all European writing for a considerable period. His peculiar combination of both Platonic and Aristotelian influences was naturally welcome to a Europe which desperately needed Aristotelian techniques and yet was deeply loyal to the Augustinian tradition.

The use which was made of Arabic sources can partly be defined negatively. A students' examination crib of the second quarter of the century gives 243 lines to Aristotle's Ethics, against 90 for physics and metaphysics combined. The rôle of Arabic is essentially in the natural sciences. The *Almagest* is the major source for astronomy. Grammar obviously is based only on Latin sources. The influence of Arabic sources in the spread of Aristotelian method and material still needs study. Renan thought that he had identified a thirteenth-century 'Averroist' school, but we now see that he did not prove his case. It has even been said that 'Averroism' was invented by St Thomas Aquinas, because the sources of the mono-psychism which he attacked are obscure. The doctrine of the 'two truths' does not appear to have been taught by anyone, although van Steenberghen pointed out that there was a conflict between what appears philosophically to be necessary and what is known theologically to be true—an obvious and much less doubtful opposition. Ibn Rushd, we have seen, was the presenter of Aristotle. Citations of him in Aquinas have been computed, and vary between nearly two hundred in the *Commentary on the Sentences* to only 21 in the *Summa Theologica*. A count of references in a work on metaphysics by Siger of Brabant, the chief of the supposed Averroists, yields 135 to Aristotle (excluding the Metaphysics), 99 to Ibn Rushd, 39 to Ibn Sina, 25 to Plato, 16 to Aquinas, 9 to Proclus, 4 to the pseudo-Aristotelian *Liber de Causis*, 3 to Zeno; there are a number of group references, to the *Dialectici*, the

Antiqui, the *Sapientes*, the *Platonici*, the *Sophistae*, and so on. To take another example, however, references in the *De Animalibus* of Albert the Great to Aristotle (148) and to Ibn Sina (138) are nearly equal, while those to Ibn Rushd are negligible. The views of the Arabs always receive the same treatment as those of the Greeks, and all are made to serve Aristotle. We cannot say that the source of unorthodox argument in the surviving works of Siger and of his colleagues Boetius of Dacia is any but Aristotle.

When we consider the famous and supposedly Averroist con-demned propositions of the University of Paris of 1277 we stumble immediately into a world of very mixed opinions, which the Bishop (or his bureaucracy) has run together haphazard, item after item. To take a few of the least technical, we have: "18. That the future resurrection should not be conceded by a philosopher, because it is impossible that it should be investigated by reason—Error, because even a philosopher must subjugate his intellect in the service of Christ." "20. That the natural law prohibits the killing of irrational animals as of rational ones, though not as much." Others are ribald, or secular, or just intended to annoy the authorities, possibly just students' chatter. "166. That the sin against nature, as being an abuse in coition, although it is against the nature of the species, is not against the nature of the individual." "168. That continence is not excellence by essence." "170. That a man deficient in good luck cannot act well in morals." "172. That delight in sexual acts does not hinder the act or use of the intellect." "174. That there are fables and untruths in the Christian religion, as in others." "175. That the Christian religion prevents learning." "176. That happiness is in this life, not another." These ideas have nothing detectable to do with Arab influence and there is every reason to presume them indigenous. A number of propositions, as in the earlier condemnation of 1270, are concerned with argu-ments about the eternity of the world, and these, together with discussions of the *summum bonum* which some of the condemned propositions reflect in a crude form, were genuinely the product of Greek thought, and a preoccupation of the condemned 'Aver-roists', Siger and Boetius.

Neither Aquinas nor Albert needed to deviate from the main line of European thought, in order to cite Ibn Sina or al-Ghazali in matters where Islam and Christianity agree. Much work has been done on Ibn Sina, and upon his Latin translators, but the last word has not yet been said on the transmission of his thought.

Bacon boasted of making "use of the eloquence of Ibn Sina" and liked to quote short passages, for example on heaven: "We can apprehend eternity—whether it is, and what it is—no more than a deaf man can the harmony of music." In the course of the thirteenth century the Arab sources were finally absorbed. They took their place as part of the inheritance from the 'gentiles' of all ages and nations. Crombie's work on Robert Grosseteste has shown how a creative scientist—the first of the great Oxford school which led Europe in the thirteenth century, as Paris did in theology—could at this date absorb his sources, both Greek and Arab, and go on to add his own very considerable contribution to experimental science. His work on optics was based on Aristotle, Euclid, a pseudo-Ptolemy, Ibn Sina and perhaps al-Kindi. It is interesting that Ibn Rushd became available in the course of Grosseteste's life and was taken into his reading as a matter of course as his works arrived. It is certain that the use of Ibn Sina did not strike Grosseteste as contaminated, and Archbishop Pecham, who went further than Tempier in Paris in condemning 'Averroist' and Thomist doctrines, himself wrote a text-book on optics which is based on Ibn al-Haytham and Witelo: "Ibn al-Haytham and Witelo teach . . . " he begins one discussion. The dissociation from Islam is sometimes explicit. Aquinas refers to "the Arabs" as a cultural-linguistic group, and directs the *contra gentiles* against the Arab and Greek philosophers with respect, but he slights Islam itself with a mere summary of the usual polemic. Dante honours alike Aquinas and Siger, with Ibn Sina, Ibn Rushd, *"que il gran comento feo,"* Aristotle, Euclid, Ptolemy and the rest, together in limbo. Salah ad-Din is also among the heroes of antiquity, but Dante's condemnation of Islam is emphatic. Both these great Europeans dismissed Islam with an indifference based on ignorance.

The range of Arab authors incorporated into the European repertory was considerable. The habit of 'name-dropping' was often in the sources the Latin writers used. Qusta ibn Luqa's *On the Distinction of the Soul and the Spirit* names Plato, Aristotle, Theophrastus, Thabit ibn Qurra, Hippocrates and Galen in one sentence. Roger Bacon's history of philosophy attempts a broad concordance of authorities, Jerome, Augustine, Isidore and Bede; Cicero, Seneca, Pliny and Josephus; Ptolemy and the *Secreta*; Abu Mashar, al-Farabi, Ibn Sina and Ibn Rushd. Bacon insisted on the prophetic justification of philosophy, and not just to avert the wrath of the authorities, so far as one can tell. He worked out a detailed correspondence of pagan philosophy and literature with the Old Testament—"under (in the time of) Gideon, Orpheus and Linus the musicians were famous; afterwards, under Samuel, was the poet Homer . . . Then, under Hosiah, the best king, the first philosopher, that is, Thales of Mileto . . . and Solon of Athens also flourished." Noe taught the "parts of philosophy" to the Chaldeans, and Abraham went to Egypt and taught the Egyptians. He reverses the actual process of events because he must see all knowledge as revealed in a special sense. On the authority of the *Secreta Secretorum* he says that God revealed all the hidden things of human wisdom to the prophets, and to others whom he had specially chosen; from these the Indians, Latins, Persians and Greeks took their fundamental principles. From Aristotle, Bacon derived the information that the "first philosophizers were the Chaldeans and the Egyptians," and that the first scholastic centre of studies was established in Egypt. He reconciles this with the notion that Noe and Abraham were in the field first, by the realistic admission that in their day "a centre of studies regularly in the scholastic manner was not set up immediately, but its order and practice grew bit by bit." Plato wrote so many fine things of God, of customs, and of the future life that "many Catholic men" reckon that he must have heard Jeremiah preach. Then Aristotle cleared up the errors of the past, and added to the sum of philosophy, but was not able to bring it to perfection.

> "For the most part, the philosophy of Aristotle rested and was silent, whether because of the disappearance and rarity of copies, or because of its difficulty, or because of jealousy; until after the times of Muhammad, when Ibn Sina and Ibn Rushd and others called back the philosophy of Aristotle into the full light of exposition."

The insistence on scriptural endorsement (except for the Arabs) marks the old familiar craving for the assurance of orthodoxy, "the affinity of theology with philosophy." As an historian of philosophy, Bacon roughly follows the actual chronology, and it is really only the gap between Ibn Sina and Ibn Rushd that he seems not to be aware of. Bacon lists the true beliefs of philosophers, not only Aristotle, but Plato, Dionysius the Areopagite before his conversion (the pseudonymous mystic interpreted according to Acts 17), Avicenna and Ethicus. He concludes that they had the *preludia fidei*, and that we cannot tell whether that would be enough for salvation. On the necessity for revelation, Bacon quoted Plato, Aristotle, Cicero, Seneca, al-Farabi and Ibn Sina. For his purely scientific works, he had read very widely among the Arabs. It is fair to say that he made no distinction between non-Christians of all ages; with him we do not feel, as we feel with some of his predecessors, that this is because he was wholly ignorant of chronology. He came as near as almost any mediaeval author to accepting all wise men as saved, and had therefore to suppose them somehow accessible to prophecy. He left unsolved the position of Ibn Sina, who could not have been informed by any prophet then acceptable to the Latin church.

The width of erudition of the thirteenth century, and its broad perspective of knowledge, is exemplified again by the translations done into Spanish at the court of Alfonso X, the Learned, many with the personal interest and intervention of the King. Around the lengthy *Libros del Saber de Astronomia* and the *Tablas Alfonsies* are grouped translations and compilations which cover astrology (including Ptolemy), the history of the world, and of Spain, and of *ultramar*, all oriented against Islam and the Arabs, but not wholly polemic; the *sirr al-asrar* in the Western form, from the Arabic direct; *Kalila wa Dimna*, the Indian fables of Bidpai in origin, and almost the sole example of translated literature of no scientific or philosophical bent; *Las Siete Partidas* is primarily a legal work. The *Lapidario* is a relation of precious stones to astrology, its scientific value justified in the name of *Aristotil*, "who was more excellent than the other philosophers." The last books of the collection were the *Libros de Ajedrez, Dados y Tablas*, on chess and other games, a subject justified by the joy that God wishes for us, to compensate for our trials. Alfonso also wrote poems in Galician, both religious and secular. His is one of the most remarkable and successful examples of government patronage. It is truly encyclopaedic, wider in interest than any single translator or author, and wider in appeal because done in the vernacular.

In the thirteenth century Europe was no longer dependent on the Arabs for knowledge of the Hellenic world or of its own philosophic tradition. In fact Europe is largely indebted for this knowledge to the Arabic, but there is no reasonable doubt that if there had been no Arabic transmission, the Greek would have been, as in fact it soon was, transmitted direct. The general development of Europe would probably not have been affected. Yet there were many more Arab and Arabic-using authors familiar and respected, and Arabic was a stronger influence, in Europe in that age, than today or at any date between. However far they might later diverge, the Arabs and Europe were then still branches of one civilization.

3. Common ground: astrology and medicine

Any science calculated to satisfy fundamental human needs will necessarily be similar everywhere. If, in addition, the cultures concerned are actually similar, the working of applied sciences will illustrate, and will be based on, a number of recurring everyday experiences. This is probably obvious in the case of medicine, and a moment's reflection will show that astrology is in the same category. Astrology is simply a discarded scientific hypothesis; whether correctly discarded does not concern us. It does concern us that it was not obviously foolish, that it was universal, and that it was complex. It may be compared to psychiatry today. Everyone who could afford a doctor could and did afford an astrologer as well, for much of the period with which we are dealing. The theory is well stated by Gerard of Cremona. He was untroubled by the idea that astrological science might be unorthodox; his defence was quietly anti-patristic and rational. The orthodox supposition, of course, was that the stars predisposed, not determined, the events of a man's life. Only a determined unbeliever would go further than that. Man, Gerard argued, is a reasoning, mortal, two-legged animal; if a man is born without legs, it does not change the definition of man. If a man is born under Piscator, he has the disposition of a fisherman, but is not necessarily a catcher of fish. The son of a king and the son of a peasant may be born under the same constellation; the two may, indeed, be born kings, but the one will succeed to his father's throne, the other dominate among peasants, stronger and tougher than his fellows. We remember Gerard's proud boast that he himself was born under the royal sign and had not served a mortal man. Stated thus, astrology was a reasonable scientific hypothesis until disproved, though possibly with revolutionary social implications. We saw that Raymund of Marseilles, an early European astronomer using Arab sources, showed some nervousness about its orthodoxy, his pious approach to astronomical detail suggests an over-reaction to criticism. The usual approach was not at all conformist, but not in intention heretical either; indeed, it was really just severely practical. The astronomical tables were constantly adjusted for latitude, at Toledo, at Marseilles, at Hereford. Roger of Hereford, responsible for this last, also wrote a concise judicial astrology for practical use, for "the conservation of good things and the avoidance of ill."

At the other end of Europe, Anna Comnena wrongly considered astrological speculation to be post-classical; the Emperor Alexis disapproved, but Anna's own attitude was equivocal. It was much the same in all three cultures, Arab, Byzantine and Latin. Among the Arabic writers, Ibn Sina disapproved. In Europe, St Augustine and St Gregory had condemned this part of the classical heritage. At the practical level, too, Salimbene, for example, jeered at an anti-papal forecast that failed: "Scorpio did them no good." Yet if the stars were only an influence, there was no necessary rejection of free will. To think of magic is to see how reasonable was the astrological hypothesis in comparison. The two were associated in treatises, and doubtless often by practitioners, but magic was quite distinct, invoking a dangerous and perhaps uncontrollable domination by alien and evil powers. William of Malmesbury, contemporary with Adelard of Bath, relates the legend of Gerbert of Aurillac in its most lurid form. He admits that Europe had need of Gerbert's skill in the regular disciplines, arithmetic, astronomy, music and geometry, and judicial astrology, but he is horrified by a pact with the devil (which Gerbert, as Pope Sylvester, forswears only at his death, when he says that he never really meant it). Malmesbury recognizes that it is reasonable to consider this tale a fiction. He says that Gerbert acquired his magical knowledge from an Arab of Seville, where the Arabs "practise divinations and incantations after the usual mode of that nation." A slightly younger contemporary, John of Salisbury, writing twenty years after Raymund of Marseilles, reviews the problem in wholly traditional terms, and sees no occasion to refer to Arabic sources of knowledge. His discussion is based on Augustine, Cicero and Latin sources exclusively; it leads on to a discussion of the fore-knowledge of God. He distinguishes ma/thesis from mathes/is, rational knowledge from condemned studies. The fictional *Turpinus* has an uncontroversial chapter on the arts, which includes sound advice on different subjects; study of music is necessary because a singer without a voice moos like a cow, dialectic makes the wise man articulate, but, once his foot is firmly set in it, he will never get it out. Astronomy foretells the future as Herod and the Magi did Christ; it is the way to know "good and evil events, present,

283

future or past" anywhere in the world; this was the means the Roman senators used, to foreknow state events. As a science, it is not necessarily contaminated by magic, but we must beware of 'nigromancia' which puts us in the power of devils. All this is set as an appendix to the main account of conflict with the Arabs of Spain, but the conscious association of astrology with the Arabs was at most remote. The thirteenth-century encyclopaedist Brunetto Latini refers to a technical conflict over the calculation of the lunar cycle as between "holy church" and the "Arabians", but this is rare.

For examples of ideas which circulated and earned church disapproval, we may again take Tempier's condemned propositions of 1277, remembering that the supposed Averroistic influence is discredited. The collected prohibitions are evidently not directed against any one school of thought, but a hotch-potch of objectionable assertions which had come to the bishop's (or his advisers') ears. The authors of the secular squibs which we have already noted are not likely to have been the same as the magicians attacked in the preamble; among others, a book of geomancy, and "books, rolls and booklets of nigromancy or containing practices of divination, invocations of demons and conjurations . . ." The propositions include: "161. That the effects of the stars on the free will are hidden;" "195. That the fate which is the disposition of the universe proceeds from divine providence not directly, but by the mediation of the notion of the higher bodies; and that this fate does not lay necessity on lower beings, which have resistance, but on higher ones;" "206. That he assigns health, illness, life and death to the position of the stars, saying that if luck smiles on him he will live, and if not, die;" "207. That at the hour of generation there inheres in a man, in his body and therefore in his soul which follows the body, a disposition to certain actions or events . . . *Error*, unless it is understood of natural events, and by way of the disposition." The reservations make it clear that a moderate position was not condemned, only such attitudes as must lead to an impossible theological position. The "astrological facts" *qua* science were not in question.

Michael Scot put forward an historical perspective which was more confused than that of Roger Bacon, but which took in more fully the world-view of the astrologers and diviners. Unlike Gerbert and Bacon, Scot wrote in a way that explains his subsequent legend as a man given to magical practices, although he carefully maintains orthodoxy. Haskins justly observed that Scot was a muddled thinker, and he stood in isolation, neither a great pupil nor a master. He holds a representative, rather than influential position as an astrologer. When he came in that capacity to the court of Frederick II he had behind him a career in Spain, not without distinction, as translator from the Arabic, his chief work being Aristotle's books on animals combined in one. This was a bond with the Emperor, whose love for zoology at least was sincere. Scot's great astrological manuscript dates from his Sicilian period, a tripartite treatise, *introductorius, particularis* and *physionomia*. A small work on alchemy attributed to Scot begins,

"As I noticed that the noble science is wholly rejected among the Latins, and I saw that no one reaches perfection, because of the confusion in the books of philosophers to be found, I decided to reveal the secrets of nature to intelligent readers."

This reminds us of the justificatory prefaces of a century earlier; by this time there remained little that was 'arcane' that was also respectable. This alchemical tract, if it is not by Scot, must surely burlesque him; it is full of references to Arabia, Alexandria, Barbary, to the alum of Aleppo, to 'Saracens' of Africa and Aleppo whose names in manuscript are unintelligible. The whole purports improbably to be dedicated to an Arab king called 'Theophilus'. Scot is genuinely a man of the Mediterranean world, and aware of it and of the Arabs.

"And the same (astrological) method as Alchandrinus describes is generally used among the Arabs and some Indians (i.e. dark-skinned people?) as can be seen in the streets and pavements of Messina and Tunis (?), in which there are trained women who invite newly arrived merchants to ask them about their situation, and their home, and their fortune in trading."

Such astrological touting was presumably at the lowest grade of the profession.

Scot cited the classic defence of astronomy, "Thabit ibn Qurra and Aristotle say that he who studies or knows philosophy and geometry and every other science, and remains without astronomy, will be occupied unprofitably." Astronomy was universally useful,

"in many things for many people, to the doctor, for the sick, to the kings and barons to know what to do, to merchants for their routes

285

and journeys, to sailors for the changeableness of winds and tides, and to alchemists and magicians and those who work the notorious art."

He defines astronomy as the "study of the stars in themselves, the rule of law", and astrology as the expression of the stars, or discussion of them "and it is called from *astro* which means star and *logos* which means word or discussion." Derivation by the roots is probably not, as it looks, an attempt at obfuscation, but is a case of pedantry. He classifies astronomy into the fabulous, the superstitious and the imaginary. The fabulous is "as among poets, how Aries and the other signs of the sky were carried up into it;" superstitious astronomy discovers the hidden past, present and future, as well as affairs of individuals, "bad and good and the bad more than good." "Imaginary" is theoretical astronomy, as

"when I say that in the south wind there are angelic spirits that are princes of carnal love, like Egyn Yazabin, and in the north wind there are angelic spirits that are princes of hatred and other evils, such as Madreth Gurgiffet Badrath."

These spirits are readily identifiable in modern Egyptian magical practices still surviving, *ajin ya azabin* and *madras jirmafit badras*, "of the upper and lower airs." Scot adds that "many sciences or arts are more or less cloaked under the name of astronomy, such as geomancy, hydromancy, aeromancy, pyromancy . . ." and so on, through the "arts or sciences of divination." Magic he sees wholly as divination, discovery of hidden knowledge by forbidden means. He takes each method separately. What he describes is certainly often most distasteful to us, and we wonder that a church which was so severe on heresy was so lukewarm in suppressing magic, until the late sixteenth century. No doubt the reason was the deeply rooted popular basis of these immemorial skills. They do not seem to have much relation with witchcraft as the various persecutions, of a later date than we are now considering, would depict it. When we read the account of Master Gilbert "whom the demons of the air easily obeyed in all the things he required of them by day and by night," and who controlled them through "prayers and fasts and almsgiving," using "books and rings and consecrated candles," we are in a world, perhaps quite harmless, which has more in common with the control of *jinn* by holy men, such as can still be found today on the periphery of Arab culture, than with that comparable survival of magic in Europe which seems to consist largely of ill-wishing. What is clear from Scot's somewhat undiscriminating account is that the different techniques of divination probably represent, not only different survivals from a remote past, but also very different levels of honesty or charlatanry, and presumably of social status, among magical practitioners. It is true that he distinguishes—compare the similar distinction of John of Salisbury—*mathesis* from *matesis*; the former included all the subjects taught normally and legitimately, and so "the mathematical art can be taught freely and publicly, but by a good Christian the 'matematical' must not be, nor can he instruct someone in it freely,"—not on account of its falsity, "as every art is true," but on account of its evil intention. For this reason, he says, the Roman church prohibits it. Yet this sharp division between the ordinary schools and the clandestine teaching of magical techniques is only justified up to a point in Scot's writings. He seems to see many kinds of magic, and he runs magic and science into one.

His history of the hidden arts brings out clearly the confusion in his mind, although the general outline harmonizes more than might be expected with a modern perspective. The story begins with Noe. Ham was "naturally a very subtle genius" and he learned the wicked arts from the demons, and practised spatulamancy and necromancy (divination with dead bodies, not raising the dead). These arts were passed from one man to another, and so developed. The world became more populated; there were villages and castles and cities. One of the descendants of Ham called Canaan went to Jerusalem, and taught two Alexandrians called Demetrius and Alexander, who in their turn taught Ptolemy, King of Egypt. He was more ingenious and learned than anyone yet, and he developed the laws of astronomy (a confusion of Claudius Ptolemy with Ptolemy Soter). The giant Athalax (Atlas) was born in Egypt, learned from Ptolemy and carried the astrolabe to Spain. There two clerics or students from France acquired the astrolabe and took it home. Master Gilbert (Gerbert of Aurillac again) was already a skilled necromancer, and, seeing the astrolabe, compelled the spirits who served him to explain its significance. He became Bishop of Rheims by diabolical art, but acquired a taste for Scripture, gave up magic and became archbishop of Ravenna and so Pope. Other historical characters appear in this story. Zoroaster is one of the first of the generation of Shem to learn magic, and the demons teach him to worship fire in Persia and "the people of that region do so to this day." Atlas is said to be contemporary with Moses, and therefore, of course, so were Ptolemy and the two Alexandrians. When Scot summarizes the great astronomer-astrologers, they represent a cross-section of Hellenistic, Arab, Jewish, and even Latin culture: "Solomon and the Sybil, Thabit ibn Qurra, Mashallah, Dorotheus, Hermes (Trismegistos), Boethius, Ibn Rushd, John of Spain, Isidore, Sahl, al-Qabizi, etcetera." This is jumbled not only chronologically but, characteristically, between astrology and magic. The first two represent magic only. What Michael Scot has to contribute of most interest is not so much his witness to the main line of the common Arab and European culture, as that submerged part of it which in his mind underlies the written sources. They rarely seem to be the actual sources he uses, but they give respectability to a subject-matter which is far from respectable and for which Scot constantly apologizes.

We may turn with real relief from the heated atmosphere of Scot's writing to the comparative sanity of ordinary practical—'judicial'—astrology. The translation of the Arabic *De Judiciis Astrorum* of Abu'l Hasan Ali ibn abi Rijal, by a Jew at the court of Alfonso, into Castilian, and thence by a Spaniard into Latin, is a good example of the common Mediterranean culture. Ibn abi Rijal, known as al-Maghrabi, left Spain and established himself in Tunis. Here was an Arab immigrant whose work passed through Jewish and European translation, who derived his material from Arab writers mostly of the East, and through them and in turn through Ptolemy, from the Babylonians, and by way of the Egyptian background of Hermetic writing from the Alexandrian Hellenes (the writer specifically preferred the 'Egyptian' school of thought). In this astrological field we are closer than in any other to the common thinking of all who have lived in the area of the Mediterranean and western Asia. There was a certain social continuity from the past, although the natural censors of two religions had excised any pagan appearance. From eleventh-century Tunis to thirteenth-century Toledo there was something approaching a complete sociological identity.

Certain topics have remained of close human interest throughout history, family relationships, pregnancies, births, friendships, marriages (how do I select a spouse, how can I be sure my child is my own? etcetera), chastity, fidelity, buying and selling, litigation, dealing in property. There has been some change in the cultural attitude to these, pregnancy becoming less desirable with rapid population increase, the scale of trade developing in historic times, the esteem for chastity fluctuating; but, on the whole, we are concerned in this type of problem with the common experience of the whole human race. This is also true of murder, robbery, war, and, apart from the changes in fashion of medical opinion, diseases and their treatment. Others of Ibn abi Rijal's problems have ceased to be relevant, at least in cultural terms that the author and translators would have understood. Monarchical government no doubt depended then, as newer systems do now, largely on the mysterious formation of public opinion, but this was expressed by the ruler's unilateral decision, rather than by the anonymous consensus of our day. Imprisonment was a hazard, perhaps more arbitrary for strangers than we would recognize; drinking remains always a normal occupation, and racing and use of horses and other sports, especially hunting, were then all common ground. Writing and sending and receiving letters was a serious enterprise, and so were journeys; astrologers must learn to answer questions about the choice of journey, about the arrival at a new city, about sea journeys and secret journeys, and so on. The great natural disasters like famine, flood and plague were universal. Slaves were a serious subject among Arabs and Europeans alike. The astrologer's interest must extend to questions about secret enemies or about the spread of rumours. Most characteristic would be to give advice about a lucky hour. Because this tradition was indeed so old, we must be careful not to take works of astrology too literally as handbooks to the social custom of the day; but we can say with assurance that all these questions had to be correctly assessed by the practising astrologer whether in the Arab World or in Europe. Yet Ibn abi Rijal is not exceptional in the range of questions for which his book offers the training, and we must assume that they met the popular demand.

Among the colleagues of Guido Bonatti of Forli, a contemporary of Frederick II, was a Baghdadi Arab who was regarded as an exceptional master. Bonatti wrote a full-length treatise for the advanced student which begins with an interesting and detailed defence of the orthodoxy and accuracy of astrology. He is much more professional in his general approach than Michael Scot, as he was in his practice. He defends his discipline against a number of criticisms with what looks like habitual skill, suggesting that the criticisms were usual. He compares the *medicus*, who deals in

corruptibles, with the astrologer, whose concern is with the unchanging bodies which shall remain till "that day which God shall
will, of which it is said that not the angels nor the Son but the
Father only, etc." He defends the profession against a diversity
of attacks, against those who say that the science of the stars is
unknowable; against those who say that the stars do not influence
this sub-lunar globe; against those who say that they do so only
in a universal way, not on particular things; against those who say
that the stars signify only what is either necessary or impossible;
against those who say that the science is harmful, and causes
sadness and anxiety to those of whom misfortunes have been foretold; against those who object that the same advice will benefit
your opponent as much as yourself. "Perhaps even some fools
will get up and ask unreasonably: 'Why do you, an astrologer, give
up something (that you think) unlucky, when you should foreknow what must happen to you?' " He tells the student to reply
that the art extends, not to casual accidents like a thorn running
into the foot, but to those things which are foreseeable; against
sudden accidents you can only take precautions, they are not
something for scientific consideration (of 'art' or 'nature'). His
most curious opponents are those who say that astrology is not
lucrative. He contrasts the rich fool, content with his folly, with
the pure scientist; astronomical art is to financial profit as the
grain to the chaff, the philistines commend nothing but the
accumulation of money, and so on. Bonatti's career was a successful one with great patrons, and we cannot really think it unprofit-
able. The attitude of the pure scientist, whether, as he says himself,
doctor or astrologer, has something of a pose of academic virtue
about it. We must recognize the total cultural absorption of the
new material which had been entering Europe from Arab sources,
adapted to a highly professional system.

The exactly comparable profession, not incompatible in one
practitioner, was the medical. Here too there was an already existing tradition, and here too the Europeans benefited greatly from
the lessons acquired from Arabic. Again the original sources were
Greek, and again the Arabs had both transmitted and improved
on them. We have seen already how the Arab sources, including
the *Liber Regalis* of Ali ibn al-Abbas, were utilized by Constantine
the African, and how a carefully corrected text was made by
Stephen of Antioch; and the maximum impact of Arab medicine
we owe to Gerard of Cremona, who translated among others the

Arabic Hippocrates, the *Liber Almansoris* (*Kitab al-mansur*) of Abu Bakr Muhammad ibn Zakariya ar-Razi with part of his *Kitab-al-Hawi* (a later and full Latin translation of this greatest of medical encyclopaedias was made by a Jew, Faraj ibn Salim, under Charles of Anjou in Sicily), the great *Qanun fit tibb* of Abu Ali al-Husain ibn Abdalla ibn Sina, literally as *Canon Medicinae*, as well as Ali ibn Ridwan and other lesser medical writers. The *Canon*, which, like the *Liber Regalis*, was of manageable size, and yet fuller than ar-Razi's *Almansoris*, was perhaps the most popular of medical treatises, and was probably the most often reprinted at the Renaissance. Ar-Razi was much appreciated as a writer on chemistry, but there can be no doubt that whatever the aberrations in mediaeval European judgement on Arab writers, Ibn Sina was the most generally admired, and over a very wide range of subjects, including even the borderland between metaphysics and religion. His opinions, we have seen, were admired, and supposed to be un-Muslim. There have been many to decry al-Ghazali, al-Hallaj and Ibn Rushd as crypto-Christian or crypto-pagan, but no judgement of Ibn Sina can assess him as other than one of the great writers of the world. The lives of the Arab medical writers who most affected the European consciousness extend over only two centuries, from the birth of ar-Razi in 865 to the death of Abu'l Hasan al-Mukhtar ibn al-Hasan ibn Abdun ibn Sadun ibn Butlan of Baghdad (*Elluchasem Elimithar filius Hahadum filius Ducellani, medicus de Baldath*) in 1063 and the Spaniard Ibn al-Wafid al-Lahmi (Albenguefit) in 1074 (Christian era).

One of the most striking aspects of the tradition which came from the Greeks through the great Arab practitioners was the emphasis on the rules of health, *regimen sanitatis*. In their treatment of medicine, disease is largely presented as an aberration; it is health that medicine is really about. The second, or practical, half of Ali ibn al-Abbas, the *Liber Regalis*, begins with a discussion of the rules of health: the chapter headings include: "The common rule for the maintenance of health, and first according to the seasons . . . The rule of health through exercise . . . The toleration of anxiety through work . . . the bath . . . through food . . . through drink, and first through water . . . through wine . . . through sleep and watching . . . through coition." The rule are also considered for infants (with the choice of wet-nurses), for boys, for adolescents and youths, for old men, for convalescents, and so on. The translator took care to give Arabic and Greek names of technical terms in addition to the Latin, and a glossary in three languages was added to the main text. Ibn Butlan's *taqwim as-sihha* was translated as *Tacuinum Sanitatis*, retaining the Arabic word with the translation *"regimen"*. It begins, "On the six things that are necessary to any man for the daily conservation of his health, with its corrections and operations." These are immediately listed.

"The first care of health is the preparation of the air, which affects the heart. The second is the regulation of food and drink. The third is the regulation of movement and rest. The fourth is the restraint of the body from sleep and from much watching. The fifth is the regulation of the relaxation and constriction of the humours. The sixth is regulation of the person to moderate joy, anger, fear and anxiety. So the preservation of health will be in these methods of balance, and the removal of these six from that balance makes illness, God the Glorious, the Almighty, permitting. And under each of these kinds there are many types, and many things necessary of which, God willing, we will describe the natures ... Let us invoke the help of God that He may make straight our mind, for human nature can scarcely be prevented from error ..."

The emphasis is more on health than on disease. Near the beginning of Ibn Sina's *Canon of Medicine* there comes this 'happy start': "I say that medicine is the science by which the dispositions of the human body are known, in order that customary health may be preserved or, being lost, may be recovered." Ibn al-Wafid's *On the Powers of Medicines and Foods*, also translated by Gerard, makes similar points:

"I have put together this book on the virtues of medicines and foods, out of the books of the ancients; for long have I wearied my mind with it ... I have poured forth prayers on it that it may come near to God, the Exalted, the Glorious ... The object of medicine is health, and according to two modes. The first is the knowledge of the complexions of the bodies of men. The second is the knowledge of medicines and foods, by the knowledge of which health is maintained in the healthy man and restored in the sick man."

Among the many parallels in the ways that astrology and medicine were viewed by both Europeans and Arabs was the solicitude to distinguish between the theoretical and the practical sides of the knowledge involved, although there was no question of a division of actual labours between pure and applied science.

As with Guido Bonatti, in astrology, we recognize the final absorption and digestion of astrology derived from and through the Arabs, so in the polymathic Arnald of Villanova, a sort of lesser and European ar-Razi, we see the same achievement in the field of medicine. His works cover every conceivable field of medicine, anatomy, physiology, aetiology, prognosis, therapy, nursing, pharmacy, psychology, even cosmetics and public health; above all, the whole is subordinated to the "philosophy". Arnald covers so large a field that he must be thought a re-editor as much as an author; some of his material comes direct from other writers. Plagiarism is meaningless in the mediaeval context, but almost the whole of the medical culture of Europe with all its acquisitions from the Arabs seems to pass through his pen. If he is indeed as much an editor as author, he gives nearly everything that he touches a personal quality. The tradition has definite characteristics which we quickly recognize, but which are distinct from those prevalent in the theological schools or even the ribald Arts faculties. There is a precision in classification which is scholastic but which must also surely represent a care in diagnosis; Arnald gives us a score of different forms of mental disturbance to consider, with sub-categories. A strictly practical re-iterated note which the Arabs had encouraged was inspired essentially by the Hippocratic corpus: for example,

"washing the head should not be left beyond twenty days, nor should it be done more than once a week, and never on a full stomach, but before dinner or supper;" "as often as people wearing tunics sweat, especially thin people, it is advisable to change the tunic, lest the body be harmed when the sweat gets cold."

The bath itself, of course, follows exercise, which, if temperate, is a source of health before meals, but impedes digestion after, "according to learned men," a phrase which emphasizes for us the sense of tradition in the writer; it also hardens the organs, apparently in a favourable sense. His little treatise, 'The adornment of women', begins with a bath but includes the chemistry of cosmetics; the remark, "there are many women who desire to adorn their faces in a wonderful way and make themselves beautiful" seems to be noted as a fact without comment.

This brings us to the next mark of this school. "The ancients say in their books that the things that preserve health are six: moderate exercise, the bath, food, drink, sleep and coition."

(We have met this in another form.) Of the last of these six he says:

> "So it is for us to say how to set about it, how it should be done, at what time, and what is harmful in it and how, and what happens to those who use it much . . ." "Immoderate coition . . . induces more weakness than any other evacuation . . ."

The tone is wholly clinical; it is far, not only from the Gregorian ideal, but equally from the antinomian. In this connection there is a classic little treatise on 'Heroic Love' (i.e. 'erotic', from *eros*, a Graeco-Arabic theme often considered scientifically). Chapter One is a description of this malady, Chapter Two is "The origin and cause of vehement desire and of fixed imagination in lovers; and the interpretation of the word;" the third chapter deals with incidental symptoms of the disease, and their causes, and the fourth with "The remedy of the said passion." There is a moral neutrality, although Arnald himself wrote religious material of a slightly non-conforming pattern.

The respect for tradition is qualified. Arnald criticizes sources linguistically, thus, "*Carabitus* is the name 'frenzy' corrupted among the Arabs, because of the uniformity of the letters with which they write"—(k-r-b-t-s for f-r-n-s-s). Although, for example, the binding effect of rhubarb on the bowels is confirmed, not by experience, but by the authority of Dioscorides, Galen and Ibn Sina, Arnald does not hesitate to reject an opinion of Ibn Rushd's alone as "irrational, mistaken and therefore not to be practised." He blames those who quote, but do not follow, the authority of Ibn Sina. His reading includes, of course, all the great Greek and Arab writers. There is a graceful appreciation of the qualities of ar-Razi which indicates also the priorities of the age:

> "a man brilliant in analysis, resolute in action, far-seeing in judgement, proved in experiment, he especially discloses the introduction to us in his little book on the agreement between the philosophers and the medical men."

On the Hippocratic 'canon', *vita brevis, ars longa*, Arnald comments with a description of the ideal professional virtues.

> "The prudent doctor is uncertain in prognostication, fair in giving assurance, careful in giving answers, so as not to promise health, for then he usurps the divine function and does God a wrong; but he does promise to be trustworthy and diligent; in visiting, he is

circumspect and attentive, in speech unassuming, in disposition, good-willed. He must be enduring, and steadfast in self-confidence, eager and consistent in persevering. The assistants must be well organized in their ways, forward-looking and careful in sentiment and thought, alert when on watch, attentive and trustworthy in execution."

We cannot say that medical and astrological writings disclose a literate class or society which is irreligious or, in any sense, an alternative society to the orthodox clergy of the periods with which we are dealing. Nor can we say that the professionalism which Arnald describes is in any way in conflict with the ideals and even the practice of the friars, though clearly far removed from the life of the great monastic lordships. Nevertheless, the society of these professional men was evidently distinct from that of the mass of other literate people and was distinguished as much by its professional quality as by its special doctrinal subject-matter and mental discipline. We must not make too much of this. So far as these professions were subsidized by provision of benefices, there was no distinction between them and the church. Michael Scot, after all, is typical enough in being a court astrologer who seems to have been conscientious in his accepting or refusing benefices. Other scientists were even less distinct. Some of Robert Grosseteste's best work in experimental physics was done after he had left the university, and when, already an old man, he had become an exceptionally conscientious bishop. The result of introducing professional skills which required extensive training was to create a special class, but this was integrated into the social pattern in much the same way among Europeans as among Arabs. The basic economy was patronage at the higher level and fee-paying at the lower.

The practical uses of the new knowledge extended, of course, to other subjects. The Arabic-Indian numerals, which remained for so long an esoteric interest of academics, were brought to life by the technical needs of the rapidly developing maritime cities. The practical studies of Leonardo Fibonacci of Pisa linked the world of theoretical science to the commercial system. His *Liber Abaci* was dedicated in 1202 to Michael Scot, and was followed a good deal later by his rather less successful *Practica Geometriae*. He did not think of himself as restoring the knowledge of the ancients, but was consciously seeking to bring Pisan practice into conformity with that of the contemporary Mediterranean

world; he had learned the uses of the algorism in study and discussions, he said, in the great trading centres of Egypt, Syria,
Greece, Sicily and Provence. The worlds of commerce, of astrology, of medicine, were all loosely connected, and their new and
secularized culture was the more like the Arab for being partly
free of ecclesiastical domination. In religion they tended to look
for new means of expression, and it was the new organization of the
friars, with their marked interest in scientific development, that
most easily bridged the contemporaneous worlds of the European
Christian community.

Another link between the Arabs and Europeans in the scientific
field was the vestigial survival of Muslim piety in Latin translations. The *basmala* is the commonest of these survivals, often
in an attenuated form, even after omitting the attestation of the
Prophet. Ketton's translation of al-Khwarismi's *Algebra* begins,
in nomine dei pii et misericordis, "in the name of God the tender and
compassionate," which is exactly the formula he uses in translating the *basmala* in the Quran. There are many other cases of the
use of the same or closely similar formula; and there are many
more elisions and paraphrases, "in the name of the Lord," "in
the name of God," or, as in the opening of Michael Scot's Aristotelian translation, *De Animalibus*: "in the name of our Lord
Jesus Christ, the almighty, the compassionate, the merciful,"
which must surely represent the Christianization of the Islamic
witness. For *inshallah* it is common to find *si deus voluerit*. Often
there are confessionally equivocal phrases, like "to God alone be
glory" or "thanks be to God the creator of all things." Some of the
most remarkable examples occur in the *Judicial Astrology* of
Ibn abi Rijal, in spite of the text's having passed through so many
changes of religion, as well as of language. Such phrases as "praised
be God in all things" naturally harmonize with any revealed
religion; more suggestive of the Islamic source are "thanks be to
the one God, the Victorious, the Honoured, the Powerful, Creator
of night and day, Uncoverer of hidden things," and, "I pray the
Almighty that of his mercy he will support and direct me in the
way of truth." Most Muslim of all is it that, of all professions, an
astrologer should end his whole work, "and what the future is,
God knows best." In one passage we find the most curious blend:

> "Ali, the son of Abu Rijal, giving thanks at the beginning of his
> books to the Lord Jesus Christ for all benefits received or to be

received, always said: 'Praised be God who is Lord of subtleties, of excellences, of rewards, of mercies; Creator of all creatures, Knower of hidden things, Understander of reasons . . .' "

Here everything up to the *semper dixit* is, of course, intruded by the European translator into his text. It seems that much scientific literature encompassed a Latin usage of Muslim piety to that strictly limited point within which nothing would strike a Christian reader as strange. Sometimes that point is most delicately calculated. Ibn Sina's *Canon* begins,

"The book of the Canon of Medicine which the prince Abu Ali ibn Sina published, translated by Master Gerard of Cremona in Toledo from Arabic into Latin. The words of Abu Ali ibn Sina: 'Let us first give thanks to God . . . whose mercies are manifest upon all the Prophets.' "

Similarly in the Latin of the *Philosophia* of al-Ghazali we read "it is necessary that there should be a prophet and that he should be believed; for the world cannot be governed except by a law which is common to all creatures;" therefore there must be prophetic revelation through angelic mediation. This comes obviously close to Islamic faith, but it is not so worded as to seem untrue to a Christian. In translations and mistranslations alike we must recognize a willingness to go far towards textual fidelity, and a sure instinctive knowledge of where to stop, in order to preclude the specifically Islamic. There is no evidence that the scientists ever quarrelled with the requirements of orthodoxy; on the contrary, they knew just how far to go, probably because this was not from outward conformity, but from inward conviction. When that is said, we may add that it is in these scientific translations that we find almost the only kind of religious accord between Arabs and Europeans—admittedly unacknowledged—in the Middle Ages. They reach across the religious barrier as well as the cultural.

What the twelfth-century translators had set out to do was achieved with complete success. Europe recovered all that it had lost in the philosophical and scientific fields at the end of the classical age; and it received this body of knowledge in a form which had been improved by centuries of Arab work on it. Europe digested a drastic and revolutionary experience apparently without pain. It was characteristic that Europeans knew from the beginning what they wanted and what they did not want, and how to take the one and leave the other. This last was perhaps the rarest ability of all. They took whatever filled a gap in their culture; they took nothing that conflicted with their existing positive ideas. In filling certain gaps, in the technological field, for example, Europe owed no significant debt to the Arabs; both Arabs and Europeans seem to have developed—once again in parallel—largely as beneficiaries of Far Eastern discoveries. Although we have seen that Europe would have recovered its lost store of learning direct from the Greek, if it had not done so first from the Arabic, it is still true that in fact it came through Arabic. Yet in the last resort it is true even in this matter, where Europe plainly owes the Arabs so much, that it is not the indebtedness which is the most interesting aspect of events or the most important, but rather the parallel development of Arabs and Europeans. The real importance of the movement of restoration of learning was that Europe once again shared with its co-heirs of antiquity this whole vast area of knowledge and skills. In other ways Europe and the Arabs would begin to diverge, after continuing along parallel paths for another century; when that happened they remained linked in learning longer than in any other way.

Chapter 11

The end of the Middle Ages

We have followed a few principal themes along the inevitable meanders of their history. Beginning with the idea that it is easy to exaggerate the differences between Islam and Christianity, and in particular between Arabs and Europeans in the eighth century, we have watched the reactions of Europe to centuries of conflict, first fighting back with little energy, and then recovering morale, and passing into a stage of aggressive hysteria before relapsing finally into lethargy and a mere habit of mind. We have seen the failure to 'recover' eastern territory for Christendom; that is, the failure of Europe to establish a Levantine colony; we have glimpsed the extermination of the Arabs as a distinct people in the northern half of the central Mediterranean, and we have noted the mood of Spain in the earlier and greater stages of the Reconquest. We have seen how the moral identity of Europe was preserved by a fiercely determined orthodoxy which wanted nothing to do with any least deviation in the whole field of religion, and how religion itself became the expression of that same sense of identity. We have seen how the doctrines were evolved that made that possible, including doctrines about what the 'true' facts of Islam must be, and doctrines which ensured that the perpetuation of the idea of war and the suppression of Arab communities within Europe should be on a legal basis. Deliberate self-isolation seems to be the key, and yet we have seen that, despite this, Europe was willing to open its ideas to everything advantageous, without touching the question of orthodoxy; that there was still a common culture, and that this was still capable of renewal. Where did all this lead? What had happened to European ideas in the course of these developments and in which direction would they now go?

1. Themes and topics

In some ways the Europe of the fourteenth century might be said to be moving in the same direction as the Arab World. It is generally thought that Duns Scotus was more clearly marked by the influence of Ibn Sina than any other Christian philosopher. His late fifteenth-century editor and commentator, Maurice O'Fihely, said that

> "he favours Ibn Sina among philosophers, everywhere, except where it might be contrary to faith; Augustine among the Catholic doctors; Paul among the apostles, and John among the evangelists; and this naturally, because, as witness Boethius, we must strive after each thing that is a likeness."

Scotus has also been said to separate philosophy from theology, in that, too, like Ibn Sina; and his well-known emphasis on the will of God, as distinct from the natural law, can be seen as parallel to normal Islamic doctrine. "There is no cause why the will (of God) wills (this particular thing), except that the will is the will." This takes us away from the concept of natural law which has been regarded as essential to 'Christian philosophy'. In Ockham also there are elements that might seem to be sympathetic to Islam, the reluctance to 'demonstrate' the truths of religion which many, Lull for example, so fondly believed would persuade Muslims to accept Christianity; the equal reluctance to discuss the divine attributes. Ethics in this system become wholly a matter of the content of revelation, and this certainly would be intelligibile to many Muslims. In contrast, Ibn Rushd seems much more of a 'Greek', and so, more fully and easily absorbed into European tradition. In 1500, O'Fihely, though devoted to Scotus, thought his use of Aristotle and of Ibn Rushd alike old-fashioned. John of Jandun, finally, represents a positive and anti-papal Averroism in the fourteenth century. We must not make too much of these diverse and almost certainly accidental tendencies. Christian and Islamic thought never wander too far from each other. We should not be surprised when parallelisms and resemblances spring up naturally. It is likely that the appearance of a great mystic like Ibn al-Arabi is linked to the last phases of Arab scholasticism, much as the fourteenth- and fifteenth-century Christian mystics were to the end of scholasticism in Europe.

There is another parallelism in the tendency of popular religion.

In the Arab and Persian, and later Turkish, world, a period of general Sufi development followed the scholastic age; it included the creation of the greater brotherhoods of mystics, some of them eccentric, who extended through all social classes. European travellers of the seventeenth century were accustomed to speak very unfavourably of the 'dervishes' as a sort of false Religious Order, and especially the wandering Qalandariya, now long defunct. In fact, many of these, other than the more highly organized ones living in community, may be compared with the enthusiastic, religious associations of European laymen, such as the Brethren of the Free Spirit, the Flagellants and Beghards and others. These were exalted people, heterodox and ecstatic in tendency; the description, whether just or not, applied by Macdonald to the darwish sects, as varying from "ascetic quietism to pantheistic antinomianism", seems certainly to have applied to the various free-spirit movements which in Europe began in the thirteenth century and reached their greatest strength in the fourteenth and the fifteenth. There was no longer the direct awareness of Islam which had given a crusading twist to some of the hysterical or revolutionary outbursts among Europeans earlier, but there seems to have been a genuine parallel between East and West. If we extend this to include the more orderly and disciplined sects, on the one side, for example, the Qadariya (Eastern, from the late eleventh century, but extending rapidly later), Shadhiliya (approximately the same dating, in North Africa), Baktashiya and Maulawiya (late thirteenth and fourteenth centuries, Anatolia), Nakshabandiya (fourteenth century, Far East), and, on the other, to include the different orders of friars, particularly the Dominicans and Franciscans, with their third orders of laity living in the world, we find that the parallelism continues. What Europe never produced was the Sufi in public life who is not professionally a mystic. On both sides there were different degrees of orthodoxy, devotion and discipline, and the parallels are not between particular orders or groupings on each side, but in general between movements over the combined area of Christendom and Islam. It seems as though there was a similar need and a similar reaction from the Netherlands to Turkestan and even further.

Though there may have been a common malaise and similar attempts at solution on both sides of the religious divide, the conscious attitude of Christian Europeans did not change radically. Something like a century passed from the end of the Latin states until the seriousness of Ottoman expansion was understood, and during that period crusading was not on a substantial scale. The new pressures by a powerful and well-organized, if still peripatetic, Turkish state had at least two results. It renewed the interest of intellectuals in Islam, and it had the linguistic result of substituting 'Turk' for 'Saracen'. 'To become a Muslim' came to be expressed in most European languages in some such form as 'to turn Turk'. Examples earlier than the late fourteenth century are rare; later the phrase became general. This marks the beginning of the time when the idea of the 'Arab' began to fade out of the image of the 'Muslim'. Europe's idea of the East would for the future, and until the twentieth century, be dominated by the Ottomans. 'Saracen', as I have argued, was an unsatisfactory term, lacking precision, but it always implied 'Arab' in some form or another, certainly never excluded it.

Basically the same polemic as was used earlier reappeared in the later Middle Ages, in the works of Denis the Carthusian (van Leeuwen), the Spaniards, Juan de Torquemada, Juan de Segovia, Alfonso a Spina and the ostensible convert from Islam, Juan Andres, and in the best of them all, Nicolas of Cusa. The new contribution made in this period to the intellectual debate—a debate which we have agreed was largely imaginary—was negligible. Pius II, Aeneas Sylvius, in neatly summarizing mediaeval polemics, truly represents the Renaissance. The most original notion of the period leading up to the Reformation was that which Southern described in his comments on Wycliff in the fourteenth century and Luther in the sixteenth (Luther was born just a century after Wycliff died). They introduced the idea of Islam as an interior state which may be imputed to the enemies of true doctrine (however the writer may define it). In doing so they in effect admitted the interiorization of Islam as the 'enemy' (undifferentiated) which it had been for so long in European imagination. Perhaps the most original idea of the age was the first glimpse of an 'ecumenic' approach. Nicolas of Cusa in his *Cribratio Alcoran* buries his thoughts in a mass of traditional matter, but in his dialogues *De Pace Fidei* he invents (e.g. 'Arabs') interlocutors of different faiths and nations who are made to present reasonable positions. For the first time there is an actual notion of debate, instead of the old wholly unreal one. The idea was picked up again in the sixteenth century by Jean Bodin, whose *Colloquium Heptaplomeres* includes among the representatives of the faiths a certain 'Octavius';

the special originality of this character is that he is conceived as a European, captured by Barbary pirates, and not an unwilling, but a convinced, convert to Islam. His captors were specifically Arabic speakers. Moreover, in the weariness of intolerance which affected northern Europe during and after the wars of religion, the Muslim example showed that the idea of toleration was practicable. This, however, was now Ottoman. The Arabs were for Europe no longer the Muslims *par excellence.*

In the fifteenth century a glimmering light of understanding persisted. If the coming Ottoman domination made it barely relevant to the Arab situation, we must look elsewhere for the serious and lasting effects of the long mediaeval European experience of the Arab World. The first and most striking is in the scientific field. The twelfth-century discovery that Europe's intellectual past could be recovered, and the sense of communion with all other ages and people (however vaguely conceived), merged gradually into a respect for the ancients which took them for granted, while still admiring the authority of antiquity. The reabsorption of the forebears had been successful in the later period; there were two tendencies. Mathematics were developed for practical purposes to a point of high, complex efficiency by the merchant class, following the earlier example set by Leonardo Fibonacci. Among some scientists, however, the *arcana* which the early translators had been so proud to uncover to all the world came to be valued because they were hidden as well as ancient. In England in the later fifteenth century, for example, we read sentences like this beginning of a chemical treatise on the *quinte essence*:

"... I write to you a tretice in englisch breuely drawe out of the book of quintis essencijs in latyn, that hermes the prophete and kyng of Egipt, after the flood of Noe, fadir of philosophris, hadde by reuelacioun of an aungil of god to him sende ..."

This is the "souereyneste secrete of all secretis" and the reader is charged, "Comounne ye not this book of deuyne secretes to wicked men and auerous, but keep it in priuytee."

A fresh sense of history survives in the *Dicts and Sayings of the Philosophers*, the first book printed in England, derived from the Arabic original of Abu'l Wafa Mubashshir ibn Fatik al-Qaid, written in the eleventh Christian century, and translated in the thirteenth into Spanish, and thence into Latin; a hundred years later the Latin was turned into French, and in the later fifteenth century three separate versions were made in English from the French. The book itself is essentially a vulgarization, a collection of sayings more or less fabulous in form, attributed to the philosophers, a kind of wisdom literature which appealed to Arabs and Europeans alike, at least until the classical revival of the Renaissance discouraged or replaced it in the West. Again the great theme is ancient wisdom, and a pride in belonging to the whole history of the human race is implicit.

> "Hermes was borne in Egipte, and asmoche to saye in Greke as Mercury, and in Ebrew as Ennoch . . . and was the firste that fonde the connynge of sterres."

Hermes Trismegistos, Thot, has now become the type of pre-Christian truth, even of preparation for the Gospel. "To the which Hermes the kingis that were in that tyme obeied, and alle her lande also and all that dwelled in iles, and constreyned hem to kepe the lawe of God, to seye trouth and dispise the werlde."

The effect of the spread of scientific information in the context of Arabic or Greek translation was not just the extension of general knowledge; it was also a gradual agglomeration of many different bits and pieces that amounted to a vast literature with its own internal consistency and character. Fragments were copied, often alchemical fragments divorced from their original context, to form little haphazard anthologies. Many undistinguished compilations on astronomy, astrology, meteorology and chemistry exist in manuscript, making constant indiscriminate use of Arab and Greek authors that happened to be available. This sort of anthologizing is natural enough in philosophical extracts; for example, to reinforce Aristotle with Avicenna. It is commonest perhaps in chemistry, and both ar-Razi and Ibn Sina were often plundered in this connection. One carefully written manuscript by Robert Greene of Welbe in 1528–9 represents a great deal of copying from a large alchemical library, with a bias towards a mystical rather than a scientific interest. It includes the great Arab writers, Greeks and mediaeval Latins. The compiler, otherwise unknown, evidently enjoyed making the collection; his signatures are fanciful and diversified. The whole shows the unchanging use of mediaeval sources in the sixteenth century, and the continuing tradition which united authors of diverse origins. A good deal earlier, manuscript anthologies had this same encyclopaedic character; one astronomical collection of extracts, for example, consists chiefly of Hermes, Umar ibn al-Farrikhan at-Tabari, al-Kindi, Dorotheus, 'the Indians', and in the aggregate it amounts to a reasonably homogeneous account of natural disasters astrologically related. A likely combination in medicine is Hippocrates with Galen and the commentary of Ali ibn Radwan. The Arabs most quoted—I hazard a guess, I do not offer a word count—were Ibn Sina, al-Kindi, al-Farabi and ar-Razi and, in their special fields, al-Khwarismi, az-Zarqali and al-Farghani. Nearly all these writers were printed, and many of them reprinted frequently, in the sixteenth and even the seventeenth century. Men's vision was necessarily extended beyond their immediate European culture. Works about astronomy made readers familiar with the Muslim calendar and with other and still older calendars. Astrological and geographical works made people familiar with place names that no one could mark upon a map; history remained vague wherever there was no means of concordance between Greek history and Jewish history, and particularly in the case of the remote civilizations of ancient Egypt and Babylonia. The result was imprecise but it was inclusive.

In technology the situation was different. Sword-making was a skill common to Arabs and Europeans, to which both contributed; but the great changes in agricultural technology effected between the ninth century and the twelfth tended to divide northern Europe from the Mediterranean, rather than Europe from the Arabs. From the twelfth century onwards, more technological developments were an exercise shared; for example, the windmill, the mariner's compass, the trebuchet, guns and gunpowder, the mechanical clock. The history of the development of these is not always certain, but there was at least a profitable interchange of experience, and so each side was at once creditor and debtor to the other, as well as the debtor to discoveries made outside the area of either. Only later did Europe draw ahead. This shared technology of the later Middle Ages had great vitality. Gunpowder and clockwork are still with us, as is the compass, not only in the latest ships, but also playing the same part in the economy as it did from the thirteenth century. For example, Egyptian vessels of traditional design, though powered by motor as well as sail, fulfil in the Red Sea the same function as lorries fill overland; but their indispensable and most valued aid is the compass, in an identical rôle for seven centuries.

Another way in which, in the later Middle Ages, Europe was

linked by experience to the rest of the world was in the reception of
story themes apparently from oriental sources. This may be de-
ceptive. We can only say that the written evidence is that the West
shared with old or distant cultures many of its amusements. The
earliest example of the 'boxed' story (the story within a story, as in
the Arabian Nights) may be Pedro de Alfonso's *Disciplina Clericalis*, already mentioned, but, though this work was popular
enough, the genre did not then catch on. Linked works of Indian
origin such as *Kalila wa Dimna* and *The Seven Sages* began to
appear in the thirteenth century, and, a little later, Don Juan
Manuel's *el Conde Lucanor*. European boxed stories include the
Confessio Amantis of Gower, the *Novelle* of Giovanni Sercambi,
Boccaccio (not only *Decameron* but *Ameto*) and, above all, Chaucer's
Canterbury Tales, as well as the *Tale of Beryn* associated for a time
with Chaucer. All these date from the later fourteenth century,
and represent at least what we have called 'Mediterranean culture';
in some cases there are Arabic and even ultimately Indian sources.
Scholars have traced a large number of miscellaneous Arabic or
oriental analogues in the *Canterbury Tales*, especially in the
Knight's Tale, the Franklyn's, the Merchant's, the Man of Law's,
the Pardoner's, the Manciple's and others. These tend to be
wonderful, or else comic and ribald, stories, or else of the moral
fable type. There is often no evidence of Chaucer's source, or of
the source of his immediate source. That we can trace no necessary
immediate Arabic source is not very important. It is more important that we should recognize in this field also the same 'inter-
nationalism' that we have seen in the scientific field. The sudden
appearance of a fictional literature is evidence of Europe's natural
links with the other cultures that derive from the ancient sources
of the Near East. Later, for example, in William Painter's *Palace
of Pleasure* in the sixteenth century, the oriental image tends increasingly to be dominated by the Turk rather than the Arab. The
Heptaméron of Marguerite de Navarre is more on the mediaeval
pattern. After the publication of Galland's version of the *Thousand
and One Nights* at the end of the seventeenth century, the vogue
switched, despite the large Arab element, to Persian stories. The
process was a gradual one. At the end of it we have so great a
fashion for oriental tales that they were manufactured in the
West; and we can trace this back through genuine translations,
to historical or fabulous tales about orientals, and so to the mere
analogues. While the fashion became more explicit with the

passage of time, that very fact marked the increasing divergence of the traditions; the charm of the quaint became more and more compelling and more alien. The past overlaps the future, and the English Charlemagne romances, which revive the world of the *chansons de geste*, are later in date than Chaucer. We must look between the two extremes of Roland and of Harun ar-Rashid or Sindbad the Sailor. It is spontaneous and unidentifiable correspondence of the mediaeval analogues which marks the real identity of matter and purpose in East and West, and so, as we should expect, the subsisting cultural unity of this kind of literature among Arabs and Europeans in the late mediaeval period.

It is curious that the passage of the centuries seems to have witnessed a steady increase in serious Arabic studies without a corresponding increase in knowledge of Arabic literature (whether history or poetry), or Islamic law or religion. It has been argued that there was a school of Arabic at Cluny or elsewhere as early as the eleventh century. This is doubtful. In the thirteenth century, both Dominicans and Franciscans supported their missions by Arabic studies, and Arabic was a regular subject of study in some Universities. It died away, except in Italy, where, in the period of early Renaissance humanism, Arabic studies still flourished. They left little literature, and may be assigned rather to the world of commerce than to that of research. It was not until the seventeenth century, under the impetus of renewed Hebrew studies, that translations from Arabic began to increase substantially in Europe. There is no apparent correlation between the mediaeval study of Arabic and the impact of Arabic works on Europe. Most of the great translators in Toledo and elsewhere in Spain appear to have worked, with a partial knowledge of Arabic, in conjunction with a native Arabic speaker, whether Arab, Mozarab, or Jewish. The later Middle Ages may even have seen simultaneously a decrease in the influence of the Arab World together with an actual increase in the numbers of Europeans who spoke or understood Arabic.

If the fourteenth and fifteenth centuries in Europe show a fading of consciousness of specifically Arab culture, there is little or no suggestion of any weakening of the common culture which I have sought to recognize at different times and in different places. In some ways it seems stronger; at least links which may always have been present now appeared openly in writing. The end of the Middle Ages and the humanist influences of the Renaissance seem barely, if at all, to have affected the strength of those Arab sources which had been absorbed into the European tradition during the preceding centuries. The two halves of a common society had barely yet diverged, although they would soon do so rapidly.

2. Geographical areas

In the central Mediterranean the fourteenth century was marked by raiding which on the Arab side was persistent, but hardly on a considerable scale. The distinction between piracy and what would later be called privateering was a fine one, and also between either and what still later would be called a commando raid. Any distinction between Arab and European pirates was subjective. There were two outstanding raids on the Christian side which are worth recalling. One is remembered in the *Canterbury Tales*, of the Knight:

> At Alisaundre he was whan it was wonne

and the capture, loot and evacuation of Alexandria in 1365 was indeed one of the most profitable as well as destructive sacks of history. Alexandria had long existed in uninterrupted peace and prosperity, though not as wealthy or as powerful as in its greatest days. The sack produced immense booty, so much that considerable quantities were jettisoned at sea.

> *Comment Alexandre fu prise,*
> *Et la menue gent occise . . .:*

vast numbers of the population were enslaved, and still greater numbers massacred, Muslim Arabs, Copts and Jews alike. Peace was achieved by the Venetians, who did not consider that raiding was good commercial policy and who were able to manœuvre Peter of Lusignan into giving up his further ambitions. Thirty years later, Nicolas of Martoni (a notary) found that European ships arriving in Alexandria were only allowed into the north harbour; he reckoned that the visible destruction still remaining amounted to one eighth of the city. In due course, in 1424 to 1426, the Egyptians had their revenge on the Lusignan dynasty, in Cyprus. A more serious expedition was that of Louis of Bourbon in 1390 against al-Mahdiya, an old victim of European attack. Froissart convincingly imagines a council of war among the defenders, which illustrates a degree of sympathy derived from a purely professional link. This abortive siege, supported by Genoa for the sake of ransom and of more favourable trading terms, inflicted damage, but was inconclusive in its results. It failed as a crusade, and the Arabs could truly claim that the Europeans had been repelled; yet the French found some colour for pretending that the money exacted by them implied the reduction of the city to a permanent tributary state. The only gainers were the Genoese. In the fifteenth century the state of trade and piracy continued, in a further degeneration.

It is evident that there continued to be a considerable movement of population. Apart from the enslavement that resulted from raiding on either side, there were voluntary changes of religion, which may well have been sincere, but which might lead to social advancement, very much as later in the seventeenth century on the Barbary Coast. In 1367, in the negotiations for peace after the capture of Alexandria, it is noted that the Sultan used one European minister:

> *Et si avoit genevois . . .*
> *Amiraus & grans druguement*
> *Estoit dou soudan.*

The Christian ambassadors to the Mameluke court travelled freely and were well received:

> *Eins avoient vin et viande,*
> *Et tout ce qu'apetis demande . . .*

although the attack was not forgotten or forgiven until new events put it out of mind. On the other hand, there were always experienced and unscrupulous mercenary soldiers ready to take expeditions in Africa or Asia; it is of these that Chaucer's knight is the type.

> . . . he loved chivalrie,
> Trouthe and honour, freedom and curteisie.

If this was not satirical, the ideal was a thin one.

In the West, the thirteenth century saw the completion of the Spanish Reconquest, though not yet, of course, the extinction of the Arab and Moorish population. Ferdinand III of Castile conquered Andalusia in the second quarter of the century, capturing Cordova in 1236 and Seville in 1248. An early policy of expulsion gave place to a renewal of the tradition of practical toleration then still alive, despite the instinct to exterminate Arab culture and the Muslim religion. The creation of the tributary state of Granada notoriously caused high productivity, to pay the tribute; this was another form of plunder. James I of Aragon, the Conqueror, occupied the Balearics in 1235 and Valencia in 1238, establishing a treatment of the conquered Arabs which was markedly better than that obtaining in Andalusia. Granada was naturally disaffected; its king, inviting his natural allies in Morocco to invade the peninsula, was 'the worst Arab', *pessimus Saracenus*, in the eyes of Europe. The last serious Moorish attempt to recover Spain in the Arab interest failed in 1340.

The autobiography of Ramon Lull, for all his eccentricity, gives us a lucid picture of the relation of Christians to their Arab subordinates in Spain, and to their neighbours in Africa, in the second half of the thirteenth century. Lull's obsession intellectually was his ability to 'prove' the Trinity by 'necessary reasons', or irrefutable arguments. Many of his published works, in both Latin and Catalan, are wholly or largely devoted to this exercise, and so are a number of still unpublished manuscripts. Behind this repetition there does not seem to lie hidden personal doubt of the efficacy of his reasoning, so much as an overflowing energy and determination to carry conviction to the multitude. Examples of his argument appear in his own *Life*; between all the different presentations of his main themes there appears very little difference to those of us who have not specialized in his thought. His other obsession was emotional, to convince the Moors of the truth of the Christian faith, and, in particular, to convince them by his Trinitarian reasoning; alternatively, to achieve martyrdom. He made one attempt to interest the King of Cyprus in an Eastern Campaign which would convert the Egyptians and Syrians and repress the anti-Nicene churches of the East, but his important contact with the Arab World was in North Africa. He may have been influenced by Saint Francis's abortive attempt to convert the Egyptian Sultan al-Kamil (later the 'friend' of Frederick II) in 1219.

Three episodes are interesting. He realized the importance of encouraging Arabic studies for the sake of any kind of communication with Arabs, and in his early thirties he "bought a Moor, that he might learn Arabic from him." They lived and studied together for nine years, and then the Moor, in Lull's absence, "blasphemed the most holy Name of Jesus." Lull ("moved by inward zeal") struck the Moor on the head and face and other parts. The Moor was "very haughty", because he had been "almost in the position of a master to his lord in teaching him the Arabic language," and attempted to kill Lull with a knife. If we interpret the facts as stated by Lull, we must say that he fell into an ungovernable rage on hearsay evidence, and treated a slave, legally without effective protection from him, with great cruelty. The 'blasphemy' itself may mean no more than an expression of Islamic piety towards Jesus as Prophet. A crowd collected and wanted to kill the Moor, but Lull had him put in a prison, and then began to reflect on the situation. His reflections do not make nice reading. He thought on the one hand that he had received the great benefit of a knowledge of Arabic from the Moor; on the other, he was afraid of being attacked again. He went to the monastery of Our Lady of La Real to pray for a solution and was astonished to find he received none; he returned home gloomily, and, when he passed the prison where he had left his victim, learned that his teacher had hanged himself with the cord that tied him. He gave thanks to the Lord for delivering him from his perplexity.

The obtuseness which made it impossible for Lull to believe that the complex arguments he had devised might fail to convince is consistent with his egocentric personality. Sometimes he seems almost to mimic or caricature Franciscan simplicity, but he also appears to have a genuine naïvety with which he freely confesses faults that he can mentally disown in consequence. When he set sail for Tunis in 1291 he was suffering from a psychosomatic disorder which disappeared when his ship sailed and he was committed to the danger which he had always boasted was the objective of his life, but which, like Tertullian or Alvaro of Cordova, he had preached without incurring. In Tunis he announced that he had studied Christianity and had now come to study Islam, and, if he found it superior, would become Muslim. He says that in consequence all the learned men of the city came to advance their strongest reasons against him, and were astonished and confounded when he refuted them. He claims that he escaped death only because the Tunisian Council thought that to execute him would make difficulties for Arabs trying to convert Europeans to Islam. He was roughly treated, but put on a Genoese ship and deported. A European who resembled him saved himself from the irritated crowd by shouting that he was not Ramon Lull; Lull estimated that this was a divine mystery. He was again expelled from North Africa in 1308, this time from Bijaya, where he had begun more aggressively than ever, by shouting publicly that the Christian religion was holy and true and the Muslim false and wrong. He was again saved by the Cadi's insistence on due process of law. The Cadi tried to help him, but was subjected to tirades of his philosophy; the public wanted him to be executed, but the majority of learned men thought he should be treated as mad. Catalan and Genoese merchants made interest that he should not be mishandled, and he was finally deported to Pisa. It was on his third attempt in North Africa that he finally resolved his tensions in a violent death. Despite his obvious eccentricity, Lull reflects much that is typical of the European attitude. He was not unimaginative in his understanding of the attitude of the Arabs to him personally, but he was quite devoid of any understanding of a different religious approach from his own. It would not be fair to say that he did not preach the Gospel, and yet by his own account it was his own compelling proofs of the Trinity that he taught, not the risen Christ. His Trinitarian rationalism was a familiar mediaeval European attitude taken to an extreme degree. He must surely be judged to have been, on his own admission, unsympathetic to the defenceless Muslim Arabs of Spain itself. The self-absorption of Europe was at once a source of strength which enabled it to shut out everything extraneous to its immediate needs, and at the same time a grave moral imperfection.

Attitudes in the west and north of Europe are further illustrated by two processes of inquisitorial law. I noted earlier that allegations of crypto-Islam took no prominent part in the case against the Templars. The accusations contrived against them show a very poor order of imagination. There was some talk of the *mahomerie* and of an idol called Bafumet. One deposition spoke of an unnamed former Grand Master who had been taken prisoner by an unnamed former sultan, and released on condition of introducing the various immoral and blasphemous practices of which the order stood accused. This evidence amounts to very little. More interesting is the case against the lepers, mostly from Pamiers, who used to meet at the leprosarium outside Toulouse. Confessions that they had poisoned springs and wells in order to infect or kill the public were extracted from them. Their motive was supposed to come from the humiliation and contempt to which they were subjected by the European public. They were induced to accuse themselves several times of having plotted with the

King of Granada and the Sultan of Egypt; having sought a good and faithful lord, they had found these two. There is a pathetic substratum of authentic fantasy beneath this absurd story. The lepers said, too, that their new masters had got them to trample on the cross; this was the routine atrocity so persistently alleged against the Arabs. No doubt, it happened sometimes in the heated atmosphere of the sack of a city, but it is certainly a stereotype. The rest of the 'plot' associated Arabs with an imagined attack on Europe, in a kind of paranoia which may be seen as a common European attitude. It is not the only attitude; these two cases, which both belong to the early fourteenth century, have contrary implications.

In Spain in the fourteenth and fifteenth centuries, social pressures steadily built up public opinion among the Christian European population against both Arabs and Jews. The culmination of mediaeval European relations with the Arabs, however, came after the Middle Ages, by the usual computation, were over; 1492 is often used to mark the beginning of the modern age, because of Columbus's first voyage to America; it was also the date of the conquest of Granada, and of the promise of freedom of worship included in the terms of surrender offered by the Catholic monarchs. (1492 was also the date of the expulsion of the Jews.) Coercion began in 1499 and soon Muslims were being offered a choice between conversion and expulsion, or, very often, were simply forced to be baptized. In 1502 Hobson's choice was extended to the Mudejares of Castile, the Arabs who had survived as practising Muslims since the Reconquest. In Aragon (including Catalonia and Valencia) the brotherhoods in rebellion in 1525 forcibly baptized large numbers of Moors. All the unhappy victims of compulsory Christianization, in Granada, Castile or Aragon, were called Moriscos, and, once baptized, were subject to the Inquisition. These 'converts', at first totally uninstructed, and later only partly instructed in the Christian religion, remained for long devoted to their own faith, and were forced to dissemble it, while remaining in touch with their co-religionists on the southern shores of the Mediterranean. Suspicion of crypto-Islam was aroused in the Inquisition by many curious circumstances. Some related to religion, like washing, particularly at work, refusing to eat pork or animals that had not been killed in the right way, or to drink wine; and others were purely customary, such as using henna, throwing sweets and cakes at a wedding, wrapping a corpse in clean linen. The Moriscos were subjected to different indignities and misfortunes in different areas, but they were universally exploited by the nobles and hated by the poor Christians. In Granada they were driven to rebellion in 1568. The Catholic clergy could force or seduce their women with impunity, because there was no effective redress. They were moved back from the sea coast, but retained contact with their fellow Muslims. The final expulsion, which began in 1609, completed the process which had lasted more than a century, and which in a sense only repeated on a larger scale the experience of Sicily. *"Il est impossible de représenter la pitié que faisoit ce pauvre peuple,"* wrote Cardinal Richelieu. Yet the final expulsion was a tribute to the pertinacity with which this persecuted people had retained their faith and their separate identity, until in fear and hatred Europe ejected them. It was even alleged in the late eighteenth century that Islam still survived in the mountains. This story which ends so late was essentially part of the earlier mediaeval process, but it was the triumph of the worst part of it. Meanwhile on the other side of the water Spaniards were themselves being assimilated. Christians were freely employed in Morocco, retaining the right to exercise their religion. Their dependence on their employer was said to ensure their loyalty. Many thousands became Muslims, some freely and some in servitude. Arab refugees from Spain and new converts alike made good military careers. The best-known example of similar traffic in the reverse direction is the Moor of Venice. Raiding continued on both sides; the most dramatic example was the invasion of Morocco by the Portuguese, and their crushing defeat in 1578.

We turn to the Eastern scene, where new situations early foreshadowed a more distant future. I earlier referred to the arrival of two peoples: the Mongols, in the thirteenth century, made a revolution in the European imagination; and the Ottoman Turks, in the fourteenth, proved a more dangerous neighbour in the long run.

The appearance of the Mongols made so great an impression because they constituted not only a danger, but, if converted to Christianity, a hope, and an alternative to Islam. Urban II had seen the Seljuk Turks as a similar menace, but they were already Muslim. The Mongols from the first appeared as a threat to both Europeans and Arabs, as an account from Palestine illustrates. The remoter corners of Europe were more vaguely apprehensive.

The annals of Melrose regret the conflict between Emperor and Pope in 1238, and then add, "Now was the first time in our country when it was heard that the unmentionable army of the Tartars had laid waste many lands; and that this was true, will appear in what follows." At about the same time the monks of Tewkesbury said that "there came a people called Tartars, sons of Ismail from out of caves, thirty thousand thousand of them, and more," who laid waste all the provinces, but were defeated by the Duke of Bavaria (the latter was not true). 'Sons of Ismail' should mean 'Arabs', and may be some reflection of the nomadic character of Tartars. Twenty years later in Cardiganshire some possible implications of this new invasion were better understood; the kingdoms of the East were destroyed, all the 'Saracens' killed, and the Tartars at the frontiers of the Roman Empire, the Christians seized by fear. At the same date in Italy the situation was more fully understood, the great Mameluke victory was known and its importance appreciated. One chronicler explains lucidly the invasion of 'Arabia' and Syria, the fear of the Sultan of Konya and the King of Armenia who paid tribute; "only the Sultan of Egypt splendidly prepared himself to resist." He briefly describes the victory of Qutuz at Ayn Jalut, in the year in which he is writing; but to Baybars this chronicle is very hostile.

An early account of the Mongols was copied by Matthew Paris in 1243 from a letter by a French traveller, quoting an Englishman employed as a Mongol representative in eastern Europe. Western ambassadors found Europeans living in Qaraqorum in the heart of the Mongol Empire. If the general public had shown no more than common sense in its apprehension of the Tartar danger, the papal and French courts had been over-hopeful that their missions would convert the Great Khans, or at least achieve some diplomatic success against the Ayyubid and, later, Mameluke state. John of Plano Carpino, a first-generation Franciscan, was sent to the Tartars and to all eastern nations as apostolic legate in 1245. On his return two years later a party of Dominicans was sent, under Ascelin or Anselm, and Simon of Tournai. The Mongols themselves sent a mission to Louis IX, then beginning his crusade. Another papal mission was sent under Andrew of Longjumeau. Finally, Louis's envoy, William of Rubruck, went in 1253. At the distance at which European diplomacy had to operate in conditions of almost total ignorance, it is hardly surprising that all the diplomatic activity proved otiose, while Mongol rulers succeeded each other and the governors the envoys encountered changed. The abortive European diplomacy is interesting in itself because it represents the attempt to break out of the dual world of the ancients, divided between Europe and the Arabs. Even more interesting is the reflection of this on a wider intellectual plane. John of Plano Carpini made an interesting study of comparative religion and social anthropology, and of hardly less interest are William of Rubruck's account and that of Ricoldo de Monte Croce. Some of the evidence was directly observed, more supplied by oriental Christians, mostly Nestorian. The effort to understand and even to sympathize with cultural difference was quite new in the European experience. Plano Carpini calmly assessed the good and bad in Mongol life. Rubruck constantly tried to explain the homely in alien terms, and vice versa (the rice beer was indistinguishable from "the best wine of Auxerre"). "A horrible and monstrous race," says Ricoldo, but he too recounts the good and the bad non-committally. He even knows there is a Mongol point of view: Christians who are shocked at the burial of living slaves with a dead Great Khan just seem cruel and mean to the Mongols. Such understanding was never extended to the Arabs. Vincent de Beauvais, the great thirteenth-century encyclopaedist, gave Plano Carpini publicity in his *Speculum Historiale*; Rubruck was cited and discussed by Roger Bacon, himself a stimulating commentator on comparative religion, morals and customs. In the fourteenth century the tradition was continued by missionaries like the Dominican, Jordan Catalani of Severac, and the Franciscan Odoric of Pordenone. Europeans now realized that there were large and influential populations who were not followers of any of the religions of Abraham, and that there was a great world beyond the barrier which Europeans and Arabs had erected between them. Europe would always afterwards be aware of an outer world. The journey of Marco Polo marked another step, because it followed a new pattern of merchant adventure, a profitable residence abroad, not a special mission; it lasted from 1271 till 1295. The Polos were glad to carry papal messages and holy oil from the Holy Sepulchre, as requested by Qubilay, but that was business. They went abroad to make their fortunes in foreign service. Marco's book lacks the analytical approach of the curial ambassadors who had made lesser journeys before him; it is simply a book of travels, by a widely ranging but not particularly methodical lay mind. His interest was wholly secular and rarely academic. It was primarily in exportable products; but he had a sharp eye for strange sexual conventions. His overseas life was a portent.

By the early fourteenth century the Il-Khans in Persia had become Muslim, and were allied to their former conquerors, the Mamelukes; the papal dream was over. The Islamic world again formed a deep barrier between Europe and the rest of the world. The advance of the Ottomans would shortly bring a greater menace to Europe than 'Saracens' or Seljuks had ever been. Turks, Persians and Mongols were none of them Arab, and this made a profound change in the European relationship with both Arabs and Muslims. 'Moor', after all, had been a kind of Arab; Berbers are not Arabs, but the culture of al-Andalus, and of Granada after it, remained always Arabic. If, in the western and central Mediterranean, the later Middle Ages saw only the completion of processes already under way, in the Levant there was a reshuffle of the pack, of which the Mongol invasions were only the beginning. It was now that 'Saracen' was replaced by 'Turk'. Yet the new situation was not much more than a reshuffle. For example, the gestures of friendship and alliance with the Ottoman sultan made first by the French monarchy, from the time of Francis I, and then by Elizabeth of England, need not be seen as just the replacement of the concept of Christendom by nationalism, but equally as the repetition on a grander scale of the innumerable Christian–Muslim alliances, usually temporary and often ineffective, which were made by nobles and even kings, in Spain in the eleventh century, or in the Latin states of the East. The pattern of relations with Muslims had taken shape in mediaeval relations with the Arabs, and continued when the Arabs no longer dominated the Levant.

The Ottomans crossed into Europe in 1357 and established their capital at Edirne (Adrianople) in 1366. The total destruction of the joint European army of the Crusade of Nicopolis in 1396, after the usual western European oppression of the local Christians, marked the end of serious military expeditions conceived as crusades. The westward movement of Timur delayed Ottoman advance in Europe for a while, but it was resoundingly resumed with the fall of Constantinople in 1453, and the transfer there of the Ottoman capital. With the extension of Ottoman suzerainty to Syria, Egypt, Tunis and Algiers early in the sixteenth century, the Arabs reached the lowest level of their fortunes. The Europeans, for their part, continued to be threatened by Turkish naval power during the sixteenth century. The successful siege of Rhodes was succeeded by the siege of Malta, which failed; the battle of Lepanto traditionally marks the moment when the Turkish tide began to turn. The vast conquests of the Turks in Europe, and the long series of wars which continued to shift the frontier forwards and backwards until in the eighteenth century the slow final Ottoman recession began, brought large numbers of Europeans into the Turkish service, usually after conversion to Islam. There is an interesting analysis, by George of Hungary, of the temptation to become Muslim, and the apologia and pious works of Murad Bay, born Hungarian, show how sincere conversion might be; but this no longer concerns European relations with the Arabs, except peripherally. The Turkish conquests, and raiding from North Africa, brought into contact with the Arab World many Europeans who followed their fortunes in Ottoman territory. The Arabs, after all, continued to exist where they had always been.

Pilgrims also had occasion specifically to observe Arabs. There are a considerable number of lively individual accounts of well observed travels that date from the fifteenth century, and before the Ottoman conquest. They were not, however, in any sense formative of the European relationship with the Arabs, and this is why I have given my space to earlier material. One passage is worth quoting from the Burgundian, Bertrandon de la Brocquière, in 1432–3, whose story reveals much about the life of the European merchants and adventurers in Syria and Asia Minor.

> "I bade adieu to my mameluke. This good man, whose name was Mohammed, had done me innumerable services. He was very charitable, and never refused alms when asked in the name of God . . . He would never accept of anything except a piece of our fine European cloth . . . I write this to recall to my reader's memory that the person who, from his love of God, did me so many and essential kindnesses, was a man not of our faith."

By this date the pilgrimage with no ulterior purpose, if it had ever existed, was becoming rare. In due course, it was derided by Erasmus, with his costive humour; the pilgrim is recognized by his "slovenly dress" and "lean gastly Carcas", coming from Jerusalem where "They shew'd us certain Monuments of Antiquity, which I look upon to be mostly Counterfeit."

3. An attempt at a final perspective

I began this book with a reminder of the difficulty in defining the Middle Ages. The Middle Ages in Europe (conventionally defined) do in fact roughly coincide with the period of Arab greatness, and this book has quoted and discussed reactions in Europe to the acts and writings of the Arabs over the period from the conversion of the English and the conquest of Spain to the rise of the Ottoman Empire. The difficulty of defining an 'age' or a group of ages is illustrated, however, by the impossibility of carrying on the continuous story to a point where it can be said to end, or even where it undergoes some radical transformation. For example, European criticism of the Arab society which was formed by the revelation of the Quran has followed the same general pattern, from the ninth century right into the twentieth. In part, this is because of a narrow Christian reaction to the actual differences between the two religions, but not entirely. Christians, whether Oriental or European, traditionally treated Islam as antinomian. What will be the attitude to Islam of those Europeans who in our own day attack Christianity in favour of antinomian ('liberal') moral theories or practice? There need be no doubt about the answer. Islam, like Christianity, can only be accused of being an oppressive and inhibiting religion. Here, then, is a change which we can date to the second half of the twentieth century. Yet it will still be open to Europeans, following Voltaire and Gibbon and others, and without adopting the stance of Christians, to apply to the Arabs of the Prophet's day the very criticisms that the Christians had earlier applied. The disgrace of the Christians was to attack Islam for so many reasons which could be, and later were, used to attack their own religion. Judgements of the sincerity of religious men are subjective. So are judgements about whether what is claimed as true is really the product of circumstances or interest, and judgements on the clarity or consistency or beauty of a doctrine or a revealed Book. Because these are subjective, they allow any enemy of any religion to hypothesize as he pleases. In this area we can only say that Europeans have on the whole maintained towards the Arabs a constant reserve which seems to run consistently through the whole mediaeval period up to the present day.

In other respects also there seems (more happily) to be no clean break, even today, with what has come from the past. The scientific attitude which comes to us from ancient Egypt and ancient Babylonia through the Hellenistic and Roman world, and to which the Arabs contributed so much before transmitting it to Europe, has been developed; and its achievement has been overlaid, but not discarded. Sailors still navigate today by Ptolemaic astronomy, and, indeed, we ordinarily live by it. It is a good working hypothesis that the sun rises and sets, although we know that the universe is not tellocentric. Mediaeval medicine, even after it had benefited by translations from the Arabic writers, may seem discontinuous with medicine today, although historians of medicine are well aware that that is not so. Much that we take for granted survives from the past, and, in the Middle Ages, was common ground to Arabs and to Europeans. The old rules of health remain very largely valid today, and if some of them seem obvious, the obvious is only yesterday's discovery, and it does not lose its validity. We can go further, and say that medicine can always learn again that disease is only a deviation from health. The attitudes inculcated by the Hippocratic tradition, if they were lost, would not be easily replaced.

This book has not been about the debt of Europe to the Arabs, and I will only touch on the subject briefly. What kind of debt is it? It is not, for example, a debt in engineering or in technology (at least in the narrow sense of the word); the most effective technology, Europe learned, as did the Arabs also, from the Far East, and developed it in its own way. It is much more a debt in ways of thought. In the earlier Middle Ages the Latin library was so restricted that Europe was incapable even of widening its understanding of its own Scriptures; it was a self-negating culture incapable of substantial development. When the Arabs gave the Europeans back their lost traditions, they also passed pagan Hellenistic thought on in a form already absorbed and adapted to make it intelligible and acceptable to a revealed Abrahamic religion. They set the example of critical appreciation and analysis. This function was also served by the Byzantines and by direct Greek sources. The Latin West was never explicitly grateful to either Arabs or Greeks. It took what it wanted and felt that it owed its capacity to develop to no single outside influence. That does not make the debt less great in fact.

Most of this book has been about a series of reactions and misunderstandings that resulted from an almost continuous condition of endemic warfare; and it is this that best explains the barrier which has always existed in spite of intellectual sympathy and shared interest. Christian intolerance, however, seems to go back to the second and third centuries, when it was a reaction to persecution, which generated hatred both of pagans and of heretics. It was to this age that the martyrs of Cordova looked back. There seems to have been an unbroken tradition of aggression in the minds of Christians, deriving precisely from their pre-existing conviction that others always persecuted them. Without comparing the Latin church of the West with the Orthodox church of Byzantium, and the various churches of the Arabic-speaking world, we can say that this tradition was so powerful in Europe that the same behaviour, considered objectively, was 'persecution' when it was perpetrated against, and not when it was perpetrated by, the Christians. Muslims, on the other hand, are required by the Quran to tolerate the peoples of the Book. Despite the aberrations of individuals or mobs, Christians and Jews survived in Arab and other Muslim countries, whereas the half-hearted attempt of canon law to define conditions which would permit Muslims to survive in Europe did not stand the strain of time. The mediaeval European urge towards homogeneity was bound up with doctrinal conformity, and could best be satisfied within a strict demarcation of frontiers. It was comforting to imagine that the Arab World was quite different, although in fact it was very similar. The sense of difference was more important than the sense of active hostility. It is less that Arabs were sometimes supposed to support heresies from without, as in the allegations against the fourteenth-century French lepers or the twelfth-century Pastoureaux; it is more that Islam was assessed as the 'sum of heresies', and so, we may say, quintessentially wrong; this helped to make Europe feel cosy, and well protected from the cold draught of outside error. In Spain the 'closed society' survived longer than anywhere else; there it was as if the former multi-cultural society had created, by reaction, a national craving for uniformity of which the Inquisition was an expression and not the cause.

Not only was the mediaeval European attitude to the Arabs rooted in the early days of persecution. It also anticipated the romantic age and the age of imperialism. The later delight in oriental glamour was adumbrated in the Middle Ages in spite of hostility to Islam, as we see in the use of poetry describing the riches of the East, and the use of quaint language for Arabs who come into historical narrative; when the Arabs and other orientals were no longer a source of fear, no inhibition operated, and from the late 1600s till the present day, but most strongly in the eighteenth century, Western orientalism has run riot, and has its own place in the story of the romantic movement. Imperialism is a more important forward reach from the Middle Ages. In one sense we can say that it first occurred to the European mind when the Mongols gave a glimpse of an outer world which might be deployed against the Muslim Arabs. From this thought to the conquest of the outer world was only one step further. In another sense we can say that the Crusades were imperialistic, but Europeans, in their own opinion, were only taking back what was theirs by right. In a third sense, however, the awareness of the Arabs that was formed in the Middle Ages contributed to the imperial movement of the nineteenth century. It provided much of the sense of being justified. In the Middle Ages, Europeans had insisted on absorb-ing the Arabs who found themselves under European rule; Arabic culture and Muslim religion were successfully extirpated. If this was right, did it not imply that Christian rule was beneficial?

Above all, imperialism has been the movement to control others for their own good, by which we mean, to force them to conform to our own patterns of behaviour, or, at least, to our ideal pattern. This seems to have been normal, whether conscious or not, and whether politically intended or not. Here it must be relevant that Europe's idea of the 'foreigner' was based for many formative centuries exclusively on the Arab World. These were centuries of mutual devastation, when the successful side always appeared inhumanly cruel to the defeated, and, to the victors, the defeated seemed incapable of suffering. That one word, *devastavit*, so often repeated in so many places and at so many times throughout the Middle Ages, either as a plaint by Europeans, or as a boast, is the key to the whole relationship. This is not, of course, to say that there was worse devastation in those days than in our own; but it does mean that during the Middle Ages devastation penetrated deeply into the European consciousness. It created, and depended on, an absolute conviction of being right. We recognize the be-haviour of the Reconquest or the Crusade again in the imperial age, a hardness and lack of sympathy or imagination which is not the invariable, but is the general, pattern. The conquered were still treated so often as though they were less than human.

Throughout the nineteenth century and the first decade of the twentieth, practical-minded imperial officials restrained the missionaries, often with difficulty, but there was always the conviction that European rule was right, and that, if it could not make Christians in a foreseeable future, yet Christian supervision was next best. If the European supervisors of empire were not convinced or keen Christians, as might and did happen, even in the nineteenth century, then their underlying conviction was that they were justified because they were European. The imperial Christians themselves thought their religion essentially European. The equation of a nation with a religion is usually considered oriental; but most Europeans have been conscious that Christianity is the religion of Europe, even when they repudiate it. It is not peculiar to Europeans to believe that theirs is the best way of life, but the Europeans and their cultural stock in America or elsewhere seem to be peculiar in their aggressive determination to do good to others whether they wish it or not. The missionary urge even remains when belief changes into disbelief. This seems to be a continuous development from the mediaeval attitude to Arabs; Europeans act from the conviction that they are right, and an imaginary moral superiority confers a real superiority in morale. They seem also, at least until very recently indeed, to have acted on the belief that it is dangerous to be passive; this was the lesson in morale learned so painfully in the period leading up to the eleventh century. Since that date, Europeans have been aggressive, and, unexpectedly, this precedes their technological superiority by many centuries.

We have seen how xenophobia and hysteria were compounded at the inception of the Crusades, and it is a mistake to view them as an isolable phenomenon. They were just one European activity. Fighting, robbing, killing, trading, making profits, taking rents or tributes, all these were closely linked to philosophical and theological analysis, to the composition of history and propaganda, and even to love of one's neighbour. The Crusades renewed the idea that we need not do as we would be done by. They were also an expression of a much older history of suspicion, as Guibert of Nogent rightly pointed out, of Hellas against Xerxes, of Rome against Parthia, Byzantium against Persia. It is largely a surprise for Europeans (or, for that matter, Arabs), even today, to discover how closely Arabs and Europeans are alike. Sometimes still they fail to recognize it. The expectation of difference goes back to the cultural intolerance of 'barbarians' which is one of the less useful legacies of Greece. What provokes symptoms of xenophobia on one occasion, and those of hospitality on another? Sometimes the answer is clear in simple cultural terms, but by no means always. What makes the difference is incalculable in advance and often unrecognized in retrospect. In the Crusades, xenophobia was indulged by the invincible knowledge of being justified; the hysteria of religious enthusiasm was never far away. The sane people were those concerned with commercial profit or professional fighting, and the good people were apt to do most harm. The experience of suppressing minorities also pandered to xenophobia. There is a natural hatred for the unlucky, and equally for those whom we have harmed. We do not love the dispossessed, least of all if the profit is ours. All the history that we have reviewed in this book tended to create suspicion between Arabs and Europeans. The encouraging thing about this is that, throughout our mediaeval period, and up to and including the present day, good personal relations between Arabs and Europeans as individuals have been maintained in spite of all.

We have seen several examples of Arab and European parallel development. The scholastic age in each one was such, independently of the influence of Arab philosophers; the succeeding age of mysticism was another; the shared ideas of courtly behaviour were yet another, the resemblance between law of *jihad* and canon law was a fourth; lyric and narrative parallels are perhaps a case of direct influence only. There is nothing surprising in the similarity of ideas, even in cases where direct influence is absent, not only because the two societies started from the same point at their first separation, but also because social developments, though far from always being parallel, often created similar conditions. The only great barrier was linguistic. When the two societies did diverge, it was a result of the political fate of the Arabs. The Turks swept across the land routes, and the Europeans circumnavigated the Arab World, to create new empires in Muslim and non-Muslim countries, on a scale beyond the experience of the mediaeval world. The Arabs subsided into a state which was far from uncultivated or without intellectual achievement, but one in which society was stable, and did not develop as Europe developed under the stimulus of imperial trade, technological invention and the resulting possibilities of investment, with its cycle of more trade, more inventions, and more investment. European industrialization and the imperialist relationships that resulted mark the final divergence. The adaptation of Arab society to the over-whelming wealth and technique of Europe from the nineteenth century onwards is another story altogether; the Arabs did not again reach a position from which they could defy Europeans till the middle of the twentieth century.

We can amuse ourselves by imagining Europeans of the Middle Ages as living their lives in a contemporary Arab setting. Nearly all the kings and knights, the merchants, the travellers, the scientists, philosophers and lawyers are quite credible imagined as Arabs. Only such prelates as Innocent III or Gregory IX are hard to translate mentally. For some time after the Middle Ages it remains easy enough to plot Arab or Turkish careers for European person-alities, and really only the architects of a religious establishment will resist the imagination, a Calvin, a Pius V, or a Cromwell; later, indeed, we can conceive a contemporary Arab Newton, but not a Voltaire; and the heroes of the industrial age, a Shaftesbury or a Garibaldi, we can imagine in the Arab World only in the twentieth century. Of the Middle Ages we must say that it was at one and the same time a period of parallel development, a period of preponderance of Arabic culture, and a period of mutual devasta-tion, with psychological results reaching forward into the im-perialist age and into our own times.

There exists no detailed and exhaustive history of Arab relations with mediaeval Europe. So much has been done to investigate Arab influence in science, philosophy and literature, in architecture, the plastic arts and military and other techniques, to examine com-mercial, political and military relations, and so much has been done to summarize and evaluate investigations in progress, and yet so much remains to do. The last word can never be spoken. Can we sum up even the impact of the Arabs on the European consciousness by adding together evidence from such a variety of sources, Eulogio or John of Gorze, or mio Cid el Campeador, Gerard of Cremona, William of Tyre or William of Tripoli, Frederick II, Roger Bacon or Guido Bonatti, Ricoldo of Monte Croce or Arnald of Villanova? I have only tried to put forward, in their own words as far as I could, some of the contemporary feelings of Europeans about the Arabs, and some of the feelings that they shared with Arabs. We cannot stress too much that Arabs and Europeans share a common inheritance, but cousinship does not preclude dislike or reluctance to understand. Arabs and Euro-peans are too alike in their differences, and too different in their resemblance, for their relationship to be an easy one, but it has developed continuously since their first encounter, and it is still capable of conferring mutual benefits if both sides so wish.

Abbreviations

AOL	*Archives de l'Orient Latin*
ARF	*Annales Regni Francorum*
Bongars	Bongars, *Gesta Dei per Francos*
Chr	Chronicon, Chronica
Chr. Sal.	*Chronicon Salernitanum*
CUP	*Chartularium Universitatis Parisiensis*
Ep	Epistola, Epistolae
ES	Henrique Florez, *España Sagrada*
Gol	Golubovich, *Biblioteca Bio-bibliografica*
Héfélé	Héfélé and Leclercq, *Histoire des Conciles*
Hist	Historia, Historiae, Historiarum
HB	Huillard-Bréholles, *Historia Diplomatica*
Itin	Itinerarium, Itinerarius
MGH Ss.	*Monumenta Germaniae Historica*, scriptores
MOFPH	*Monumenta Ordinis Fratrum Praedicatorum Historica*
MP. CM	Matthew Paris, *Chronica Majora*, RS 57
MPG	Migne, *Patrologia Graeca*
MPL	Migne, *Patrologia Latina*
Muratori	Muratori, *Rerum Italicarum Scriptores*
RHC	*Recueil des Historiens des Croisades* (except where other-wise stated, *historiens occidentaux*)
Rod. Tolet.	Rodericus Toletanus
ROL	*Revue de l'Orient Latin*
RS	Rolls Series
SOL	Société de l'Orient Latin
s.a.	*sub anno*

Gesta where there is no contrary indication, refers to *Gesta Francorum*.

Notes

Small capitals indicate topics.

Chapter 1

p. 1　　　　C. S. Lewis, *Selected Literary Essays*, Cambridge, 1969, p. 11

p. 7　　　　Gibbon, *Decline and Fall*, LII

pp. 8–9　　Lynn White, *Mediaeval Technology and Social Change*, Oxford, 1962

p. 11　　　ST OSWALD: Bede, *Ecclesiastical History*, III, 11; ETHELDREDA: *ibid.*, IV, 19; DRYCHTELM: *ibid.*, V, 12

p. 12　　　MUSLIM MARTYRDOM: *Shorter Encyclopedia of Islam*, s.v. *shahid*, but the reference there to Maqrizi (*Khitat*, l. 68) does not exactly represent the sense of the text, which describes how the Christians threw relics of martyrs in coffins into the river, to bring about the flood

pp. 13–14　Peter the Venerable, *Contra sectam Saracenorum*, I, 13; see note to pp. 237–8; JEWS: C. & J. Héfélé and H. Leclerc, *Histoire des Conciles*, Paris, 1907–38, III, p. 204, can. 13, 14, 15, and footnotes

pp. 14–15　ST AUGUSTINE: Bede, *op. cit.*, I, 27

pp. 15–16　PILGRIM: *Vita S. Willibaldi* or *Hodoeporicon*, Library of Palestine Pilgrims Text Society, London, 1897, based on T. Tobler, *Descriptiones Terrae Sanctae*, Leipzig, 1874, and T. Wright, *Early Travels in Palestine*, London, 1848, cf. W. Levison, *op. cit.*, *infra* (from whose guidance I have diverged a little in interpretation); DEANA, etc: Text printed by W. Levison, *England and the Continent in the Eighth Century*, Oxford, 1946, app. X

p. 16　　　ST BONIFACE: Tangle, MGH *Ep. Sel.*, Berlin, 1916, vol. I, No. 78, p. 169; Bede, *op. cit.*, IV, 25

pp. 17–18　Isidore Pacensis, MPL 96, col. 1253 ff.

pp. 18–19　CADWALLA: Bede, *op. cit.*, III, 1; Gregory of Tours, *Hist. Franc.*, IX, 24

p. 20　　　ALCUIN: MPL 101, col. 234

Chapter 2

p. 23   This chapter is the product of a close analysis of the following texts:
Eulogio, *Memoriale Sanctorum, Liber Apologeticus Martyrum, Documentum Martyriale, Epistolae* and *De vita et passione SS. Florae et Mariae*, all in Migne, *Patrologia Latina*, 115. Alvarus Cordubiensis, *Indiculus Luminosus* and *Epistolae* in MPL 221, and *Vita vel Passio S. Eulogii* in MPL 115. The column references in Volume 115 fall in the sequence 703–870, and those in Volume 221 in the sequence 500–556. I shall make all references therefore to the columns only

pp. 23–4   Perfectus, 766–7, 518; Gospel, *Matthew* 24:24 (not Vulgate)

pp. 24–5   519, 520, 746, 768

pp. 25–6   736–7–8, 770

p. 26   527, 738

pp. 26–7   836–8
text, *Matthew* 10:33

pp. 28–9   838, 831, 844, 841, 842, 832, 843

p. 30   717; 714–18 *passim*

pp. 30–1   861–2; *Psalms* 82(83):1 and 96(97):7; accusations of idolatry, cf. p. 231, also pp. 95, 132, 235–7

pp. 31–2   754–6; Arnobius, *Adversus Gentes*, MPL 5; 523, 529, 535

pp. 32–3   761, 759, 524, 801–3, 714, 796, 532, 801; VISIGOTHIC: the claim to senatorial and so Roman descent (707) not incompatible with aristocratic status in the Visigothic kingdom

pp. 33–4   803, 527, 761, 770, 529, 765 cf. 768, 850, 791, 802, 811, 866, 726, 712, 735, 748, 795, 751, 525–6, ELVIRA: Héfélé, vol. 1, pt 1, p. 255 (canon 60). Classical language: cf. Richer, *Histoire de France*, ed. R. Latouche, Paris, 1964–7, *passim*

pp. 34–5   (military) 527–8, 530, 536, 559, 738, 750–2, 756, 758, 761, 771–4, 781, 783, 796, 804–5, 822, 839

pp. 35–6   815, 839, 775, 714, 854 ff., 862, 864, 777 ff.

pp. 36–7   771, 815, 793, 792

pp. 37–8   737–8, 784. LULL: compare below, p. 223 and pp. 310–312

p. 39   707, 858; *Romans* 1:18, 21; 2 *Peter* 1:21, 2:2; *Matthew* 24:11

p. 40   859–60

pp. 40–1   861 cf. Alvaro 523

pp. 41–2   551, 523, 543 cf. 546, 539–40, *Daniel* 11:38; 767, 544

pp. 42–3   538, 552, 539, 542; *Ezekiel* 23:20, *Jeremiah* 5:8, *Job*

40:10, 12, 13 (Vulgate numbering; RSV 15, 17, 18). The whole section on Job 451–551, *Job* 40:10–41:25 = RSV 40:15–41:34

pp. 43–4   552, *Psalms* 67:31 (= 68:30), 768, 545, 737

pp. 44–5   708, 745

pp. 45–6   534, 518, 530

pp. 46–7   748–51, 752, 754; *Matthew* 5:44, *Luke* 3:14, 1 *Peter* 2:23, 1 *Cor.* 6:10, 1 *Cor.* 5:6, 1 *Tim.* 1:6, *Jeremiah* 9:5; *Matthew* 8:38 with *Mark* 10:32, cf. *Luke* 9:26

p. 47   761, 762

p. 48   General: "Significance of the Voluntary Martyrs of Ninth-Century Cordoba", J. Waltz, in *Muslim World*, IX, 1970 (not seen by me before writing this chapter). See also Dozy's *Mussulmans d'Espagne*, Leyden, 1861, and Lévi-Provençal, *L'Espagne musulmane*, Paris, 1959–3, and others

Chapter 3

p. 49   Willibald, *loc. cit.* 'Rex' appears to refer to the caliph.

p. 50   ARF, G. H. Pertz, *Scriptores Rerum Germanicarum ad usum Scholarum*, Hannover, 1895, s.a. 810; cf. *Annales Fuldenses*, 1891, *s.a.* 810; ARF, *s.a.* 816 and 817

p. 51   *ibid.*, *s.a.* 801; and Eginhard, ed. L. Halphen, Paris, 1938, 16 (pp. 48–9). Fredegar, *Fourth Book of the Chronicle of*, *with its continuations*, ed. J. M. Wallace-Hadrill, London and Edinburgh, 1960, *s.a.* 737 and 732 (continuator); *Annales Mettenses Priores*, Hanover/Leipzig, 1905, and cf. *Fuldenses*

pp. 51–2   ARF, *loc. cit.*; Liutprand, *Antapodosis* (MGH Scriptores III) 1:4, 11:43, 44

p. 53   *Ibid.*, 11:47–54. GREEK USAGE: e.g. Sozomen 6:38, Socrates 4:36; Latin, Ammianus Marcellinus, XIV:v:1–7, XXII:xv:2 ("Arabs whom we now call Saracens"), XXIII:vi:13 (Loeb); cf. Pliny, vi:32, 'Arraceni'. (An Arabic source, *sharqiyin*, for 'Easterners', has been conjectured.) Fredegar, *loc. cit.*

p. 54   Gregory of Tours, *Hist. Francorum*, preface

pp. 56–7   ERCHEMBERT: Heremberti *Epitome Chronologica*, Muratori 5:18D, 19C, E, 21C; and MGH Ss. 3; *Chronicon Salernitanum* MGH Ss. 3, pp. 503, 529; Iohannis *Chronicon Venetum*, MGH Ss. 7, p. 17; Rodulfi Glabri *Historiarum sui temporis libri* V, 1:5 and 4:7, MPL 142 and MGH Ss. 7; BABYLON IN EGYPT: named, according to Strabo, XVII:1:30, by the Babylonian invaders of Egypt

pp. 57–8   DESERT: Benedicti *Chronicon*, MGH Ss. 3, p. 713; *Chr. Sal.*, *loc. cit.*, p. 538; TENTH CENTURY: Lupi Protospatae

Chronicon, s.a. cit., Muratori 5, MGH Ss. 5; LUNI:
Thietmari *Chronicon*, MGH Ss. 3, VII:31, p. 850;
ROME: *Chr. Venetum, loc. cit.*, p. 18; Benedicti *Chr., loc.
cit.*, pp. 712–13; cf. Glaber, *op. cit.*, 3:7, MPL col. 623,
682 ff.

pp. 58–9 Hincmar, *Annales Bertiniani*, ed. A. Waitz, Hanover,
1883, *s.a.* 846; Liutprand, *op. cit.*, 11:44, 46, 43, IV:4, 6;
Le Couronnement de Louis, ed. E. Langlois, Paris, 1925,
I. 2239; *De Ortu et Obitu Justorum Coenobii Casinensis
Liber* Petri Diaconi, MPL 173, col. 1070; Lynn White,
Latin Monasticism in Norman Sicily, Cambridge, Mass.,
1938, pp. 9–10, with further references

p. 60 Fredegar, *loc. cit.*; *Annales Mettenses Priores s.a.* 799;
ARF *s.a.* 807, 810

pp. 60–1 Bernard the Wise, Palestine Pilgrims Text Society, vol.
III, London, 1897, ch. 3–7 from Tobler, *op. cit.*, and T.
Wright, *Early Travels, loc. cit.*; Liutprand, *op. cit.*, 11:26

p. 61 VERCELLI: *Chronicon Novaliciense*, V.9, MGH Ss. VII,
pp. 112–13

pp. 62–4 Raoul Glaber, *Historiae*, I, *s a.* 973, MGH Ss. VII, pp.
54–5; cf. ex Syri *Vita S. Maioli*, MGH Ss. IV, *s.a.* 973,
pp. 652–3

pp. 64–5 RECAMUND: *Antapodosis*, I:1–2; V.2
pp. 64–9 *Vita Iohannis Gorziensis*, 115 *et seq.* (950–6); MGH Ss.
IV., p. 369 *et seq.*; reluctantly, I cannot accept the interpretation of the Latin text by Abdurrahman Ali El-Hajji,
Andalusian Diplomatic Relations, Beirut, 1970, p. 313 ff.

pp. 70–1 *Chr. Sal.*, para. 113, 114, pp. 530–1 (871)
pp. 71–2 WAIFAR: *ibid.*, para. 110, p. 528
pp. 72–3 SICILY: *ibid.*, para. 60, p. 498; ABDALLA: *ibid.*, para. 112,
pp. 528–30 (872)

p. 73 AIMO: *Chron. Novaliciense*, V:18, pp. 114–15
pp. 73–4 RELATIONSHIP: *Chr. Sal.*, paras. 109, 112, pp. 528–9;
SALERNO: A. Mieli, *La Science Arabe*, para. 52, ed.
Leiden, 1966, p. 219; RICHER: *op. cit.*, II:59, vol. 1, p. 224,
IV:50, vol. 2, p. 224; CARZIMASIA: Antapodosis, VI:6

p. 75 Erchembert, *loc. cit.*, 19E; SALERNO: *Chr. Sal.*, para. 126,
p. 537

p. 76 LEO: Mansi (*Sacrorum Conciliorum Amplissima Collectio*,
1759–98), XVI, col. 888; Liutprand, *op. cit.*, II.26

pp. 76–7 JOHN: in MPL 126, ep. CCCXIX, CCCXXI, col. 928–30
pp. 77–8 *Chr. Sal.*, para. 130, p. 538; *Epistolae Joannis Papae VIII
loc. cit.*, LXXIX, LXII, LVIII, LIX, LX, LXXVIII,
LXXII, LXXI, LXII, LXVIII, LVII, LVIII, LIV,
LXVII, LXXIII, LXIV, CLXXXVI

Chapter 4

p. 81   R. Dozy, *Récherches sur l'histoire et la littérature de l'Espagne pendant le moyen age*, 2nd ed., Leiden, 1860, 3rd ed., Paris/Leyden, 1881; R. Menendez Pidal, *La España del Cid*, Madrid, 1929; Dozy, 2nd ed., p. 18

pp. 81–3   POEMA DEL CID; R. Menendez Pidal, *Cantar de Mio Cid*, Madrid, 1913. References to section numbers. ASMARON: 25; BOOTY: 23, 25, 29, 31, 32, 45, 47, 68, 72, 74, 95, 96, 99, 119, 121—not exhaustive; BLOOD: 24, 95, 119; Jerome, 78; SI CON MOROS: 34; TERROR: 27, 28, 72; MOORS: 113, 148, 26, 46, 126, 83, 132, 118; MOOR NOR CHRISTIAN: 9 (2X), 76, 49, 128, 150; BUEN ORA: *passim*; SANCHO: Dozy, *op. cit.*, 2nd ed., pt 3, p. 220, from Llorente, Prov. Vascong. III, p. 456; IBN BASSAM: Dozy, *op. cit.*, 3rd ed., pp. 338–48, 2nd ed., pp. 357–68

p. 84   CID: *Poema*, 122; *Historia Roderici* printed by R. Menendez Pidal, *op. cit.*, tomo 2, pp. 957, 958, 961, 964–5; PRAYER: 957; *Primera Cronica General de España*, ed. R. Menendez Pidal &c., Madrid, 1955, cap. 921

p. 85   ALFONSO VII: *Cronica Adefonsi Imperatoris*, ed. L. Sanchez Belda, Madrid, 1950, paras 131, 133, 134, 161, 169, 174

pp. 86–7   ES, vol. 37, p. 311; app. VII; *ibid.*, vol. 33, p. 466, app. XI; *ibid.*, vol. 25, p. 223, app. XVII; TOLEDO: Mansi, *op. cit.*, XX. 615, cf. *Cronica General*, cap. 871

p. 87   Osbernus, *De expugnatione Lyxbonensi* (RS 38, with *Itinerarium Regis Ricardi*), pp. clxii–clxiii

p. 88   Salimbene, *Cronica* pp. 28–9, *s.a.* 1212, MGH Ss. XXXII

pp. 88–9   ZAIDA: *Cronica General*, cap. 883, p. 553 ff.

pp. 89–90   LATER CHAPTERS: *ibid.*, cap. 886, and cf. "Fuentes de la Cronica", in edition cited, pp. clxxx–clxxxii; TOLEDO: Rod. Tolet., *De rebus Hispaniae* (A. Schottus, *Hispaniae illustratae scriptores*, Frankfurt, 1603, vol. II), VI.xxv and *Cronica General*, cap. 871, p. 540

p. 90   Dozy, *op. cit.*, 2nd ed., p. 59; *Cronica*, cap. 877–92. Fuentes, p. clxxxii

pp. 91–2   Rod. Tolet., *Historia Arabum* (same edition), cap. XLIV, cf. *Cronica*, cap. 887: *Cronica Adefonsi, ed. cit.*, and ES, vol. 21, pp. 394 and 373, 396–7

pp. 92–3   Rod. Tolet., *De rebus Hispaniae*, X.vii, and *Cronica*, cap. 979

p. 94   Rod. Tolet., *Historia Arabum*, cap. 1–6; *Cronica*, 467–94

pp. 94–5   *Cronica Adefonsi*, paras 175, 176; *Cronica General*, cap. 908

pp. 96–7   *Roland* (ed. J. Bédier), lines 3490–4; lines 3172, 4–5;

lines 3633–47; 3261 and lines preceding, J. Bédier, *Les Légendes Épiques* (3rd ed., Paris, 1929), vol. III. H. Grégoire, "Les Dieux Cahu, Baraton, Tervagant..." in *Annuaire de l'Institut de Philologie et d'Histoire Orientales et Slaves*, VII (New York), and "L'Étymologie de Tervagant" in *Mélanges offerts à Gustave Cohen*, Paris, 1950; the canonists considered 'Saracens' the same as the pagans of antiquity; see pp. 256–9n and compare p. 34

p. 97   *Cronica, loc. cit.*; *Roland*, lines 3661–5

pp. 98–100   Turpinus text VI, XV, XXV, XXXIV in H. M. Smyser, *The Pseudo-Turpin* (Cambridge, Mass., 1937) cf. *Historia Caroli Magni*, ed. C. Meredith Jones, Paris, 1936; *Roland*, 3858–61; 1132–4, 1138–40 cf. 2365, 2383–8; 1015; 3668–74, 3985–7; *Gormont*, ed. A. Bayot, Paris, 1921, 472; *Anseïs von Karthago*, ed. Johann Alton, Tübingen, 1892, 6670; cf. Bédier, *loc. cit.*, p. 143; cf. also the stories of Bohemund and Sancho, p. 201 below, and note, and a number of other *chansons*

pp. 101–3   SPANISH ARABIC CONTROVERSY AND BACKGROUND: consult inter alia R. Dozy, *Histoire des Mussulmans de'Espagne*, Leiden, 1932; A. Jeanroy, *La Poésie Lyrique des Troubadours*, Toulouse and Paris, 1934; E. Lévi-Provençal, *Islam d'Occident*, Paris, 1948; R. Mendendez Pidal, *Poesia arabe y poesia europea*, Madrid, 1941; R. Nelli, *L'Érotique des Troubadours*, Toulouse, 1963; A. R. Nykl, *Hispano-Arabic Poetry*, Baltimore, 1946; J. J. Parry, *Art of Courtly Love by Andreas Capellanus*, New York, 1941; H. Pérès, *La Poésie Andalouse au XIe Siècle*, Paris, 1953; J. P. Roux, *L'Islam en Occident*, Paris, 1959; W. M. Watt and P. Cachia, *History of Islamic Spain*, Edinburgh, 1967

p. 101   KHARJAS: E. Carcia Gomez, "Veinticuatro kharjas" in *Al-Andalus*, Madrid, 1952, and S. M. Stern, *Les chansons mozarabes*, Palermo, 1953; in general on language, W. D. Elcock, *The Romance Languages*, London, 1960. The quotation is Garcia Gomez 23, Stern 39

pp. 103–4   Bertran de Born in J. Audiau, *Nouvelle Anthologie des Troubadours*, Paris, 1928, p. 144; Piere Vidal, "all goes ill", ed. J. Anglade, Paris, 1923, p. 59; MARCABRU: Audiau, *op. cit.*, p. 266, and J.-M.-L. Dejeanne, *Poésies Complètes du Troubadour Marcabru*, Toulouse, 1909, pp. 108–9; cf. *Les Chansons de Guillaume IX*, ed. A. Jeanroy, Paris, 1927

pp. 104–5   IBN HAZM: Nykl, *op. cit.*; Nelli, *op. cit.*, cf. Pérès, *op. cit.*, G. Duby, "Les 'jeunes' dans la société aristocratique",

Annales, Économies Sociétiés, Civilisations, Paris, 1964; ANDREAS CAPELLANUS in Parry, *op. cit.*

pp. 105–6   Wolfram von Eschenbach, *Werke*, ed. A. Leitzmann, Tübingen, 1961, vol. 2, VIII.25–9 (p. 62) and IX.453.11–14 (pp. 91–2). English translation by Jessie L. Weston, London, 1894, 2 vols, 8.319–20, 9.351–3; *Disciplina Clericalis*, MPL 157, col. 671; see C. Haskins, *Studies in the History of Mediaeval Science*, New York, 1927, pp. 115–19, and Mieli, *op. cit.*, 59

pp. 106–7   Roberti de Monte *Cronica*, MGH Ss. 6, *s.a.* 1180 (1179); Roger of Wendover *Chronica*, RS 84, vol. 1, p. 131; Coggeshall, *Chronicon Anglicanum*, RS 66, p. 67; Orderici Vitalis *Historia Ecclesiastica* III.13.1, MPL 188; see also pp. 200–1n (Hoveden)

pp. 107–9   PROPHECIES: Hoveden, RS 51, *s.a.* 1184, p. 297; other prophecies were associated with Damietta, pp. 208–9n; ST ALBANS: Roger of Wendover, *Flores Historiarum*, lectiones variae, p. 167 ff. (RS 84), and Matthew Paris, *loc. cit.*, *s.a.* 1213; HENRY II: Geraldus, *De principis instructione*, pp. 157–8 (RS 21); (for Spain in the 13th century, see chapter 11)

Chapter 5

p. 112   GIBBON: see p. 119n; TALLEYRAND: in *Mémoires du Prince de Talleyrand*, Paris, 1891, I, pp. 77–8, and "Situation de la République" (An VI) in G. Pallain, *Correspondance diplomatique*, Paris, 1891

p. 113   Malmesbury, *De regum gestis*, RS 90, IV.2, and MPL 151, col. 571

pp. 114–15   GESTA FRANCORUM: *Histoire anonyme de la Première Croisade*, ed. L. Bréhier, Paris, 1924, p. 22; GUIBERT: Guiberti de Novigento *Gesta Dei per Francos*, 1.1, MPL 156; RHC, vol. IV

pp. 115–16   Urban, col. 565 *et seq.*, MPL 151, cf. Fulcheri Carnotensis *Historia Hierosolymitana*, H. Hagenmeyer, Heidelberg, 1913, I.92; WILLIAM OF TYRE: *Historia Rerum in Partibus Transmarinis Gestarum*, MPL 201, IX.10, cf.–2. Gesta, *ed. cit.*, p. 217. COLLECT: John of Würzburg, in Tolber, *Descriptiones* (*cit.*), and MPL 155, cap. XIII; and cf. *secreta*. For further references, N. Daniel, *Islam and the West, the Making of an Image*, Edinburgh, 3rd ed., 1966, p. 348

p. 116   Cafari Genuensis *Liberatio Orientis*, RHC, vol. V, cap. XV, and MGH Ss. XVIII, p. 13

pp. 116–17   *Gesta*, pp. 148–50

pp. 117–18	Fulcher, *op. cit.*, II.60. Embrico of Mainz, see note to pp. 232–3; Guibert, *op. cit.*, I.3, col. 689
p. 118	COROZAN: p. 232 ff. below; Guibert, *op. cit.*, I.1
p. 119	Robert, *Hist. Hieros*, RHC, vol. III; MPL 155, col. 671; bk 1, ch. 1, Gibbon, Everyman ed., VI, p. 45, cf. *Chron. Montis Casinensis* auctore Petro, MGH Ss. VII, p. 765
p. 120	Guibert, *op. cit.*, II.3; *Gesta*, 2–4; modern analyses with further references; K. Setton, *History of the Crusades*, vol. I, ch. 7 and 8; S. Runciman, *History of the Crusades*, vol. I, bk 2
pp. 121–2	Robert, *loc. cit.*; Baudry, *Hist. Hierosolymitana* in RHC, vol. IV, and MPL 166, col. 1070 (lib. I, cap. 1); Guibert, *op. cit.*, L.I and II.3 and 4
p. 122	Albert, *Hist. Hierosolymitanae Expeditionis*, RHC IV and MPL 166, lib. I, cap. 1; Glaber, *Hist.*, MGH Ss. VII, *s.a.* 1009; Adhemar, *Historiarum lib.*, MGH Ss. IV, *s.a.* 1010
pp. 122–3	TREVES (Trier): *Gesta Trevirensium archiepiscoporum* in *amplissima collectio* of E. Martène and U. Durand, Paris, 1724; Albert, *loc. cit.*, lib. I, cap. 24–31; Setton, *op. cit.*, vol. I, ch. 8; Runciman, *op. cit.*, vol. I, bk 3
p. 124	Guibert, *loc. cit.*, Albert, *loc. cit.*; EMPEROR: MPL 155, col. 465–70, and incorporated by Robert of Rheims (*ibid.*, coll. 670–2) in Urban's sermon; cf. Guibert, *op. cit.*, I.4 (coll. 693–5)
p. 126	*Roland*, 1132–8; Albert, II.43
pp. 126–7	*Gesta (Francorum)*, *ed. cit.*, pp. 28, 162, 216; *Gesta Ludovici*, A. and F. Duchesne, *Historiae Francorum scriptores*, vol. IV, Paris, 1636 &C Robert, IX.4
p. 127	*Gesta*, pp. 42, 11, 93; for 'martyrdom' used loosely, cf. MP. CM, II, p. 419; IV, p. 160; V, p. 169. ANTIOCHE: e.g. 8.22; Albert, VIII.12
p. 128	Fulcher, *op. cit.*, I.10; Raymund of Aguilers, *Hist. Francorum*, RHC, vol. III, MPL 155, cap. XIV, XV, XXVII, XXVIII; *Gesta*, pp. 132, 146
p. 129	Robert, *op. cit.*, III.4; Albert, *op. cit.*, V.7; Raymund, XXIII; *Gesta*, 46, 52; Fulcher, 11.5
pp. 129–30	*Gesta*, pp. 50, 150; Fulcher, 1.5, III.37, and on Turks, II.51 (1115)
pp. 130–1	Albert, III.57; *Gesta*, p. 46; *Antioche*, 8.22; Guibert, *op. cit.*, VII.20, V.35; Tyre, 4.23
pp. 131–2	*Chanson d'Antioche*, ed. P. Paris, Paris, 1848; and *La Conquête de Jérusalem*, ed. C. Hippeau, Paris, 1868. *Jérusalem*, VII.13, 14; Fulcher, at Caesarea, II.8 and also at Jerusalem, I.18; *Gesta*, 114. For the relation

of popular movements to Crusading in general, consult
N. Cohn, *The Pursuit of the Millennium*, London, 1957;
see also A. Hatem, *Les Poèmes Épiques des Croisades*,
Paris, 1932

p. 133   *Gesta*, 212, 178; Fulcher, *op. cit.*, I.18, II.8

pp. 133–4   Fulcher, *loc. cit.*, and II.11

pp. 134–5   *Gesta*, 108, 166, 176, 202; Raymund, *op. cit.*, XXXVIII;
TEMPLE: *Gesta*, 202–6

pp. 135–6   Albert, *op. cit.*, VI, 23, 25, 28, 29, 30; William of Tyre,
op. cit., VIII.20; Runciman, *op. cit.*, vol. 1, bk V, ch. II

pp. 136–7   *Gesta*, 176; Fulcher, II.8; *Gesta*, 164; Albert, VI.29;
Fulcher, II.5; Richard of England kills the prisoners
contra fas et licitum: Sicardi Cremonensis *Chronicon, s.a.*
1191, MGH Ss. 31; and massacre at Damietta *christianis
ipsis displicuit*: Ryccardi de S. Germano, *Chronica, s.a.*
1219, MGH Ss. 19, p. 340 (both in Muratori, vol. 7)

pp. 137–8   *Chronique d'Ernoul*, ed. M. L. de Mas Latrie, Paris, 1871,
p. 25 *et seq.*

p. 138   Albert, *loc. cit.* and *passim*

Chapter 6

pp. 140–1   *Hreimskingla Saga*, translated in Penguin edition; M.
Magnusson and H. Palsson, *King Harald's Saga*, pp. 51,
57–8, London, 1966

pp. 141–2   MAINLAND: e.g. Romualdi *Annales*, MGH XIX, p. 420;
AL-HAKIM; Ademari *historiarum libri tres, s.a.* 1010,
III,137, MGH IV

p. 142   *ibid.*, p. 139 (1020); *Annales Cavenses*, MGH III, p. 191

pp. 142–3   Hugo Falcandus, *Liber de regno Siciliae*, ed. G. B.
Siragusa, Rome, 1897, preface pp. 5–6 (also attributed to
Roberto di San Giovanni; cf. G. A. Garufi, *Archivio
Storico per la Sicilia*, 1942); Roberti de Monte *Cronica*,
MGH Ss. VI, p. 528; Joinville 734 cf. 732; Salimbene,
op. cit., p. 484. In general, refer K. Setton, *op. cit.*, vol. I,
p. 52 and vol. II, p. 27 ff.

pp. 143–4   Peter the Deacon, *op. cit.*, MPL 173, coll. 1034–5; and
MGH VII, pp. 728–9; Muratori IV (*Chronicon* only)

pp. 144–6   Gaufridi Malaterrae *Historia Sicula*: Muratori V; MPL
149, coll. 1121–9, 1136–52, 1174, 1184–7, 1209

pp. 146–7   Generally refer M. Amari, *Storia dei Musulmani di
Sicilia*, Florence, 1854–72; C. H. Haskins, *Studies in the
History of Mediaeval Science*, New York, 1927 reprinted,
ch. 9; and A. Mieli, *Science Arabe*, reprinted Leiden,
1966, para. 54; see also below, chapter 10. Hugo Falcandus
op. cit., p. 6

p. 147   Ibn Jubayr, *Travels*, ed. R. J. C. Broadhurst, London, 1952, pp. 340–3, and RHC, historiens orientaux, vol. 3

p. 148   William of Apulia, *De rebus Normanorum in Sicilia*, line 1057; Muratori V, MPL 149; cf. *Brevis Historia liberationis Messanae*, Muratori VI, coll. 613–26. BUILDING: Alexander Telesinus, *De rebus gestis Rogerii Siciliae Regis* in Muratori V, and other editions; DEFERTARII: Hugo, *op. cit.*, p. 69 (XXI); OATH: Lynn White, *Latin Monasticism*, p. 140; cf. references on pp. 58–9; MASMUDA: Hugo, *loc. cit.*, p. 25 (X); cf. p. 99 (XXVI) and Romuald, *loc. cit.*, p. 429

pp. 149–52   Romuald, *loc. cit.*, pp. 426–7, 431–2, 435–6; Hugo, *loc. cit.*, pp. 25, 27 (X), 56–7 (XIV), 69–70 (XXI), 73 (XXII), 80 (XXIV), 108–10 (XXXIII–IV), 115–19 (XLI–XLIV), 173 (ep.)

pp. 152–3   HAUTEVILLES: Malaterra 1137; Hugo 89 (XXV) and p. 8 (preface); Romuald, 425–7, 435

p. 153   Haskins, *op. cit.*, ch. 8

pp. 153–4   J. L. A. Huillard-Bréholles, *Historia Diplomatica Friderici Secundi*, Paris, 1861–72, vol. I.1, p. 118, vol. II.1, p. 393, vol. V.1, pp. 626–7; *Annales Siculi*, in MGH Ss. XIX, *s.a.* 1224, 1245, cf. Ernoul, *op. cit.*, pp. 437–8

pp. 154–5   INEVITABLE CONFLICT: HB, vol. IV.1, pp. 452, 457–8, vol. V.1, p. 628, vol. V.2, pp. 764, 905; see also index, s.v. Lucera; Ryccardi de Sancto Germano notarii *Chronica*, a. 1242, cf. *Annales S. Iustinae Patavini*, a. 1220, both in MGH Ss. XIX

p. 155   SARACEN TROOPS: Rolandini Patavini *Chronica*, IV.9, a. 1238; VII.13, a. 1255; II.6–7, a. 1224; V.22, a. 1248; *Annales Veronenses*, a. 1237, both in MGH Ss. XIX; cf. Manfred, *Annales S. Iustinae Patavini*, *ibid.*, p. 188 *s.a.* 1266; Regnier, Cardinal of Viterbo, in MP. CM (RS 57), *s.a.* 1249, vol. V, p. 61 *et seq.*; Otto of Freising, *Chronicon* 258 in MGH Ss. XX; *Gli Diurnali di Messer Mattheo di Giovenazzo*, para. 2, p. 470 and para. 163, p. 489; a. 1265 in MGH Ss. XIX; cf. paras 19, 24, 44, 51, 55, 61, 69, 93, 96, 117, 125, 135, 144, 146, 148, 153, 160, 178; and Ryccardus de Sancto Germano, *op. cit.*, a. 1266; Brunetto Latini, *Li Livres dou Tresor*, ed. F. J. Carmody, Berkeley and Los Angeles, 1948, 1.98. In general, see HB, introduction, Chapter VI, Part I. Compare the Spanish *almogavars*, who were, indeed, used by the Catalans in Sicily

p. 156   CHARLES II: *Codice Diplomatico dei Saraceni di Lucera* dall 'anno 1285 al 1343, ed. P. Egidi, Naples, 1917, pp. 290–4; 330–2; 404–5

pp. 157–8   PATRIARCH: HB, vol. III, a. 1229 (18 Feb.), p. 86 ff. and 102 (also MGH Ss. IV, p. 260); TEUTONIC MASTER: *ibid.*, p. 90 ff. (101–2)

p. 158   FREDERICK: *loc. cit.*, a. 1229 (March), p. 93 ff.; Pope Gregory's summary of his case, *loc. cit.*, p. 147 ff., July 1229, to King of France; Ernoul, pp. 458–64, cf. HB III, p. 485, a. 1228

pp. 158–9   GREGORY: *ibid.*, and MP. CM, vol. 3, p. 590, *s.a.* 1239; PROPHECY: Salimbene, *op. cit.*, *s.a.* 1250, p. 440; the *Dicta Merlini* associated Frederick with the Moors, *ibid.*, *s.a.* 1250, pp. 359–60; cf. Ryccardus, *op. cit.*, *s.a.* 1230; and cf. pp. 107–9n and 208–9n; also Radulphi de Diceto *Ymagines Historiarum*, RS 68, *s.a.* 1189, p. 60

p. 159   SHEPHERDS: Salimbene, *op. cit.*, *s.a.* 1251, pp. 444–5; cf. Cohn, *op. cit.*, pp. 77, 82–7; MP. CM, vol. III, a. 1238

pp. 160–1   GREGORY: HB, pp. 339–40, vol. V.1; Salimbene: *op. cit.*, p. 350, a. 1250

p. 161   Haskins, *op. cit.*, pp. 264, 298; cf. Mieli, *op. cit.*, section 54 (9)

p. 162   Haskins, *op. cit.*, pp. 311, 318; *De animalibus*, MS Cambridge U.L. Dd. 4.30 & Ii. 3.16; TREATY: HB, vol. III, p. 276, and J. M. L. de Mas Latrie, *Traités de Paix et de Commerce et Documents divers concernant les relations des chrétiens avec les Arabes de l'Afrique Septentrionale au Moyen Âge* (Paris, 1866–72)

p. 163   DIPLOMATA: HB, e.g. vol. V.1, pp. 626, vol. V.2, 907

pp. 163–4   MP. CM, *s.a.* 1249, *loc. cit.*; *op. cit.*, vol. III, p. 521, *s.a.* 1238; vol. IV, p. 268 *s.a.* 1243, p. 635, *s.a.* 1247; vol. V, pp. 216–17, *s.a.* 1251. For the use of Arab girl acrobats and entertainers, see e.g. HB III, p. 104 and MP. CM IV, p. 147, and also Notes on Illustrations, p. ix

p. 165   De Mas Latrie, *op. cit.*, *documents*, and in MPL 148, col. 305–8, 449–52

Chapter 7

p. 168   See especially G. Mathew, "Ideals of Knighthood in late Fourteenth Century England" in *Studies in Mediaeval History presented to Frederick Maurice Powicke* (ed. R. W. Hunt, W. A. Pantin, R. W. Southern), Oxford, 1948, and *The Court of Richard II*, London, 1968, ch. XIII for general European background

pp. 169–70   ANTHROPOLOGIST: T. Asad, *The Kababish Arabs*, London, 1970, p. 187; MUHASSIN: *Table-talk of a Mesopotamian Judge*, tr. D. S. Margoliouth, London, 1922, pp. 13, 14

p. 170   AL-MUTANABBI: A. J. Arberry, *Poems of al-Mutanabbi Selections with . . . translations*, Cambridge, 1967, p. 30

pp. 170–1   Al-Farabi, *Fusul al Madani*, ed. with translation, D. M. Dunlop, Cambridge, 1961; *L'Histoire de Guillaume le Maréchal*, ed. P. Meyer, Paris, 1901, lines 7277–9

pp. 171–2   SECRETA: as edited by R. Bacon, *Opera hactenus inedita* &c., fasc. V, ed. R. Steele, Oxford, 1920, pp. 43–6, 49, 58, 153–4. As left by the translator (Philip of Tripoli) only in MS, e.g. Cambridge Mm. 3.11, fo. 161v, Gg. 4.25, fo. 13v, Gg. 4.29, fo. 1v

pp. 172–3   Fulcher, *op. cit.*, in MPL 155, II.3, 5, 17–18, 10, 31 (ed. H. Hagenmeyer, 3, 6, 18, 11, 32)

pp. 173–4   Tyre, *op. cit.*, IX.22 (MPL 201, col. 454); X.2 (456)

pp. 174–5   *Ibid.*, X.11 (464); CAESAREA: Fulcher, *op. cit.*, II.8

pp. 175–7   BALDWIN I and II: Tyre XII.1 & 4 (521, 524); XIV.3 (582), XVI.2 (640 ff.)

pp. 177–8   AMALRIC: *ibid.*, XIX.2 & 3 (718 ff.); Haskins, *op. cit.*, p. 136

p. 179   BALDWIN IV: Tyre, *op. cit.*, XXI.1 (814–15)

pp. 179–80   Malmesbury, *De regum gestis* (RS 90) *s.a.* 1087, 1093, 1104, 1119, 1123; Bohn Library translation, London, 1847

pp. 180–1   FULK: Tyre, XV.1 & 27

pp. 181–2   Joinville, *Histoire de St Louis*, ed. N. de Wailly, Paris, 1906, paragraphs in order utilized: 386–8, 343, 436–7, 60, 469, 604–5, 594, 517, 582, 561, 286, 261, 527–38, 516, 735, 758. Outside Joinville, the image of Louis was much coloured by the contrast between his rumoured success (the Sultan's pro-Christian brother wants to surrender Cairo; all Egypt captured, MP. CM V, p. 138 and VI, p. 169) and actual disaster

pp. 182–3   *Itinerarium Peregrinorum et Gesta Regis Ricardi*, RS 38, VI.xxxiv (pp. 437–8)

p. 183   Joinville, *op. cit.*, para. 558; Ernoul, *op. cit.*, p. 282; Richard of Devizes, *Chronicon*, ed. J. T. Appleby, London, 1963, pp. 74–5; Guillaume le Maréchal, *loc. cit.*, lines 11823–5

p. 184   Tyre, XVI.7 (646); XX.33 (814)

pp. 185–7   SHIRKUH: *ibid.*, XIX.5 (753). SALADIN: *ibid.*, XX.12 (789); *Life of Saladin by Beha ed-Din*, Palestine Pilgrims Text Society, London 1897; *Itinerarium* I.18, p. 39, VI.27, p. 428, VI.32, p. 434; and Gerald of Wales, *De principum instructione*, RS 21, III.17 et alibi; *De expugnatione Terrae Sanctae libellus*, p. 25 (RS 66); GESTA: Benedict of Peterborough, RS 49, vol. 2, p. 189; Sicard of Cremona, *loc. cit.*; *libellus*, p. 250; Ernoul, *op. cit.*, pp. 228–9, 232–4, 173–4; romanticized history in MS, text in J. F. Michaud, *Bibliothèque des Croisades*, vol. 3, Paris, 1829, pp. 341–3; Salimbene, *op. cit.*, *s.a.* 1187, pp. 4–6; Joinville, *op. cit.*, 330, 331. For Saladin legend, see G. Paris, "La légende de Saladin" in *Journal des Savants*, 1893

pp. 187–8   *The Theologus Autodidactus of Ibn an-Nafis*, ed. M. Meyerhof and J. Schacht, Oxford, 1968, pp. 67–70, 60–2, 52, 65; Tripoli, *De statu Saracenorum* in Prutz, *Kulturgeschichte der Kreuzzüge*, Berlin, 1883 (there is a good MS accessible in Cambridge, Dd. 1.17). Chapter references as in Prutz's arrangement: XIX–XXII

pp. 188–90   Fidenzio, *Liber recuperationis Terrae Sanctae*, in Gol, *Biblioteca Bio-bibliografica della Terra Santa e dell' oriente Francescano* (Quaracchi, 1906–), vol. 2; chs XV, XXI, VII, VIII, IX, XI, XVII, XVI, XXI, XLVIII–LVII; cf. Lull's faith in a *bellator rex*—*Liber de fine*, 2.1; text in A. Gotron, *Ramon Lulls Kreuzzugsideen*, Berlin and Leipzig, 1912

p. 190   VILAIN REPROCHE: Joinville, *op. cit.*, 198, 199; ARAB KNIGHTS: Ernoul, *op. cit.*, p. 144; L. A. Meyer, *Saracenic Heraldry*, Oxford, 1933; TROUBADOUR REPERTORY: P. Meyer, *Le Roman de Flamenca*, Paris, 1865, lines 680–9 (pp. 21–2)

Chapter 8

p. 192   Fulcher, *op. cit.*, III.37 (MPL ed., col. 925)

p. 193   *Gesta*, 158; cf. Raymund of Aguilers, *op. cit.*, 18 (MPL 155), and Fulcher, I.15. Historians, e.g. Runciman, *op. cit.*, vol. I, p. 249; Raymund, 24; *Gesta*, 180; Albert of Aix, *op. cit.*, V.5–12; Raymund, 19

pp. 193–4   AZAZ: Albert, V.5 (cf. Runciman, vol. I, IV.IV). Albert, III.25; *Gesta*, 130, 158, 180; Fulcher, II.62 and I.23 (text in Hagenmeyer only)

pp. 194–5   TRUCES: Tyre: XXI.5–10 and 32 (col. 783–7, 811–12); Ernoul, *op. cit.*, pp. 54–5, 96–7; RAYMUND II OF TRIPOLI: cf. Ernoul, p. 141 and the MS cited by Michaud, *op. cit.*, vol. 3, p. 340

pp. 195–6   Usama ibn Munqidh, *Memoirs of an Arab Syrian Gentleman* (kitab al-Itibar), tr. P. K. Hitti, New York, 1927, reprinted Beirut, 1964; Albert, *op. cit.*, III.3 (English forest law punished infringement by nobles less severely); ROBERT: Benedict of Peterborough, *Gesta Regis Henrici Secundi*, RS 49, vol. 1, pp. 341–2, a. 1185 pp. 196–7   *Gesta*, 150 (Kerbogha) and 10 (Xerigordo); Odo, *De profectione Ludovici VII in orientem*, ed. V. G. Berry, New York, 1948, p. 140

pp. 197–8   WOMEN PRISONERS: Albert, *op. cit.*, III.46; VIII.18 & 31; V.5

p. 198   CAPTURED WIFE: *ibid.*, II.37

pp. 198–9   GREEK MONK: Arsenius in Bartholomaei de Neocastro *Historia Sicula*, cap. CXX; RICOLDO: AOL, vol. II, Paris, 1884; *Epistolae V de commentatorie de perditione Acconis*, ed. R. Rohricht, pp. 272, 279, 293

p. 199   MARGARET: A. Manrique, *Cisterciensium seu verius Ecclesiasticorum annalium a condito Cistercio*, tomus tertius, Lyons, 1649, pp. 198–9, 226–7, 262–3 (cf. Michaud, *op. cit.*, vol. 3, pp. 369 *et seq.*)

pp. 199–200   KING'S SPY: *Itinerarium Peregrinorum et Gesta Regis Ricardi*, VI.3; cf. Joinville, p. 2, 3 below; *Gestes des Chiprois*, SOL, Série historique, vol. 5, pp. 240–1; TRANSLATIONS: see pp. 171–2, 264, 276; APPRECIATION: Tripoli, *op. cit.*, see p. 208 below, and Ricoldo, *Itinerarius* (sic), in J. C. M. Laurent, *Peregrinatores medii aevi quatuor*, Leipzig, 1864; see also pp. 215–17 and 243 below; Tyre, *op. cit.*, prologus col. 212

pp. 200–1   EXOTICISM: MP. CM, *s.a.* 1246, vol. IV, p. 566; Diceto (RS 68), *Ymagines Historiarum*, p. 25; *Gestes des Chiprois*, ed. *cit.*, p. 242; AOL, "Correspondance fausse du sultan", ed. W. Wattenbach, vol. 1, pp. 299–300; Orderic, *Historia Ecclesiastica*, in MPL 188, coll. 776–7. Compare the story of Sancho of Navarre and the princess of Morocco, Hoveden, *Chron.*, RS 51, vol. 3, pp. 90–2

p. 202   Walter, *Bella Antiochena*, MPL 155, col. 997. Joinville, XCVIII.502; Ernoul, *ed. cit.*, pp. 86–7, cf. 101

pp. 202–3   Vitry, *Epistolae II*, in *Lettres de Jacques de Vitry*, ed. R. B. L. Huygens, Leiden, 1960, pp. 86–8; Tyre, *op. cit.*, XIX.3, coll. 750–1

pp. 203–4   DANGER: Tyre, XXI.7 and XXIII praef.; MPL 201, coll. 820, 889–90; Vitry, *op. cit.*, II, p. 96; *Job* 21:14; *Hosea* 4:9; *Isaiah* 1:6 (adapted)

pp. 204–6   Vitry, *op. cit.*, II and *Historia Hierosolimitana* in J. Bongars, *Gesta Dei per Francos*, Hanover, 1611, p. 1085 *et seq.* and 1097. Other descriptions of the nations of the East in travellers cited below, pp. 227 and 316. Cf. also Thomas of Bethlehem in Michaud, *op. cit.*, vol. 3, p. 348

pp. 207–8   Fidenzio, *op. cit.*, ch. VII, p. 13

pp. 208–9   Tripoli, *op. cit.*, XXI, XXII, XXIII, XXIV, LI, LII;

cf. Jacques de Vitry, *Ep. II, ed. cit.*, pp. 88 and 96; Diceto, *s.a.* 1189, *loc. cit.*; MP. CM III, pp. 11 and 55. Many prophecies were associated with the first capture of Damietta, examples in SOL, série historique, vol. 2, p. 305 *et seq.*

p. 209   Templar, *Gestes des Chiprois, ed. cit.*, p. 252; Ricoldo, *Epistolae V*, pp. 278, 289, 291. Interpretations of the disaster, e.g. G. Villani (Historia Fiorentine, Muratori XIII, 7.144), as a blow to trade, caused by sinful men and dissolute women; but John of Ypres (Chron. S. Bertini, LIII.VI, coll. 772–3, in *Thesaurus anecdotorum*, ed. G. Martene and U. Durand, Paris, 1717, vol. 3) sees in the troubled succession to Qalaun God's judgement on the sultans also

p. 210   TEMPLE: cf. p. 157, above; Ricoldo, *ibid.*, p. 273; *Gestes des Chiprois* p. 162; cf. Runciman, *op. cit.*, vol. 3, p. 216, and Setton, *op. cit.*, vol. 2, p. 28, cf. 2, p. 34

p. 211   *Gesta, ed. cit.*, p. 50 and cf. above, 5, p. 23; Fulcher, *op. cit.*, II.30 (MPL) (Hagenmeyer 31); Tyre, *op. cit.*, XIX.14 and 23. For Memphis, cf. Malmesbury, *op. cit.*, *s.a.* 1099. Burchard of Mount Sion, however, thought that ancient Memphis was Damietta (Laurent, *op. cit.*, p. 158)

pp. 211–12   CAIRO EMBASSY: Tyre, *op. cit.*, XIX.17–18; LAMARTINE: original albums, *Voyage en Orient*, ed. Lotfy Fam, Paris, n.d., pp. 316–20; cf. an Ayyubid parallel in Ryccardus de S. Germano, *op. cit.*, Muratori VII, coll. 986–8

pp. 212–13   Joinville, *op. cit.*, paras 148, 324, 335–6, 348–53, 358–9, 372–3, 394–6

pp. 213–15   GERARD: Arnold of Lübeck, *Chronicon Slavorum*, in MGH Ss. XXI, pp. 235–41

pp. 215–17   Ricoldo, *Itinerarius, ed. cit.*, chs XXI to XXIX, and cf. *Ep. II*; also Philippe de Mezières, *Le Songe du Vieil Pélérin*, ed. G. W. Coopland, Cambridge, 1969, vol. 1, p. 331, with its recognition of Arab charity by a theoretically fanatical Crusader

pp. 217–18   *Correspondance fausse, ed. cit.*, pp. 299–300; cf. Ricoldo, *Ep. I*, pp. 266–7; DIVIDED: e.g. v. Andreae Danduli *Chronicon Venetum*, Muratori 12, Milan, 1728, lib. 24, cap. 22; SELF-QUESTIONING: cf. *infra*, pp. 248–9

p. 219   MONGOLS: pp. 314–17 and *n*, below; MERCENARIES: Ernoul, *op. cit.*, p. 458, and Tyre, continuation, MPL 201. LXXXVI, col. 1005

pp. 219–20   W. von Heyd, *Commerce du Levant*, vol. 2, Leipzig, 1885–6, Supp. 1; De Mas Latrie, *Traités, cit.* p. 73 ff. and p. 83, para. 26. From the beginning, the canons forbade Christian experts to serve as master on Arab ships (pp. 256–9n). For Lull's absurdly optimistic assessment of the boycott, see *Liber de fine, loc. cit.*, 2.5. For list of commodities traded, see Francesco Balducci Pegolotti, *La Pratica della Mercatura*, ed. A. Evans, Cambridge (Mass.), 1936

p. 220   FONDACOS: De Mas Latrie, *op. cit.*, Supp. 36–8, and p. 23

pp. 220–2   William of Adam, *De modo Saracenos extirpandi* in RHC, Documents Arméniens, vol. 2, pp. 523–5. He accuses the Genoese, Segurano Salvago, of being addressed by the sultan as 'brother', of permitting buggery on his ships, and of flying the sultan's flag (p. 525)

p. 222   PAPAL LETTERS: de Mas Latrie, *op. cit.*, pt I, Gregory IX (1233), cf. Innocent III (1198); Honorius III (1226); Innocent IV (1251). Papal canonical instructions in *Raymundiana* (p. 260 below). The fullest contemporary picture is given by Marino Sanudo (*Secreta Fidelium Crucis*, in Bongars), a defender of the papal position, although he was Venetian. Fourteenth-century papal relations with the Italian cities were very complex

pp. 222–4   Salimbene, *loc. cit.*, *s.a.* 1279 (p. 314); cf. Angelo di Spoleto, *De fratribus minoribus visitantibus captivos in Babilonia* (1303–4) in Gol. vol. 3, p. 68 ff.; LULL: *A Life of Roman Lull*, tr. E. A. Peers, London, 1925, and see pp. 310–2; TREBIZOND: in Gol., *op. cit.*, 2, pp. 66–7, other cases p. 61 *et seq.*, p. 110 *et seq.*; p. 143 *et seq.*, *Chronica* fr. Johannis Vitodurani who praises sultan an-Nasir Muhammad for protecting the Latins; vol. 4, pp. 390–4, Livin and Martinozzi; vol. 5, p. 282 ff., B. Nicolo de Tavileis, and *passim*; CARMELITES: *Chronicle . . . of the Carmelites in Mesopotamia*, ed. H. Gollancz, London, 1927

pp. 224–8   Simon, in Gol. vol. 3, pp. 246, 262–75; Jacopo di Verona, *Liber Peregrinationis* (1335), ed. R. Rohricht in *Revue de l'Orient Latin*, vol. 3 (1895), pp. 240, 244–5; comparable accounts, Antonio de' Reboldi, *Itinerarium in Sepulchrum Domini et ad montem Sinai* (1327–30) in Gol. vol. 3, p. 331 ff.; Peter de Pennis, *Libellus de locis transmarinis* (*c.* 1350), ed. C. Kohler, in ROL, vol. 9 (1902); Ludolf of Sudheim, *De itinere Terrae Sanctae* (1348) in AOL vol. 2 (Paris, 1884), ed. C. A. Neumann; Odoric of Pordenone (Frimli) (1330) in Laurent, *op. cit.*; rather later, Nicolas de Martoni, *Liber Peregrinationis ad loca sancta* (1394–5), ed. L. le Grand, ROL, vol. 3, and earlier, Willibrand of Oldenburg, *Peregrinatio* (1211) and Burcardi de Monte Sion *Descriptio Terre Sancte* (*c.* 1283), both in Laurent, *op. cit.*, and Magistri Thietmari *Peregrinatio* (1217) also ed. Laurent, Hamburg, 1857. See also *De passagiis in Terram Sanctam ex chronologia magna excerpta*, ed. G. M. Thomas, Venice, 1879, and Pegolotti (pp. 219–20n above)

p. 228   Fear of spies or of being taken for a spy was widespread, as was fear of reprisals. For an example of the latter, see Matteo Villani, *Istorie*, Muratori XIV, 7.3 (coll. 406–7)

Chapter 9

pp. 230–1   These points are discussed very fully in my *Islam and the West, ed. cit., passim*

pp. 232–3   Southern, R. W., *Western Views of Islam in the Middle Ages*, Cambridge, Mass., 1962. Walter of Compiègne, *Poema de Machomete*, in M. E. du Méril, *Poésies populaires latines du moyen âge*, Paris, 1847; Alexandre du Pont, *Roman de Mahomet*, ed. J. T. Reinaud and F. Michel, Paris, 1831; Embrico of Mainz, *Historia de Mahumete*, under Hildebert of Lavardin, in MPL 171, coll. 1345 ff. Hugh, Hugonis Floriacensis *Cronicon*, ed. B. Rottendorff, Münster, 1638; *Gesta, ed. cit.*, index, s.v. *Khorasan*; Sigebert, MPL 160, coll. 119–22

p. 233   Guibert, *op. cit.*, coll. 689–93; Anastasius, *Historia Ecclesiastica* in *Corpus Scriptorum Historiae Byzantinae*, vol. 2. Vincent *Speculum Historiale*, 23.40 in *Bibliotheca Mundi*, Douai, 1629, vol. 5

p. 234   *Cronica de Espana*, CXI, cf. Roderick, *Historia Arabum*, III; *De generatione*, in Bibliander, *Machumetis Saracenorum principis . . . doctrina ac ipse Alcoran*, Basle, 1550. For this, and for all questions relating to the corpus of Cluniac translations, see M. T. d'Alverny, "Deux Traductions latines du Coran au Moyen Âge" in *Archives d'histoire doctrinale et littéraire du Moyen Âge*, Paris, 1948, and J. Kritzeck, *Peter the Venerable and Islam*, Princeton, 1964

p. 235   Gerald of Wales, *op. cit.*, p. 70; Guibert, *loc. cit.*, col. 691. Alan of Lille, *De fide catholica*, MPL 210, coll. 425–6. Walter, *op. cit.*, p. 381; du Pont, *loc. cit.*

pp. 235–6   JOKE: Guibert, *loc. cit.*, coll. 692–3. On idols, see Daniel, *op. cit.*, app. A. Byzantines and Muslims are accused jointly in Diceto, *loc. cit.*

p. 236   Turpinus, *loc. cit.*, ch. VI; *Gesta*, pp. 118, 216; *Couronnement de Louis*, ed, E. Langlois, Paris, 1925, line 848 and passage following

pp. 237-8   PEDRO: *Dialogus*, MPL 157. PETER THE VENERABLE:
             references at p. 234n above. Texts in MPL 189 and Bibli-
             ander, *op. cit.*; for full text of Latin translation of al-
             Kindi, see MSS, e.g. Bodley CCC.d.184. Critical edition
             of *contra sectam* and some others of the texts, in Kritzeck
             op. cit.

p. 238   M. T. D'ALVERNY: "Marc de Tolède" in *Al-Andalus*,
             1951-2, and p. 234n above

pp. 238-9   *Contrarietas* (cf. d'Alverny, *loc. cit.*) known in only one
             MS (Paris, Bibliotheque nationale, lat. 3394). *Refutatio* or
             Disputatio of Ricoldo, in MS, e.g. BM Royal 13.E.ix and
             BN lat. 4230; translation into Greek with retranslation
             into Latin in MPG 104. *Quadruplex reprobatio*, in MS, e.g.
             Cambridge Dd.1.17 and BN lat. 4230; printed as *Galensis
             de origine et progressu* .... *Machometis*, ed. W. Dreschsler,
             Strasburg, 1550. Tripoli, *op. cit.*, ch. 1-17; Pascual,
             in *Obras*, ed. P. Armengol Valenzuela, Rome, 1905-8.
             Vitry, *Hist. Hieros*, *ed. cit.*, 1.6; cf. Melkite position at
             same date; Paul d'Antioche, *Lettre aux Musulmans*, ed.
             P. Khoury, Beirut, 1964

pp. 239-40   SIRA: English version by A. Guillaume, *The Life of
             Muhammad*, London, 1955, pp. 188-9. Mark, printed by
             d'Alverny, *loc. cit. Quadruplex reprobatio*, *ed. cit.* ('Galen-
             sis'), ch. VII, p. 19, Cambridge MS Dd.1.17, fo. 72b,
             col. 1

pp. 240-1   Brunetto, *op. cit.*, I.25; Tripoli, *loc. cit.* (ch. 2). Auvergne,
             De fide et legibus in *opera omnia* (several editions; e.g.
             Nuremberg, 1497, fo. 37r, 18M). Roderick, *loc. cit.*,
             Pedro, *loc. cit.*, *Dialogi*, No. V.

pp. 241-2   Lull, *Doctrina Pueril* 71.3 and 8, ed. M. Obrador y
             Bennassar, Palma de Mallorca, 1906

p. 242   BACON: examples in *Opus Majus*, ed. J. H. Bridges, Oxford,
             1897, pars secunda, vol. 3, p. 72 and elsewhere, and *Moralis
             Philosophia*, ed. F. Delorme and E. Massa, Zurich, 1953,
             e.g. pp. 72 and 187-8, see also index, s.v. Algazel, Alphara-
             bius, Avicenna; *De Viciis contractis in studio theologie*,
             ed. R. Steele, Oxford, 1905, *passim*: MARTI: *Explanatio
             Simboli* in J. M. March, *En Roman Marti*, Barcelona,
             1908; see also *Pugio Fidei*, Leipzig, 1687, Tripoli, *op. cit.*,
             ch. 50

pp. 243-5   Ricoldo, *Itinerarius*, *ed. cit.*, X, XVII, XVIII, XX and
             XXX-XXXII (pp. 117, 125, 126-8, 130, 135-6). *Libellus
             ad nationes orientales*, Oxford MS Bodley Can. Pat. lat. 142

p. 246   UTHRED: in D. Knowles, "The censured opinions of
             Uthred of Boldon", *Proceedings of the British Academy*,

XXXVII (1951), and *The Historian and Character*, Cambridge, 1963, cf. Langland, *Piers Plowman*, texts B, Passus XII, 275 ff., and C. Passus XV, 200 ff. (cf. B.III.323 ff.), ed. W. W. Skeat, London, 1869 and 1873; ARGUMENT BROUGHT FORWARD: see the cases of Lull and various Franciscans on pp. 222–3n, and 310–12, but contrast Peter Thomas, Gol. vol. 5, pp. 79–80; further references, Daniel, *op. cit.*, chs 8 and 9. PASTOUREAUX: *Annales de Burton* in *Annales Monastici*, RS 36, vol. 1, pp. 290–3

pp. 246–7   TEMPLARS: p. 312 below. "1277": CUP, vol. 1, n. 473, p. 543 ff. (ed. H. Derifle and A. Chatelain, Paris, 1889–1897)

p. 247   "HONEY": *Summula quaedam brevis*, ed. Kritzeck (p. 234n, above), p. 206; Auvergne, *De legibus*, fo. 17v.R in *opera omnia*, Nuremberg, 1497. INTENDED TO CONVINCE: this again I argue more fully: Daniel, *op. cit.*, p. 229 ff. COMMON GROUND: *ibid.*, ch. 6 (p. 163 ff.)

p. 248   Joinville, *op. cit.*, para. 53, cf. above, 5.6

pp. 248–9   Joachim, *Expositio in Apocalypsim*, Venice, 1527, reprinted Frankfurt, 1964, f. 163v. For an example of Crusade preaching set in the whole historical perspective of holy war, see *Tractatus solemnis* fratris Humberti... ordinis praedicatorum, *de predicatione Sancte Cruis*, 1490. This work, though not, like the same author's *Opus Tripartitum,* in *Appendix ad Fasciculum Rerum Expetendarum et Fugiendarum*, Tomus secundus... scriptorum veterum, ed. E. Brown, London, 1690, intended specifically in preparation for the Council of Lyons in 1274, belongs to the period of ecumenical thinking (on Latin terms, and not for Muslims) which hoped to restore traditional Crusading theology. From the earlier Crusading period, cf. Malmesbury, p. 113n, also MPL 151, coll. 571–2. Cf. Quodam *itinerarium Terre Sancte* (1463) in ROL, vol. 12 (1909–11), cap. XIII; or much earlier, Auvergne, *op. cit.*, fo. 37r–v, 18N. These are examples of a general tendency. See also the Venetian excerpts *De passagiis* (above 224–8)

pp. 250–1   GREGORY: MPL 148, col. 484 and 450–1 citing *John* 1:9 and 1 *Tim.* 2:4, *Quran* 1:1; cf. 37.182. Gregory claimed suzerainty over Spain. For Urban's attitude before 1095, see for example ES, vol. 25, Ap. XII, pp. 215–16

pp. 251–2   Guibert, *op. cit.*, col. 700; Lateran IV, Héfélé, vol. V, pp. 1390–5; BERNARD: MPL 182, col. 653 cf. 651; see also *Dictionnaire de Théologie Catholique*, s.v. *indulgences*, for further references

pp. 252–3   Bernard, *loc. cit.*, coll. 652, 924
pp. 253–4   Humbert, *Opus*, I.xi and xii; tractatus, *passim.* CRITICISM:
e.g. *Collectio de Scandalis* (by Gilbert of Tournay?),
ed. P. A. Stroick in *Archivum Franciscanum Historicum*
(XXIV), 1931; Pierre Dubois, *De recuperatione Terre
Sancte*, ed. Ch. V. Langlois, Paris, 1891; Galvanus de
Levanto, *Pro recuperatione Terrae Sanctae*, ed. Ch. Kohler,
in ROL, vol. 6 (1898); Andreae Danduli, *op. cit.* See also
A. S. Atiya, *The Crusade in the Later Middle Ages*,
London, 1938, and P. A. Throop, *Criticism of the Crusade*,
Amsterdam, 1940
p. 255   HOLCOT: R. Holkot, *In librum Sapientie*, Basle, 1560,
Lectio LXV (cap. v). ROLAND: lines 3668–70
pp. 256–9   Héfélé, *op. cit.*, vol. V: 1st Lateran, p. 630 ff. Lateran III,
pp. 1104–5 and Lateran IV, p. 1386 ff., cf. Valladolid and
Lerida, pp. 1504–5. For pre-Islamic canons controlling
Jews, cf. *ibid.*, vol. III, p. 204 (Macon AD 583). Canons
relating to classical paganism applied to Muslims and
assuming continuity of descent, Penaforte, *Summa canon-
um*, Verona, 1744, I.iv.2 cf. pp. 219–20n). Collections of
canons, *Decretalium Gregorii liber*, Antwerp, 1573, and
many other editions, with commentary by John of Andrew:
lib. V tit. vi cap. v, vi, x, xi, xii, xv, xvi, xvii, xviii and
passim; *Clementinae*, tit 2 (cap. unicum); *Extravagantes*,
Ioannis XXII, tit. viii (cap. unic.) and *Communes*, lib. V
tit. 2 cap. 1 (see always *de Judaeis et Saracenis*); cf. *Bullarum
diplomatum et privilegiorum* . . . ed. A. Tomasetti, Turin,
1857–72, vols 2 and 3
p. 260   Penaforte, *loc. cit.*, I.iv *passim*, and *Raymundiana* in
MORPH, Rome and Stuttgart, 1898, vol. VI, fasc. 1,
Documents, VIII
p. 261   For Spanish laws: *Las Siete Partidas*, Madrid, 1807
p. 262   PETER: Kritzeck, *ed. cit.*, p. 253

Chapter 10

p. 263   Tannery, P., *Mémoires scientifiques V*—"Sciences exactes
au Moyen Âge", Toulouse and Paris, 1922, p. 79; cf.
p. 229, and see also *Mémoires scientifiques X* (supplément
au tome vi), Toulouse and Paris, 1930, No. 3, Oct. 1900—
"Histoire des sciences— mathématiques", p. 25. "Algorism' is Chaucer's "augrim". Gerbert, MPL 139, vol. 85
et seq. Isidore, *Etymologiarum sive Originum libri*, Oxford,
1911; Bedae *opera omnia*, MPL 90–5; AFFLACIUS: Mieli,
op. cit., para. 52. CONSTANTINE: above, pp. 143–4
p. 264   Stephen of Antioch, *Liber Regalis*, printed text, Lyons,

              1523, fo. 5r, cf. 136r and MS Vat. lat. 2429, cf. Haskins, *op. cit.*, p. 131

pp. 265–8   ADELARD: ed. Willner, *Des Adelard von Bath Traktat De eodem et diverso*, Münster, 1903, p. 1, and ed. M. Müller, *Die Quaestiones Naturales des Adelardus von Bath*, Münster, 1934, pp. 1, 5, 8, 9, 11, 12, 23, 42–3 (Series: *Beiträge zur Geschichte der Philosophie und Theologie des Mittelalters*, IV.1 and XXXI.2); Haskins, *op. cit.*, p. 20 *et seq.*

p. 268   HUGH: texts in Haskins, *op. cit.*, pp. 70–9. I am indebted to Dr Henry Riad, Director of the Cairo Museum, for access to his unpublished work on Hermanubis

p. 269   STEPHEN: text in Haskins, *op. cit.*, pp. 99–100

pp. 269–70   RAYMUND: Bodley MS CCC 243 fo. 53r *et seq.*; Haskins, *op. cit.*, pp. 96–8; R. Lemay, *Abu Ma'shar and Latin Aristotelianism in the Twelfth Century*, Beirut, 1962, p. 143

pp. 270–2   KETTON, HERMANN: texts in Bodley MS, 243, fo. 92r–v, 105r, and Haskins, *op. cit.*, pp. 45–7, 48–9, 57–8, 121–2; MPL 189 (coll. 657–60), and Bibliander, *op. cit.*; Lemay, *op. cit.*, pp. 23–4 and 212 and cf. *passim.* Quran, 4:169 (171). Abu Ma'shar ('Albumasar'), *Introductorium in astronomiam*, Venice, 1506. Auvergne, *ed. cit.*, fo. 40v and 41r, 19 ff. Cf. Bacon, *De Viciis, ed. cit.*, p. 42. Haskins identifies Robert as 'Chester', not 'Ketton', but see d'Alverny, "Deux Traductions", *loc. cit.* In general, cf. Haskins and Lemay, *op. cit.*, and L. Thorndyke, *History of Magic and Experimental Science*, London, 1923, vol. I; G. Sarton, *Introduction to the History of Science*, Baltimore, 1927, vol. I

p. 272   FORMER AGES: Hugh, *loc. cit.*; Adelard, *De eodem, loc. cit.*, Gundisalvo, *de scientiis*, ed. M. A. Alonso, Madrid and Grenada, 1954, pp. 55–6, and *De divisione*, ed. C. Baur, Münster, 1903, p. 3

pp. 272–3   GERARD: texts in K. Sudhoff, "Die kurze 'Vita' und das Verzeichnis der Arbeiten Gerhards von Cremona" (text: *Sicut lucerna relucens*, p. 75 ff.) in *Archiv für Geschichte der Medizin*, Band VIII, Nov. 1914, and K. Sudhoff, "Daniels von Morley Liber de naturis inferiorum et superiorum", text from p. 40, in *Archiv f. d. Geschichte der Naturwissenschaften u. d. Technik*, Band VIII; cf. also G. Sarton, *op. cit.*

pp. 273–4   Salisbury, *Metalogicon*, ed. C. C. I. Webb, Oxford, 1929, I.vi (p. 21) and IV.vi (p. 171); also, MPL 199; Sylvester, *De mundi universitate*, ed. C. Barach, Innsbruck, 1876,

1.3, pp. 22 and 24; lines 241, 235–6, 311–12. BURY ST EDMUNDS: *The Chronicle of Jocelin of Brakelond*, tr. and ed. H. E. Butler, London, 1949, p. 130. Ibn Butlan, *Tacuinum Sanitatis*, opening phrases, printed with *Liber Albenguefit* (ibn Wafid) in *De Virtutibus Medicinarum*, Strasburg, 1531; many MSS, e.g. BM, Sloane 3097

p. 275   For the Greek sources it it most convenient to consult Mieli, *op. cit.*

p. 276   PHILIP: reference at pp. 171–2n, above

pp. 277–8   STUDENTS' GUIDE: M. Grabmann, *I Papi del Duecento e l'Aristotelismo*, 1; *I Divieti ecclesiastici di Aristotele sotto Innocenzo III e Gregorio IX*, Rome, 1941 (*Miscellanea Historiae Pontificiae*, vol. V); restated at length by F. van Steenberghen, *Aristotle en Occident*, Louvain, 1946, pp. 93–8. AQUINAS: C. Vansteenkiste, "San Tommaso d'Aquino ed Averroe" in *Rivista degli Studi Orientale*, 32, Rome, 1957; SIGER: C. A. Graeff, *Siger de Brabant, Questions sur la Métaphysique*, texte inédit, Louvain, 1943; cf. F. van Steenberghen, *Siger de Brabant d'après ses œuvres inédites*, Louvain, 1931, and J. J. Duin, *La Doctrine de la Providence dans les écrits*, Louvain, 1954. Alberti Magni, *De animalibus libri XXVI*, ed. H. Stadler, Münster, 1916, 2 vols. On the Averroistic controversy, E. Renan, *Averroes et l'Averroisme*, Paris, 1852 and F. Mandonnet, *Siger de Brabant*, Louvain, 1911, put the orthodox case

p. 278   CUP, reference at pp. 246–7n; *s.a.* 1277. On ibn Sina see M. T. d'Alverny, *Les Traductions d'Avicenne*, Rome, 1957—Accademia Nazionale dei Lincei

p. 279   Bacon, Delorme, *loc. cit.* (see above 9.14–15) and *De viciis*, ed. *cit.*, pp. 17, 36; A. Crombie, *Robert Grosseteste and the Origins of Experimental Science*, Oxford, 1953, pp. 48–9, 116–17 and *passim*; Pecham, *ibid.*, p. 165. Aquinas, *Summa contra Gentiles*, I.vi, Rome, 1934; reference to Arabs in *Quaestiones de Spiritualibus Creaturis*, ed. L. Keeler, Rome, 1938. Dante, *Commedia Divina, Inferno*, IV.143–4 cf. XXVIII.22 ff.; *Paradiso*, X.82–138. Salah ad-Din with the heroes of antiquity in Limbo 'solo in parte', inferno IV.129. Qusta ibn Luqa, *De Differentia Animae et Spiritus*, ed. C. Barach, Innsbruck, 1878

pp. 279–81   Bacon, *Opus Majus, vol. cit.* (ch. 9, pp. 14–15), pp. 54–5, 64, 66, *De viciis*, as cited

p. 281   ALFONSO: anthologized in *Alfonso X el Sabio*, ed. A. G. Solalinde, with bibliography of editions; reprinted Buenos Aires, 1940, p. 166. A useful summary of the Alfonsine corpus in Mieli, *op. cit.*, para. 59 n. 6

p. 282   GERARD: references at pp. 272–3n. above

pp. 282–3   RAYMUND: note on pp. 8–9 above; see Lemay, *op. cit.*, pp.
              141–2, and Haskins, *op. cit.*, pp. 82 *et seq.*, 113 *et seq.*
              Roger, *De tribus generalibus iudiciis astronomie*, Cambridge
              University Library, Ii.1.1, fo. 41r. ANNA: *Alexiade*, Tome
              2, Paris, 1943, ed. B. Leib, p. 57, VI, vii.2; Penguin
              translation by E. R. A. Sewter, London, 1969, pp. 193–4.
              Augustine, *De civitate Dei*, V.1–8. Salimbene, *op. cit.*, *s.a.*
              1284, p. 547. Malmesbury, *op. cit.*, *s.a.* 1002

pp. 283–4   Salisbury, *Polycraticus* 2.18, ed. C. C. I. Webb, Oxford,
              1909; also MPL 199. Turpinus, *loc. cit.*, XXXIV. Bru-
              netto, *loc. cit.*, I.118

p. 284   PROHIBITIONS: CUP, *loc. cit.*, No. 206, "That *he* assigns"
              —sic. I omit only the words *et aspectui fortune*

pp. 284–8   Scot, *De animalibus*, reference at p. 162 above. Haskins,
              loc. cit., p. 245 ff. and p. 272 ff. Text cited from p. 290.
              For the astrology, MSS: Bodley 266 fo. 20v–25r and
              Edinburgh University Library, 132 fo. 34r–v; and cf.
              Mieli, *op. cit.*, para. 54n.9 and Lemay, *op. cit.*, p. 243. I am
              indebted to my colleague, Mr Hassan al-Khalifa, for
              the identification of the spirit in modern magical practice,
              which he was able to achieve without putting a leading
              question. In general, cf. Lane's *Modern Egyptians*, Chapter
              XII; note also MP. CM IV, p. 62

pp. 288–9   ALI IBN ABI RIJAL: *De iudiciis astrologie*, Basle, 1551 (first
              printed Venice, 1485); cf. Cambridge University Library,
              MS Mm.4.43, fo. 1 *et seq.*, fo. 217v *et seq.* Cf. F. Cumont,
              L'Égypte des Astrologues, Brussels, 1937, and A. J.
              Festugière, *La révélation d'Hermes Trismégiste*, *L'Astro-
              logie et les sciences occultes*, Paris, 1944. For 'Sahl' in the
              text understand 'Ibn Sahl'

pp. 289–90   Bonatti, *Decem continens Tractatus Astronomie*, Venice,
              1506, Cap. IV–X. *Matthew* 24:36. Bonatti placed by
              Dante in *Inferno*, canto XX.118 (Michael Scot appears
              above at line 116)

pp. 291–2   LIBER REGALIS: see p. 264n, above; fo. 136; IBN BUTLAN:
              see pp. 273–4n, above; also for IBN WAFID. Ibn Sina,
              Canon, Strasburg, 1475, Venice, 1555, and many other
              printed editions and MSS. Cf. *Cantica Avicennae* a
              Magistro Armengaudo Blasii de Montepesulano in
              Latinam translatus, in Avicenne, *Poème de la Medecine*,
              ed. H. Jahier and Abdelkader Noureddine, Paris, 1956,
              pars prima, *medicina est conservatio sanitatis*, &c.

pp. 293–5   ARNALD: Arnaldi Villanovani Philosophi et Medici, *Opera
              Omnia*, ed. N. Tavrelli, Basle, 1585. *Aphorismi*, col. 237

et seq., *De regimine sanitatis*, col. 657; *De coitu*, 839–42; *De Balneis*, 691; *De exercitio*, 687; *De ornatu mulierum*, 1646; *De amore heroico*, 1523; *Phrenesis*, 262; ar-Razi, 639–40; Avicenna, 879; Averroes, 555–8; *super canonem vita brevis*, 1677 *et seq.*, 1722. PLAGIARISM: cf. R. Bacon, *De retardatione*, ed. A. G. Little and E. Withington, Oxford, 1928, *De conservatione juventutis*. 'HEROIC' LOVE: cf. Chaucer, Knight's Tale, II.1372–6

p. 295   Fibonacci, *Scritte di Leonardo Pisano*, ed. Baldassare Boncompagni, Rome, 1962

pp. 296–7   Ketton (as 'Chester'), *Liber Algebrae et Almucabolae* in *Robert of Chester's translation of the Algebra of al-Khowarizmi*, ed. L. C. Karpinski, New York, 1915. 'Ali ibn Abi Rijal, *ed. cit.*, pp. 1, 144, 296, 352, 410. *Liber introductorius . . . Alquindi*, ed. A. Nagy, Beiträge, z.r., Münster, 1896. Ibn Sina, Scot, Ketton and Mark, all *loc. cit.* and Mark also in his Quran translation, Vienna, cod. 4297. AL-GHAZALI: *Logica et Philosophia Algazelis Arabis*, ed. P. Liechtenstein, Venice (?), 1506 (tr. Gundisalvo), lib. II, cap. 10 and 11. Other examples in the following Cambridge MSS: Kk.1.1, fo. 117v, 222v, al-Zarqali, *ibid.*, fo. 125r; and cf. Ff.4.13, fo. 7r, 8r; also British Museum, Royal 12.F.VII (ibn Ridwan), fo. 1r, and Sloane 3097, fo. 102v; Arundel 115, fo. 3r; Cotton, App. VI, fo. 163r

Chapter 11

p. 300   SCOTUS: Maurice O'Fihely ('de portu'), in Wadding, *Annales Minorum* cited as vol. IV by E. Gilson, in "Avicenne et le point de départ de Duns Scotus", *Archives d'histoire doctrinale &C*, Paris, 1927, vol. 2 (I have not traced this in editions available to me). Second reference, in Ioannis Duns Scoti, *opera omnia*, ed. L. Wadding, Lyons, 1689, vol. IV, annotationes p. 508. 'THERE IS NO CAUSE': Gilson, *loc. cit.* On Ockham, cf. D. Knowles, *Evolution of Medieval Thought*, London, 1962, p. 318 ff. LULL: full references in Daniel, *loc. cit.*, pp. 178–80. John of Jandun, *Opera*, Venice, 1552–86

p. 301   Macdonald: in *Encyclopaedia of Islam* (1), s.v. *derwish*. Beghards, &c. cf. M. Cohn, *op. cit.* and G. Leff, *Heresy in the Later Middle Ages*, Manchester, 1967

pp. 302–3   Nicolas of Cusa, *Cribratio* in Bibliander, *op. cit.*, and *De pace*, ed. R. Klibansky and H. Bascour, London, 1956; Pius II, *Epistola ad Morbisanum* in Bibliander. Further references, Daniel, *op. cit.*, pp. 276–9. Bodin, *Colloquium*, Schwerin, 1857. Cf. G. Postel, *De orbis Terrae Concordia*,

Basle, 1544, *Alcorani et Evangelistarum Concordiae liber* and other works; and J. Lecler, *Histoire de la Tolérance au siècle de la Réforme*, Paris, 1955; English version, *Tolerance and the Reformation*, London, 1960

p. 303   *The Booke of Quinte Essence*, ed. F. J. Furnivall, London, 1866, 1889, pp. 1, 3–4, 25

p. 304   *Dicts*, ed. C. F. Buhler, London, 1941 and 1961, pp. 8–11

pp. 304–5   GREENE: Cambridge University Library Ff.412 and 13; other MSS specified, Cambridge University Library II.1.13 and BM Arundel 162; other examples, Cambridge, Mm.3.11, Ff.6.50 and BM Sloane 1933 (from Walsingham Priory), Royal 12.C.XV, Cotton App. VI, Arundel 115. Arab science contributed to a wider range of subjects, Royal 15.B.IV and Cotton Vespasian B.X. The collection in Lansdowne 209 was perhaps made for antiquarian (rather than, as in Greene's case, scientific) reasons

p. 306   DISCIPLINA: pp. 105–6n, above. G. Sercambi, *Novelle*, ed. A. d'Ancona, Bologna, 1871 and 1882; DON JUAN MANUEL: ed. F. J. Sanchez Canton, Madrid, 1920. W. Painter, *Palace of Pleasure*, London, 1566–7; Marguerite de Navarre, *L'Heptaméron*, ed. M. Francois, Paris, 1906. A. Galland, *Mille et Une Nuits*, ed. G. Picard, Paris, 1960

p. 307   CHARLEMAGNE: *The Sowdone of Babylone*, ed. E. Hausknecht, London, 1861. ARABIC STUDIES: probably no one would question that the most interesting as well as the fullest mediaeval discussion of education, study of Arabic, and Crusade in conjunction, is P. Dubois, *De recuperatione Terre Sancte*, ed. Ch.–V. Langlois, Paris, 1891 (also English translation with introduction by W. Brandt (Records of Civilisation No. 51), *The Recovery &c.*, New York, 1956. CLUNY: see A. Cutler, "Who was the Monk of France?" and the important articles, D. M. Dunlop, "A Christian Mission to Muslim Spain", and Abdelmagid Turki, "La Lettre du Moine de France", all in *Al-Andalus*, respectively vols XVII, XXVIII and XXXI, 1952, 1963 and 1966. For Renaissance Arabic Studies, see K. H. Dannenfeldt, "The Renaissance, Humanists and the Knowledge of Arabic" in *Studies in the Renaissance*, vol. 2, New York, 1955. Franciscan Studia, Gol. vol. 13, ed. P. A. Kelinhaus, Quaracchi, 1930; Dominicans, A. Cortabarria, "L'Étude des langues" in Mélanges de l'Institut Dominicain d'Études Orientales, No. 10, Cairo, 1970; papal studium in Paris, CUP, vol. 1, p. 212, No. 180

p. 308   Chaucer, *Canterbury Tales*, Prologue, line 51; Guillaume le Machaut, SOL, Série Historique, vol. 1, 6040–1, cf. P. de Mezières, *Life of St Peter Thomas*, ed. J. Smet, Rome, 1954, text at pp. 128–34. Martoni, *loc. cit.*, p. 587 refers to what is generally called the West harbour, and is roughly South-West, as the Southern, and by implication the East would be the North harbour; cf. Lannoy (below, p. 318n), p. 70. AL-MAHDIYA: Froissart, *Les Chroniques*, ed. K. de Lettenhove, vol. XIV, pp. 218–20, Brussels, 1870–6; Berners' translation, ed. G. C. Macaulay, London, 1930, p. 401. Similarly for Turkish projects, *ed. cit.*, vol. XV, pp. 252, 262 ff., 309 ff., Berners pp. 438–40

p. 309   Guillaume, *loc. cit.*, Chaucer, *loc. cit.*, lines 45–6

p. 310   JAMES I: many details of capitulations (both observed and breached) in *Chronicle of James I*, ed. P. de Gayangos, tr. J. Forster, London, 1883; e.g. chs 121, 184, 251, 254, 283, 295, 330, 361–5, 416–21, 436–50. SARACENUS: *Annales S. Iustinae Patavini*, *s.a.* 1264, MGH Ss. XIX, p. 187

pp. 310–12   Lull, *Vida Coetania, ed. cit.* (Eng. tr.), chs 2, 4, 5, 6, 7. Polemic works, references Daniel, *op. cit.* See also 8.85 above. ST FRANCIS, *Vita*, by Bonaventure, in B. Francisci, *Opera omnia*, ed. v. der Bush, Cologne, 1849

pp. 312–13   TEMPLARS: pp. 246–7 above, and H. C. Lea, *History of the Inquisition in the Middle Ages*, New York, 1906, vol. 3, pp. 256–302; G. Lizerand, *Le Dossier de l'Affaire des Templiers*, vol. 2, p. 92 cf. p. 152; LEPERS: *Registre de Jacques Fournier*, ed. J. Duvernoy, Toulouse, 1964, pp. 135–45; but cf. P. Ponsoye, *L'Islam et le Graal*, Paris, 1957, ch. VI

pp. 313–14   H. C. Lea, *History of the Inquisition in Spain*, New York, 1907, vol. III, bk VIII, ch. II, and *The Moriscos of Spain*, London, 1901; H. Kamen, *The Spanish Inquisition*, London, 1965, reprinted 1968; E. W. Bovill, *The Golden Trade of the Moors*, London, 1958, reprinted 1968, pp. 155, 168; Richelieu, *Mémoires*, vol. 1, Paris, 1907. Cervantes (*Don Quixote*, II.65) only appears ambiguous. F. Braudel, *La Méditerranée et le monde a l'époque de Philippe II*, 2 vols, Paris, 2nd ed., 1966

pp. 314–15   PALESTINE ACCOUNT: Guy de Basainville, in A. and F. Duchesne, *Historiae Francorum Scriptores*, Paris, 1649, V, p. 272; Melrose, MGH, Ss. XXVII, p. 439; Tewkesbury (*s.a.* 1240), *ibid.*, p. 468; *Annales Meneviae et Stratae Floridae*, *ibid.*, *s.a.* 1260, p. 444. CHRONICLER: *Annales S. Iustinae Patavini*, MGH Ss. XIX, pp. 191–2 *s.a.* 1268, cf. *Annales Burtonensibus* MGH Ss. XXVII, pp. 474–5,

Examinatio de Tartaris, p. 474. Further examples in MP. CM, IV, p. 9, V, p. 87, VI, pp. 78–83, 113–15; John of Ypres, *op. cit.*, chs 49, 51, 53

pp. 315–17   Plano Carpini, *et al.*, texts in *Sinica Franciscana*, vol. I *Itinera et Relationes Saeculi XIII et XIV*, ed. A. van den Wyngaert, Quaracchi, 1929 (pp. 45, 244 here quoted), used by Vincent de Beauvais, *Speculum Historiale*, *loc. cit.*, bk 31, ch. 2 ff.; cf. 29, ch. 49ff. ('Nestorian evidence 31.2) and translated in C. Dawson, *The Mongol Mission*, London, 1955, and A. T'Serstevens, *Les Précurseurs de Marco Polo*, Paris, 1959; MARCO POLO: editions most convenient for reference in English translation are Everyman and Penguin. Cf. Jourdain Catalani de Severac, *Mirabilia Descripta*, in H. Cordier, *Les Merveilles de l'Asie*, Paris, 1925. Ivo of Narbonne in Matthew Paris, *op. cit.*, vol. 4, *s.a.* 1243 (pp. 270–7). Ricoldo, *Itinerarius, ed. cit.*, cap. IX– XII cap. pp. 114, 117. Cf. Dubois, *op. cit.*, 25 (p. 18), and Michaud, *op. cit.*, vol. 3, p. 317, et alibi; Joinville, *op. cit.*, 471–92

p. 318   George of Hungary, as *Septemcastrensis*, in Bibliander, *loc. cit.*, *Tractatus de Moribus, Conditionibus et Nequitia Turcorum*. Murad Bey wrote trilingually in Turkish, Latin and Hungarian; the full text of his main work, without title and first called in English *A Treatise on the Mohammedan Religion*, is available only in MS, BM Additional 19894; his praise of the Prophet (*codes supra tres linguas*) is Bodley, Marsh 179. De la Brocquière, *Voyage d'Outremer*, ed. L. D'Aussy in Hakluyt, London, 1811, vol. IV, supplement, p. 487, and T. Wright, *coll. cit.*, p. 327, translation quoted, by Roger l'Estrange, 1680 (reprinted, London, n.d.), p. 32. Another edition of the original, ed. Ch. Schefer, Paris, 1892. There are many textual variants. "A man not of our faith"—"Je escrips cecy affin que il me souviengne que ung homme hors de nostre foy, pour l'onneur de Dieu, m'a faict tant de biens." La Brocquière is the most natural and most generous of travellers. For the end of the fifteenth and early sixteenth centuries there are a number of very interesting Palestine pilgrims, of which perhaps the best are Santo Brasca, *Viaggio in Terra Santa*, ed. A. L. M. Lepschy, Milan, 1966; Francesco Suriano, *Il trattado di terra Santa*, ed. G. Golubovich, Milan, 1900 (Suriano was at one time prior in Jerusalem and was resident for some time in the Near East); Bernhard von Breydenbach, *Opus Transmarine Peregrinationis*, Mainz, 1486; Pietro Casola,

English translation *Pilgrimage to Jerusalem* by M. M.
Newett, Manchester, 1907; F. Fabri, *Evagatorium in
Peregrinationem*, ed. C. D. Hassler, Stuttgart, 1843-9,
with summary and commentary in *Jerusalem Journey*, by
H. F. M. Prescott, London, 1954; and Ludovico da
Varthema, *Travels*, London, Hakluyt Society, 1863, ed.
and tr. J. W. Jones and G. F. Badger. For the late mid-
fifteenth century, Roberto da Sanseverino, *Viaggio in
Terra Santa* ed. G. Maruffi and Quodam *Itinerarium Terre
Sancte Promissionis* auctore anonymo ordinis fratum
minoram religioso, ROL, vol. 12 (1909-11), Bologna,
1888. Earlier again, and contemporary with La Brocquière, are Guillebert de Lannoy, *Voyages et Ambassades*,
ed. C.-P. Serrure, Mons, 1840, and Nompar de Gaumont,
Voyaige d'Oultremer, ed. de la Grange, Paris, 1858

pp. 321-2 The present writer's fuller views on imperialism in
relation to the Muslim World, Daniel, *Islam, Europe
and Empire*, Edinburgh, 1966. The transition from the
'colonialism' of the Crusades to true colonialism is marked
by Dubois, *op. cit.*, especially sections 3-4, 18-22, 63,
67-70 and 110 *et seq.* with his detailed project for conquest and settlement, including planned intermarriage,
under French leadership

Bibliographical note

The history of ideas, sentiments and attitudes requires the use of old-fashioned source material—straight narratives, such as chronicles and travels—even more than of contemporary documents. However inaccurate or mistaken an author may be about the facts he alleges, he cannot but indicate truly his own reactions to them, if we can only read him correctly. I have made extensive use of the great nineteenth-century collections, the *Monumenta Germaniae Historica*, Migne's *Patrologia Latina*, the Rolls Series and the *Recueil des Historiens des Croisades* in particular, as well as other valuable collections of more specialized character, such as the publications of the Société de l'Orient Latin and Golubovich's *Biblioteca Bio-bibliografica*. Certain collections of documents were relevant to my purpose, notably Héfélé's *Conciles*, de Mas Latrie's *Traités* and Huillard-Bréholles' *Historia Diplomatica*. Individual classics exist in more than one edition, and often in translation too; for example, Liutprand of Cremona, the *Poema del Cid*, the *Chanson de Roland*, the *Gesta Francorum*, Joinville. In the notes I have indicated the sources I have actually used, with all the care possible; I hope that there is no serious mistake.

Wherever I depended on a secondary authority, I have stated it in the notes, and, where I was conscious of additional obligation, in the main text as well. Of course it is impossible to acknowledge, or even to remember, all the books that contribute, many only remotely, to the formation of ideas. A few books are relevant in general, rather than at specific points. For Arab rulers I have relied on C. E. Bosworth, *The Islamic Dynasties* (Edinburgh, 1967). For further reading on the theme of Chapter 7 see F. R. C. Bagley's introduction to a translation of *Ghazali's Book of Counsel for Kings* (London, 1964). For the Arab background to the mediaeval travellers in Cairo in Chapter 8, see Stanley Lane-Poole's *History of Egypt in the Middle Ages* (London, 1901). For the relation of Muslim and Christian thought, the great study in comparative theology, *Introduction à la Théologie Musulmane*, by L. Gardet and M.-M. (G. C.) Anawati (Paris, 1948) is cardinal. In the field of Muslim–Christian relations more and more is being written; I mention the classic *The Preaching of Islam* by Thomas Arnold (London, 1929), and two recent books, Y. Moubarac, *Pentalogie Islamo-Chrétienne* (5 vols, Beirut, 1972–3), which ranges over the whole field, from the

Quran to the situation of Arabs at the present day, and W. M. Watt, *The Influence of Islam on Mediaeval Europe* (Edinburgh, 1972) which is a short summary of the state of scholarship in this subject. For the holy war, M. Khadduri's *War and Peace in the Law of Islam* (Baltimore, 1955) is illuminating. When I finished my book, I had not seen D. M. Dunlop's *Arab Civilization to AD 1500* (in the same series), which gives a parallel history of Arab culture. Other recent books which relate somewhat to my subject are J. Riley-Smith's *The Feudal Nobility and the Kingdom of Jerusalem* (London, 1973) and J. Prawer's *Histoire du Royaume Latin de Jérusalem* (Paris, 1969–70). For a fuller examination of the subject of my Chapter 2, see E. P. Colbert, *The Martyrs of Cordoba* (Washington, 1962).

I have not supplied a full bibliography, even when citing some secondary authorities, but the sources I have used are many, and the first index following should make it easier and quicker to refer to the bibliographical entries in the Notes.

Bibliographical references

Quick reference index to main bibliographical entries under page numbers used in the notes

Abu Mashar, 270–2
Adefonsi Cronica, 85
Adelard, 265–8
Ademar, 122
Alan of Lille, 235
Albert of Aix, 122
Albert the Great, 277–8
Alcuin, 20
Alexander du Pont, 232–3
Alexander Telesinus, 148
Alfonso X (1), 261
    (2), 281
Alvaro, 23
d'Alverny, M. T. (1), 234
    (2), 238
    (3), 278
Amari, M., 146–7
Ammianus, 53
Anastasius, 233
Angelo di Spoleto, 222–4
Annales de Burton, 246
Annales Cavenses, 142
Annales Fuldenses, 50
Annales Meneviae, 314–15
Annales Mettenses, 51
Annales Regni Francorum, 50
Annales S. Iustinae Patavini, 154–5
Annales Siculi, 153–4
Annales Veronenses, 155
Anseis, 98–100
Antioche, chanson, 131–2
Arnald of Villanova, 293–5
Arnobius, 31–2
Arnold of Lubeck, 213–15
Asad, T., 169–70
Atiya, A. A., 253–4
Augustine of Hippo, 282–3

Bacon, Roger (1), 171–2
    (2, 3), 242
Bartholomew of Neocastro, 198–9
Basainville, 314–15
Baudry, 121–2
Bede (1), 11
    (2), 263
Bédier, 96–7
Beha ad-Din, 185–7
Benedict of Monte Soracte, 57–8
Benedict of Peterborough (1), 185–7
    (2), 195–6
Bernard of Clairvaux, 251–2
Bernard Sylvester, 273–4
Bernard the Wise, 60–1
Bertrand de Born, 103–4

Bibliander, 234
Bodin, 302–3
Bonatti, 289–90
Bonaventura, 310–12
Bongars, 204–6
Boniface, 16
Bovill, E. W., 313–14
Braudel, F., 313–14
Brevis Historia Messanae, 144–6
von Breydenbach, 318
la Brocquière, 318
Burchard, 211

Cachia, P., 101–3
Cafaro, 116
canons, 256–9
Carmelite Chronicle, 224–5
Caroli Magni Historia, 98–100
Casola, 318
Cetalani de Sévérac, 315–17
de Caumont, 318
Carvantes, 313–14
Chartularium (CUP), 246–7
Chaucer, 308
Chronicon Novaliciense, 61
Chronicon Salernitanum, 56–7
Cid, poema del, 81–2
Codice dei Saraceni, 156
Coggeshall, 106–7
Cohn, N., 131–2
Comnena, Anna, 282–3
Contrarietas, 238–9
Correspondance fausse, 200–1
Cortabarria, A. 307
Couronnement de Louis, 58–9
Crombie, A. C., 279
Cumont, F., 288–9
Cutler, A., 307

Dandalo, 217–18
Daniel, N. (1), 115–16
    (2), 321–2
Daniel of Morley, 272–3
Dannenfeldt, K. H., 307
Dante, 279
Dawson, C., 315–17
Diceto, 158–9
Dictionnaire de théologie, 251–2
Dicts and Sayings, 304
Dozy, R. (1), 47
    (2), 81
Dubois, 253–4
Duby, G., 104–5

Duin, J. J., 277–8
Dunlop, D. M., 307

Eginhard, 51
Elcock, W. D., 101
Embrico, 232–3
Erchembert, 56–7
Ernoul, 137–8
Eulogio, 23
de Expugnatione libellus, 185–7
de Expugnatione Lyxbonensi, 87

Faber, 318
al-Farabi, 170–1
Festugière, A. J., 288–9
Fidenzio, 188–9
Flamenca, roman de, 190
Fournier, 312–13
Franciscan miscellanea, 222–4
Fredegar, 51
Froissart, 308
Fulcher, 115–16

Galland, 306
Galvanus de Levanto, 253–4
Garcia Gomez, E., 101
Garufi, G. A., 142–3
de Generatione, 234
George of Hungary, 318
Gerald of Wales, 107–9
Gerard of Cremona, 272–3
Gerbert, 263
Gesta Francorum, 114–15
Gesta Ludovici, 126–7
Gesta Trevirensium, 122–3
Gestes des Chiprois, 199–200
al-Ghazali, 296–7
Gibbon, 119
Glaber, 56–7
Golubovich, 188–90
Gormont, 98–100
Grabmann, 277–8
Grégoire, 96–7
Gregory VII, 250–1
Gregory IX, 222
Gregory of Tours, 18–19
Guibert, 114–15
Guillaume le Machaut, 308
Guillaume le Maréchal, 170–1
Gundisalvo, 272

el-Hajji, 64–9
Haskins, 105–6
Héfélé and Leclercq, 13–14
von Heyd, 219–20
Hincmar, 58–9
Holcot, 255
Honorius III, 222
Hoveden, 107–9
Hreimskringla Saga, 140–1
Hugh of Falco, 142–3
Hugh of Fleury, 232–3

Hugh of Santalla, 268
Huillard-Bréholles, 153–4
Humbert, 248–9

Ibn Butlan, 273–4
Ibn Ishaq, 239–40
Ibn Jubayr, 147
Ibn an-Nafis, 187–8
Ibn Ridwan, 296–7
Ibn abi Rijal, 288–9
Ibn Sina, 291–2
Ibn al-Wafid, 273–4
Innocent III, 222
Isidore of Beja, 17–18
Isidore of Seville, 263
Itinerarium Regis Ricardi, 182–3
Itinerarium Terre Sancte, 318

James I of Aragon, 310
James of Verona, 224–8
Jeanroy, 101–3
Jérusalem, Conquête de, 131–2
Joachim, 248–9
Jocelin of Brakelond, 273–4
John VIII, 76–7
John of Gorze (life), 64–9
John of Jandun, 300
John of Salisbury (1), 273–4
              (2), 283–4
John of Venice, 57–8
John of Ypres, 209
Joinville, 181–2

Kamen, H., 313–14
Ketton (1), 237–8
       (2), 270–2
       (3), 296–7
al-Kindi, 296–7
al-Kindi, pseudonym, 237–8
Knowles, D., 300
Kritzeck, J., 234

Lamartine, 211–12
Langland, 246
de Lannoy, 318
Latini, Brunetto, 155
Lea, H. C. (1), 312–13
          (2), 313–14
Lecler, J., 302–3
Leff, G., 301
Lemay, R., 269–70
Leo IV, 76
Lévi-Provençal (1), 47
              (2), 101–3
Levison, W., 15–16
Lewis, C. S., 1
Liutprand, 51–2
Ludolf of Sudheim, 224–8
Lull (1), 188–90
     (2), 241–2
     (3), 310–12

Lupus Protospata, 57–8

Macdonald, D. B., 301
Malaterra, 143–4
Mandonnet, 277–8
Mansi, 76
Manuel, Don Juan, 306
Maqrizi, 12
Marcabru, 103–4
Marguerite de Navarre, 306
Mark of Toledo, 296–7
Marti (1) and (2), 242
Martoni, 224–8
de Mas Latrie, 162
Mathew, G. (1) and (2), 168
Mattheo di Giovenazzo, 155
Menendez Pidal (1), 81
    (2), 101–3
Meyer, L. A., 190
de Mezières (1), 215–17
    (2), 308
Michaud, 185–7
Mieli, A., 73–4
Murad Bey, 318
al-Mutanabbi, 170

Nelli, R., 101–3
Nicolas of Cusa, 302–3
Nykl, A. R., 101–3

Odo of Deuil, 196–7
Odoric of Pordenone, 224–8
Orderic Vital, 106–7
Otto of Freising, 155

Paris, G., 185–7
Paris, Matthew, *abbreviations*
Parry, J. J., 101–3
Pascual, Peter, 238–9
de Passagiis, 224–8
Paul of Antioch, 238–9
Pegolotti, 219–20
Penaforte (1), 256–9
    (2), 260
Pérès, H., 101–3
Peter of Alfonso, 237–8
Peter the Deacon (1), 58–9
    (2), 119
Peter de Pennis, 224–8
Peter Thomas, 246
Peter the Venerable, 13–14
Peter Vidal, 103–4
Philip of Tripoli, 171–2
Pisano, Leonardo, 295
Pius II, 302–3
Plano Carpini, 315–17
Pliny, 53
Ponsoye, P., 312–13
Postel, 302–3
Primera Cronica General, 84

Quadruplex reprobatio, 238–9

Quinte Essence, Booke of, 303
Qusta ibn Luqa, 279

Raymund of Aguilers, 128
Raymund of Marseilles, 269–70
de' Reboldi, Antonio, 224–8
Renan, 277–8
Richard of Devizes, 183
Richelieu, 213–14
Richer, 33–4
Ricoldo (1), 198–9
    (2), 199–200
    (3), 238–9
    (4), 243–5
Robert de Monte, 106–7
Robert of Rheims, 119
Robert of S. Giovanni, 142–3
Roderici Historia, 84
Roderick of Toledo, 89–90
Roger of Hereford, 282–3
Roger of Wendover, 106–7
Roland, 96–7
Rolandin of Padua, 155
Romuald, 141–2
Roux, J. P., 101–3
Runciman, S., 120
Ryccardus de S. Germano, 136–7

Salimbene, 88
Sanserverino, 318
Santo Brasca, 318
Sanudo, 222
Sarton, G., 270–2
de Scandalis collectio, 253–4
science MSS, 304–5
Scot, Michael (1), 162
    (2), 284–8
Scotus, 300
Secreta Secretorum, 171–2
Sercambi, 306
Setton, K. M., 120
Sicard, 136–7
Sigebert, 232–3
Siger, 277–8
Simon Semeon, 224–8
Socrates, 53
Southern, R. W., 232–3
Sowdone of Babylone, 306
Sozomen, 53
van Steenberghen, F., 277–8
Stephen of Antioch, 264
Stern, S. M., 101
Strabo, 57–8
Summula quaedam brevis, 247
Suriano, 318
Syrus the monk, 62–4

Talleyrand, 112
Tannery, 263
Templar documents, 312–13
Thietmar of Walbeck, 57–8
Thietmar, magister, 224–8

Thomas Aquinas, 279
Thomas of Bethlehem, 204–6
Thomas of Froimont, 199
Thorndyke, L., 270–2
Throop, P. A., 253–4
T'Sterstevens, A., 315–17
Turki, A., 307
Turpin, 98–100

Urban II, 115–16
Usama, 195–6
Uthred, 246

Vansteenkiste, C., 277–8
Villani, Giovanni, 209
Villani, Matteo, 228
Vincent of Beauvais, 233
Vitodurani, 222–4

Vitry (1), 202–3
   (2), 204–6

Walter the Chancellor, 202
Walter of Compiègne, 232–3
Waltz, J., 47
Watt, W. M., 101–3
White, L. (1), 8–9
   (2), 58–9
William of Adam, 220–2
William of Apulia, 148
William of Auvergne, 240–1
William of Malmesbury, 179–80
William of Rubruk, 315–17
William of Tripoli, 187–8
William of Tyre, 115–16
Willibald, 15–16
Willibrand, 224–8
Wolfram, 105–6
Wurzburg, 115–16

Index

Aachen, 50–1
Abana, river, 274
Abbasids, 7, 21, 75
Abdalla, a Cordovan, 23; another, 35; a founder of Salerno, 74; a general, 72; a Spanish envoy, 50; of Lucera, 155
Abd al-Aziz, nephew of Abu Zakariya, 162
Abd al-Mumin, the Almohad, 92, 148
Abd ar-Rahman I ad-Dakhil, ruler of Spain, 17
Abd ar-Rahman III an-Nasir, first Umayyad Caliph in Spain, 50, 64–70
Abd ar-Rahman, Spanish Arab commander, invader of France, 51
Abelard, Peter, 274
Abenguefit, see Ibn al-Wafid
Abenragel, see Ibn Abi Rijal
Ablaudius the Babylonian, 268
Abraham the Patriarch, 26, 27, 122, 240, 249, 255, 280
Abraham of Tunis, see Ibrahim
Abu Abdalla ibn Abd al-Aziz, of Tunis, 220
Abubacer, see Ibn Tufayl
Abu Bakr as-Siddiq, first caliph, 40
Abu'l Wafa Mubashshir ibn Fatik al-Qaid, 303
Abu Mashar, Jafar ibn Muhammad ibn Umar al-Balkhi, 268, 270, 271, 274, 279
Abu Yaqub Yusuf, Almohad caliph, 108
Abu Yusuf Yaqub al-Mansur, Almohad caliph, 108
Abu Zakariya Yahya I, Hafsid ruler of Tunis, 162, 219
Acqui (Italy), 59
Acre (Palestine), 181; Bishop of, 204; hospital, 186; fall of, 112, 198, 208–9, 215–16, 261, see also illustration; Kingdom of (Jerusalem), 172
Acrobats, 163–4n and illustration
Adalbero, Archdeacon of Metz, 197
Adam, William of, see William
Adela, Countess of Blois, 100
Adelard of Bath, 146, 265–8, 272, 283
Adhemar of Chabannes, historian, 122, 141
Adhemar of Monteil, Bishop of Le Puy, 128, 131
al-Adid, Fatimid caliph, 212; see also Dedication
al-Adil, al Malik, Sayf ad-Din, 162, 183, 185, 186

Adolf, a Cordovan, 35
adoptionism, 20, 50
Aeneid, 34
al-Afdal, Abu al Qasim Shahinshah, Fatimid wazir, 126
Afflacius, John 263
Africa, North, 6–11 passim, 58, 165, 199, 219, 249, 273, 312; attacks and wars, 60, 71–2, 143; ostriches in, 162; see also Ifriqiya, and illustration
Agarene, 53, 73, 76, 85, 271
Aghlabids, 52, 53, 55, 72
Agrigento (Sicily), 145
Aguilers, see Raymund
Ahmed ibn Marwan of Antioch, 193
Aigoland, character in the fictional Turpinus, 99, 100
Ain Jalut, battle of, 315
Alan of Lille, theologian, 235
Alarcos, campaign, 107
Albelda, (Spain), 86
Albert of Aix, 122–4 passim, 135, 137, 138, 195, 197–8
Albert the Great, St, 144, 278
Albi (France), 36
Albigensians, 246
Alchandrinus, 285
Alcobaza, massacre, 107
Alcuin, Abbot of Tours, 20, 50
Aldhelm, Bishop of Sherborne, 19, 34
Aleppo, 127, 285
Alexander the Great, 17, 115, 119, 171, 190, 276
Alexander II, Pope, 146
Alexander, an Alexandrian magician, 287
Alexandria, 186, 214, 224–7, 256, 259, 285, 308–9, 308n
Alfonso II, the Chaste, King of Asturias, 86
Alfonso VI, King of Castile, 85, 89–90, 97, 101, 106, 237; see also Pedro
Alfonso VII, King of Castile, 85, 91, 94, 238, 264
Alfonso X, the Learned, King of Castile, 88, 281, 288
Alfonso a Spina, polemist, 302
Alfred, King of Wessex, 55
Algazel, see al-Ghazali
Algiers, 317
algorism, 263 and n, 296; see also al-Khwarizmi
Alhazen, see Ibn al-Haytham
Ali ibn Abi Talib, fourth caliph, 244

Ali ibn al-Abbas al-Majusi, 144, 199, 264, 277, 290, 291
Ali ibn Yusuf ibn Tashufin, 89, 91
Almagest, 147, 272, 275, 277
Almogovars, *155n*
Almohads, 80, 88, 91–3, 101, 108–9, 148, 162, 165
Almoravids, 80–2 *passim*, 85, 88–92, 94, 101, 104
Alodia, a Cordovan, 35
Alvaro of Cordova, 26, 29, 30; attacks Islam, 41–4; his character, 38–9; his concept of Islam, 39; hates *muezzin*, 41; later parallels, 67, 311; his Latinism, 32, 34; military terminology, 34; opposes compromise, 32–3, 38, 46
d'Alverny, M. T., 238
Amalarius of Metz, liturgiologist, 20
Amalric I, King of Jerusalem, 137, 177–178, 183, 195, 203, 211
America, 323
amirez, 59, 109
Amirulmuminin, 18, 89, 109, 222
Anastasius Bibliotecarius, antipope, 74, 118, 233
al-Andalus, 317; *see also* Andalusia
Andalusia, 309, 310; *see also* al-Andalus
Andreas Capellanus, courtly author, 105
Andres, Juan, polemist, 302
Andrew, St, 127
Angevins, 156, 180; *and see* rulers by name: Fulk; Charles; Henry
Anglo-Saxons, 11–12, 16–18 *passim*, 21; *see also* English
animals, study of, 162, 285; camels a cultural survival, 155
Annales Siculi, 154
Annals of the Frankish Kingdom, 51
Anseis de Cartage, poem, 100
Antioch, 118, 127, 128, 197; siege of, 116, 134, 192–4 *passim*; prince of, 210; *see also* Poème d'Antioche
Antioch, *see* Stephen
Antioche, poem, 96, 121, 127, 131, 172, 236
Antiochene, 130
Anubis, ancient Egyptian god, 268
Apollin, supposed idol, 95, 132, 235–6
Apulia, 52, 58, 275; Apulians, 155
al-Aqsa, mosque, 134–6, 157
Aquinas, St Thomas, 277–9 *passim*
Aquitaine, *see* Eudo; William
Arabia, 11, 18, 142, 239–43, 273, 315
Arabian Nights, 200, 306–7
Arab history, 2, 4–10, 16–17, 88–95, 239–42, 249 and *n*, 319–26
Arabic calendar, 267, 270, 284, 305
Arabic culture, 8; in Cordoba, 33–4, 38; in the East, 205, 213–14, 321; in 8th and 9th centuries, 17–22; influence on Europe, *see* Arabs, Science; mixed, 36,

101; not tolerated in Europe, *see* Arabs, Chaldeans
Arabic language and literature: European study of, 199, 307 and *n*; failure in East to translate, 199, 201; learned by Lull, 310; in Spain, 33–4, 38, 84, 90, 101–5; spoken in the East, 199, 213; style in reported speech, authentic, 72 73, not authentic, 200–1; titles, confused, 75; translations of, 264–77, 281, 290–1, 296–8; treaties written in, 219; used in Sicily, 148
Arabs: as Agarenes and Saracens, 53, 76, 85, 213, 216, 242, 266, 271; character and manner, of, 91, 178–9, 199–200, 215–17 and *n*; chivalry and chivalric ideals of, 167–72, 174–6; Christian, *see* Christians; equated with ancient pagans, 33–4, 94–8 *passim*, 235–7, 269, 274; expansion of, 6–8; and Frederick II, *see* Frederick II; influence on Europe, 5, 8, 80, 228, 320; and Mongols, 218, 314; "pagan" used to denote, 66, 78, 115, 142, 146, 149, 237; relations with Europe, 2, 62–3, 70–5 *passim*, 195–6, 254–62, 320–2; alliances and treatises, 51–3 *passim*, 62, 75–8 *passim*, 193, 219–20, 317; debauch Europeans, 72, 73, 83, 150, 155; debauched by Europeans, 83, 124, 131, 149, 314; devastate Europe, 56–60 *passim*, 155, 163, 189, 209, 248–249; devastated by Europeans, 82, 85, 88, 133–6, 149, 151–2, 156, 308; love of hunting shared, 195–6; as masters, 219; not tolerated in Europe, 151, 153–7, 254–62, 309–10, 312–14, 321; prisoners, 142, 186, 189
sexual relations with Europeans: debauchery, 149–50, 314; rapes, 72–3, 124, 131, 155, 189, 197; unions, 89, 101, 198, 257
rulers of, 128–9, 184–91; and Turks, 5, 130, 317–18
Aragon, 219, 313; *see also* James I
Argemirus, a Cordovan, 36
Arianism, 242, 248, 249
Aristippus, Henry, 147, 150
aristocracy, and hunting, 195 and *n*
Aristotle, 3, 162, 171, 190, 269, 272–81 *passim*, 285, 300, 304; Aristotelian, 277
Armenia, King of, 137, 315; Armenians, 137, 192, 201, 205
Arnald of Villanova, 293–5, 325
Arnobius, theologian, 34
Arnulf, Frankish leader, 55
Arrian, historian, 34
Arsuf (Palestine), 194
Artemia, a Cordovan, 35
Arthur of Britain, 119
Asad, T., 169 *n*
Ascelin or Anselm, Dominican, 315

Index

Ascalon (Palestine), 133, 194
asceticism, 12, 16; as death wish, 35, 37, 38
al-Ashari, Abu al-Hasan Ali ibn Ismail, 20
al-Ashraf, Salah ad-Din Khalil, son of Qalaun, 200–1, 209n; *see also* illustration
Asia Minor, 103
Assassins, 195, 214; Old Man of the Mountain (Sheikh el-Jebel), 190
Assyrians, supposed, 92, 201
Astalius, name associated with Hermes (Thot), 271
astrology, astrologers, 107–8, 169, 177, 208, 243, 276, 282–90, 304–5; defended, 282, 285–6, 289–90; defined, 283–4, 286–7; *see also* illustration
astronomy, 269, 271, 275, 281, 282; defined, 283–4, 304–5
Asturias, 86
Athanasius, Bishop and ruler of Naples, 76–8
Athens, 115
Atlas (Athalax), 287–8
Augustine of Canterbury, St, 10, 14, 235
Augustine of Hippo, St, 38, 279, 283, 300; Augustinian, 277; *City of God* of 30
St Augustine's Abbey, 232
Augustinians, 228
Aurea, a Cordovan, 35
Aurelius, a Cordovan, 35
Auxerre, wine of, 316
Avars, 97
Avempace, *see* Ibn Bajja
Avenzoar, *see* Ibn Zuhr
Averroes, *see* Ibn Rushd
Averroism, alleged, 247, 274, 278–9, 284; Averroes hardly Averroist, 276; said invented by Aquinas, 277; anti-papal, 300
Avicebron, *see* Ibn Jabirul
Avicenna, *see* Ibn Sina
Avignon, 51
awqaf, 216
Ayyubids, 167, 183, 184, 212 and n, 315
Azaz (Syria), 193

Babylon, in Egypt, 56, 75, 118, 141–3 *passim*, 167, 211, 214, 226 and 56–7n; in Mesopotamia, 274; (Babylonia), 305
Babylonians, 288; supposed, 201
Bacon, Roger, 144, 171, 243, 276, 279–281, 284, 325
Baghdad, 6, 167, 185, 209, 215, 216, 245
Bahira, monk in Muslim tradition, 40
Bairen, battle of, 84
Bait ad-Din, 212
Baktashiya, sufis, 301

Baldwin I, King of Jerusalem, 112, 117, 128, 172–5, 180, 193, 194
Baldwin II, King of Jerusalem, 175
Baldwin III, King of Jerusalem, 175–7, 183
Baldwin IV, King of Jerusalem, the Leper, 173, 179; *and see Dedication*
Baldwin d'Ibelin, 213
Balearics, 60, 113, 300; Majorca, 219
Balian d'Ibelin, 186
Balthasar, fictional sultan, 201
al-Bara (Syria), 134
barbari, 58, 61, 73, 115, 323–4; Latins barbarians, 204; not barbarians, 212
Barbary Coast, 196, 285, 303, 309; *see also* Africa, North, and places by name
Barbastro (Spain), 83, 101
Barcelona, 51
Bari, 57, 60, 61
basmala, 200, 220, 296
Basques, 96
al-Battani, Abu Abdalla Muhammad ibn Jabir, al Harrani, 276
Baudry of Borgeuil, 121
Baybars al-Bunduqdari, ez-Zahir, 5, 187–8, 189, 208, 239, 315
Becket, Thomas, 199
Bede, St, 12, 19, 263, 279
Bédier, J., 97
Bedouin, 53, 213
Beghards, 301
Behemoth, 43
Benedict, Monk of Monte Soracte, 57, 58
Benedict, St, 59
Benedictines, 232; *see also* Monte Cassino and other houses by name
Benevento (Italy), 56, 58, 77
Berbers, 7, 22, 109, 140, 145, 148, 242; invasions of, 80, 82, 88
Berengar, theologian, 144
Berengaria, Queen of Castile, 85
Bernard, the king's spy, 199
Bernard the Wise, monk of St Michel, 60–1
Bernard of Clairvaux, 112, 147, 238, 252–3, 274
Bernard Sylvester, 274
Beverley, *see* Margaret
Bijaya (Algeria) 223, 250, 312
Bilbais (Egypt), 195
Birinus, Bishop of Dorchester, 10
al-Biruni, Abu Rayhan Muhammad ibn Ahmed, 21, 268
al-Bitruji, Nur ad-Din Abu Ishaq al-Ishbili, 277
Bodin, Jean, 302
Boethius, 288, 300
Boetius of Dacia, 278
Bohemund I, of Taranto, prince of Antioch, 112, 114, 116, 131, 134, 136, 193, 201

Boldon, see Uthred
Bonaparte, General (Napoleon I), 2
Bonatti, Guido, of Forli, 289–90 (and *n*),
    293, 325
Bone (Buna, Algeria), 165, 223
Boniface (Wynfrith), St, 16
Boniface, Count, 60
Borgueil, see Bandry
Bouillon, see Godfrey
boycott, see commerce
Bramidonie, character in *Roland*, 96, 100
Brethren of the Free Spirit, 301
Bretons, 19, 130
Britons, 18–9, 155, 204; Britain, 55
Brunetto Latini, 240, 284
al-Bukharo, Islamic traditionist, 239
Bulgars, 221
Buna, see Bone
Burgundians, 8, 318 and *n*
Bury St Edmunds, Abbot of (Sampson),
    274
Byzantines, Byzantium, 7–9 *passim*, 22,
    50–1, 126, 165, 173, 323; astrology in,
    283; in central Mediterranean, 50, 72,
    76–8 *passim* 140; culture of, 12, 17, 64,
    152; cultural influence of, 104, 146,
    264, 320; and Latins, 114, 124, 192;
    in war with Arabs, 52, 58

Cadi, 24–5, 27–30, 34, 37, 44, 45, 136,
    223, 312
Cadwalla, King of Gwynnedd, 18
Caesarea (Palestine), 116, 133, 175; *and
    see* Hugh
Caffaro, Genoese historian, 116, 172
Cairo, 118, 199, 214, 224–8; called
    Masr, 211; Cairene, 182; *and see*
    Babylon, Fustat
Calabria, 52, 56, 58
Calatabiano, see Robert
Calendar, Muslim, 267, 270, 284, 305;
    Christian, 18–19
Caliph, 49, 65–9, 75, 185; *and see*
    Abbasids, Fatimids, Umayyads and
    individuals by name
Calistus II, Pope, 89
Calvin, John, Reformer, 325
Canaan, supposed descendant of Ham,
    287; Canaanites, supposed, 97
canon law, 254–62, 321
Canterbury, 11; *and see* archbishops by
    name
Canute, King of England, 13
Caractacus, British King, 211
Cardiganshire, 315
Carmelites, 224
Carolingians, 6, 20–1, 59
Carthage, Carthaginians, 6, 53, 56, 60,
    100; *see also* Africa, North, *and
    Anseis*
Caserta, see Richard
Castile, 313; *see also* kings by name

Castilian, 106
Catalan, 103, 106, 310
Catalani, Jordan, of Sévérac, 316
Catalonia, 107, 219, 313; Catalans, 162,
    312
Catania (Sicily), 150
Cato, 34
Celtic, 18, 104
"Chaldeans", 143, 155, 268, 269, 271,
    274, 280; 'Chaldean', used for 'Arabic',
    32, 34, 86
Chansons de Geste, 95–100; do not
    exclude romance, 100–1; poetic cycle,
    235, 307; *see also* poems by name
Charlemagne, Emperor, 20, 50–1, 54,
    75, 96, 98–100 *passim*, 119, 170, 190;
    coronation of, 6, 55
Charles I, of Anjou, King of Sicily, 143,
    156, 166, 291
Charles II, of Salerno, King of Sicily,
    156
Charles Martel, 7, 8, 51, 60
Charles the Bald, I, King of France, and
    II, Emperor, 77
Chartres, 130
Chatillon, see Raynald
Chaucer, Geoffrey, 307; *Canterbury
    Tales*, 306; Knight's Tale, 229, 308–9;
    Sir Topaz, 236
chess, 281
Childeric III, King of the Franks, 7
China, 6, 11
Chiriaco (Italy), 57
chivalry, 167–72, 177–9, 180–6 *passim*, 190
Christ Jesus, 130, 157, 269, 283;
    Christian attitudes to divinity of, 23,
    49; Christian polemic can be turned
    against, 231; Christian public
    confession of, 23, 47; and holy war,
    84, 99, 104, 120, 249; Islamic respect
    for, based on Quran, 41, 64, 216, 247;
    as Prophet, 63, 236; as son of Mary,
    72, 75; supposed blasphemed, 310–11;
    see also martyrdom
Christians, Christianity: Arab, 18, 118,
    194, 207, 209, 214, 235, and Latins,
    114–15, 138, 168, 205, their rites,
    204–5, 226–7, 244–5, 310; canon law
    and Islam, 254–60; despised by
    Muslims, 188–9; as Europeans, 100,
    248, 323; heretical movements, 246–7;
    and Islam, 10–17, 41, 179, Ch. 9; lose
    Africa and Asia, 113, 249; under
    Muslim rule, 13–14, 80, 214, 223, 250,
    255, 314, 321; orthodoxy of, 245–6,
    248, 297, 299; and pilgrimage, 15, 16;
    shrines shared in Cairo, 12, 214, 226;
    see also Crusades; martyrdom;
    pilgrimage; prisoners; polemic;
    toleration
churches, turned into mosques, *see*
    mosques

Index

Cicero, 34, 279, 281, 283
Cid, el (Ruy Diaz of Bivar), 81–2, 84–5, 89, 95, 325; the poem, 81–2, 103
Cirencester, 100
Cistercians, in Spain, 107; *see also* St Bernard
civilization, shared; 5–10, 184, 216, 299, 320, 323–5; in astrology, 288, 290; in courtly ideals, Ch. 7 *passim*, 190–1; in learning, 279–82, 297–8, 303–5; in literary themes, 21, 89, 100–6, 306–7; in magic, 209, 286; in medicine, 92–5, 290–5, 320; in Mediterranean, 49–50, 70; in methods of war, 72–3, 82, 85–6, 99, 107, 136–9, 209–10, 248–62 *passim*, 322–4, *and see* loot; in morals, 75, 145, 186–9, 194, 215, 230; in music, 73–4, 83, 101; in mysticism, 300–1; in philosophy, 272–4, 275–8, 280, 300; in religion, 12–16, 20–1, 41, 63, 75, 208–9, 231, 247, 251; in social life, 83, 147–51, 175, 190, 213, 288–9, 32ı
Civita Vecchia (Italy), 58
Clement V, Pope, 217, 258, 259
Clermont, 111
Clonmel (Ireland), 228
Cluny, 122, 324*n*
Coggeshall, Ralph of, 107
Cologne, 122; *and see* Raimband
colonization, 59, 130, 137–8, 201, 220, 299; Pullani, 206; decolonization, 218; proposals, 321–2*n*; *see also* imperialism
commerce: European trade with Arabs, 9, 112, 207, 208, 218–21, 229, 324, with Far East, 316; in Fatimid Egypt, 214; Frederick II and, 164; link with arithmetic, 296; merchant communities in Arab cities, 210, 218–21, 224–5 and *n*, 260, in Latin states, 204; papal boycott of, 164, 219–20 and *n*, 221–2 and *n*, 224, 225, 256, 259–60; regulated by treaties, 162, 219–20; trade and raid, 142–3, 195, 308–9, *see also* illustration; trade in slaves, 9, 74, 220–2, 260; *see also* Italian cities by name; Mediterranean
Comnena, Anna, 283
Compiègne, 50; *see also* Walter
Compostela, 98, 107
Conradin, Hohenstaufen, King of Jerusalem, 155
Constantine, Emperor, donation of, 21
Constantine the African, 143, 144, 263, 264, 290
Constantinople, 7, 10, 50, 249, 317; trade in eunuchs, 74; Emperor of, 124; *see also* Byzantines
contrarietas, 238
conversions, 13; of Christians to Islam, in general, 197, 198–9, 210, 224, 227, 309; individual cases, 33, 117, 196–8

passim, 213, 318; of Muslims to Christianity, in general, 313–14; individual cases, 29, 52, 72–3, 193, 195; recommended by Pope, 154–5, 163; "secret Christians", at Cordova, 27, 35–6; "secret Muslims", at Palermo, 147, 149; Moriscos, 313–14; of Jews to Christianity, 123; Pedro de Alfonso, 106, 237; of Mongols, potentially, 244; Turks supposed converts from Christianity, 130; phrases to describe, 130, 302
Copts, 226–7, 308; Coptic, 114, 226
Cordova, 7, 19, 23–48, 85, 104, 223, 250, 309
Coria (Spain), 85
Corozan, *see* Khorasan
Corsica, 60, 213
Cosmas and Damian, Sts, martyrs, 70
Couronnement de Louis, 59, 236
Crassus, 274
Cremona, *see* Gerard, Liutprand
Cromwell, Oliver, 325
Cronica General, 88–94, 97, 234, 239
Crusaders: behaviour in the East, 130–9, 192–210; behaviour in Europe, 114, 118–24; ideals of, 167–91 *passim*; lack of interest in Arab world, 119, 247–8; lively accounts by, 211; and profit motive, 112, 195
Crusades, 2, 113, 173, 248–9, 254, 323–4; Arab troops used in, 154; Army of, 126–32; Charlemagne no Crusader, 51; the Cid no Crusader, 81–2, 84; compared with *jihad*, 136, 230, 261–2; as defence, 99–100, 104, 115–18, 243, 248–9; development of ideas of, 53–4, 76–81, 83, 85–7, 98–9, 108–24 *passim*, 146, 152, 218, 249–54; and Eastern Christians, 114–15, 138; end of, 209, 217–18, 242, 317–18; and Frederick II, 157–8; law of, 251–62 *passim*, 310 and *n*; leaders of, 125, 171–3 *passim*, 189–90; as martyrdom, 38, 115, 125–7 and *n*, 132; and Pastoureaux, 159, 246; problem of defeat and failure, 100, 207, 209*n*, 215, 217; secular element in, 127, 131–2, 172; in secular verse, 104; warfare of, 133–9; world rule conceived, 183–4; *see also* commerce; pilgrimage; Reconquest; and end-papers, x
Cuarte, battle, 84
Cuenca, (Spain), 89
Cusa, Nicolas of, 302
Cuthbert, archbishop of Canterbury, 16

Daimbert of Pisa, Patriarch of Jerusalem, 116
Damascus, 10, 12, 17, 126, 210, 212, 215, 274; *see also* John, St

Damietta, (Egypt), 163, 213, 228, and
    208–9*n*
Daniel of Morley, 272
Dante, 279
Demetrius, St, 127; the Alexandrian, 287
Demosthenes, 34
Denis van Leeuwen the Carthusian, 302;
    see also Dionysius
Deuil, *see* Odo
Devizes, Richard of, historian, 183
Diana, Roman goddess, 15
Dionysius the Areopagite, pseudo, 280
Disciplina Clericalis, 106, 306
Dominicans, 154, 165, 208, 209, 216,
    244–5, 301, 307, 315, 316
Domnoulos, Shabbetai b. Abraham, of
    Salerno, 74
Donatism, 34
Dorotheus of Sidon, 288, 305
Dorylaeum (Turkey), 126, 131
Dozy, R., 81, 82, 83
Druzes, 141
Drycthelm, monk of Melrose, 12
Duby, G., 105
Duns Scotus, 300

East Anglia, 54; East Angles, 10; *see also*
    Anglo-Saxons
Edirne (Turkey), 317
Edmund the Martyr, St, King of East
    Anglia, 13
Edmund Rich, Archbishop of
    Canterbury, recipient of a letter, 158
Eginhard, historian, 51
Egypt, 2, 8, 167, 249, 317; in ancient
    history, 280, 305; attacked by
    Crusaders, 115, 126, 177, 181, 195,
    239; base for attacks on Italy, 56–8
    passim; beauty of, 225; boycott of, 164,
    219, 221–5 and *n*, 256, 259; delta,
    225, 228; embassy to, 213–14;
    Europeans in, 221, 223 and *n*;
    legendary rents from, 186; Louis IX
    in, 181, 239; in mediaeval
    historiography, 75, 241, 249, 280;
    pilgrim travel in, 61, 224–8, 318*n*;
    symbolic, 273; *see also* Egyptians;
    dynasties and places by name
Egyptians, 22; ancient, in vague sense,
    143, 268, 269, 271, 280, 288; actual,
    129, 181, 212–13; Arabic and, 211; *see
    also* Egypt
Elamites, supposed, 201
Elipandus, Archbishop of Toledo, 20
Elluchasen Elimithar, *see* Ibn Butlan
Elvira, Council of, 34; *see also*
    Recamund
Embassies, 50–1, 64–70, 182, 211–12,
    309; imaginary, 108–9; *see also*
    prisoners (redemption)
Embrico of Mainz, 118, 232, 234
Emich, Count of Leisingen, 123

Emila, a Cordovan, 36
Engels, Frederick, 4
English, 204, 273
Enlightenment, 1, 119
Erasmus, 318
Erchembert, historian, 56, 75
Erigena, John Scotus, 20
Ernoul, historian, 137, 172, 183, 190, 202
eryahiya, 175
Eschenbach, *see* Wolfram
Etheldreda, Queen of Northumbria and
    Abbess of Ely, 12
Ethicus of Istria, philosopher, 280
Ethiopia, 159; Ethiopians, 270
Euclid, 267, 272, 279
Eudo, Duke of Aquitaine, 51
Eulogio of Cordova, Archbishop elect of
    Toledo, source for martyrs' movement,
    26 ff., 325; and Flora, 26–9; and
    Leocritia, 29; execution, 29–30; and
    the *muezzin*, 31, 41; on
    discrimination, 31–2; illiterate in
    Arabic, 32; on moderation, 32–3, 38,
    46–7; and Latinism, 33–4; uses
    military imagery, 34; his praise of
    asceticism, 37; exhortation to death,
    28; his pupils, 36; contradictions in
    character of, 28, 38; concept of Islam,
    39–40, 42–5, 231; reveals opponents'
    views, 46–7; later parallels, 37, 65–7
eunuchs, European–Byzantine–Arab
    trade in, 74; at Sicilian court, 149–50;
    at Fatimid court, 212; in Spanish
    poetry, 105
Euphemius, Byzantine who invited the
    Aghlabids to Sicily, 72
Euphrates, river, 274
Europe, Europeans: Arab invasions, 52–
    62 *passim*; Arabs, relations with, *see*
    Arabs: relations with Europe; Arabs,
    suppressed, in, 144–57, 254–62, 313–
    314; communities, in East, 210, 218–
    220, 260, at Qaraqorum, 315, *see also*
    commerce; identity expressed by
    Christian orthodoxy, 245–6, 248, 297,
    312; imperialism of, 321–2*n*, 322–3,
    324–5; intellectual heritage recovered
    through Arabs, 297–8, 319–20;
    interest in Arabs, 199–200, 307; and
    Mongols, 314–17; and Ottoman
    Turks, 317–18; seapower of, 142–3;
    in service of Arabs, 25–33, 91–2,
    155*n*, 218–19, 220–2*n*, 229, 309, 314,
    318; Spain, attitude to, 105–10;
    unions with Arabs, 83, 89, 100–1, 163,
    197–9; xenophobia in, 113–14, 121,
    122, 124, 168, 323–4; *see also*
    civilization, shared
excommunication, 207, 255, 260; of
    Frederick II, 157
exoticism imputed to the Arab World,
    51, 200–1, 212, 214, 307, 321–2

Index

Falco, Hugh of, historian, 147, 152
al-Farabi, Abu Nasr Muhammad ibn Tarkhan, 21, 170, 243, 272, 279, 281, 305
Faraj ibn Salim, translator, 291
al-Farghani, Abu al-Abbas Ahmed ibn Muhammad ibn Kathir, 21, 273, 276, 305
Fatimids, 55, 115, 122, 126, 141-2, 167, 184, 212
Felix, Bishop of Urgel, 20
Felix, a Cordovan, 36
Ferdinand III, King of Castile, 309
Ferrando, Toledan prisoner, 108
Fibonacci, Leonardo, of Pisa, mathematician, 295, 303
Fidenzio of Padua, 189-90, 207-8
flagellants, 301
Flanders, 51, 159
Fleury, Hugh of, 232-4 *passim*
Flora, a Cordovan, 26-9
fondacos, 220, 224
Fourfold Condemnation, 239, 240
France, 8, 9, 24, 97, 121, 140, 159, 219; (Gaul), 8, 10, 16; leper plot, 312-13; *see also* La Garde—Freinet
Francis of Assisi, St, 310
Franciscans, 165, 207, 209, 223, 227, 301, 307, 315, 316
Franks, Frankish, in original sense, 8, 11, 17, 21, 55, 58, 76; in later sense: and courtly ideal, 171-2, 183, 189-90; in Spain, 81, 83, 95; in East, *see* Crusaders; *see also* Europeans, commerce: merchant communities
Fredegar, historian, continuator of, 53
Frederick I, Emperor, 109, 185, 213
Frederick II, Emperor, 107, 140, 141, 147, 200, 325; and Sicilian Arabs, 153-5; condemned for negotiating, 195; and Crusade, 157-8; and papacy, 158-9, 160-1; and animals, 162, 285; and girls, 163; and Mediterranean, 164, 219; and secularism, 160-1; and Arab rulers, 162-4; reputation, 163-4; and Arab science, 161, 165; and Bonatti, 289; and M. Scot, 101, 285
Fulcher of Chartres, historian, 129, 137; reports Urban II, 113, 118; describes Crusading society, 130, 132, 192; his preference for peace, 117, 133-4; criticizes Christians, 117-18; recounts Adhemar's disbelief in Holy Lance, 128; assesses crusading leaders, 172-3, 180; describes looting and killing, 133, 136, 194
Fulk of Anjou, King of Jerusalem, 180-1, 183
Fustat, 17, 51, 211

Galen, 144, 279
Galician, 106, 281

Galland, Antoine, 200, 306
la Garde-Freinet, 52, 53, 55, 59, 64-5, 73
Garibaldi, Giuseppe, 325
Garigliano, river, 52, 55, 58, 77
Gascony, 121
Geber, *see* Jabir
Genoa, Genoese, 59, 116, 142, 204, 219, 309, 312
gentiles, 34, 115; *gentes*, 142
George, St, 127
George of Hungary, 318
Gerald, *see* Giraldus; Gerald of Lausanne, Patriarch of Jerusalem, 157-8
Gerard of Cremona, 272-3, 276, 282, 292, 325
Gerard of Strasbourg, 213, 217
Gerbert of Aurillac (Sylvester II, Pope), 144, 263, 283, 284; as "Gilbert", 286-7
Germans, 9, 10, 21, 77. 130, 204; Germanic, 104, 105, 128, 169
Gesta Francorum, history, 114-16 *passim*, 120, 126-9 *passim*, 131-2, 134, 137, 172, 197, 201, 236
al-Ghazali (or Ghazzali), Abu Hamid Muhammad, at-Tusi, 21, 243, 272, 276, 278, 291, 297
Gibbon, E., 1, 3, 7, 112, 119, 319
Gideon, 280
Giraldus Cambrensis, 109, 180
Glaber, Rudolf, historian, 63, 64, 122
Godfrey of Bouillon, Advocate of the Holy Sepulchre, 5, 112, 128, 135, 172-4, 193
Gormont, chanson de geste, 100
Gottschalk, monk of Orbais, theologian, 20
Gottschalk, disreputable Crusader, priest, 123
Grail, holy, 105
Granada, 259, 310, 313-14, 317
Greek: language, 22, 161, 264, 276, 291-2; culture, 8, 17, 74, 145-7 *passim*, 200, 279-81 *passim*, 304, 320, in Sicily, 55, 145-7, 152-3, 166; Greek alternative to Arabic, 146-7, 165, 265, 281, 304, 320; history, 144, 305; Orthodox church, 114, 207, 245; Greeks as source of knowledge, 265, 268-72 *passim*, 278, 280, 304, 320; ancient Greeks, 6, 115, 205, 269, 272; Hellenes, 271; mediaeval, 50, 52, 59, 124, 130, 145, 152, 153, 155, 166, 197, 221; Greek monk at fall of Acre, 198; Ibn Rushd a "Greek", 300; *see also* Byzantines, Hellenistic
Greene, R., of Welbe, 304
Grégoire, H., 97
Gregory I, the Great, Pope, 14, 235, 283
Gregory IV, Pope, 58

Gregory VII, Pope, 86, 165, 222, 233, 250–1 and *n*

Gregory IX, Pope, 154, 158, 164, 200, 222, 325; Decretals, 255, 257

Gregory, Bishop of Tours, historian, 19, 55, 249

Grosseteste, Robert, Bishop of Lincoln, 279, 295

Guibert, Abbot of Nogent, historian, 118–24 *passim*, 233, 235

Gundisalvo, Dominic, 272

Hadrian the African, abbot, 19

Hafsids, 143, 162

Hagar, mother of Ismail, 53

al-Hakim, Fatimid caliph, 122, 141

Halim, Arab soldier at Salerno, 71

al-Hallaj, Abu al-Mughith al-Husain ibn Mansur ibn Muhammad al-Baidawi, mystic, 291

Haly Abbas, *see* Ali ibn al-Abbas

Ham, son of Noe, 287

Hama (Syria), 193

Hamud (Ibn Hammud), Sicilian Arab lord, 145

Harald Hardradi (Hardraade), King of Norway, 140, 141

Harran (Syria), 14

Harun ar-Rashid, Abbasid caliph, 50

al-Hasan al-Basri, religious leader, 12, 16

Hasan ibn Ali ibn Zaid, astrologer, 169

Haskins, C. H., 153, 161, 177, 269, 285

Hattin, battle of horns of, 186

de Hautevilles, 141, 152

Hebrew, 106, 159; *and see* Jews

Hellenistic, 5, 10, 21–2, 144, 266, 273, 281; *see also* Greek; Alexander

Henry I, King of Saxony, 61

Henry IV, Emperor, 233

Henry I, King of England, 106, 180

Henry II, King of England, 109, 185

Henry of Anjou, "III", son of Henry II of England, 266

Heraclius, Patriarch of Jerusalem, 186, 202

Hereford, 283; *see also* Roger

Heretics, 246–7, 255; *see also* heresies by name

Herluin, Arabic-speaking Crusader, 116

Hermann of Carinthia, translator, 270–1

Hermanubis, 268 and *n*

Hermes Trismegistus, 268, 288, 304, 305; Hermetic, 275, 288

Herod, 283

Hijra year, 18, 267

Hincmar, Archbishop of Rheims, theologian, 20

Hincmar, monk of Rheims, historian, 58

Hijaz, 240; *see also* Arabic, Mecca, Medina

Hippo, *see* Bone

Hippocrates, 144, 279, 291; Hippocratic, 293, 294, 320

historiography, iii, 4

Hohenstaufen, 158; *see also* Frederick I, Frederick II, Manfred, Conradin

Holcot, Robert, theologian, 255

Holofernes, supposed Assyrian general, 94

Holy Land, *see* Palestine

Homer, 280

homosexuality, 231, 247; Arabs in Sicily accused of, 150; Turks accused of, 124; Mamelukes accused of, 221–2; Salvago accused of permitting, *220–2n*; taken for granted, 227; reproved by Ibn an-Nafis, 187–8; by William of Tripoli, 188 cf. p. 74

Homs (Syria), 49, 193

Honorius IV, Pope, 222

Horace, 34

Hosiah, 280

Hoveden, Roger of, historian, 108

Hubert, Walter, Bishop of Salisbury 182

Hugh, Count of Arles and King of Italy, 53

Hugh, Lord of Caesarea, 211

Hugh of Santalla, translator, 268–9, 272

Hugh the Illuminator, pilgrim, 224

humanism, 273–4, 274–5, 307

Humbert of the Romans, Dominican, writer, 253–4, 262

Hunayn, Abu Zayd ibn Ishaq al-Ibadi, 144

Hungary, 123; *see also* Magyars

Huns, 50, 97

Ibelin; *see* Baldwin; *see* Balian

Ibn Abi Rijal, Abu'l Hasan Ali al-Maghribi, 288–9, 296–7; and illustration

Ibn (al-) Arabi, Abu Bakr Muhammad ibn Ali Muhyi ad-Din al-Andalusi, mystic, 300

Ibn al-Arabi, Spanish amir, 50

Ibn Bajja, Abu Bakr Muhammad ibn Yahya ibn al-Saigh, 277

Ibn al-Batriq, Yuhanna (Yahya) abu Zakariya, 276

Ibn Butlan, Abu al-Hasan al-Mukhtar ibn al-Hasan, 274, 277, 291, 292

Ibn al-Haytham, Abu Ali al-Hasan, 21, 279

Ibn Hazm, Abu Muhammad Ali ibn Ahmed ibn Said, 104

Ibn Ishaq, Abu Abdalla Muhammad, traditionalist, 239–41 *passim*

Ibn Jabirol, Solomon ibn Yudah; *see* Ibn Jabirul

Ibn Jabirul, Abu Ayyub Sulayman ibn Yahya, 277

Index

Ibn Jubayr, Abu al-Husain Muhammad ibn Ahmad, al-Kinani, traveller, 147–148, 149, 150
Ibn an-Nafis, Ala ad-Din, Ali ibn Abi al-Haram, physician and historian, 187, 222
Ibn Qurra, Thabit Abu al-Hasan ibn Marwan al-Harrani, 273, 276, 279, 285, 288
Ibn Ridwan, Ali Abu al-Hasan, 273, 277, 291
Ibn Rushd, Abu al-Walid Muhammad ibn Ahmed, 93, 274, 276–80, 288, 291; a "Greek", 300; see also Averroism
Ibn Sabin, Abu Muhammad Abd al-Haqq ibn Ibrahim al-Ishbili, 161
Ibn Sahl, Ali Abu al-Hasan Rabban at-Tabari, 288
Ibn Sina, Abu Ali al-Husayn ibn Abdalla, 21, 272, 273, 277, 278, 281, 283, 304, 305; in Bacon's historiography, 280; on immortality, 243, 246, 279; his Canon, 291, 297; most admired, 291, 300
Ibn Tufayl, Abu Bakr Muhammad ibn, Abd al-Malik, al Qaysi, 93, 277
Ibn Tumart, Amghar, religious reformer, 88, 92, 97, 148, 234, 238
Ibn at-Tumna, Sicilian Arab amir, 144
Ibn al-Wafid, Abu al-Mutarrif Abd ar-Rahman, al-Lahmi, 292
Ibn Zuhr, Abu Marwan Abd al-Malik ibn Abi al-Ala Zuhr, medical writer, 106
Ibrahim ibn al-Aghlab, ruler of Ifriqiya, 51
idolatry, Islam misinterpreted as, 31, 95, 98, 132, 231, 235–7; idolators, 255
al-Idrisi, 146
Ifriqiya, 51, 56–61, 220; title, "King of Africa", 142; and see Africa, North
immortality, Ibn Sina's doctrine of, 243, 246, 279, 291
imperialism, 321–2n, 322–3, 324; see also colonization
India, 11, 143, 226, 229, 285; Indies, 2, 164; Indian(s), 306; supposed, 143, 201, 227, 268, 269, 271, 280, 305; Indo-Arabic numerals, 295; Indian Ocean, 6
indulgences, 86, 87, 126, 181, 251–2
Indus, river, 274
Innocent III, Pope, 153, 165, 222, 259, 325
Iohannitus, see Hunayn
Iranians, 22; see also Persians
Iraq, 6, 9, 18; see also Baghdad, Samarra
Ireland, 224, 226
Isaac the Patriarch, 63, 240; see also Ishaq
Isaac, ambassador of Charlemagne, 51

Isaac Iudaeus; see Ishaq al-Israili
Ishaq, Abu Yacub ibn Sulayman al-Israili, 144, 272
Ishaq, a Cordovan monk, 25–6, 28, 33, 35–7 passim
Isidore of Seville, 17, 263, 279, 288; Etymologies of, 272
Isidore of Beja ("Pacensis"), 17
Islam: Abrahamic, 7; and Bible, 63–4, 231; and canon law, 254–62, 321; Christian praise of, 215–17; European polemical approach to, 39–45, 127, 230–1, 237–48, 302; European popular approach to, 100, 232–7; as heresy, 242, 245, 321; interest in, 248; and Jews, 13, 214, 230; jihad, see separate entry; Kabah, 235; martyrdom and saints in, 12–13; modes of sex, forbidden, 197–8, 247, supposedly indulged, 43, 72, 78, 189, 230, 234–5; Muslim communities in Europe, see La Garde-Freinet, Italy, Moriscos, Sicily; Muslim schools of thought: Khariji, 18, Shia, 13, 18, 244, Sufi, 142, 300–1, Sunni, 274; not associated with Christian heresies, 246–7, 278; as pagan survival, 34, 97–8, 235–7, 250, 256; pilgrimage, 15, 149, 258–60; prayer, 14, 215–16; prohibition of wine, 187–8; respect for Christ, see Christ Jesus; rise of, 6–7, 173; salvation in, 246 and n; shares belief with Christians, 2, 10–16, 20–1, 209, 230–2, 251; shares pagan elements, 16; shares worship, 12, 226; see also conversions; Muhammad; polemic, anti-islamic; Quran; toleration
Ismailite, 53, 59
Israel, ancient, 111
Italy, 7–8, 51, 120, 121, 159, 162, 222; Arabs in, 52, 55–7, 74, 75–8, 88, 102, 140, 154–6; Italians, 186, 197, 219; see also individual cities
Iunae-Minerva, supposed Roman goddess, 15

Jabir ibn Aflah, Abu Muhammad, 277
Jacobites, 205, 241, 244
Jaen, 85
Jaffa (Palestine), 182, 189
Jaffa, Walter of Brienne, Count of, 182
James I, the Conqueror, of Aragon, 220, 310 and n
James of Verona, pilgrim, 228; see also Vitry
Jandun, John of, 300
Jeremiah, 280
Jeremiah, a Cordovan, 36
Jerome, St, 279
Jerusalem, holy city of Palestine, 15, 60, 80, 99, 100; in First Crusade, 112, 115, 116, 121, 123, 129, 133, 192–4,

197, 199; massacre in, 134–5, 209, 253; late twelfth century, 182, 186; under Frederick II, 157–8; Latin Kingdom of, 172–81, 192–210; Holy Sepulchre, 104, 122, 157, 162; *see also* Pilgrimage, Temple; patriarchs of, by name

Jérusalem, poem of, 96, 121, 131–2, 236

Jews, ancient, 63, 170, 279–80, 287–8, 305; fight the Apostles, 248; in Arabia, 242; astrologically described, 271; alleged allied to Egypt, 122; mediaeval, attacked, 122–3, 124, 141, 144, 308; salvation of, 246; survive in Europe, 321 cf. 2; protected by Islam, 13; in canon law, 14, 249, 254–62; language and culture, 25, 106, 161, 272, 307; in Cairo, 214, 227; anonymous individuals, 68, 83

Jihad, 7, 13, 154, 209, 230, 248–9, 261; compared with Crusade, 136, 230, 248–9, 261

Joachim of Flora, Abbot of Fiore, 248

Job, 43

John, St the Evangelist, 300

John, St of Damascus, 7, 17, 18, 20

John VIII, Pope, 76–8, 250

John X, Pope, 52

John, King of England, 108–9, 196

John of Andrew, canonist, 256–7

John of Capua, translator, 106

John of Gorze, ambassador for Otto I, 64–70, 325

John of Plano Carpini, traveller, 218, 315, 316

John of Salisbury, 273–4, 283, 287

John Scotus, *see* Erigena

John of Seville, translator, 270; perhaps identical with J. of Spain, q.v.

John of Spain, uncertain writer, 288; perhaps identified with J. of Seville, q.v.

John of Toledo, astrologer, 159

John, a Cordovan merchant, 24–5, 31; another Cordovan, 35

John the Treasurer, 259

John, *see also* Joinville, Segovia, Torquemada, Manuel

Joinville, John, lord of, 143, 172, 181, 183, 187, 190, 212–13, 248

Jordan, river, 174

Joscelin II, Count of Edessa, 175

Josephus, 204, 279

Judas Maccabeus, 94, 115

Jupiter, Roman god, 15, 271

Juvenal, 34

Kababish, tribe, 169

Kabah, 235, 241; *see also* Islam

Kalila wa Dimna, 21, 106, 281, 306

al-Kamil, al-Malik, Nasir ad-Din, sultan

of Egypt, 157, 162–4 *passim*, 200, 219 310

al-Kamil ('Perfectus'), Cordovan monk, 23–4, 31

Kerbogha, ruler of Mosul, 116, 117, 131, 132, 193, 194, 196

Khadija, wife of the Prophet, 234, 241

al-Khalifa, H., *284–8n*

Kharja, 101

Khorasan (Corozan), 6, 118, 127, 197, 232–4 *passim*, 240

al-Khwarizmi, Abu Abdalla Muhammad ibn Musa, 263, 266, 276, 296, 305

al-Kindi, Abd al Masih ibn Ishaq, pseudonym, 238

al-Kindi, Abu Yusuf Yaqub ibn Ishaq ibn as-Sabbah, 21, 272, 273, 276, 279, 305

Konya (Turkey), 315

Kufa (Iraq), 17

La Brocquière, Bertrandon de, 318

Lamartine, A. M. L. de, 211

Lance, supposed holy, 127–8

Landemar, a Salernitan, 71

Lanfranc, Archbishop of Canterbury, 144

Laon (France), 267

Lateran Councils, 251, 255

Latin, Latin Europe, 8, 52, 166, 169, 269; language and culture, 11, 17, 19, 33–4, and *n*, 36, 161, 200, 280; translations into, 21, 74, 106, 144, 220, 263–4, 268–9, 276, 278, 288, 290–1, 296–7; *see also* scientific learning

Latin rite, 78, 204–8, 250, 321; *see also* Rome; Popes

Latins: in East Europe, 114, 122–3; in the Levant, 138, 168, 189, 192, 205–8, 221, 225–6, 229, 265; in Sicily, 55, 72; *see also* crusades; Franks; Jerusalem; merchants

Lemay, R., 267, 270, 273

Leo III, the Isaurian, Emperor, 7

Leo V, "the Armenian", Emperor, 51

Leo IV, Pope, 58

Leo X, Pope, 222

Leocritia, a Cordovan, 29, 30–5

Lepanto, battle of, 318

lepers, accused of plotting, 312–13, 321

Levison, W., 15

Lewis, C. S., 1

Liliosa, a Cordovan, 36

Lille, see Alan

Linus, ancient musician, 280

Lisbon, 87

Liutprand, Bishop of Cremona, historian, 52, 53, 56, 58, 59, 61, 64, 69, 74

Livy, 34, 204

Loewen, battle of, 55

Lombard, *see* Peter

Index

Lombards, invaders of Europe, 7, 8; in Europe, 50, 55; in Salerno, 71; on Crusade, 193; in Sicily, 151; in service of Frederick II, 155

Lombardy, 16

Longjumeau, Andrew of, 315

loot, object of war, 81–3, 103, 107, 124, 133, 136, 146, 182, 186, 195

Lothair (Lothar) I, Emperor, 60

Louis I, the Pious, King of France and Emperor, 119

Louis VII, King of France, 126

Louis IX, King of France, 5, 143, 159, 181–4 and n, 196, 202, 223, 239, 248, 315; image outside Joinville, 181–2n

Louis II de Bourbon (duke), 308

Lucera (Italy), 154–7, 163

Lupus, Servatus, Abbot of Ferrières, 20

Luther, M., 302

Lyons, Council of, 253

Maarra (Syria), 134, 136, 137

Macaulay, Thomas Babington, first baron, 3

Maccabees, 190; *and see* Judas

Macdonald, D. B., 301

Magi, 270, 283

Magic, 268, 271, 283–4, 286–8 and n; attributed to the Prophet, 94, 100, 234, 243, to Ibn Tumart, 92, 97

Magyars, 8, 61, 97; Hungarians, 221

Mahdi, 89

al-Mahdiya, 142, 308

Mahom, imaginary idol, 44, 95–6, 132, 235

Maimonides, 277

Mainz, 122

Maiolus, Abbot of Cluny, 62–4

Malaterra, Geoffrey, historian, 144–5

Malta, 213, 318

Mamelukes, 136, 167, 182, 184, 187, 218, 221–2, 226, 315

Mandeville, John, travel author, pseudonym, 208, 239

Manfred, son of Frederick II, governor and King of Sicily, 155, 162

Maniakes, George, Byzantine general 140, 165

Manuel I, Emperor, 109

Manuel, Don Juan, 306

Map, Walter, writer, 180

Marathon, 52, 112

Marcabru, poet, 104

Marco Polo, 218, 316

Margaret of Beverley, nun, 199

Marguerite de Navarre, Queen, 306

Mark of Toledo, translator, 234, 238, 240

Maronites, 205

Mars, Roman god, 15, 271

Marseilles, 219, 225, 226, 283

Martoni, Nicolas of, pilgrim, 308

martyrdom, Muslim and Christian concepts of, 12 and n, 15; voluntary martyrdom 23–48, 223, 311; imaginary, 65; parallel cases, 37, 65, 67; involuntary, in Crusade, 38, 115, 125–7 and n, 132; evaded, 132

Marx, Karl, 4

Mary, mother of Christ, 72, 75, 225; praised by Quran, 41, 247; appeal to name of, 199; alleged attack on by Frederick II, 160; Spring at Matariya, near Cairo, 214, 223, 226; church at Palermo converted from mosque, 148; Lucera renamed for, 156; altar at Tunis, 220

Mary, a Cordovan, 28–9, 35

Mashallah, astrologer, 288

Maslama, Abu al-Qasim ibn Ahmad al-Majriti, 266

de Mas Latrie, M. L., scholar, 219

Matthew, St, Evangelist, 63

Matthew Paris, 160, 163–4, 200, 238, 315

Maulawiya, 301

Mauretania, *see* Morocco

Maurice, St, 127

Mazzara, Val di, 153

Mecca, holy city, 194, 241, 245, 258; Meccans, 240–2; *see also* Hijaz

Medes, 155

Medicine, 74, 290–5

Medina, Holy city, 243

Mediterranean, unity of, 5 ff., 70, 73, 140–4, 164, 167, 214, 228–9, 285, 288; linked by arithmetic, 296; *and see* civilisation, shared; areas within, 8, 79, 112, 165, 218; Frederick II and, 157, 162, 164; Arab–European encounter in, 5–10, 11, 54–60, 79, 100, 111–13, 138–9, 165; *and see* Crusades, Reconquest; commerce in, 2, 218–20, 296, *and see* commerce, pilgrimage; Northern Europe in relation to, 11, 19, 49, 54, 169, 215, 263, 305; Mongols in relation to, 218

Melkites, 205

Melrose, 12, 315

Memphis, 118, 211 and n

Menedez Pidal, R., historian, 81

Meno, 147

mercenaries, 145, 229, 232, 309; European soldiers in Arab service, 92, 219, 314, 220–2n; others, 25, 33, 309, 318; Arab, 152, 155, 159, 314; almogavars, 155n; *see also* Europeans: in Arab service

merchants: Meccan, 241; Italian, 210, 218–21, 256, 259, 260–1, 316; *see also* commerce

Merovingians, 6, 7

Messina (Sicily), 285

Metz, Annals of, 51; *see also* Amalarius

Michael I Rangabe, Emperor, 51

Michael, *see* Scot
Middle Ages, definition of, 1–5, 319;
limits of European expansion in, 143,
319–26
Minerva, Roman goddess, 370; *see also*
Iunae-Minerva
missionaries, 165, 223–4, 256, 323; as
chaplains, 218, 220, 224
Moabites, supposed, 85, 94–5
monasticism, 14, 16, 37
Monastir (Serbia), 114
Mongols: threaten invasion from East,
80, 314–15; as a world power, 218,
314, 322; converted to Islam, 218, 317;
believed convertible to Christianity,
244; enslaved, 221, 244, 314, 317;
assessed as people, 244, 316; *see also*
Tartar
Monophysites, 205, 207, 244; *see also*
Copts; Jacobites
monotheism, 31, 231
Mons (France), 112
Monte Cassino, monastery, 59, 143, 144,
263
Montiel, battle of, 85
Monumenta Germaniae Historica, 3
Moors, attack Europe, 58, 142, 310; in
Spain, 81, 82, 85, 86, 242, 268, *see also*
Reconquest; persecuted, 255, 309,
see also Islam, toleration, *and* Moriscos;
Lull and, 310; kind of Arab, 317; *see*
also Arabs, Morocco, Spain
Moriscos, 254, 313–14
Morley, *see* Daniel
Morocco, 50, 88, 106, 143, 222, 310,
314; king of, 196, 222; Marrakush, 91,
108–9; Mauretania, 249
Moses Farachi, *see* Faraj
Moses Maimonides, *see* Maimonides
Moses Sefardi, *see* Pedro de Alfonso
mosques, turned into churches, 90, 97,
148, 150, 156; returned to use as
mosques, 157–8; mutual desecration,
210; destroyed, 85
Mozarabs, 19, 23–48, 66–7, 94, 205,
239, 247, 250, 307
Muawiya II, caliph, 18
al-Muazzam, al-Malik Sharaf ad-Din,
Sultan of Damascus, 219
Mudejares, 313
muezzin, 31, 41–2, 158, 258–60, 262
Muhammad the Prophet, 8, 118, 271,
280; occasional part-understanding of,
41, 100–1, 235, 236, 249, 251; life of,
18, 239–42; genealogy of, 240; tomb
believed object of Hajj, 149, 258;
alleged a magus, 94, 97, 100, 234, cf.
243; abused and misrepresented, 23,
24, 40, 43, 53, 94, 223, 228, 232–5;
243, 246; misrepresentation analysed,
230–1; and *muezzin*, 258, *see also*
muezzin; Quran

Muhammad II al-Mutamid ibn Abbad,
ruler of Seville, 89
Muhammad an-Nasir, Almohad caliph,
108
Muhassin ibn Ali, 169
al-Murabitin, *see* Almoravids
Murad Bey, Terjuman, 318
Muratori, L., 3
Murviedro (Spain), 84
Musa ibn Maymun, *see* Maimonides
al-Mustansir, Abu Abdalla Muhammad
I, ruler of Tunis, 143
al-Mutanabbi, Abu at-Taiyib Ahmad ibn
al-Husain, 170
al-Muwahhidin, *see* Almohads
muwashshah, 101

Nakshabandiya, sufis, 301
Naples, 76, 77
Narbonne (France), 51, 142
an-Nasir, al-Malik Salah ad-Din Daud,
219
an-Nasir Muhammad ibn Qalaun,
Mameluke sultan, 222–4*n*, and
illustration
an-Nasir, Hammadid ruler in North
Africa, 250–1
Las Navas de Tolosa, battle of, 88, 108,
109
Nebuchadnezzar, supposed king of
Assyria (Judith), 94; King of Babylon,
used symbolically, 141
Nelli, R., 104
Nelson, Admiral Lord, 46
Nestorians, 205, 241, 244–5, 316
Netherlands, 301
Newton, Isaac, 325
Nicaea, 129, 198
Nicephorus I, Emperor, 51
Nicetas, procurator of Sicily, 50
Nicopolis, battle of, 317
Nile, river, 214, 228; *see also* Egypt,
Roda
Nilus Doxopatres, historian, 147
Nimes (France), 51
Noe, 280, 287
Normans, 9, 128, 129, 140, 144–53, 146,
162, 165–6
Northumbrians, 10
Nubians, 211, 227
Nunilo, a Cordovan, 35
nuns, captured, 198–9, 209
Nur Muhammadi, 234
Nur ad-Din Mahmud ibn Zangi, atabeg
of Syria, 109, 184, 185
Nykl, A. R., 102

Ockham, William, philosopher, 300
Odo of Deuil, historian, 197
Odoric of Pordenone, traveller, 316
O'Fihely, Maurice, church writer, 300

Index

Olaf, St Haraldsson, King of Norway, 13
Orderic Vitalis, historian, 107, 201
Orleans, 122
Orpheus, 280
Oswald, St, King of Northumbria, 13
Otranto, 74
Otto I, Emperor, 64, 65
Oxford, 7; University of, 279

Padua, *see* Fidenzio
Pahlevi, 11, 22
Painter, William, writer, 306
Palermo, 146, 150
Palestine, Holy Land, 118, 158, 161–3
   passim, 199, 249, 314; under Franks,
   115, 129; *see also* Acre; Crusades;
   Jerusalem; pilgrimage
Pamplona, manuscript attacking Islam
   found at, 19, 34, 40, 231, 232
Pantellaria, island, 60, 162, 213
Paris, 55, 226; University of,
   propositions condemned, 278–9, 284
Parthian, supposed, 199
Pascal II, Pope, 233
Paschasius Radbertus, Abbot of Corbie,
   theologian, 20
Paske de Riveri, Patriarch's mistress, 202
Pastoureaux (Shepherds), 159, 246, 301,
   321
Paul, St, 33, 39, 109, 300; church of, 57
Pedro de Alfonso (Moses Sefardi), 106,
   237, 241, 306
Pepin of Heristal, Duke of the Franks,
   50
Pepin, the short, King of the Franks, 7,
   51
Penaforte, Raymund of, canonist, 260
Perfectus, a Cordovan monk, *see* Kamil
persecution, 55, 113–18, 151–7, 209–10;
   theory of, 14, 30–1, 76, 78, 139, 154,
   324
Persian(s), 271, 301; mediaeval idea of,
   geographical, 75, 127; as a culture,
   143, 272, 276, 280; il-khans, 317
Peter, St, 33, 39, 116, 117; church of,
   57, 58, 76
Peter I of Lusignan, King of Cyprus
   "and Jerusalem", 308
Peter Bartholomew, visionary
   Crusading priest, 127
Peter the Deacon, of Monte Cassino,
   historian and fiction writer, 59, 143
Peter the Hermit, Crusading leader, 114,
   116, 123–5 *passim*; character, 120–1,
   122; fictional character, 131–2
Peter Lombard, 275
Peter Pascual, Mercedarian and writer,
   239
Peter the Venerable, Abbot of Cluny,
   13, 237–8, 262, 270
Peter, a Salernitan soldier, 70
Peter, a caid, in Sicily, 151

Phaedo, 147
Philip of Novara, historian, lawyer, 172
Philip of Tripoli, 199, 276
Philip, Sicilian eunuch, 149
Phoenicia, 249
Picardy, 159
Pilet, Raymund, Crusading leader, 193
Pilgrimage, pilgrims, Christian, unarmed,
   15, 49, 60, 207, 224, 226, 318 and *n*;
   under boycott, 225; *see also* Egypt:
   boycott; commerce: boycott; in
   arms, 112, 126, 192; *see also* Crusades;
   for Muslims, *see* Islam, Mecca
Pirenne, H., 7
Pisa, Pisan, 142, 146, 204, 219, 220, 295,
   312
Pius II, Pope, 302
Pius V, Pope, 325
Placidus, fictional saint, 59
Plato, Platonic, Platonists, 3, 180, 265,
   266, 274, 277, 279–81 *passim*;
   Platonic influence, 277
Pliny, 279
Poitiers, Alphonse, Count of, 182
polemic, anti-islamic: content and
   methods, 31, 39–45, 65–7, 99–100, 223,
   237–9, 242–5, 302; discussed, 45–8,
   217, 230–1, 245–8; frivolous, 233,
   235, 237; historical argument, 248–9;
   Jewish element, 106, 237; Spain as
   source of, 45, 94, 106, 199, 215, 231,
   233, 235–6, 238–40; Trinitarian, 310,
   312; *see also* Islam; Muhammad the
   Prophet (life of)
du Pont, Alexandre, 232, 234, 235
Pontus, a legendary founder of Salerno,
   74
Popes: approach to Arab rulers, 222,
   250–1; attacked by Arabs, 57–8;
   hostile policy to Arabs, 74–9, 124,
   155–6, 158–9, 164, 166; *see also*
   commerce (papal boycott); Latin;
   Rome
Pordenone, Odoric of, *see* Odoric
Portugal, 257, 261; Portuguese, 2, 106,
   314
predestination, 20
preludia fidei, 280–1, 304
prisoners: Arab, 81, 83, 136–7, 142, 203,
   216, 308, 311; European, 61, 76, 159–
   160, 197–8, 209, 221–3, 260; killing
   of, 134–7 and *n*; Louis IX, 159, 181;
   redemption of, 61–2, 136, 165, 216,
   222, 250; as slaves, 61, 73, 83, 101,
   136–7, 142, 159–60, 197–9, 203, 209,
   227, 260, 308–9; trade in slaves, 9, 74,
   220–2, 260
Proclus, 277
prophecies, 108 and *n*, 158–9 and *n*,
   208–9 and *n*
Provence, Provençal, 101–4, 128; *see also*
   La Garde-Freinet

Ptolemy, Claudius, 268, 272, 275, 279, 287, 288; Ptolemaic, 320; pseudo-Ptolemy, 279
Ptolemy Soter, King of Egypt, 287
Pullani, 195, 204, 206–7
pyramids, 214, 226
Pythagoras, 263; Pythagoreans, 274

al-Qabisi, Abu as-Saqr Abd al-Aziz ibn Uthman ibn Ali, 288
Qadar, 20
Qadariya, sufis, 301
Qalandariya, sufis, 301
Qalaun, al-Mansur Sayf ad-Din, al-Alfi, Mameluke Sultan, 189, 221, 222, and illustration
Qaraqorum, 315
Qubbat as-Sakhra, 12, 134, 157, 210
Qubilay, Great Khan, 316
Quintilian, 34
Quran, holy, 7, 11, 44, 216, 217, 228, 231, 234, 246, 255, 270–1, 296, 319
Quraysh, 241, 242; *see also* Mecca, Hijaz, Medina
Qusayy, 240
Qusta ibn Luqa al-Balabakki, 276, 279
Qutuz, al-Muzaffar Sayf ad-Din, Mameluke Sultan, 315

Rabanus Maurus, Abbot of Fulda and Archbishop of Mainz, theolgian, 20
Raimbaud of Cologne, scholar, 263
Rainald, Langobardic commander of Crusade, 117
Ramadan, 24, 31
Ramla (Palestine), 175
Raoul de Wanou, Crusader with Louis IX, 213
Ratramnus, monk of Corbie, theologian, 20
Ravenna, 7, 50
Raymund, Count of Toulouse, or Count of St Gilles, 112, 128, 134, 193, 194
Raymund, Count of Tripoli, 195
Raymund of Aguilers, historian, 128, 134
Raymund of Marseilles, 269–70, 282, 283
Raymund Lull, 37, 223, 241, 300, 310–12
Raymund Marti, 239, 243
Raynald of Chatillon, 186–7, 194
ar-Razi, Abu Bakr Muhammad ibn Zakariya, 21, 273, 277, 291, 293, 304, 305
Recamund, Bishop of Elvira, 64–9
Reccafred, Bishop of Seville, 33
Reconquest (*reconquista*), 98, 107, 120, 140, 242, 268; completion of, 309–10, 313; principles and practice of, 48, 80–8, 125, 322; *see also* Moriscos; Spain
Red Sea, 6, 194, 305
Reformation, 1

Refutation, 238
Regnier, Cardinal Capocci, of Viterbo, 163
relics, in the Cordovan cult, 24, 29, 30
Renaissance, 1, 119, 291, 307
Renan, E., 247
Revolution, French, 1–3 *passim*
Rheims (Reims), 130; *and see* Robert
Rhodes, 318
Rhone, river, 214
Riad, H., 268*n*
Richard I, King of England, 162, 182–4, 185, 195, 199
Richard, Count of Caserta, 154
Richelieu, Armand Jean Duplessis, Cardinal Duc de, 314
Richer, monk of Rheims, historian, 74
Ricoldo da Monte Croce, polemist, traveller, 198–9, 209, 210, 215–17, 239, 243–5, 316, 325
Ridwan, atabeg of Mosul, 193
Risala, 243
Riveri, *see* Paske de
Robald, Count of Cimera or Nice, 73
Robert, King of Sicily (Naples), 156
Robert of Calatabiano, 150–1
Robert of Ketton, translator, 238, 270–1, 296
Robert of London, 108, 109
Robert of Rheims, historian, 119, 121, 127
Robert of St Albans, convert, 196
Roberter (Robert?), European mercenary leader in Morocco, 92
Roda, Island of, 227
Roderick, Archbishop of Toledo (Jimenez de Rada), 88, 90–3 *passim*, 239, 241, 242
Roderick, a Cordovan, 35
Roger, *see* Bacon
Roger I, Count of Sicily, "the Great Count", 141, 144–5, 146, 155
Roger II, King of Sicily, 142, 146, 149, 152; *see also* illustration
Roger, son of Roger II of Sicily, 152
Roger of Hereford, astrologer, 283
Roland, chanson de geste, 96–8, 100, 126, 236, 255, 307; imputes idolatry, 95–6, 235–6
Rolls Series, 3
Romance, 102
Romania, 115; *see also* Byzantium
Rome, 15, 55, 59, 115, 244; ancient, 5, 10, 205; attacked, 57, 58, 76, 77; Romans, 50, 58, 130, 258, 266, 271; Roman church, 19, 166; *see also* Latin, Popes
Romuald, Archbishop of Salerno, historian, 152
Roncevaux, Roncesvalles, 51, 96
Runciman, S., 136
Russia, 9

Index

Sabaeans, 14
Sabigotho, a Cordovan, 35
Safet (Safad, Palestine), 189
St Albans, 107; *and see* Robert of, *also*
Matthew Paris
saints, 12–13, 16; *see also* martyrdom
Saladin, *see* Salah ad-Din
Salah ad-Din (Saladin) al-Malik an-Nasir,
5, 109, 159, 167, 182–3, 196–9, 202,
213; legend of, 185–7; in Dante, 279
Salerno, 59, 70–2, 73, 75, 77; medical
school, 74, 144, 263
Salernus, supposed eponymous founder
of Salerno, 74
Salimbene, Adam of, historian, 88, 106,
159–61 *passim*, 187, 222–3
Salisbury, *see* Hubert, Bishop of; John
of
Samaritans, supposed, 201, 205
Samarra (Iraq), ruins of, 244
Sancho I, King of Navarre, 86
Sancho I Ramirez, King of Aragon and
Navarre, 82
Sancho VI, King of Navarre, 200–1*n*
Santalla, *see* Hugh
Sanudo, Marino, Crusade apologist,
222*n* and end-papers
Saraceni, usage discussed, 53 and *n*,
240–1, 242–3, 266, 302
Saragossa (Zaragoza), 50, 97
Sarah, mother of Isaac, 53, 241
Sardinia, 51, 60
Sarmatians, 155
Saruj (Turkey), 193
Sassanians, 6
Scandinavia, 9
science, Arabic, Ch. 10
scientific learning, Arab influence on,
74, 106, 109, 143, 146–7, 161, 164,
165, 303–5, 319–20; manuscript
collections, 296–7*n*, 304–5*n*
Seine, river, 52
Scot, Michael, 144, 161, 162, 274, 284–8,
289, 295, 296
Scots, join Crusade, 121
Scott, Sir Walter, 187
Scythians, 273
Secreta Secretorum, 21, 171, 190, 199,
276, 279–81 *passim*
secularism, of Frederick II, 160; of
Crusades, 172, 175, 202–4; of Europe,
278, 296
Segovia, John of, 302
Semites, 22
Seneca, 279, 281
Sepulchre, Holy, 104, 122, 157, 316; *see
also* Jerusalem
Sercambi, Giovanni, 306
Sergius II, Pope, 58
Servandus, Bishop of Hippo, 250, *see
also* Bone
Seville, 89, 283, 309; *see also* John of

Shadhiliya, Sufi sect, 301
Shaftesbury, the Earl of, 325
Shaizar (Syria), 193
Shia, 13, 18, 244
Shirkuh, Asad ad-Din, general serving
Ibn Zangi, finally wazir of Egypt, 185
Sicily, Arabs in, 72, 249; rule in, 55, 76;
Christians of, 85; Normans in, 140,
142–3, 144–53, 199; Frederick II and,
157, 164; Arabs expelled from, 153–4,
164, 314; sea power of, 142–3; trade
of, 219; translations made in, 264, 275,
291; Adelard of Bath in, 265
Sigebert of Gembloux, historian, 232,
233
Siger of Brabant, philosopher, 277–9
passim
Simon Simeon, pilgrim and writer, 224–
228
Simon of Tournai, traveller, 315
Sira Rasul Allah, 239, 240
slaves, slavery, *see* prisoners
Slavs, 9, 50, 97
Solomon, 288
Solon of Athens, 280
Spain, Arabs in, 7, 51, ch. 4, 113, 249,
261–2, 284, 317; knowledge of Arabs
in, 88–95; European knowledge of,
105–10; vehicle for Arab influence,
95–105, 264, 268–73; channel for
trade, 9; Christians under Arabs in,
13, 17–18, 23–48, 223, 250–1, *see also*
prisoners; Charlemagne in, 50–1;
Bishops of, 33, 50, 66, 67–8; learning
in, 263–4, 273, 275; *see also* Toledo;
Reconquest, *see* separate entry;
Cordova martyrs, 23–48; sources of
traditional polemic, 45, 94, 106, 199,
231, 232, 233, 236, 238–40, 247
spies, 71, 199, 224, 228, and *n*
Stephen, a translator, 269
Stephen of Antioch, translator, 199, 264,
290
Stephen of Perche, Chancellor of Sicily,
150
Stephen, visionary priest, 128, 194
Stubbs, William, Bishop of Oxford, 3
Sudanese, 227; *see also* Nubians
Suetonius, Roman historian, 51
Sufism, 142, 300–1
Sulayman, a Cordovan, 35
Sunnis, 244
Suriani, 205, 206, 207–8; *see also* Syria
Sybil, Jewish, 288
Sylvester II, Pope *see* Gerbert
Syracuse, 265
Syria, 8, 12, 18, 241, 249, 315, 317;
Crusades and, 123, 171,192, 195, 242;
life in, 318; polemic originates in, 233;
Syrian desert, 6; Syriac church, 114;
Syriac, 11, 276; *see also* Crusades,
Damascus, Palestine, Latin'

Tafurs, 131–2
Taifas, 101, 103
Talleyrand-Perigord, C. M. de, Prince of Benevento, 112
Tamim, Zirid ruler of Ifriqiya, 142
Tancred, Prince of Tiberias and of Edessa, Regent of Antioch, 112, 135, 194
Tancred, Count of Lecce and King of Sicily, 153
Tannery, P., 263
Tarazona (Spain), 268
Tarsus (Turkey), 265
Tartars (Tatars), usually designating Mongols indiscriminately, as exotic, 155, 201; defeated by Mamelukes, 201, (*see also* Ain Jalut); sold as slaves, 221; as a menace, 110, 164, 315; *see also* Mongols
Tashufin ibn Ali ibn Yusuf, 91, 94; *see also* Ali ibn Yusuf
at-Tawaif, Muluk, *see* Taifas
technology and development, 8–9, 11 305, 324
Tempier, Etienne, Bishop of Paris, 278, 279, 284
Templar of Tyre, historian, 209
Templars, 246–7, 252–3, 312; *see also* Temple
Temple, "Solomon's", *see* al-Aqsa; "the Lord's", *see* Qubbat as-Sakhra; at Acre, 209
Tertullian, 311
Tervagan (Termagaunt), imaginary idol, 95, 132, 235–6
Teutonic Knights, Master of, 157
Tewkesbury, monks of, 315
Thales of Mileto, 280
Theoctitus, Sicilian procurator's legate, 50
Theodore of Tarsus, Archbishop of Canterbury, 11, 19
Theophanes, Byzantine historian, 118
"Theophilus", 285
Theophrastus of Eresos, 279
Theseus, Greek hero, 52
Thoros II, King of (Cilician) Armenia, 137
Thot, ancient Egyptian god, 268, 271, 304
Thrace, 114
Tiber, river, 58
Timur (Tamerlane), 317
Tlemcen (Tilimsan, Algeria), 222
Toledo, 26, 29, 89, 159, 234, 264, 272–5 *passim*, 283, 288, 307; Council of, 86; *see also* John, Mark, Roderick
Toleration, 87, 136, 147–9, 165, 208–9, 214, 310; defended, 66; recommended, 302–3; alliances imply, 75, 84, 193; lack of animosity, 49; *see also* civilization, shared; conversions;

persecution; toleration rejected by recipient, 32–3; *see also* Crusades, *jihad*, martyrdom, Mediterranean
Torquemada, John of, 312
Tota, Queen of Navarre, 86
Toulouse, 312
Tournay, *see* Simon
treaties, *see* Arabs; commerce; embassies
Trebizond, 223
Trier (Treves), 122, 198
Trinity, Holy, argument about, 231, 238, 310, 312
Tripoli (Syria, now Lebanon), 188, 193; (Libya) 61; *and see* Philip, William, Raymund
troubadour verse, 101–5
Troy, 119
Tunis, 56, 146, 162, 219, 220, 222, 285, 288, 311, 317; under Aghlabids, 51, 55; *see also* Ifriqiya
Turanshah, al-Malik al Muazzam, Sultan of Egypt, 181, 213
Turkestan, 301
Turks, 53, 115; Seljuk, 80, 109, 314, 317; seen as a menace, 284, 314; accused of atrocities, 124; admired, 117, 130, 211; compared to Franks, 130; preferred to Greeks, 197; and Arabs, 130; rulers, weakness of, 128; Tafurs and, 131; Ottomans, 5, 80, 167, 218, 224–49, 254, 301–3 *passim*, 314, 317–18; term replaces 'Saracen', 302, 317; 'to become Turk', 130, 302; Turks replace Arabs, 302, 306, 317–18, 324; confused with Magyars, 61
Turpinus, fiction, 98–100, 283
Tyre, *see* William, Templar

Umar ibn al-Khattab, caliph, 10, 119, 157
Umar ibn Abd al-Aziz, caliph, 11
Umar ibn al-Farrikhan at-Tabari, 305
Umayyads, 11, 49; mosque of, 210; of Spain, 7, 101; *see also* rulers by name
Urban II, Pope, 79, 111–13 *passim*, 115, 118–20 *passim*, 146, 249, 250, 314
Urgel (Catalonia), Count of, 107; *and see* Felix
Usama ibn Munqidh of Shayzar, writer of recollections, 168–9, 193, 195, 204
Uthred of Boldon, theologian, 246

Valencia, 81, 82, 90, 91, 95, 310, 313
Van Steenberghen, F. 277
Varangians, 141
Venice, Venetian, 9, 58, 204, 219, 308, 222*n*
Venus, Roman goddess, 15–16, 43, 271
Vercelli (Italy), 61
Verdun (France), 74

Index

Verona, *see* James
Vienne, Council of, 258
Vikings (Danes, Northmen, Norsemen),
    8, 9, 51, 54, 55, 72, 100
Villanova, *see* Arnald
Vincent of Beauvais, 233, 238, 316
Virgil, 265
Visigoths, 7, 8, 11, 75; Visigothic, 33
    and *n*
Vita Karoli Magni, 51
Vitry, James of, 172, 204–6, 207, 238,
    239
Voltaire, 319, 325
Vulcan, Roman god, 43

Waifar (Guaifar), Prince of Salerno, 71
Waimar (Guaimar), Prince of Salerno, 77
Walabonso, a Cordovan, 35
Walafrid Strabo, Abbot of Reichenau, 20
Waldensians, 246
Walter of Compiègne, 232, 234, 235
Walter Sans Avoir, crusading leader, 114
Walter the Chancellor, historian, 202
Walter, *see* Map
Waraqa, 258
West Saxons, 10; *see also* Alfred;
    Anglo-Saxons
William I, King of England, 171, 179,
    232
William II, King of England, 180
William I, King of Sicily, "the Bad",
    149–50, 151, 152
William II, King of Sicily, "the Good",
    142, 147, 152, 153, 156
William, Prince of Orange, 119, 236
William, Count of Arles, 64
William IX, Duke of Aquitaine, Count
    of Poitou, 102–4 *passim*, 128
William of Adam, titular Bishop of
    Sultaniya, 220–1

William of Apulia, historian, 148
William of Auvergne, theologian, 241,
    247, 271
William of Malmesbury, 113, 179–80,
    283
William of Rubruck, 218, 315, 316
William of Tripoli, Dominican writer,
    187–8, 208–9, 239, 241, 243, 325
William of Tyre, historian, 93, 115, 131,
    135, 170–82, 184, 195, 200, 203–4,
    211–12, 325
William the Marshal, 171, 184, 185
Willibald, Bishop of Eichstadt, 49
Witelo, Silesian writer on optics, 279
Wolfram von Eschenbach, 105
Wycliff, John, 302

xenophobia, 113–14, 121, 122, 124, 168,
    323–4
Xerigordo, 117, 197

Yahya ibn Ghaniya, Murabiti governor
    in Spain, 91, 94
Yathrib, *see* Medina
Yazid I, caliph, 49

Zaida bint Muhammad ibn Mutamid of
    Seville, 89, 101
Zajal, 101
Zakat, 216
Zangi, Imad ad-Din ibn Aq Sonqur,
    atabeg of Mosul, 184
az-Zarqali, Abu Ishaq Ibrahim ibn
    Yahya ibn an-Naqqas, 277, 305
Zayd ibn Haritha, 40
Zeno, 277
Zirids, 142
Zoroastrians, 14, 144; *see also* Magi

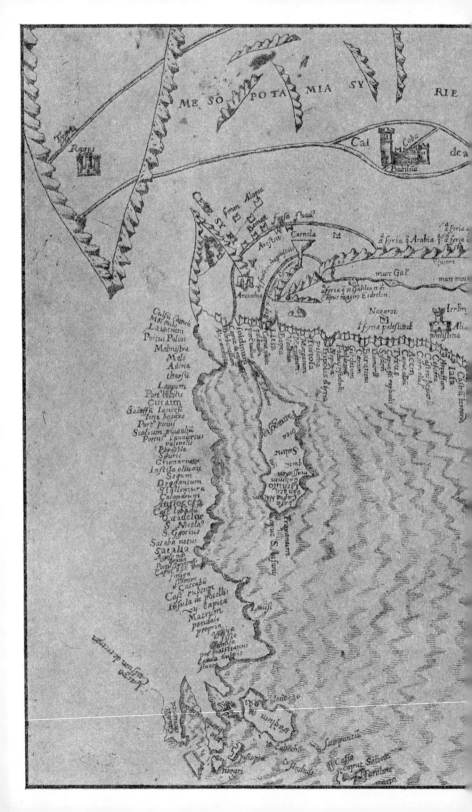